Word Smart
for Business

Word Smart
for Business

by Paul Westbrook

Random House, Inc.
New York

Princeton Review Publishing, L.L.C.
2315 Broadway
New York, NY 10024
Email: comments@review.com
Copyright ©1999 by Princeton Review Publishing, L.L.C.

ISBN 0-679-78391-1

Editor: Tom Russell
Production Editor: Kristen Azzara
Production Coordinator: Stephanie Martin

9 8 7 6 5

Acknowledgments

Special thanks to Al Silverman and Brigitte Weeks for their valuable assistance in getting me started in writing.

My good friends and business associates were extremely helpful in gathering and verifying definitions. Thanks, in alphabetical order, to Bill Arnone, Jesse Birnbaum, John Feldtmose, Karin Fredrickson, Jeremy Gold, John Halak, Frank Hardy, Donald Lindgren, Larry Smiley, Rose-Marie Stock, Ruth Westbrook, and Ransom Widmer.

Thanks go to the following expert reviewers: Larisa Avner, Certified Public Accountant; Dr. Israel Blumenfruct, Chairperson of the Department of Accounting and Information Systems, Queens College; Jacob Borenstein, Esquire; Elayne Brown, Director of Human Resources, The Princeton Review.

In particular, I want to thank Evan Schnittman, Editor-in-Chief at The Princeton Review for his overall direction and guidance, and Tom Russell for his nitty-gritty editing that made this book better.

Finally, I want to thank Liz Buffa, the author of the first edition of this book, entitled *Word Smart Executive Edition*, which was a valuable starting point for this book.

Introduction

> *"After I contribute to the **Roth IRA**, buy a new **I bond**, consider the **Y2K** problem, hope my company will **reprice** my options, and wonder if the **Big 5** (once the **Big 8**) will become the Big 4 (knowing that the **Big Three** are the **Big Two** to stay), then I'll finally consider if there is a **brightline** between a rock and a hard place."*

Two years have passed since our last edition, and new words keep springing up, although we haven't quite figured out what to call the next decade, which seems to me a more immediate task. We're in the 1990s, but what do you call the 2000s? Could we be headed to the "ohs," or "zeros," or "aught aught." For the sake of GenX and the Millennium folks, we won't even consider the "nothings."

In this edition, we added a ton of new words and updated many entries. You should now find this as complete and current a business dictionary as exists on the shelves. Perhaps unique to a business dictionary are the business slang entries—from **dead-cat bounce** to the old favorite **garbage in/garbage out**.

There are two appendices. The first is a list of acronyms and abbreviations, and the second is a list of governmental organizations with their addresses, phone numbers, and web sites.

To make it easier for you, we've indicated the disciplines the words in this book are used in as shown below:

[A]   Accounting

[B]   Business and management

[C]   Computers and communications

[E]   Economics

[F]   Finance and Wall Street

[HR]   Human Resources, benefits, and compensation

[I]   Insurance

[L]   Legal

[M]   Math and statistics

[RE]   Real estate

[S]   Business slang

[T]   Taxes and estate planning

The Alphabetical Convention used

The words in this book have been alphabetized without regard to hyphens. For example, **asset allocation** comes before **asset-backed bond**. Numbers are converted to words, so that **forward slash** comes just before **401(k)** (because the popular benefit plan begins with "four").

A

AAA, AA, A ratings [F] Standard & Poor's and Moody's are two of the prominent firms that rate bonds for investors. These ratings refer to the financial stability of the bond issuer. The two rating systems are similar; for example, an AAA from Standard & Poor's is equivalent to Aaa from Moody's.

The city's *AAA rating* from Standard & Poor's made its bonds an attractive investment.

Rating the Bonds

Highest quality or investment grade:

AAA or Aaa	Best quality
AA or Aa	High quality
A	High-medium quality
BBB or Baa	Medium quality

Lower quality, high yield, or junk bonds:

BB or Ba	Moderate, but not well-guarded
B	Risk of future problems
CCC or Caa	Poor quality
CC or Ca	Often in default
C	Lowest rated, poor prospects
D	In default

---

abatement [L] A reduction or suspension of a charge, or a termination of a lawsuit.

[T] A decrease in taxes, or a tax rebate.

Because its building burned down, BradCo. received an *abatement* of the penalties it normally would have had to pay for late filing of income taxes.

ABC inventory analysis or management [B] A system of tracking and controlling inventory by classifying it into three categories: A (high value), B (medium value), and C (low value).

[A] A method of valuing inventory that gives more weight to expensive merchandise. A is the most expensive inventory, B is less expensive, and C is the least expensive.

> Using ABC management, the accounting department determined that a small number of items represented the major costs of the company's large inventory.

ability to pay [B] A policy for charging for services on a sliding scale in which people who earn a smaller income would pay less for a service than would those who earn a larger income.

> The Smiths liked to use Dr. Jones, whose services were offered on an *ability-to-pay* scale.

[HR] The ability of a company to meet the demands of a collective bargaining agreement.

> After the rumors of financial mismanagement, the local chapter of the Amalgamated Workers' Union was concerned about Acme Corporation's *ability to pay*.

above the line [T] An adjective to describe tax deductions or adjustments made before arriving at the adjusted gross income. These deduction are operating expenses for businesses or adjustments for individuals such as IRA, Keogh, and alimony payments.

[B] Refers to a star or creative person involved in advertising or media.

abrogate [L] A synonym for repeal, rescind, or void.

> Both parties *abrogated* the contract after deciding to cancel the deal.

abscissa [M] In graphing, the horizontal distance from the y-axis to a point. See *ordinate*.

absenteeism [HR] Days or hours that an employee doesn't report to work—Monday and Friday are often the most frequent days.

absolute advantage [E] An asset held by a particular company or country because of patents, ownership of natural resources, skills of its people, or some other factor. Sometimes called "absolute cost advantage."

> The tiny country of Alabascar had an absolute advantage in its climate and terrain which were ideal for raising sheep whose wool was prized.

absolute cell reference [C] In computer spreadsheets, it is a reference to a specific cell, not a relative one. It is often written with dollar signs before the number and letter references to a cell.

absolute value [M] The numerical, or positive, value of a number or expression. It is written with bars before and after the number, such as $|4|$. For example, the absolute value of -4 is 4.

absorption costing [A] The practice of allocating manufacturing costs to the products being produced. This includes materials, labor, and overhead. It is also called *full costing*.

> The electric company's rate increase forced Sponge Inc. to practice *absorption costing* and raise the price of its sponges.

abstract of title [L] A condensed history of the legal actions concerning a specific piece of land.

accelerated depreciation [A] [RE] [T] A practice in which a larger amount of an asset's cost is written off in early years than in the later years. This method is often used for real estate assets. See *depreciation*.

> Although he had twenty years to depreciate the asset on his tax returns, Mario opted for an *accelerated depreciation* schedule that allowed him to take a higher tax deduction now, when he really needed it.

access code [C] A password containing numbers, letters, or both used to gain entry to computer systems or files.

accessory [L] A person who helps another person commit a crime but is not present when the crime is committed, or one who is present when a crime is taking place but does nothing to stop it.

access privileges [C] Authorization to read or copy information from another computer network or site, usually with an ID number and password.

access time [C] The time the computer takes to find and retrieve data.

accidental death and dismemberment (AD&D) [HR] Insurance providing a benefit to workers who suffer a job-related accident in which a loss of life or limb (arms, legs, or eyes) occurs.

accomplice [L] A person who joins with another person to commit a crime and bears equal responsibility for it.

accord and satisfaction [B] Payment of money or other consideration to absolve a debt, usually less than the amount owed. The accord is the agreement, and the satisfaction is the settlement of an obligation.

> Since Acme Corp. would never pay off its debt, L-Mart accepted two thousand "slime balls" as *accord and satisfaction* and wiped the debt from its records.

account [A] A record of the entries and changes to a specific accounting item, such as cash, inventory, or sales.

[B] A company that is a customer of a consulting or advertising firm, or of a supplier or vendor of services or goods.

> The consolidation of all advertising by Acme Chemicals with Zoo Advertising meant one major *account* for Zoo.

accountability [B] A management system of assigning responsibility. An associate vice president may be accountable to a senior vice president, who is accountable to an executive vice president. Each person in the chain must answer for his or her actions to the next person higher in the chain.

> Jane was *accountable* to her senior loan officer for her weekly budget and operations report.

accountant [A] A person trained in one or more fields of accounting. A certified public accountant (CPA) practices accounting through auditing and expressing an independent opinion on whether a company's statements follow generally accepted accounting principles (GAAP).

account executive [B] The person in charge of an account at a consulting or advertising firm.

accounting [A] The general activities of a company relating to capturing financial data, bookkeeping, preparing financial statements, and analyzing costs. The head of the accounting department is usually called the "controller" (or the outdated term "comptroller"), who usually reports to the chief financial officer.

accounting firms [A] See *Big 5.*

Accounting Principles Board (APB) [A] The organization that used to determine accounting procedures and principles for the accounting field and issued APB Opinions. In 1973, APB was replaced by the Financial Accounting Standards Board (FASB), which issues FASB Statements.

accounts payable [A] Money a company owes to other companies, usually suppliers, for materials, supplies, and other items used in the regular production of its products. It usually does not include regular ongoing administrative or labor expenses such as salary, rent, and debt service.

> The assistant bookkeeper printed out a list of *accounts payable* for her boss; it included bills for paper clips, copy paper, and paper cups.

accounts receivable [A] The money that is owed to a company from the sale of its goods or services.

> Even though Zippy Corp. didn't have much money in its accounts, it was able to get a line of credit because the amount of its *accounts receivable* was so high.

accretion [B] A growth in an asset due to outside forces. Accretion in a business may occur due to expansion or an increase in the value of the company's investments.

> The Diamond Hotel experienced an *accretion* because sand was naturally accumulating on its beaches, tripling its value.

accrual accounting; accrual basis [A] A method of accounting in which revenue and expenses are recorded when earned or incurred. This is in contrast to *cash accounting*, in which revenue and expenses are recorded only when money is received or paid out.

accrued liability [HR] The present value of pensions or other benefits earned by employees. It is the amount for which the company is responsible in its pension plan.

accumulated depreciation [A] The total decrease in value recorded for an asset since the date of the asset's acquisition.

accumulated dividends [A] See *cumulative dividends*.

acid test [A] A term that refers to the measurement of how many times current assets (minus inventories) can pay current liabilities. The acid test is a measure of a company's ability to meet current obligations. Also called the "quick ratio."

acquisition [B] The taking over of an organization by another. This is usually accomplished by buying the controlling portion of common stock.

acquit; acquittal [L] The legal verdict that a person or company is not guilty of a specific crime.

acre [RE] A standard unit of land measurement equaling 43,560 square feet, or 4,840 square yards, or 160 square rods. (A rod is a linear measurement of 16.5 feet, 5.5 yards, or 5.03 meters.)

across the board [B] An event or action that affects all aspects of a company or group.

> Budget cuts affected the employees at Acme Corp. *across the board*.

action item [S] A topic, idea, or task that needs attention.

> The Vice President for human resources felt overwhelmed by the numerous *action items* given to her by the president.

active cell [C] In a computer spreadsheet, it is the cell highlighted by the cursor.

act of God [I] [L] An unforeseen and catastrophic event caused by forces of nature.

actuarial equivalent [I] A mathematically equal alternative, such as a lump-sum distribution from a pension plan that is equivalent to an annuity distribution. It is equivalent because an actuary has determined that the present values of both are the same.

actuarial table [I] Produced by actuaries, a table that charts life expectancies for different age groups or other groups of people, such as smokers.

actuary [HR] [I] A mathematician specializing in insurance or pensions. Actuaries deal with mortality tables (the number of persons who die at different ages), probability, and present and future value calculations.

The *actuary* was called on by the board of directors to determine the total costs for restructuring the company's pension plan.

actus reus [L] A criminal act, pronounced ACT-us RAY-us. It is a wrongful act, as opposed to wrongful thoughts and intentions, which is called *mens rea*, meaning a guilty mind, pronounced MENS RAY-a. In a murder, the actual homicide is the *actus reus,* while the intention behind it is the *mens rea.*

ad agency; advertising agency [B] A firm specializing in the planning, preparing, and placing of advertising in a variety of media for a company. At an agency, an account executive oversees a particular company account to help determine the message the company wants to communicate and then implements that strategy through the layout of advertising pages or the production of radio or television spots.

addendum [L] An item added to a legal document either at the time it was first signed or afterwards.

address [C] The electronic location of a person or a business in the online world. All addresses follow a similar pattern: a person's screen name (also called a "user ID"), followed by @, followed by a domain name, followed by the three-letter domain type abbreviation (com, edu, gov, org).

The *address* for the president is President@Whitehouse.gov.

The @ sign is pronounced "at," and periods are pronounced "dot."

ad hoc [L] Term meaning "for a specific purpose." Pronounced Add-HOCK and means *for this* in Latin.

The *ad hoc* committee was formed to determine if the company should have a baseball team.

adjudication [L] The process of rendering a final judgment in a legal action.

adjustable life [I] A life insurance policy that allows for the adjustment of premiums, and accordingly, the face value of the insurance. See *life insurance*.

adjustable rate mortgage (ARM) [RE] A mortgage with an interest rate that may change periodically (usually every one to three years) during the life of the loan and is tied to some index or formula. It usually has a low first-year rate, which is also known as an "introductory rate."

> Because they believed that interest rates might fall in the next few years, Donny and Marie felt it would be smart to get an *adjustable rate mortgage*.

adjusted basis [T] The increasing or decreasing of an asset's tax basis for the purpose of determining capital gains. It is frequently adjusted because of depreciation or depletion. See *basis*.

adjusted gross income (AGI) [T] Gross income minus any above-the-line deductions or adjustments.

> Jay had an annual salary of $50,000, but his alimony payments reduced his *adjusted gross income* to about $20,000.

adjuster [I] The insurance company employee who decides the amount the company will pay for a claim.

> The *adjuster* was on the site immediately after the fire to calculate the damages and offer an initial payment until the full settlement was made.

administrator [L] A person appointed by a court to settle an estate when an executor is not qualified or not available to do so, or when there is no will.

ADR (American depository receipt) [F] A substitute stock that is available on an American stock exchange and is held in custody overseas. This allows a foreign company, for instance the Sony Corp., to have its stock traded in the United States as well as on its home turf, in this case the Nikkei Exchange.

adr (alternative dispute resolution) [HR] A nonlegal but hopefully effective method of resolving an internal dispute, usually between employee and supervisor. It is an in-place method, often using outside arbitrators to resolve internal matters.

ad valorem tax [T] Latin for *according to value*, it's a tax that's a percentage of a value rather than a dollar amount per unit. It is commonly used in customs duties. It is also used in connection with real estate where the higher the assessed value, the higher taxes due.

> All raw materials for import in Alabascar carried a 3 percent *ad valorem tax*, collected as the goods arrived at the border checkpoints.

advanced technologies [B] A term usually applied to highly scientific fields such as chemistry, biology, physics, computers, and mathematics.

adverse possession [RE] A term that refers to a situation in which someone continuously, openly, and spitefully occupies and possesses a piece of real estate.

advertising [B] Paid announcements of products or services to attract buyers. A company determines, often with an ad agency, what its message should be and what media will be used. The communication is often mass media. Advertising provides most of the revenues for magazines and virtually all of the revenues for nonpublic radio and television.

ADV form (investment advisor) [F] The SEC (Securities and Exchange Commission) form that generally describes the investment portion of what a financial planner does and how that planner is compensated. As of July 8, 1997, only major firms are generally registered with the SEC, and individual planners are registered with the state(s) in which they operate.

affidavit [L] A legal document, made under oath or affirmation, that attests to some fact.

> The lawyers told the employee to file an *affidavit* with the court attesting to her complaints of unfair hiring practices at Acme Corp.

affirmative action [HR] A program that requires a certain percentage of minority hiring, to overcome some past or present discriminatory actions on the part of an employer.

> When the local court ruled that the city's hiring programs had been discriminatory, it instituted a plan of *affirmative action* that required its future hiring to reflect the percentage of minority population in the city.

AFL-CIO [B] See *American Federation of Labor—Congress of Industrial Organizations.*

after-tax income [B][T] Income after taxes have been deducted or paid.

> Because they were in the highest tax bracket, the Bramleys' *after-tax income* was only about half of their before-tax income.

Age Discrimination in Employment Act (ADEA) [HR] The 1967 legislation that protects employees aged forty to sixty-five. It prohibits age discrimination in pay, benefits, and continued employment. In 1978 the upper age was raised from sixty-five to seventy. In 1986, amendments effectively ended mandatory retirement by age.

agent [L] A person authorized to act on behalf of another person or a company.

[I] A person licensed to sell insurance. An exclusive agent, often called a "general" or "captive agent," sells only one insurance company's policies. An independent agent sells for any number of insurance companies, claiming to get the best deal for you. Both types receive a commission for selling insurance policies.

[RE] In real estate, a person who has been given authority to act for the buyer or seller.

age of consent [L] The age at which a person may marry without their parents' consent, which varies by state. Commonly, it's sixteen or eighteen, but in a few states it is as low as fourteen.

age of majority [L] The age at which a person is considered legally responsible for all of his activities, including their ability to manage his own money. It is usually age twenty-one, but is eighteen in some states.

agglomeration [B] The act of putting together different companies into one large conglomeration.

> The *agglomeration* of Acme Corp,, MM Corp., and Zippy Corp. formed the AMZ Corp.

aggregate; aggregate income; aggregate demand/supply [E] The term aggregate refers to the sum of the parts. Aggregate income is the total income a country produces. Aggregate supply is an economic term for the total goods and services supplied to a market at a given time. Aggregate demand is the total demand for goods and services in a market.

> GDP (gross domestic production) is one example of an *aggregate income*. Economists like to compare the *aggregate demand* with the *aggregate supply* in a country to gauge its economic status.

aggressive growth fund [F] A mutual fund usually comprised of smaller companies that hopes for maximum capital gains. See *mutual funds*.

aging schedule [A] A list of outstanding accounts receivable usually grouped by length of time payments are overdue.

agreement of sale [RE] A written contract between a buyer and a seller that comes before the actual closing takes place. It lays out all the terms that have been agreed upon for the sale to close.

> They signed an *agreement of sale*, which stipulated that the seller would be responsible for the cleanup of the environmental hazards, and the buyer would take care of the flood damage.

AI (artificial intelligence) [C] See *artificial intelligence*.

AICPA (American Institute of Certified Public Accountants) [A] The professional association of certified public accountants (CPAs).

air bill; airway bill [B] The air freight version of a bill of lading.

> States Air Shipping always had *airway bills* attached to each carton to ensure that the contents were correct.

air freight [B] A term that refers to using airplanes to transport freight. Air freight is faster but much more expensive than truck or rail freight.

FedEx is one of the largest *air freight* shippers in the country.

air rights [RE] The rights of owners to the air above their property. These rights may come into conflict with the rights of the public to "paths in the sky" for airplanes.

algebra [M] Math that uses letters or symbols to represent numbers or values in a general case. Algebra also has rules for the manipulation of values. For instance, the general case for determining the future value of an investment, or any future value, is:

$$FV = PV(1 + i)^n$$

Each letter or group of letters represents a value. In this formula the two letters FV represent the future value and PV the present value. The letter i is designated to represent the interest rate, and n designates the number of years. See *formula*.

algorithm [M] A step-by-step mathematical or problem-solving procedure.

alibi [L] An excuse as to why a person could not have been at the scene of the crime.

alien [HR] A person who resides in a country but is not a legal citizen of it. A resident alien has permanent residence status but no citizenship. An illegal alien has not been given permission to reside in a country.

alienation [RE] The voluntary transfer of real property from one person to another.

align [S] To coordinate and move in the same direction, such as getting separate units within a company to pull in the same direction.

alimony [T] Payments made from one former spouse to another due to separation or divorce.

A-list [S] A term to describe the important items on a boss's mind or a company's objectives.

alliance [B] The teaming up of companies to provide a wider array of services to customers than any one can offer alone. For instance, an accounting firm may form an alliance with a law firm to provide legal services to its clients. This would allow the accounting firm to control more business than just its core activities, making it more valuable to its clients. Domestic airlines have formed alliances with foreign carriers; for example, Continental has an alliance with Virgin Atlantic Airways.

allocation [A] To disperse costs to different accounts over time.

allocation of resources [E] The term used to describe the dispersion of a limited amount of resources (both physical and human) among the people and companies who need them to make products and services. It is also the dispersion of products and services from the producers to the consumers.

allowance [B] A price reduction given to a retailer in compensation for something. A brokerage allowance assumes, for example, that a certain number of items may be broken in shipping. Retail display allowance is a price break in exchange for a better selling spot on the shelves.

> Zippy Corp. was willing to give L-Mart a generous retail display *allowance* if L-Mart displayed Zippy merchandise at the front register.

allowances [T] A number reported by an employee that determines how much tax money will be withheld from an employee's paycheck. The fewer allowances reported, the larger the employee's paycheck. If not enough taxes are withheld because a person claims too many allowances, a penalty and additional taxes might be owed.

> Because Kurt had three children and owned his own home, he took the maximum number of *allowances* on his W-4 form.

all-risk policy [I] A property insurance policy covering everything except perils specifically excluded.

alpha [F] A sophisticated measurement of mutual funds that calculates the difference between the fund's actual performance and an expected performance in light of its risk factor, usually as measured by beta. Alpha is said to measure the performance of the manager, whereas beta measures the market. See *beta*.

alphanumeric [C] An adjective describing something comprised of both letters and numbers.

alternative minimum tax (AMT) [T] A tax designed to make sure the wealthy pay taxes. At a certain income level, people must calculate both their regular income tax and, with Form 6251, the alternative minimum tax. They must pay whichever is more. To calculate the amount of the tax, the taxpayer must add tax adjustments and preference items, such as incentive stock options, and passive investment activities.

alternative mortgage instrument (AMI) [RE] Any mortgage that is different from a standard, fixed-rate, level-payment mortgage; for example, a gradual payment loan, an adjustable rate mortgage, or a reverse annuity mortgage.

alternative work arrangements [HR] Any of a number of work schedules other than 9 A.M. to 5 P.M., such as flextime, part time, job sharing, or telecommuting.

Alt key [C] A key on a computer keyboard used to trigger certain functions. In general, the Alt key (alternate key) is used with another key to carry out a function.

amended return [T] A tax form filed to correct a mistake on a previously submitted form.

> Because the accountants miscalculated the charitable deductions for Whammo, the company had to file an *amended return*.

amenity [RE] A nice feature, convenience, or luxury that improves the quality of a property, such as architectural uniqueness or scenic beauty.

> *Amenities* on the property included a tennis court, swimming pool, Jacuzzi, and sauna.

American Accounting Association (AAA) [A] An organization of accountants, accounting teachers, and accounting researchers who develop theories and techniques.

American Compensation Association (ACA) [HR] A professional association for compensation specialists.

American Federation of Labor—Congress of Industrial Organizations (AFL-CIO) [B] The largest labor union in the United States.

American Institute of Certified Public Accountants (AICPA) [A] See *AICPA*.

American Institute of Real Estate Appraisers (AIREA) [RE] The Appraisal Institute, as it is commonly known, is one of the main professional organizations for real estate appraisers; they confer the MAI and RM designations for appraisers.

American Management Association (AMA) [B] A general association of executives, managers, and supervisors in industry, commerce, government, and nonprofit organizations. It offers many training seminars to its members on subjects such as how to better manage and communicate.

America Online (AOL) [C] The largest commercial online service with approximately 15 million subscribers.

American Society for Training and Development (ASTD) [HR] A professional association for people who are involved with company training.

American Society of Real Estate Counselors (ASREC) [RE] A professional organization for real estate appraisers that confers the CRE designation on its members.

American Stock Exchange (AMEX) [F] The second-oldest stock exchange in the United States. AMEX was founded in 1842 and originally called the New York Curb Exchange because business was actually conducted on the street curb. Its rival is the New York Stock Exchange (NYSE). New York's Wall Street is the home to both the AMEX and the NYSE. Early in 1998, the NASDAQ system reached an agreement with the American Stock Exchange and the Philadelphia Stock Exchange to form a joint association.

Americans with Disabilities Act (ADA) [HR] The 1990 legislation that extended the same employment protection to disabled people that the Civil Rights Act of 1964 extended to African Americans and other minorities.

amicus curiae [L] Pronounced a-Mi-cus CURE-e-i, it's a legal term referring to a third party who submits information or arguments to the court concerning a case. It's Latin for *friend of the court* and is often used in cases of a controversial or a widely publicized case.

amnesty [L] An act of state or federal government that forgives people for actions. For example, during a tax amnesty, states give people a certain window of opportunity to come forward to pay taxes owed. No penalties are assessed during the amnesty period.

amortization; amortize [A] To write off the cost of an asset gradually and systematically over time. For instance, accountants amortize the cost of an asset through depreciation.

   [RE] To pay off a mortgage or any debt with regular, scheduled payments. An amortized mortgage requires regular payments of the principal plus interest on the loan. A conventional thirty-year mortgage requires the exact same payment for all thirty years, although the amount of the interest declines and the principal represented increases in each payment. The amortization schedule is the schedule of payments to retire the debt. See *mortgage*.

ampersand (&) [C] The symbol for "and." It comes from the term "and per se and."

AMT bonds [F] Municipal bonds that are subject to the AMT tax. AMT stands for the alternative minimum tax. Certain municipal bonds, which are generally tax-free, have this feature and will not be tax-free to an investor who is in a high tax bracket.

analog [C] Transmission of data by varying frequency or voltage, as opposed to digital, which is the transmission of data by varying the digits. For example, an analog clock has hands, whereas a digital clock has only numbers.

analysis [M] The application of common sense as well as mathematical and statistical calculations to describe, understand, contrast, hypothesize, solve, and make decisions about a problem.

analysis paralysis [S] The inability to make a decision or solve a problem because of getting mired in the details or the technical aspects of the situation.

analytical geometry [M] Geometry primarily using algebraic expressions defined in terms of position coordinates on a graph.

annual benefit statement [HR] An individual benefit report generated at the end of the year showing the specific benefits for an employee. It also serves to advertise what the company has contributed to these various benefits. Usually the benefit statement will summarize such items as the current amount invested in the 401(k) plan and the amount of pension earned. It can also show the company's medical and life insurance programs and how much it costs the company to provide those benefits.

annualized or effective rate [M] To take any rate given in a certain time frame and convert it to a rate for the year.

> When Rip-Off Retailers offered a "low, low" interest rate of only 2 percent, Marty was quick to point out that it was a monthly rate and that the *annualized rate* would be 26.82 percent—no bargain.

annualized return [F] A one-year return. To calculate an annualized investment return, a period less than a year or more than a year, is converted it into a one-year result. This allows for a standard comparison that is recognizable and understood.

> To get the *annualized return* for the JAMS Corporation, we took the returns for a five-year period and averaged them.

annual percentage rate (APR) [RE] The amount—as a percentage—of interest paid each year. Even if an advertisement screams out "2 percent monthly interest!" it must report the APR. The Truth in Lending Act makes showing the APR as well as the periodic interest mandatory.

annual renewable term [I] Term insurance that is renewable year by year. See *life insurance.*

annual report [F] A report on a company's status that includes what the company did the year before, its ideas and business outlook, and a full financial report including a balance sheet and a summary of the audit done by a public accounting firm. Companies provide annual reports for their investors. Because they are designed to make investors feel all warm and cozy about their investments, annual reports are usually big, glossy productions.

annuitant [HR] A name some companies call their retired employees. It comes from the term *annuity*, which is how traditional pensions are paid, versus a lump sum.

annuity [HR] A standard form of a pension payout. It is a payment of equal monthly payments for the rest of the retiree's life. This is in contrast to a lump-sum payout. For the different forms of payouts from pensions, see *pension plan*.

[I] An insurance product that provides a yearly income for the holder of the annuity.

> Because his company did not have a retirement plan, Jack bought an *annuity* from his life insurance company to pay out when he retired.

[M] In financial calculations, a stream of usually equal payments, although payments can be variable or increasing. If money is paid out (or in) at the *beginning* of the period, it is called an "annuity due." If money is paid out (or in) at the *end* of the period it is called an "ordinary annuity."

anonymous FTP [C] A term used on the internet referring to the ability to get files without having an account. Using this, one may copy files from thousands of different computers around the world.

anticipation note [F] A short-term municipal note offered in anticipation of obtaining full legislative approval for longer-term financing.

anticipatory breach [L] The notification of a person or company that a party cannot meet its obligations under a contract, making the contract invalid.

antitrust; antitrust laws [B] Laws designed to promote fair trade practices by outlawing price fixing, monopolies, price discrimination, and similar unfair business practices. The term "trust" was used by large firms in the early 1900s, such as Standard Oil, which led to antitrust action by the government to break them up. A more recent example of government antitrust action involved IBM, and most recently Microsoft.

> A small segment of zipper producers was brought up on charges of price fixing, illegal under *antitrust laws*.

AOL (America Online) [C] See *America Online*.

appeal [L] A request made to a higher court to review a decision of a lower court.

appellate court [L] A court whose sole function is to review cases of lower courts.

apples and oranges [S] One of the most common business phrases used to distinguish between two alternatives. "We need to compare apples to apples, not apples to oranges," is a common expression used when attempting to keep a comparison accurate.

applet [C] A small utility program used within the Java programming language, such as a retirement calculator. This is opposed to major software applications such as word processor or spreadsheet programs.

applicable federal rate (AFR) [T] A rate of interest determined monthly by the Treasury Department, used to calculate the interest on unpaid taxes.

application [C] Another word for a type of computer program. There are spreadsheet applications, graphics applications, word-processing applications, and database applications.

> Microsoft Word is a type of word-processing *application*.

applications software [C] Software for the computer, including word-processing, spreadsheet, database, and communications applications.

appraisal [I] A valuation of damages, which is typically needed after an accident. Who performs this appraisal and how it is done is specified by the insurance company. An outside appraiser is often hired by the insurance company to perform this valuation.

[RE] An unbiased estimate of a property's value. Most banks require a real estate appraisal before they will give a mortgage on the property. The lender usually refers to the result of this appraisal as "the appraised value."

> The *appraisal* put the value of the property at $150,000, even though Ziggy paid $200,000 for it.

Professional Designations
for Real Estate Appraisers

Those considering purchasing, financing, or insuring real estate usually need the services of a real estate appraiser. Most people are unfamiliar with the types of appraisers out there. Banks generally maintain an "approved list" of appraisers on file—this means that they will accept an appraisal from someone on that list for the purposes of receiving financing from their institution. Some of the most common terms used in reference to real estate appraisers are:

State certified: Some states now require that real estate appraisers pass an exam to receive state certification.

MAI: Member, Appraisal Institute. The Appraisal Institute is one of the major professional real estate appraisal organizations. They educate and certify their member appraisers. The MAI designation is one of the highest an appraiser can receive. It indicates that he or she has passed a series of classes and exams and has submitted a sample appraisal for approval.

---

appreciation [F] [RE] An increase in the value of an investment or other asset, like real estate property.

appropriation [A] An amount set aside for a specific business purpose.

approximation [M] The process of guessing or ball-parking a number rather than precisely calculating it.

appurtenance [RE] Something that is added to the property and passed along to the buyer with the property itself.

The tool shed was an unsightly but useful *appurtenance*.

arable [RE] Land that is suitable for farming.

After the effects of the drought and toxic waste, that land was no longer considered *arable*.

arbiter; arbitrator [B] Impartial third parties used to settle disputes. They have become very popular in labor disputes in recent years. Arbiters must bring their decision to the court that appointed them for a final okay; arbitrators have authority to make a final decision.

> The *arbitrator* for the contract negotiations between the employees and Acme Corp. sat up all night with both sides trying to compromise on the issue of overtime.

arbitrage [F] The practice of buying an investment or commodity in one market and selling in another market in order to make a profit, the sophisticated investor's dream. It doesn't often happen and it takes a sharp eye to find what are called these inefficiencies in the markets. For example, indexes, and futures contracts on indexes, may move at slightly different rates. An arbitrageur may then buy huge quantities of lower-priced contracts while selling the higher priced ones. (As the price changes are so small, it involves trading a great number of contracts to make any profit.)

arbitration [B] A method of settling a dispute through an impartial third party, used commonly in labor-management relations. Usually the arbitrator has the authority to dictate the terms of a settlement, versus a mediator who attempts through argument to get agreement between parties.

Archie [C] An internet program used to search for anonymous sites and content. It has largely been replaced by newer search engines. It originated at McGill University where all the FTP sites were organized for easy browsing.

architecture [C] The overall design and structure of a computer system.

archive [C] To copy or save computer files, usually for storage.

> Louise downloaded all the files as a single *archive*.

archive site [C] A machine that provides access to a collection of files across the internet.

> The anonymous FTP *archive site* allowed Mario to access a range of material through the FTP protocol.

arithmetic [M] The mathematics of primarily addition, subtraction, multiplication, and division. Arithmetic does not denote the more complex forms of mathematics such as calculus.

arithmetic progression [M] See *geometric progression*.

arm's length transaction [L] The relatively equal bargaining position of two parties in which the agreement reached is free of one-sidedness or duress placed on either party.

[RE] Term refering to a deal between a buyer and seller in which both buyer and seller are out on the open market, are not related, and are under no pressure to buy or sell.

> Because the sale price was very fair, one can assume it was an *arm's length transaction*.

arraignment [L] A formal court procedure in which a person is officially charged with a crime.

arrears [A] A term refering to an overdue payment.

> The business manager finally turned over all the accounts in *arrears* to a collection agency.

arrow keys [C] The keys of the computer keyboard that can direct the movement of the cursor on the screen horizontally or vertically.

artificial intelligence (AI) [C] Computer programming that attempts to duplicate characteristics of human intelligence through expert systems, voice recognition, and robotics.

ASAP or asap [S] As soon as possible, in other words, now. When spoken, each letter is pronounced, as in "A-S-A-P."

ASCII (American Standard Code for Information Interchange) [C] Pronounced as As-key, it is the most common character code used by computers today, consisting of a basic 128 upper and lower case letters. Along with the addition of the Extended Character Set, technical graphic and non-Western letter characters are included. ASCII files can be used from computer to computer because the basic text is the same from program to program.

> To send a Word for Windows file to someone without Windows, save it as MS-DOS text and it will be converted to *ASCII* format.

Asean [E] The Southeast Asian political and economic bloc. It consists of such countries as Brunei, Malaysia, the Phillipines, Singapore, Thailand, and Vietnam. In 1997 the three countries of Cambodia, Laos, and Myanmar (formerly Burma), were added.

Asian basin; Asian rim; Asian tigers [E] The geographic area in Asia along the western Pacific, particularly Hong Kong, Indonesia, Japan, Malaysia, and South Korea. These countries have had dynamic and modern economies, although since the middle and fall of 1997 this has not been so. Japan's is by far the most advanced of these economies. The original "little tigers" were Hong Kong, Singapore, South Korea, and Taiwan. They were joined by the "new tigers" of Indonesia, Malaysia, the Philippines, and Thailand.

Asian contagion [E] The negative economic results that affected the countries in the Asian basin starting in the summer of 1997, and that affected other economies around the world.

assault [L] An attempt, or threat, to do physical harm to another person. Aggravated assault is a reckless attempt to physically harm another person.

assembly language [C] The computer language that translates easy-to-use English syntax computer code into binary machine language.

assembly line [B] A method of mass production usually along a conveyer belt that gives each worker one or only a few tasks to be completed on the material or equipment.

> When Zippy Corp. changed to an *assembly line* manufacturing process, each worker, who previously had made one complete zipper, had to be retrained to perform just one step in the production of zippers.

assessed valuation [RE] The value placed on a house or property for tax purposes. Real estate taxes are a percentage of assessed valuation, which may or may not be close to the actual market value.

> With an annual tax rate of 7 percent and an *assessed valuation* of $20,000, the property owner would have $1,400 a year in real estate taxes on the property.

assessor [RE] A person, employed by a taxing authority, who determines the value of property.

asset [A] Something of monetary value to a business, such as equipment, inventory, trademark, or real estate. The balance sheet is the financial statement that lists assets and liabilities.

asset allocation [F] The percentage of each broad category of investments in a portfolio. For instance, 50 percent large-cap stocks, 40 percent intermediate bonds, and 10 percent money market funds would be an example of asset allocation. The allocation of these basic categories is considered the basic strategy of setting up a portfolio. Definable categories in stocks include large-cap, mid-cap, small-cap, and international stocks. Categories in bonds include long-term corporate and treasury bonds, intermediate-term corporate and treasury bonds, high yield bonds (junk bonds), and municipal bonds.

asset-backed bond [F] A bond that is secured against a specific asset of the company that issues it, sometimes called a "mortgage bond."

> Weehawken Village issued an *asset-backed bond* against the real estate owned by the village.

asset turnover [A] An accounting ratio calculated by sales revenues divided by average total assets for a period of time, usually for a year. It is used to analyze how effective a company is in using assets to generate sales.

assignee/assignor [L] The person who receives or gives property or agrees to a contract.

assignment [L] The transferring of benefits and perhaps the obligations of a contract to another party.

assumable mortgage [RE] A mortgage that can be transferred from the seller of a property directly to the purchaser whereby the purchaser continues payments. Not all mortgages are assumable.

> The fact that old Mr. Lapine had an *assumable mortgage* helped clinch the deal; the buyer was able to take over the mortgage at a below market interest rate.

assumpsit [L] An agreement or promise where there is no formal contract. It also refers to legal action to enforce or recover damages for nonperformance.

assumption [M] A variable, or parameter, in a mathematical or statistical argument. For example, estimates of inflation, unemployment, and productivity are assumptions in economic models.

assumption of risk [L] An agreement by a company or individual to perform certain duties that are known to be risky. Thus, if a lawsuit later arises, it can be claimed that the risks were assumed.

asterisk (*) [C] A star-shaped symbol, often called "star," commonly used to represent multiplication in computer spreadsheets. It is also used in DOS applications, such as in *.*, which denotes all files and is pronounced "star-dot-star." It has even been called "splat" by hackers. The formal symbol is pronounced: AS-ta-risk.

asymmetric information [E] A newer term in economics referring to one side in a negotiation having more information than the other. This term came to the fore after the 1996 Nobel prizes were awarded to William Vickrey and James Mirrless, whose work dealt with this concept. For instance, a used-car dealer has more information about the car than a buyer, unfortunately for the buyer.

asynchronous [C] A nonsynchronized, or intermittent, flow of information, common in modems.

AT&T WorldNet [C] One of the commercial online services.

ATM (automated teller machine) [F] The ubiquitous machines using bank or credit cards that allow one to perform many of the transactions that formerly required standing on line in a bank, such as withdrawing cash or transfering funds.

at sign (@) [C] A commonly used symbol in computer spreadsheets and within internet addresses. It was originally a general business symbol meaning "each," as in: twelve staplers @ $10.50 = $126. But it was available on the computer keyboard and adopted for several computer uses. It can be described as an *a* with a tail wrapped around it or an *a* within a circle.

attachment [L] A court order to seize property to pay for a legal judgment.

at the market [F] A buy order for investment securities at whatever market price is available.

at the money [F] A term used to describe an option whose strike price for a call or a put is exactly the price of the underlying security. That is, it is not "out of the money" (the investor hasn't made money yet) or "in the money" (the investor has made money); it's sort of at the break-even point.

attitude [S] Generally, a negative demeanor. Often suggests an uncooperative or combative person.

attorney [L] Commonly, a lawyer who is qualified to practice law in a jurisdiction. This can also refer to a person who can act for another, such as a person who has power of attorney.

attorney-client privilege [L] A term referring to the legally private communications between an attorney and client. Other privileged communications include those with doctors, psychologists, and priests.

attributes [C] A computer file's defining features; for example, a read-only file, which a user cannot do anything to other than read it, has a read-only attribute. In a database, the tables are divided into rows and fields, which are also called attributes.

audit [A] An accountant's formal review of the books and financial statements of a company. The accuracy of transactions is tested and samples are verified to determine if generally accepted accounting principles (GAAP) were followed.

[T] The process by which the Internal Revenue Service examines a number of tax returns each year. This whole process is designed to check all the numbers a person has reported to ensure the income tax payment is correct. Some taxpayers are chosen for an audit completely at random.

auditor [A] An accountant who performs an audit of a portion or the entirety of a company's books. The auditor's work, including the auditor's opinion, allows investors to have confidence that a company's statements can be relied upon for accuracy.

auditor's opinion [A] The statement by a certified public accountant that the company's statements were examined and the expression of an opinion of the fairness of those statements. If an auditor gives an unqualified opinion, there have been no irregularities or exceptions found; this is often called a standard opinion. However, an auditor can give a qualified opinion that contains phrases such as "except for" or "subject to."

audit trail [A] A chain of records or documentation that shows the sequence of details back to the origin of a transaction. For instance, the audit trail of marketing expenses can show the account balances back through the journal entries and back to paid checks or payments by check. The purpose of the audit trail is to allow the auditors to verify transactions and to catch any errors.

Austrian school [E] Ideas of economics originating from the Austrian economist Carl Menger (1840–1921). Menger argued that humans do not act like rigid mathematical models. He developed the marginal utility theory and attacked socialism, supporting instead ideas of laissez-faire capitalism. See *laissez-faire, marginal utility, socialism,* and *utility.*

autoexec.bat file [C] A DOS file that automatically initiates a "batch" of key startup functions when the computer is turned on. It stands for automatic execute batch. See *config.sys file.*

auto insurance [I] A general form of insurance covering auto accidents, especially medical expenses and body repairs to the car.

auto redial [C] A feature on telephones, faxes, or modems that redials a designated number when there is a busy signal.

auxiliary storage [C] Devices on which a computer stores data and programs not being used. Auxiliary storage is nonvolatile memory, meaning that the stuff packed away there will not be lost when the power is turned off.

average (mean) [M] The value obtained by adding each value and dividing that total by the number of values. See *mean, median,* and *mode.*

B

baby bells [B] The seven local telephone companies that emerged from the 1984 breakup of AT&T. They were Ameritech, Bell Atlantic, Bell South, Nynex, Pacific Telesis, Southwest Bell, and U.S. West. Due to mergers, they are soon to become four.

baby boomers [B] The group of people generally born between 1946 and 1964. They form a major group of consumers for business markets because of their sheer numbers, about 76 million. It is a generation of people who have been characterized as spenders, ideal for business. The term "baby boom" came from the simple fact of the great increase, or boom, in births starting after World War II. In his 1980 book *Great Expectations, America and the Baby Boom Generation*, Landon Y. Jones, former managing editor of *People Magazine*, coined the phrase. See *generations*.

backdating [I] A procedure in the insurance industry to make the effective date of a policy earlier than the application date, usually to provide the policy holder a lower age and therefore a lower rate.

back-end load [F] [I] A load is a commission charged on a mutual fund by a stock broker, insurance agent, or other financial salesperson. Often there are no initial sales charges if there is a back-end fee, but a fee is assessed if you sell the fund within several years of purchasing it. This is referred to as a back-end load, redemption fee, deferred sales charge, or exit fee.

> If only Mary Anne had realized that Class B mutual funds have a *back-end load* when she invested—the 5 percent commission reduced her profit on the sale by $250.

backfill [RE] Refers to the process of filling in dirt around a structure or foundation for support.

[S] Refers to recouping one's position after having been taken off guard by some information.

> After it had been revealed at the board-of-director's meeting that the company's loans were in trouble, the treasurer quickly *backfilled* by indicating that the company had a contingency plan for that eventuality.

background [C] The backdrop of color on a computer screen or, in a multitasking environment like Windows, the programs that are held behind the scenes while other programs are being actively used.

> Ashley was entering data in Lotus 1-2-3, which was running in the foreground, while WordPerfect was active in the *background*.

background noise [C] Extraneous sounds such as static that creep into communication lines.

backlog [B] The accumulation of orders that can't immediately be filled because production can't satisfy demand. This term also refers to the monetary value of any orders a business holds but has yet to fill. Looking at the backlog is a good way for a company to assess how efficient or timely it is and how much income it can expect in the short term.

> "Our business is doing well!" insisted the CEO of Acme Corp. at the board meeting. "Just take a look at our *backlog*—we have orders of almost a million dollars waiting to be filled."

back of the envelope [S] A quick calculation or analysis, as one would do on the back of an envelope (because no other paper was available at the time).

back order [B] Those goods that are not available but have already been ordered.

back slash (\) [C] A symbol most commonly used in MS DOS programs to separate directories and programs. The backslash is not found on a conventional typewriter's keyboard, only on a computer keyboard. Think of it as a vertical line that is leaning backward. Don't confuse it with a regular slash (/), which is leaning forward and appropriately called the forward slash.

> Example: c:\MSDOS\wp\file.bat.

back stabbing [S] A term referring to a person's attempt to do another person political harm within an organization.

backup; back up [C] A copy of an original file or disk, made in case anything happens to the original file or disk. May be used as a verb or a noun:

> The supervisor advised his crew to *back up* their files during the storm in case the electricity went out.

> I'm so glad I made a *backup* of that file—that coffee spill damaged my original disk.

back-up plan or procedure [S] A secondary plan, in case the primary plan doesn't work out.

bad debt [A] An accounts receivable that is not collectible because of a customer's inability or unwillingness to pay.

bail [L] The amount of money required to release a defendant until the date of his or her court appearance. In some cases, a defendant can be released on his or her own recognizance with the promise to appear in court when directed, and thus no bail is necessary. See *release on one's own recognizance*.

bailiff [L] A court attendant who is responsible for keeping order or custody of prisoners while in court.

bait and switch [B] An unethical (and often illegal) practice of enticing unwary consumers with the promise of a certain product or price and then either talking them out of purchasing that product or conveniently not having it in stock, with the intent of selling a more expensive one.

balanced fund [F] A mutual fund balanced between stocks and bonds. Typically stocks comprise about 60 percent of the fund while the remaining 40 percent are mostly in bonds, with some cash or money market funds.

balance of payments [E] The accounting of the flow of goods and money from one country to another. In the aggregate, it is the accounting of all the money that flows into and out of an economy. If consumers in the United States buy more goods from Japan, then Japanese businesses receive more dollars during the year than American businesses receive yen. Americans have more Japanese goods, and the Japanese have more American dollars. The balance of payments is divided into two: the current account, which refers to the goods, and the capital account, which refers to the money.

balance of trade [E] The difference between exports and imports for a given country at a given time. If the country exports more than it imports, it has a favorable balance of trade. If it imports more, the balance is unfavorable.

When the small country of Zeenomaland suddenly found a booming worldwide market for its hand-woven baskets, it benefited from a favorable *balance of trade*.

balance sheet [A] A key financial statement listing all of a company's assets balanced against its liabilities and stockholder equity. It is sometimes called the "statement of financial position." It represents the financial condition of a company at a particular point in time, usually at the end of the year, whereas an income statement shows the results of a company's operation over a period of time, such as a year. The balance sheet shows the assets of the company on the left, which are its productive assets, balanced by its liabilities and equity on the right, which are the claims against the company.

Balance Sheet

MacSoftware, Inc.
As of December 31,1998
(in thousand of dollars)

Assets:		Liabilities and Shareholders' Equity:	
Cash	$ 5,000	Notes	$ 5,000
Accounts Receivable	10,000	Accounts Payable	12,500
Market Securities	3,500		
		Total Liability	17,500
Property, Plant and Equipment	6,500	Common Stock	7,500
Total Assets	$ 25,000	Liabilities and Shareholders' Equity	$ 25,000

balloon mortgage; balloon payment [RE] A loan that has a big final payment, called the *balloon payment*. It is sometimes structured so that only interest payments are made monthly and principal is paid as a lump-sum balloon payment.

> The *balloon mortgage* had a monthly payment of $1,000 for five years, with a final *balloon payment* of $20,000.

balls [S] A terms that refers to having guts or utter nerve.

> Smithers expressed what everyone felt: "She sure has *balls* for telling off the boss."

bandwidth [C] The capacity of computer connection or network to carry data. Bandwidth is the range of upper and lower transmission frequencies.

banker's acceptance [F] A short-term promissory note issued by a company and guaranteed by a bank. Used widely in international trade. It can be traded before its maturity date.

bank failure [E] The bankruptcy of a bank. Although not many banks have failed recently, during the 1980s the Thrifts Savings and Loan banks failed at an alarming rate. The organization overseeing them, the FSLIC (Federal Savings and Loan Insurance Corporation) itself became insolvent in 1989 and was taken over by the main banking regulatory organization, the FDIC (Federal Deposit Insurance Corporation). The RTC (Resolution Trust Corporation) was set up to temporarily deal with this crisis, which it did. It is estimated that the S&L problem has cost taxpayers $165 billion.

banking [E] The business of accepting money as deposits and then lending money to other businesses and individuals.

bankruptcy [L] Legal declaration of one's inability to meet financial obligations. When a person or company files for bankruptcy, a court oversees the liquidation and satisfaction of creditors. Chapter 11 bankruptcy is voluntary bankruptcy; chapter 7 is involuntary. In either case, a court helps the company or individual to settle debts. In bankruptcy a company may be able to settle its debts for less than owed, for instance, paying only 10¢ on the dollar.

Know Your Bankruptcy

Chapter 7 The most common form of bankruptcy, where a court appoints a trustee to sell assets to pay creditors. This is for either individuals or businesses. The advantage is that most of the debts are erased.

Chapter 9 An unusual form involving a municipality, where there is a reorganization and an adjustment of debt.

Chapter 11 A court leaves the business in the hands of the owners to reorganize and keep the business going. If after a period of time the court decides that the business cannot repay its creditors, the court may order the liquidation of assets.

Chapter 12 A special form of bankruptcy for farmers, where a farmer can keep his farm going while restructuring his debt.

Chapter 13 Under this form of bankruptcy, a person with regular income is allowed to tailor a plan for the eventual repayment of debt. This is usually for unsecured debt under $250,000 and secured debt under $750,000. Debts are not erased but must be negotiated with creditors.

---

bar, the [L] A term that refers to attorneys as a group. The word derives from the time when there was a physical bar in front of the judge's bench, where lawyers and their clients would stand.

bar code [B] Those zebra-like lines and numbers seen on just about every product in the world. A computer scans a bar code for data such as price and inventory information. Technically, it is called a "universal product code" or "UPC." Here's an example of a bar code.

ISBN 0-679-77356-8

digits represent the actual item (Math Smart for Business)

first digit (5) means U.S. dollars
next four digits is price ($12)

digits represent the company (The Princeton Review)

bargaining unit [B] A group of employees within a company who are represented by a particular union.

bargain sale [T] The sale of property or stock at a below market value. The amount of the bargain is often called the "bargain element."

bar graph or bar chart [M] See *graphs*.

barren [RE] Lacking any vegetation.

The land had been *barren* for years since the devastating fire.

barriers to entry [E] Factors that tend to prevent or make difficult the entry of other companies into a market, usually because of existing advantages to particular companies. These factors may be economies of scale, patents, or rights to certain raw materials.

barrister [L] In England, the barrister is the person who presents the case in court, while the "solicitor" prepares it and may even settle the case before it gets to court. Thus, the barrister, as the name implies, only practices at the bar.

Barron's [F] A popular weekly publication for professional and active investors on all aspects of investments and the economy.

bartering [B] [F] The trading of goods or services without the use of actual dollars. Goods or services received through bartering are taxable to the recipient.

> Peter Minuit *bartered* beads and trinkets with the Native Americans for the island of Manhattan in 1626.

Basel Accords [E] The 1988 international agreement, in Basel, Switzerland, that pressured banks to lend more to governments and less to businesses and individuals. In the United States, this led to a credit crunch in which companies could not get the necessary loans to expand.

basement [RE] The lowest level of a building, either fully or partially below the ground.

base 10 [M] A number system using only 10 symbols, which are added to and repeated for numbers over 10. It is the number system in use today. In contrast, a number system to the base 4 would have only four symbols and would look like this: 0, 1 ,2 ,3, 10, 11, 12, 13, 20, 21, 22, 23, 30, 31, 32, 33…and so forth.

base-year analysis [E] A method of analyzing economic trends that uses one year as the yardstick against which all others are measured. Using the "constant dollars" from one year allows analysts to see how much things have gone up or down, without inflation.

BASIC [C] A popular and widely used programming language. It stands for Beginners All-purpose Symbolic Instruction Code.

basic input/output system (BIOS) [C] A set of instructions and routines that allows a computer to control, communicate, and command the various devices connected to it, such as the disk drives, hard drive(s), memory, printer, keyboard, and communications ports. Just as an operating system allows application programs to interact with all of the devices, the BIOS system allows that same interaction between the operating system and hardware.

basis [T] A key tax concept, it is the original cost of an item or investment that may be adjusted for tax purposes. When an investor sells an investment, he or she subtracts the tax basis from the proceeds to determine the capital gains, and thus the tax owed. The lower the tax basis, the higher the gain, and therefore, the greater the tax liability. Tax basis can be increased by acquisition costs, for instance brokerage fees and legal fees. Tax basis can be decreased by depreciation.

basis point [M] One-hundredth of one percent. For instance, if treasury bonds are paying 7.50 percent interest, an increase to 7.51 percent is said to be an increase of one basis point. An increase to 7.60 percent would be an increase of ten points basis points, and to 8.50 percent would be an increase of 100 basis points or one full percentage point.

batch file [C] A DOS-based command to execute several, or many, operations with only one command.

battery [L] The actual physical contact with another person that may follow an assault, as in assault and battery. See *assault*.

baud [C] A unit of data transmission speed equal to one bit per second (bps).

baud rate [C] The speed-in bits per second (bps)-at which a modem can send data through the phone line. The higher the number, the faster the modem can transfer data. Typical baud rates are 14,400, 28,800, 33,600, and 57,600.

> I just got a modem with a *baud rate* of 33,600, although my internet service provider can only handle 14,400. But I'm prepared for their upgrade!

Bayes theorem [M] A statistical method by which the number of false positives are estimated. This is used for procedures that are not 100 percent precise. Thomas Bayes was a minister in England in the 1700s.

bean counter [S] A sometimes unflattering, sometimes flattering reference to a person who primarily does accounting or bookkeeping work all day. It is sometimes implied that the person doesn't have a sense of the big picture. It may also refer to someone who is admired for her ability with numbers.

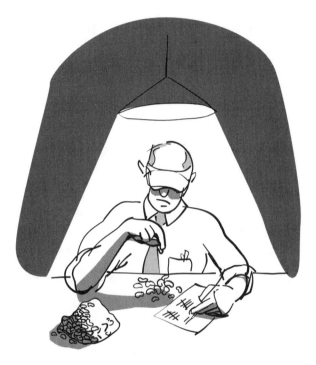

bear; bear market [F] A market characterized by falling prices or an investor who acts with the expectation that prices will fall. In technical terms, a bear market is defined when stock prices fall at least 20 percent. The opposite of a bear market is a bull market.

The *bear markets* of 1973 and 1974, losing 14 percent and 26 percent respectively, rightfully discouraged many investors.

bearer bond [F] A bond without registration by investor names. These are no longer allowed, as bonds must now be registered. Years ago, bonds did not have names registered to them. The bearer of them owned them. They were generally kept in safe deposit boxes, because they were like currency, and once every six months the coupons were clipped from them for interest payments.

bear hug [B] A takeover offer that is well above the current market value of stock.

> When the board of trustees at Irate Corp. tried to resist the *bear hug* takeover attempt made by Acme Corp., shareholders reminded the board that they had to accept an offer that was in the best interests of the investors.

bearing wall; bearing partition [RE] A wall or partition that actually supports a part of the building. If a wall is a bearing wall, it cannot be knocked down in a renovation without compromising the safety of the building.

bedroom community [RE] A community outside a major city from which many residents commute to the city to work.

> The *bedroom community* of Seascape was only a 20-minute commute to the city where Mary worked.

beige book [E] An important Federal Reserve anecdotal report on various economic conditions from each of the district banks. It contains interviews with key business leaders, economists, and other sources. The beige book is so called because it has a beige-colored cover. It is published for internal Federal Reserve purposes and is issued eight times a year.

bells and whistles [S] A phrase describing something, such as a computer or dishwasher, that has all the features and embellishments one could imagine.

> Hector reminded his staff that the presentation tomorrow was to be elaborate with all the *bells and whistles.*

bell-shaped curve [M] The most common curve in statistics. It represents the ideal distribution. It is sometimes called the "normal curve" or "normal distribution". There are surprisingly many examples of bell-shaped type distributions in nature, business, and everyday activities.

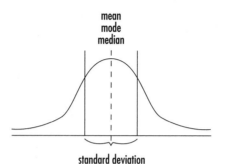

bellwether [B] An individual or company who leads or initiates a product or service. A trend-setter. Derived from olden days when the lead sheep had a bell that led the flock. A wether is a male sheep.

> Since McSoftware Inc. owned 80 percent of the software market, its performance was considered a *bellwether* of the software industry.

bench [L] A term referring either specifically to the place where the judge sits, or collectively to the courts and judges.

benchmark [B] A standard to judge one's performance, as an individual or company.

benchmarking [B] The measuring of a company's products or services against the best in the field.

bench warrant [L] An order by a judge for a person to appear in court on a specific charge.

beneficiary [HR] [I] The person who is named in a benefit or insurance plan to receive specified money if the employee dies. It is recommended that employees review the beneficiaries of their benefits if they have a change in life situation, such as divorce.

> Mr. Smith named Mrs. Smith as *beneficiary* of his $1 million life-insurance policy.

benefit [HR] A nonsalary aspect of compensation, such as a pension, 401(k), or health plan. These are all benefits of the job besides basic compensation.

[S] Any positive effect on a company or organization.

MacSoftware *benefited* from the popularity of the internet.

benefit accrual [HR] The amount of a benefit that is considered owned, such as a pension plan, although it could be paid later. For instance, an annual benefit statement from a company may say that at the end of the year one has a pension accrued benefit of $543 per month, payable at age sixty-five. That means that if one quit the company now his pension at age sixty-five would be $543 a month. The longer one works, however, the greater the benefit accrual.

bequest [T] A gift of personal property through a will. This is in contrast to "devise," which is a gift of what is called "real property," in particular real estate.

Bernouilli Box [C] A specific mass storage device that uses cartridges. It was introduced by the Iomega Corp. in 1983.

best defense is a good offense [S] An expression that means to take preemptive action instead of waiting for something to happen and then responding to it. A competitor who is anticipating a price war can plan for it by initiating it first.

Best insurance report [I] A rating of health and life insurance companies by the A.M. Best firm. It's highest rating, an A++, is only given to a little over 10 percent of all companies. Best Insurance Reports are available at the library, or at A.M. Best's website at: www.ambest.com/bestline ($4.95 for each rating). Other firms that rate insurance companies are: Duff & Phelps, Moody's, Standard & Poor's, and Weiss Research.

beta; beta coefficient [F] A sophisticated investment calculation measuring a mutual fund's volatility versus the volatility of the stock market as a whole. A beta value of 1.00 would mean that the fund has the exact same volatility as the S&P 500, which is the normal standard for measuring the market. If the fund has a beta of 1.10 then it is anticipated that it will have a 10 percent greater volatility than the market when the market goes up or down.

beta program [C] A software program in its final testing stage before official release. It may contain some bugs, which is why it is offered in this preview form.

Use that *beta* program at your own risk.

beta test [C] The actual testing of a beta, or almost final, software program.

Better Business Bureau (BBB) [B] An association designed to protect customers and businesses from illegal or questionable practices.

beyond a reasonable doubt [L] In a criminal trial, the degree of certainty required of a juror before a valid decision can be made. In a criminal case, the certainty required is higher than in a civil case. In a civil case, the standard is "preponderance of the evidence."

bias [M] A statistical concept that deals with the purity of information. If a pollster asks questions that are nonobjective, the results can be biased, or slanted.

bid and asked [F] The price a willing buyer will pay (bid), and the price a willing seller wants (ask).

Big Bang [F] A monumental day for London's financial markets, October 27, 1986, when it opened up to foreign firms. It also refers to a Japanese effort beginning in April 1998 to open up its financial markets. See *May Day*.

Big Blue [B] The nickname for IBM (International Business Machines) because of its blue corporate color and the size of the company.

big board [F] A casual term for the New York Stock Exchange (NYSE).

Big 8 accounting firms [A] The original eight major public accounting firms. Now after merging, there are only five. See *Big 5 accounting firms.*

The eight original firms were:

Arthur Andersen	Ernst & Whinney
Arthur Young	Peat, Marwick, Mitchell
Coopers & Lybrand	Price Waterhouse
Deloitte, Haskins & Sells	Touche Ross

---

big enchilada; big kahuna [S] The top dog, the top banana. In other words, the top boss. It could also mean a real big deal.

Everybody knew Drew was the *big enchilada* even though he was quiet during the meeting.

Big 5 accounting firms [A] The five remaining major public accounting firms. Just yesterday, it seems, there were six major public accounting firms, down from the original eight, with many regional and local firms as well. See *Big 8 accounting firms.*

The remaining five firms:

Arthur Andersen
Deloitte & Touche Tohmatsu
KPMG Peat Marwick
Ernst & Young
Price Waterhouse Coopers

Big Three [S] A nickname for the three American auto companies: General Motors, Ford, and Chrysler. Chrysler has been bought by Daimler Benz, so perhaps it is down to the Big Two.

big-ticket items [B] Expensive retail items that are almost always purchased on credit.

Retail sales at Cheapo Stores, Inc. were up in the third quarter due to the interest-free financing it offered on such *big-ticket items* as washer-dryers, entertainment systems, and refrigerators.

bilateral agreement [E] An agreement between two countries on international trade issues. This is in contrast to "multilateralism," which is an agreement between a number of countries.

billing records [A] The documentation of the bills a company has sent to clients, especially a services company.

bill of lading (BOL) [B] The document detailing the contents, by amount and weight, of goods being shipped. The bill of lading is not a bill at all but rather a table of contents for the shipment.

> Before accepting the shipment, Tizzy Corp. employees were supposed to check the contents of all packages against the *bill of lading* to be sure that everything was in the shipment.

bill of particulars [L] In a criminal case, a detailed listing of the allegations against a defendant or defendants.

bimodal distribution [M] A statistical distribution in which there are two peaks, or modes, of data, in contrast to the typical bell-shaped curve, which has only one peak.

binary [M] [C] A number system using only two symbols, or digits, commonly 1 and 0. It is used as the basis of computer logic.

binder [I] An agreement by an insurance agent to immediately cover property, such as a house, even before an actual insurance policy is issued.

[RE] A legal agreement between the buyer and seller of real estate to cover the down payment before the final contract is signed.

> They signed a *binder* so that the seller wouldn't entertain any more offers on the house.

binding letter of intent [L] A letter of intent that a court of law would generally uphold as an actual lease or contract.

binomial [M] A mathematical or algebraic expression of two terms connected by a plus or minus sign. An example of a binomial is $3x + 4y$. A *monomial* has one term, such as $5xy$. A *trinomial* has three terms, such as $6x + 7y + 8z$. Any algebraic expression of more than two terms is called a *polynomial*.

binomial formula (or theorem) [M] The rule for the expansion of the power of a binomial. As an example, $(a + b)^2$ can be expanded to: $a^2 + 2ab + b^2$.

biotechnology [B] The field of business that concentrates on the newest discoveries in microorganisms and genetics.

bit [C] The smallest element of value inside a computer. It is the single digit, such as 0 or 1. Billions of bits form the basis of memory in a PC. The word "bit" was formed as an abbreviation of the two words binary and digit.

> A group of eight *bits* is called a byte.

bit map or bitmap [C] A set of dots, or bits, on a screen that represent an image. A bit map is also a specific type of image file, abbreviated by the three-letter suffix .bmp.

bitnet [C] A worldwide network similar to but separate from the internet.

> Bitnet, started in 1981 at the City University of New York, stands for "Because It's Time Network."

bits per second (bps) [C] See *baud* and *baud rate*.

black box [S] A term referring to computers' complex processes that are unfathomable by most people. Thus, the computer is considered a mysterious box of complexity.

> Tami just looked at the computer and exclaimed that after becoming the top salesperson in the region, she would like to begin understanding what was in that *black box*.

blackmail [L] The illegal demand for money or other property under threat of harm.

black market [B] Items that are sold illegally are said to be sold on the black market. Usually, black market items are expensive because they are restricted by the government or some shortage of supply.

> Jan had to pay top dollar for the cigarettes she bought on the *black market* during the government's rationing.

Black-Sholes formula [M] [F] A complicated mathematical formula to determine the present value of stock options that are traded on the various option markets. This is the most common method of determining the present value of stock options given to company executives.

blanket mortgage [RE] A mortgage for more than one piece of property.

> When the contractor built fifty houses on that property, he took out a *blanket mortgage* rather than fifty individual mortgages.

block [C] In word-processing software, a whole section of text that will be moved, deleted, have a special font, or have some other operation performed on it. In communications software, a section of data transmitted at one time.

blockade [E] The blocking of a country's trade by other countries. It is meant to isolate that country.

blow-in cards [B] Those irritating loose promotional inserts in magazines. The term refers to the process of blowing them into the magazine.

blow off [F] Very strong, almost frenzied, stock market buying, propelling the market to new highs, likely to be corrected in the future.

blowout [F] The instant sale of an initial stock offering due to strong demand.

blue chip [F] A stock of very high quality. It is usually considered a lower risk stock because it is from a large, established, and consistently profitable corporation. Companies like GE, Exxon, and Ford are examples of blue chip companies. The term "blue chip" originates from 1904 when it was first used to refer to the most consistently profitable corporations. The term is borrowed from poker, where the blue chip is the most valuable.

Cicely's father gave her a gift of some *blue-chip* stocks when she graduated from business school. He felt it was the foundation of a stable portfolio.

blue-collar worker [B] Tradespeople. Typically, a blue-collar worker performs manual labor, such as a delivery person, a construction worker, or a plumber.

The hourly wages for *blue-collar workers* in our company increased when the union renegotiated their contract.

blueprint [RE] An architectural plan for construction or renovation of a piece of property. It is called a blueprint because the special paper they are printed on is blue.

They needed *blueprints* drawn up for their renovation before they could even think about beginning any of the work.

blue sky laws [L] [F] State regulation of the offering and sale of securities within the state. The term is derived from investors buying something worthless, like a piece of the blue sky. States hope that these laws limit the amount of securities that are without value.

board of directors [B] The group of individuals selected by stockholders to oversee the management of a corporation. Usually some board members are outside directors, while some may be officers of the company, such as the president, executive vice president, and vice president of operations, among others.

body language [S] The physical movements or positions one makes in response to someone or something. People try to read into this body language meaning, and often, but not always, are right. A firm handshake usually means a confident person. A tapping finger on a desktop probably means impatience. People can, however, learn to exhibit body behavior that camouflages their true feelings. At best, body language can offer clues to inner reactions or feelings, but it's not an exact science.

boilerplate [L] Legal language that appears as a fixture in certain types of documents. For instance, a record company's contract with a certain musician will include standard clauses found in all of that company's contracts, along with stipulations particular to that deal. *Boilerplate* may refer either to a document as a whole, or to standard language found within.

> When you go over those leases, don't bother reading the introductory clauses; they're all just legal *boilerplate*.

boiler-room operation [F] An illegal operation selling small-cap stocks that are thinly traded and therefore sensitive to market fluctuations. A bank of phones is set up with telemarketers pushing specific small stocks, thereby pushing the prices of those stocks artificially high. The operators then sell their own stock, making a profit, before the prices fall back down to realistic levels.

boldface [C] In word-processing software, thicker and darker characters that stand out from other text.

bona fide sale [RE] An arm's length transaction in which both buyer and seller are acting in good faith.

bond [F] A long-term liability of a company, municipality, or government, usually with a specific interest rate (coupon rate) and for a specific length of time (maturity). A bond is essentially a loan made by investors to an organization. The investors earn interest while the corporation or government gets the cash it needs for major projects. Corporate bonds are usually sold in units of $1,000, municipals in $5,000, and Treasury notes and bonds can be of different denominations. A zero coupon bond pays no interest, but the initial value is greatly reduced, increasing in value to the date of maturity where it equals the full value of the bond.

> The school district floated a *bond* to finance the construction of a new gymnasium.

How Long Will My Bond Live?

Short-term:	Usually one to two years
Intermediate-term:	Three to ten years
Long-term:	Twenty to thirty years, or more

bond fund [F] A mutual fund of bonds, either of a specific type, like long-term treasury bonds or municipal bonds, or a mixture of corporate and treasury bonds, usually of similar maturities.

bonus [HR] A lump-sum payment for work well done. It can be paid to selected employees or to an entire department. There is usually a formula established to determine how much will be paid.

bookmark [C] A process that allows an internet user to "mark" a document or web site in order to easily return to that place. Different browsers have different names for this process, including "hotlists" and "favorites."

books, the [A] A company's accounting journals, ledgers, and other accounting records.

book-to-bill ratio [A] A ratio comparing new orders against shipments of specific goods.

> The Semiconductor Industry Association's book-to-bill ratio monthly movements are an indication of strength or weakness in the computer business because it shows the current demand for computer chips.

book value [A] A company's worth if all its assets were sold and its debts were paid off, or more technically, its total assets minus total liabilities, sometimes referred to as "net book value." It is also the value at which assets are carried on the balance sheet. A book value of an asset is the cost of the asset less any accumulated depreciation or amortization. Book value is usually based on the historical cost of assets and may vary significantly from market value.

> The *book value* on Zippy Corp. would certainly be great if it were to liquidate—it has such valuable property with practically no debt at all.

Boolean algebra or logic [M] A mathematical logic based on two elements, 1 and 0, or true and false. There are several operations that are then applied to these elements, such as *and, or,* and *if...then.* It is the logic used in computers. George Boole was a British mathematician who developed this form of logic in the mid-nineteenth century.

> For instance, the sentence "If the person lives in Pennsylvania, then send letter C," would be translated into *Boolean logic* as "if p then C," and expressed as "p → C."

boom-and-bust cycle [B] See *business cycle*.

boondoggle [B] An unnecessary business or civic project. Boondoggles are sometimes created to give someone a job or do someone a favor.

> "That whole Shmendrick Project is just a *boondoggle* to keep the boss's nephew employed," Smithers told her new secretary.

boot [C] The process by which a computer loads up the operating system when it is initally turned on. This is also called a "cold boot." If a user hits the reset button while the computer is already running, the system will reboot, which is also called a "warm" or "soft boot."

[T] Money or property that exchanges hands. When property is exchanged, one party may have to pay a certain amount of additional money to even up the transaction. This additional payment is called boot, as in *money to boot*.

bottleneck [S] A point or area that is a problem and creates slowdowns.

> Cruthers was the real *bottleneck* to approving the requisitions because of his tendency to overanalyze each one.

bottom fishing [F] The buying of low priced, out-of-fashion stocks that are hoped-for bargains.

bottom line [B] The final profit or loss on a project; a plan's cost to a company.

> After listening to a sales pitch on the necessity of water coolers in each office, the president of Zippy asked the salesperson, "What's the *bottom line* here? What will this cost me?"

[S] The profit in an activity, or the core idea in an action.

> After everyone had a say in the matter, Smithers summarized sarcastically, "Apparently the *bottom line* here is getting the job done at any cost, rather than doing the best job."

bottom up [S] Term that refers to the setting of company objectives by asking for suggestions from lower staff members, versus the *top down* authoritarian method.

bounce-back card [B] Those loose promotional inserts in magazines that allow you to fill out your name and address and receive free information. See *blow-in cards*.

bounded description [RE] See *metes and bounds description*.

bracket [T] See *tax brackets*.

bracket creep [T] The built-in adjustment to the tax brackets, so that if one receives an increase in salary she will not automatically pay more in taxes.

Brady bonds [F] Named for former Treasury Secretary Nicholas Brady, these bonds are the restructured debt of Latin American and other emerging countries. Initially the interest rates were quite high because of their inherent risk, but they have decreased since then because there have been few problems. The principal is guaranteed but not the interest payments. Brady bonds are primarily traded by institutions.

brain drain [E] The exodus of technically trained people from a country or countries. Many foreign students study in the United States and then stay and work here, causing a brain drain in their countries of origin.

brainstorming [B] The process of a group generating as many ideas as possible by allowing members of the group a lot of creative freedom. Rules of brainstorming allow members to offer ideas without criticism or challenge from other members. Usually employed to solve thorny problems or to find creative solutions to old problems, the method was originated by Alex Osborn in 1939 at the advertising agency of Batten, Barton, Durstine & Osborn (BBDO).

brand (name); brand association; brand loyalty [B] A name, symbol, or phrase that identifies a product as from a specific company. If a product has a high *Brand association*, occurs when one company is associated with a product more than any other. Band-Aids, Kleenex, Singer, and Xerox are all brands that have such high brand association that their names are synonymous with the products they represent. *Brand loyalty* occurs when people are loyal to a brand name and associate it with quality and value.

> Because her family always bought Buicks, Alice had a great deal of *brand loyalty* to those cars.

breach of contract [L] Failure to perform certain duties as detailed in a contract.

break [T] See *tax break.*

breakeven analysis; breakeven point [A] The analysis of profits by determining the relationship between the costs and revenues, often illustrated by a breakeven graph. In a simple breakeven graph the fixed costs are shown as a horizontal line, with the variable costs starting at the fixed costs and moving on an upward slope. That is, whereas fixed costs are flat (the cost of the basic factory), variable costs increase as more products are made (the costs of materials and labor). The revenue line increases from zero and eventually will cross the variable cost line at the breakeven point. It is at that point that profit is then made on all additional products. The real world is not this simple. In the real world each of the lines are not straight but will have jumps and squiggles in them. But the simple graph gives the basic idea from which real world inferences are then drawn.

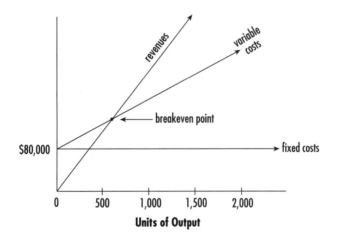

break in service [HR] A term referring to an employee who has worked for a company, leaves, and then returns, thus having already provided service for that company.

break key [C] A key on the computer keyboard that either stops or pauses an operation.

break-up value [A] The estimated value of assets if a company were to liquidate. Also called *liquidating value.*

breath [F] See *market breath*.

Bretton Woods agreement [E] An international conference and the resultant agreement between forty-five countries in July 1944, in Bretton Woods, New Hampshire. The agreement created the International Monetary Fund (IMF) and the International Bank for Reconstruction and Development, more commonly known as the "World Bank." One aspect of the agreement was the requirement that each country's central bank buy and sell its currency to keep the value of its currency in line with the others. This fixed-rate agreement stayed in effect until 1973, when floating rates of currencies were established.

bridge loan [RE] A short-term loan to cover the brief period of time between the buying of one property and the selling of another. This is a typical situation for a homeowner who purchases a new home before selling the old one.

brief [L] The document in which a lawyer makes a legal case against a defendant.

brightline [S] A new business and law term that is meant to delineate a certainty, as a line in the sand.

> The court responded by setting *brightline* standards, so businesses would know what to do in the future.

broadband [C] A general term for a very fast means of data transmission, such as fiber optics.

broad-banding [HR] The compensation practice of reducing the number of salary grades so that each grade has more latitude to provide for more raises. It provides a broader band or range for giving raises, which should give employees a broader grin.

broker [F] A person who arranges for the buying and selling of investments. A full-service broker gives advice on investments and carries out transactions but also charges a higher commission for the service. A discount broker places a buy or sell order with generally no advice, thus charging a lower commission. A deep-discount broker offers the cheapest service of all but usually just for investors who trade in large amounts or very frequently.

> Since Sal knew exactly what he wanted to buy, he preferred to deal with a discount *broker*.

[RE] A real estate agent, usually licensed, who typically acts on the seller's behalf to find a buyer for the property. The broker charges the seller a commission if he or she makes the sale.

> Although they didn't want to pay a commission, the Jayhawks listed their house with a *broker* because they didn't have time to sell it themselves.

brokerage allowance [B] See *allowance*.

broker commission [F] See *commission*.

broker dealer (BD) [F] See *dealer*.

brownian motion or movement [M] Random motion, originally referring to molecular movements, but now also referring to random motion observed in business activities, such as consumer buying habits.

browse (or surf) [C] To travel between different sites on the internet.

browser [C] A program that allows a user to seek and find internet web sites. A browser will also allow a user to access and navigate through a hypertext document. On the internet, the World Wide Web may lead one through different types of resources (newsgroups, gopher, telnet, etc.). A browser is the tool needed to move effortlessly from one type of document to another. See *web browser*.

B-school [B] Graduate business school. The main degree is an MBA, which is a master's of business administration. Graduates are often sought after by consulting firms and companies.

bubble market; bubble economy [B] Any market, stock market, real estate market, or economy that increases dramatically, like a bubble. Unfortunately, like a soap bubble, these market bubbles do burst. History has recorded several notable bubbles:

> **May We Burst Your Bubble?**
>
> ---
>
> **Tuplipmania**:   Holland 1637. Tulips became an obsession as early as the 1630s, and in 1636 one bulb was sold for about $5,000 in today's dollars.

bucket shop [F] The illegal activity of taking orders to buy or sell but either never executing the orders or executing them only when it is advantageous to the broker.

buck slip [S] A routing slip usually attached to a memo or article that is circulated within an office. It could have come from the slang term "to pass the buck."

budget [A] A financial plan estimating revenues and expenses for a project, company unit, or the entire company.

[E] A plan for annual expenditures and revenues for a government. A balanced budget is being proposed for many of the developed countries and was actually achieved in the United States for the fiscal year that ended September 30, 1998. The final tally was that the U.S. government took in more than $70 billion than it spent (without counting the Social Security excess payments).

buffer [C] A holding place in a PC's memory that stores something the user just used or is about to use.

bug [C] A glitch in a computer program.

building codes [RE] State or local regulations for the design, construction, and use of real estate. May be referred to simply as *code*.

Because the inspectors found that the building's electrical system was not up to *code*, they would not grant a certificate of occupancy.

building permit [RE] An official authorization to build or alter a structure, obtained by submitting a plan to the local or state government.

> "You don't even have a *building permit*!" cried the inspector. "You'll have to tear this building down."

built-in [S] A term describing a feature already in place. If something is built-in, it is part and parcel of the main product.

> The new computer system had a *built-in* program to track telephone usage.

bull; bull market [F] A market characterized by rising prices, or an investor who expects the market to rise and invests according to that expectation. The opposite of bull market is a bear market.

> The market from the 1980s through the late-1990s has been an extended *bull market*.

bulletin board system (BBS) [C] A collection of message boards and files devoted to a particular topic. Many BBSs are maintained by individuals or small organizations. Some require a fee to use; others are free. They allow a user in many cases to leave or review messages, play games, download software, and chat with other users. A BBS is more like a community newspaper than a commercial online system.

bunsha [B] See *Japanese business words*.

burden of proof [L] The requirement of proving a fact or facts in dispute in a case. In a criminal case, each fact must be proven, whereas in a civil case, only the majority of evidence need be proven.

bureaucracy; bureaucratic [S] Burdensome administrative procedures or organization.

burglary [L] The unlawful presence of a person in a building or on property, usually to commit theft.

burn in [C] The operation of a computer system for a continuous period of time to see if it will fail, usually 24 or 48 hours. It also refers to the permanent etching of an image on a monitor by having had that image on the screen too long.

burnout [HR] A general term for an employee, usually in a stressful job, who has a decrease in energy and motivation for a job. This can be temporary for individuals such as nurses or therapists who deal with personal stresses of others on a daily basis. It can also refer to an employee who becomes frustrated after doing the same job for a number of years and needs a respite.

bus [C] A computer pathway between devices.

business [B] Any company, firm, enterprise, activity, or transaction designed to provide products, goods, or services for a profit.

business cycle [B] A recurring period of business activity that begins with an increase, reaches a plateau, and ends with an eventual falling off of business. It has sometimes been referred to as the "boom-and-bust cycle." Some businesses are called cyclical, such as airlines and automobile companies, because their sales increase and decrease with the business cycle. Others are called noncyclical, such as the food and basic clothing industries, because they are in demand regardless of the business cycle.

[E] A recurring period of increased business activity with a slowdown occurring after a number of years. Traditionally there are four periods of the cycle: expansion, prosperity, contraction, and recession. Since World War II, the business cycle occurred in three to five year segments (or cycles) in the United States. In the 1980s, the business cycle lasted about eight years, and it seems that it might be duplicating or extending that in the 1990s.

business plan [B] A formal report that analyzes in detail a new business venture. It is usually prepared for management approval but can be for bank loan purposes as well. An outline of a plan includes the description of the new business products or services, the analysis of customers and opportunities, the projected financial revenues and expenses, and a timetable for the business to be a success.

business risk [F] There are several risks that investors consider: market risk, inflation risk, and business risk. Business risk is the risk that a business faces within its industry. A business that is well-positioned within its industry has a greater market share (and, perhaps, proprietary products) and has a lower business risk than one that is not well-positioned.

business travel accident insurance [HR] A special travel insurance carried by a company for anyone traveling on company business. Although rarely used, it provides an extra benefit for employees.

business unit [B] A part of a company that is a business unto itself.

> MacWorld Enterprises has three *business units*: magazine publishing, cable television, and parking lots. The parking lot business unit was far removed from the rest of the company.

Business Week [B] A major weekly news magazine in business.

button [C] A circle or square on a computer screen that represents an option. When one is pushed by the click of the mouse, an operation is performed. Sometimes called a radio button, since when one button is selected, the others are deselected.

buttress [RE] An exterior wall or building support that gives support by pushing in on it.

> The *buttresses* on the church were actually quite beautiful.

buy American [E] A campaign by American companies or unions promoting the buying of goods made by American workers.

buy-and-hold strategy [F] An investment approach of buying high-quality stocks and then holding them for many years. Since good solid stocks should continue to grow, this is a realistic and generally sound strategy.

buyback agreement [B] Any clause in a contract that guarantees that the seller will buy the item back from the purchaser in a certain time frame.

> L-Mart insisted on a *buyback agreement* so that Acme Corp. would buy back any unsold slime balls within six months.

buydown [RE] An additional chunk of money—a percentage of the loan, or points—offered at a closing in exchange for a reduced loan rate.

buyers' market [S] The market condition where buyers have the upper hand in which prices are usually lower and buyers can negotiate on their terms. This is the opposite of a "sellers' market," in which the prices are high and sellers control the market.

buy out [B] The purchasing of the controlling share of a company's stock.

> XYZ Corp. tried to *buy out* ABC Corp. by purchasing up large blocks of ABC stock.

buzzwords [S] Business- or management-type words that are in vogue. Words such as *monitor, parallel, integrate, contingency, functional, system*, and *total* are common management buzzwords.

> "I don't mind the use of *buzzwords* around here," Jenkins cautioned, "but I don't want to hear the word 'seamless' anymore! Is that understood?"

bylaws [L] The legal rules for operating a company that were established at the time of incorporation, or have been added since then.

> The *bylaws* of McSoftware Inc. specified that the board of directors would meet every quarter.

bypass trust [T] Also called a "credit shelter trust," it is an estate tax strategy that allows a surviving spouse to receive income from certain assets, the principal of which will not be taxed in the spouse's estate.

by-product [B] An output of a process that is designed for another product but useful in its own right.

byte [C] A group of eight bits; bytes are used as a measure of a computer's capacity and are usually expressed as megabytes and gigabytes. See *bit*.

How about some numbers

One kilobyte equals 1,024 bytes (2^{10})

(a little more than 1,000, precisely 2 to the 10th power)

One megabyte equals 1,048,576 bytes (2^{20})

One gigabyte equals 1,073,741,824 bytes (2^{30})

One gigabyte also equals 1,024 megabytes

What's next? A terabyte, or 1,099,511,627,776 bytes (2^{40}).

C

C [C] See *C language*.

cache [C] Pronounced "cash," it is an area of computer storage devoted to high speed retrieval of frequently used data or information.

CAD/CAM (computer-aided design/computer-aided manufacturing) [C] Engineering and manufacturing software used not only to design products, but also to manufacture them. They can be used separately but are quite potent when used together.

cafeteria plan [HR] Employee options that allow an employer to take money out of a paycheck for things like retirement plans, insurance, and day care. Just like in a cafeteria, employees are allowed to select options they wish to pay for. These plans are sometimes called "flexible benefit plans." The IRS defines a cafeteria plan as providing employees the choice between cash and qualifying benefits. The money taken out reduces the amount of taxable income and is therefore sometimes called a "salary reduction plan."

> Dominick's company offered a *cafeteria plan*, giving options to contribute to a retirement plan, life insurance, or child care, that enabled him to pay less in taxes.

calculated risk [S] A knowingly risky strategy taken with the hope of a positive outcome.

> Smith took a *calculated risk* in asking for a raise at this time because, unbeknownst to his boss, he had an offer in his pocket from another company.

calculator [C] Besides the small hand-held type on everyone's desk, it can also refer to a computer program available to perform basic math functions while using another program. The computer version often resembles a simple hand-held calculator on the screen.

calculator, use of [M] Many business applications of mathematics, such as figuring ratios, taxes, costs, and revenues, require only a simple hand-held calculator. Some applications, such as financial calculations of present and future value, require a more substantial calculator, but these machines can still be somewhat small and hand-held. Only in more complicated applications, such as statistics or spreadsheets, are computers necessary.

calculus [M] An advanced method of calculation based on the rate of change of a variable. There are two methods of calculus that are the opposite of each other: derivative and integral. The process of finding the derivative is called "differentiation"; finding the integral is known as "integration." Just as there are the paired and opposite calculations of addition and subtraction, or multiplication and division, so there are the paired calculations of differentiation and integration. A typical derivative calculates the minimum or maximum of a formula, whereas a typical integral calculates the area under a curve. These two calculations allow for complex and useful calculations in engineering, science, and business. Calculus was discovered in the late 1600s by two mathematicians, Isaac Newton and Gottfried Leibniz.

callable bond [F] A bond that can be called in before its maturity date, typically five to ten years from the issue date. Treasury notes and bonds are generally not callable. Companies and municipalities call bonds early to reissue them at lower interest rates, saving considerable amounts of money. This only happens when interest rates decline. Investors often think they will be getting high interest until maturity, only to be surprised and disappointed when bonds are called.

call feature [A] The provision built into bonds that allows a company or organization to call them in early. This occurs when interest rates drop so that the company will save considerable money by calling in existing issues and then reissuing the debt at the lower interest rates.

call option [F] An option to buy a stock at a specified price. In contrast, a put option is a right to sell stock at a specific price. See *put option*.

Calpers [HR] The nation's largest public pension fund. It stands for The California Public Employees' Retirement System but is known simply as Calpers.

cancellation [I] The termination of any insurance policy.

can-do attitude [S] A positive and assertive demeanor, no matter what the task. Marines are trained to exhibit this trait.

cap [F] A stock-market term that refers to a company's size, such as large cap, small cap, or mid-cap. See *capitalization rate*.

[RE] A limit on mortgage rate increases. For instance, if there is a six-point cap on the interest rate of an adjustable mortgage and the initial rate was 8 percent, then the rate could never be raised above 14 percent.

capacity [B] Generally, the maximum goods that can be produced with the existing plants and equipment of a company. It also can refer to different levels of production.

What's Zippy Corp.'s Capacity?

Zippy's capacity may be measured in one of five ways:

1. **Deal capacity.** How much Zippy Corp. would produce if everything were perfect—with no waste or breakdown.

2. **Normal capacity.** The average of Zippy's actual production over several years.

3. **Planned capacity.** What Zippy can expect to make in one average year.

4. **Operating capacity.** What Zippy makes in a specific time period (part of a year: monthly, weekly, daily operating capacity).

5. **Practical capacity.** How well Zippy could do, taking into account some inefficiency and losses.

[C] The number of bytes that can be used or stored in a computer's memory or hard drive. This number used to be expressed as kilobytes but is now expressed in megabytes or gigabytes.

I have to get a new computer with more *capacity*—the games I play have taken up all the space I have.

[L] The ability to understand the facts and charges brought against a defendant. A defendant cannot be convicted of a crime that he cannot legally understand.

capital [A] Owners' equity in a company. That is, the amount of funds the owners invested in the company. It can also mean the total productive assets of a company.

[E] Money or, in economic theory, assets capable of producing income that is more broadly defined than money. It can mean physical capital, such as machinery, equipment, or factories, in addition to money, investments, or securities. It is considered one of the three factors of production: labor, capital, and land.

[F] Money ready for investment or already invested in a company or financial venture.

Widget Corp. needed to raise more *capital* before it could make the improvements that were so sorely needed for the future.

capital account [E] The part of the balance of payment between countries that refers to the flow of money between them. The other part is called the "current account," which is the actual flow of goods and services between countries. See *balance of payments*.

capital asset [A] A long-term productive asset such as equipment, buildings, and plants.

capital asset pricing model (CAPM) [F] A prominent mathematical formulation of how securities should be priced based on their riskiness relative to riskless treasury investments.

$$R = r_f + \beta \ (r_m - r_f)$$

R   is the return

r_f is the risk-free return

r_m is the market rate return

β is beta, or its riskiness

capital budgeting [A] The plans for buying long-term productive assets such as equipment and plant improvements.

capital expenditures [A] The amount spent for long-term productive assets.

[B] An outlay of cash used to buy an asset.

The *capital expenditures* for Jiffy Corp. were high that year; it expanded the company by buying five more buildings.

capital expenses [A] The money used to pay off the interest and amortization of a loan.

capital formation [E] The process of increasing the amount of machinery, equipment, and factories in an economy. Implementing more efficient means of production helps the economy remain competitive and thus strong.

capital gains and losses [T] The profit or loss made on an investment. The selling price minus the tax basis equals the amount of capital gains or losses. If an investor purchases a stock for $50 and sells it for $90, $40 is her capital gain, or profit. After July 28, 1997, if the investment or property is owned for more than eighteen months, then it is a long-term capital gain or loss. If owned for a shorter period, it is a short-term capital gain or loss. An investor who has several gains and losses during the year should follow this saying: Net your longs, net your shorts, net your nets. The result is the amount of gains or losses, short-term or long-term, she can take on her taxes. Currently only $3,000 of long-term capital losses can be taken each year. See *capital loss carryover.*

capital improvements [A] Improvements made to a company's main long-term assets, such as plants and buildings.

After modernizing the plant with a number of capital expenditures and *capital improvements*, ABC Corp. went to the bank to ask for more capital.

capital intensive [B] Term used to describe industries that require more capital than average to either start or sustain them, such as oil refineries, chemical plants, or wineries. This is in contrast to "labor-intensive" industries, such as the automotive industry.

capitalism [E] An economic system based on the principles of free competition, private ownership, and profit maximization. Individuals own the means of production. This is in contrast to socialism, in which the government owns the means of production of all goods and services.

The transition from a socialist economy to *capitalism* was difficult: The citizens were not used to profit-making and competition.

capitalization [A] The sum of all debt and equity of a company. It is also considered the amount and structure of the capital of a company.

The *capitalization* of Miracle Drugs, Inc. was complete, so it could now build its production facilities, hire employees, and proceed to make its profits.

capitalization rate (cap rate) [F] A method used to indicate a company's size relative to other companies. The "cap rate" is determined by multiplying the number of shares of stock by the price of shares.

[RE] A method used in real estate to quickly evaluate an income producing property. The cap rate is determined by dividing a property's net operating income by its purchase price.

capitalize [A] To record an expenditure as a long-term asset versus an immediate expense.

[B] To determine the present value of an asset by dividing the income expected from that asset by an interest (or capitalization) rate.

[S] To take advantage of a situation.

Acme Corp. *capitalized* on the new slime craze after the success of the children's movie *The Slime King*.

capital loss carryover [T] Practice by which a tax-payer can re-port part of his current capital losses on the following year's tax return. There is a limit, generally $3,000, of capital losses that can be taken on an individual tax return per year. If a tax-payer has more than that, he can carry them over to next year, or several years if necessary, until he uses them up.

capital market [E] The financial markets for investments. Businesses raise capital by selling securities, stocks, and bonds, and individuals buy investments as a means of income, savings, and growth for their future wealth.

capital markets [F] Stock and bond markets where long-term securities are traded, such as the New York Stock Exchange. This is in contrast to short-term markets such as commercial paper and treasury bills, called the "money market."

capital stock [A] Shares of a company, representing ownership of a business. Often referred to as "common stock" when there is only one class of stock issued.

[E] The total amount of physical capital in an economy, such as equipment, machinery, or factories.

capital structure [A] The mix of long-term capital, equity, and debt of a company, such as common stock (equity) and bonds (debt). A firm with little or no debt is considered to be capitalized very conservatively.

capitation [HR] A per person charge for service, such as with a managed care organization. An HMO charges a flat rate per employee times the number of employees in the medical plan. The term comes from *per capita*, Latin for "per head."

Caps Lock key [C] The key on the keyboard that allows the user to type all uppercase letters.

captive agent [I] An insurance agent that represents one insurer. Often called a "general agent." This is in contrast to an "independent agent" who will represent several insurers.

cardinal number [M] A number that represents quantity but not the order. For instance, AOL (America Online) has 13 million (cardinal number) customers and is the number one (ordinal number) internet service. An ordinal gives the position or order, such as first, second, third, and so forth.

career counseling [HR] Assessment, discussions, and advice about one's career, sometimes from someone in the human resources department or a consultant outside the company.

career ladder [HR] A set of organized steps for promotion to higher and higher levels of responsibility within a company, often accompanied by specific training to prepare for each step.

carpal tunnel syndrome [HR] An affliction affecting the wrists, hands, and forearms, usually from the overuse of a computer keyboard.

carrot and stick [S] A negotiating strategy that offers the opposing party a reward as inducement toward reaching a final agreement. Whether or not the promised reward is ultimately delivered is sometimes another story.

cartel [E] An organization of independent companies formed to set group trade restrictions. Perhaps the best known international cartel is OPEC (Organization of Petroleum Exporting Countries), which attempts to set oil prices.

> OPEC, the oil *cartel*, agreed to restrict the amount of oil that would be released on the market.

[L] A generally illegal arrangement between companies to fix prices and the availability of products.

case studies [B] A method commonly used in graduate business schools to analyze business decisions. Some case studies present hypothetical situations, but often they present a real present-day or past business dilemma. Students look at the information, analyze the data, and decide what to do. Then, typically the instructor explains how the situation played out in real life.

> The most important class Jane took her first year in business school was *Case Studies*—it gave her a sense of real business decisions and their consequences.

case, upper/lower [C] Refers to letters as being either upper case (ABCDE) or lower case (abcde). Some computer programs are case sensitive, meaning that a command of "D" will be different than a command of "d." If a program is not case sensitive, then upper or lower case letters don't affect the operations.

cash [A] Currency, bank accounts, or other "near-cash" instruments that are very liquid and can easily be converted to cash.

[F] Another name for money market instruments or money market funds. Used when an investor doesn't know in what stocks to invest. Interest is earned in these short-term safe securities, like T-bills. Sometimes also referred to as a "parking place" or a holding place, until an attractive stock investment is found. Occasionally these money market investments are held when there is great uncertainty in the stock and bond markets because they are considered the safest.

cash accounting; cash basis [A] A basic method of accounting in which revenue and expenses are recorded only when money is received or paid out. This is in contrast to "accrual accounting" in which revenue and expenses are recorded when earned or incurred.

cash budget [A] A projected schedule of cash receipts and expenses over a given period of time.

cash cow [B] A business, or business unit, that generates lots and lots of money.

> That division of Zippy Corp. is a real *cash cow*—they can't pay out dividends fast enough!

cash flow [A] The amount of cash generated from a particular business activity or project.

cash-flow analysis [A] A report that looks at how the cash reserves in a company are affected during a specified period, such as where the cash came from (sources) and how it was spent.

> The accountants at ABC Corp. provided the CEO a *cash-flow analysis* so she could see how money had been spent in that quarter.

cashier [A] The business function, usually under the treasurer or accounting department, that issues cash when necessary, such as cash advances or checks for the purchase of materials.

cash method [A] See *cash accounting.*

cash or deferred arrangement (CODA). [HR] Another name for a 401(k) plan. See *401(k) plan.*

cash surrender value [I] The amount of money a life-insurance policy holder would receive if he or she were to stop (surrender) the insurance and take whatever value is in the policy.

cash value [I] The amount of money accumulated in a whole life-insurance policy that can be withdrawn while still keeping the policy in force.

casual dress [S] The relaxation of a company's dress code to include more casual wear, such as khakis and sweaters. Companies sometimes permit it during the summer or on Fridays. Some companies have adopted it year-round.

casualty; casualty insurance; casualty loss [I] Casualty insurance covers unexpected losses, called casualty losses, due to an accident, fire, catastrophe, or company negligence.

> That *casualty insurance* saved ABC Corp. after the huge fire wiped out its plant.

catastrophic medical coverage [HR] A form of medical insurance that provides significant payments for very costly medical conditions. It is considered the most critical type of health insurance because it is unlikely that an individual would have enough money to cover these conditions. This form of payment is usually built in to major medical or general medical coverage.

catch-22 [S] A contradiction that makes the overcoming of an obstacle impossible. The term comes from the 1961 book *Catch-22* by Joseph Heller about a bomber squadron in Italy in World War II. In the book, a soldier can avoid being sent into combat if he is deemed to be mentally insane. However, the catch is that if he wants to get out of combat then he couldn't be insane.

> Annie couldn't get a job without experience, and she couldn't get experience without a job. It was a *catch-22* situation.

cathode ray tube (CRT) [C] The basic tube that forms a computer monitor.

CATS [F] A trademarked security, originated by Salomon Brothers and Bache, that stands for Certificate of Accrual on Treasury Securities. It involves taking apart treasury securities and selling pieces to investors. A number of these treasury dissections have been performed by the major brokerage houses, and each usually has a trademark name.

CATV [C] Cable television.

cause-and-effect diagram [M] A graphic technique showing the results of alternatives. It also is known as the "fishbone diagram," because it looks like the skeleton of a fish.

caveat emptor [B] Latin for "Let the buyer beware." In other words, consumers buy things at their own risk—and need to be cautious of what the seller says about the product or service. The term is commonly pronounced KA-vee-ot EMP-tor.

> Although *caveat emptor* is a smart way to do business, a seller is usually bound by law to inform the purchaser of any problems with a product.

cc [S] To send a copy of a letter or memo to someone. It stands for "carbon copy," which is an outdated way of making copies. Carbon paper was inked on one side and positioned ink-side down between sheets of paper, then typed on. Although the method is clearly outdated (has anyone even seen a typewriter lately?), the term cc has survived. It is usually written at the bottom of a letter with a colon after the double 'c' followed with the name of the person who is to receive the copy, as in "cc: Cruthers."

C corporation [B] A regular corporation, in contrast to a corporation that has elected an *S corporate* status. S corporate status, often referred to as a subchapter S corporation, allows for the pass-through of income and expenses to the owner(s). See *corporation*.

CD (certificate of deposit) [F] A popular bank interest investment, usually with a maturity of six months to five years, primarily used by conservative investors.

CD (compact disc) [C] The popular small plastic discs that contain recorded music. The disc is read by optical lasers that contain digitized music or information. By the way, in this case the word *disc* is spelled with a "c" versus the "k" that is used for a disk utilized for computer purposes. See *CD-ROM*.

CD-ROM (compact disk-read only memory) [C] Called CDs for short, CD-ROMS look just like audio CDs, but they store all sorts of computer programs, from games to entire encyclopedias (complete with audio and video clips). What's that Read Only Memory part? Well, unlike regular computer programs, a user cannot write on or modify a CD-ROM. CD-ROMS require a special drive.

cease-and-desist order [L] A legal order stopping a person or company from doing something. Also referred to as an "injunction."

cell [C] In a spreadsheet, the rectangular area where a row and column intersect.

> The spreadsheet for the sales force had sixty *cells*, formed by twelve columns representing the months and five rows representing the five sales regions.

cellular phone [C] A relatively new and highly popular method of phone service requiring no wires! Currently there are over 50 million users with about 1 million signing up each month. The phones use small geographic sites, or cells, to transmit and receive phone calls. The service is quickly including data transmission as well as phone communication.

central bank [E] The governmental bank that controls and regulates banks, banking, and the money supply in a country. It also coordinates international matters with other central banks as necessary. The Federal Reserve Bank is that official bank in the United States. In France, it's the Bank of France; in Germany, it's the Bundesbank; and in Canada, it's the Bank of Canada.

centralization [B] An organizational method in which the control and decision-making are shared by only a few top executives. This is in contrast to decentralization, in which an organization delegates decision-making downward.

central processing unit (CPU) [C] The computer's brain or microprocessor. As technology develops, manufacturers are finding ways to make the CPU smaller, faster, and more powerful.

CERN [C] The Conseil European pour la Recherche Nucleaire (CERN), which is translated as the European Laboratory for Nuclear Research. It is where the World Wide Web all began.

certainty [M] In probability, the concept that something is certain to happen. In a race it is certain there will be a winner (as long as the race is not rained out), and in a coin toss it is certain that either heads or tails will result (as long as it doesn't land on its edge).

certificate of incorporation [B] The legal document that certifies that a corporation has been established.

certificate of occupancy (CO or C of O) [RE] A certificate issued by a local government that officially allows a building to be occupied. It means that the building has been inspected and that it is up to code. See *building codes*.

> When the Binks sold their business, the buyers realized that there was no *CO* for the small building in the back. The buyers would not be able to use it until they legalized it.

certificate of title [RE] See *title*.

certificates [F] In the world of stock market investments, the stock certificate is the actual piece of paper with all the information about the stock, such as the issuer, the number of shares the certificate represents, and the CUSIP number. A "bond certificate" is the corresponding record of a bond.

certified employee benefits specialist (CEBS) [HR] A professional designation for benefit specialists.

certified financial planner (CFP) [F] The main certification of financial planners. CFPs must meet certain requirements of knowledge and experience in investments, insurance, taxes, and financial calculations.

certified management accountant (CMA) [A] One who has passed the CMA exams. Applies to accountants who have not met the statutory state requirement for a CPA.

certified public accountant (CPA) [A] One who has passed the CPA exams and met the state statutory requirements to practice accounting in that state. Only those who meet these requirements are able to use the initials CPA. A CPA audits the books of a company and gives an expression of the accuracy of the company's financial statements.

certiorari [L] Pronounced sir-she-ah-RAR-e, it is an order from a higher court requiring a lower court to provide the records and proceedings of a case so it can decide if an appeal is warranted.

ceteris paribus [E] Pronounced KA-ter-is PAIR-e-bus, it is a Latin term meaning holding other things equal. The term is applied to economics when one variable or a specific relationship is studied. For instance, it could be said that as the price of wine increases, fewer bottles of wine will be sold, ceteris paribus, or other things being equal. However, if at the same time doctors announced that wine is good for people's health, then all other things are not equal, and wine may increase in sales even though the price increases.

CGA [C] See *monitor*.

CGI (common gateway interface) [C] Software that allows web sites to be interactive, as in chat rooms and bulletin boards.

chairman [B] Typically the chief executive officer of a company. Often the chairman is the top executive in the company, responsible for policy and overall direction of the company, whereas the president, who reports to the chairman, is responsible for the day-to-day operations of the company.

chairman of the board [B] The presiding officer of the company's board of directors.

chamber of commerce [B] Local business people who organize, meet, and promote business interests in their area. They are part of a national group that coordinates business interests in Washington D.C. and in major business centers.

change agent [HR] See *organization development*.

change in management [B] Major new players in a company who are charged with pursuing different policies. Often occurs when the company is facing difficulties, and it is felt that new management is needed to solve its problems.

channels of distribution [B] The paths products follow from manufacturer to distributor and finally retailer, including the transportation and storage of the products.

chaos theory [M] A new mathematical method still in its developmental stage that involves complicated real-life applications. It attempts to find connections within disorder and irregularity to make them understandable. Predicting weather patterns is an example. Within the seemingly chaotic movement of wind, moisture, temperature, and pressure comes a certain order called weather.

chapter 7, 11, and 13, etc. [L] See *bankruptcy*.

character [C] A letter, number, or symbol that occupies one byte of information.

character witness [L] A person who testifies at a trial on behalf of another person. Usually it is someone who has known the person on trial for some time and can vouch with credibility for his or her character.

charitable deduction [T] Money donated to a charity or non-profit organization; these gifts are tax-deductible.

> The money that XYZ Corp. donated to the local civic organization enabled XYZ to take a sizable *charitable deduction* on its corporate tax.

charitable lead trust (CLT) or remainder trust (CRT) [L] Money or property given to a trust that receives some tax benefit. A lead trust refers to a trust where the charity receives income while a person is alive, but the principal is returned to the family at the person's death. A remainder trust is one where the trust receives the remainder, what's left, after the person dies, but the person making the donation receives an income up to his or her death. In either case the person making the donation receives a current tax deduction.

chart [M] See *graph*.

charter [B] Primarily an official document of incorporation, it can also mean the general purpose of a business.

> Mr. Gathers, chairman of McSoftware Inc., told the employees that their *charter* was to make the very best software available anywhere.

chartered financial analyst (CFA) [F] A financial analyst who has met certain requirements of knowledge and experience in economics, security analysis, portfolio management, and financial accounting.

chartered life underwriter (CLU) [I] A person who has passed the certification of the American College for Life Insurance, which is a school specializing in insurance.

chartered property and casualty underwriter (CPCU) [I] A person who has passed the certification of the American College for Property and Casualty Insurance, which is a school specializing in insurance.

chart of accounts [A] A list of accounts used by a company for accounting purposes, with each account usually given a number or code.

chat room [C] An internet site that allows a person to enter into a "conversation" with one or more people who are online at the same time. This involves typing a message and waiting for other people to respond. Some sites are hosted, sometimes with an author or well-known person and revolve around a topic ("The New Tax Increase"); others are more free-form.

Don't Be a PITA—Chat Acronyms

AFK Away from keyboard
BAK Back at keyboard
BRB Be right back
BTW By the way
GMTA Great minds think alike
GTSY Good to see you
IMHO In my humble opinion
L8R Later
LTNS Long time no see
LOL Laughing out loud
OIC Oh, I see
OMG Oh, my God!
PITA Pain in the ass
ReHi Hi again
ROTFL Rolling on the floor laughing
RTFM Read the #$%&*@ manual!
WRT With respect to
:::POOF::: Signing off now

---

chattel [L] Personal property, goods or possessions, in contrast to real estate, which is real property.

chattel mortgage [RE] A mortgage on personal property, as opposed to the typical mortgage on real estate. It is generally used to secure the payment of money or performance of an obligation.

cherry picking [S] Term that refers to selective in order to get only the best.

Chicago Board of Trade (CBT) [F] Established in 1848, it was first an exchange to trade forward grain contracts but now trades in many futures and options.

Chicago Board Options Exchange (COBE) [F] The first organized trading exchange for options, established in 1973.

Chicago Mercantile Exchange (CME) [F] Started in 1919, it is an exchange trading in many agricultural commodities.

Chicago school [E] Milton Friedman and other economists who either taught at the University of Chicago or who promote the ideas of macroeconomics, monetarism, and free markets.

Chicken Little, the sky is falling [S] A person who thinks calamities are frequently afoot. He will communicate these impending disasters to others in the organization and will be labeled as either a worry wart, or someone who is trying too hard to get things right.

chief executive officer (CEO) [B] The head honcho in a company. The CEO reports only to the board of directors.

chief financial officer (CFO) [A] The senior company officer in charge of all accounting and financial reporting, usually reporting directly to the president of the company.

chief operating officer (COO) [B] The person who runs the day-to-day operations of a company. The COO often holds the title of president.

> The *COO* at Zippy Corp. oversees all acquisitions and hiring done in the company.

Chinese wall [S] Protective barriers between departments for security, objectivity or other reasons. Such barriers are usually set up between the traders of a Wall Street firm and the group handling individual clients.

chip [C] The integrated circuit that forms the basis of a computer; it is so small it could rest on a finger tip. Some of the well-known chips are the 386, 486, and Pentium for IBM-compatible computers and the 68000 series and PowerPC for the Macintosh computers from Apple. The Pentium II chip has 7.5 million transistors!

chip shot [S] An easy task to accomplish.

chi-square test [M] A statistical test comparing the frequencies of two distributions to see if they are alike. It helps decide whether a sample distribution could be a random sample from a specific population. It is written as c^2. It is named from the Greek letter *chi*. To use the results, the degrees of freedom of the sample is required. The degrees of freedom is usually the number of observations minus one. A table usually called the "values of c^2" is consulted. See *statistics*.

churn; churning [F] An unethical, and illegal, activity by which a broker actively over trades an account so as to increase brokerage commissions instead of trying to increase the profit of the account.

chutzpah [S] A term meaning to have guts or utter nerve. "Chutzpah" can have both positive and negative connotations. It is pronounced without the initial "c" as in HUTZ-pah. From the Yiddish *khutspe*.

circle [M] A perfect round 360-degree curve with all points equally distant from the center.

circle the wagons [S] To close ranks within a group, protecting each other against some outside pressure or attack. It comes from the old Western method of actually making a circle of wagons, affording the best protection from outside marauders.

circuit breaker [F] An official halt of trading to cool down markets, just as fuses or circuit breakers halt the flow of electricity when an electrical system is overheating. If and when markets plunge, the circuit breaker allows for a breather and, hopefully, for cooler heads to prevail. These rules were established after the October 19, 1997, plunge of 508 points in the Dow Jones industrial average (a 22.6 percent drop.) Several rules were established: After a 50-point drop from the previous day's close (frequently invoked), a 350-point drop (stops the trading of all stocks for 30 minutes), or a 550-point drop (halts the trading of all stocks for one hour).

circular file [S] Slang for waste basket.

Smithers promptly filed the promotional material in the *circular file.*

circularization [A] The audit process of confirming accounts payable and accounts receivable by directly contacting customers and creditors.

circumstantial evidence [L] Evidence implied from the facts of the case, in contrast to direct evidence.

The defense attorney argued that while his client had in fact donated money to the senator's campaign, there was no direct evidence that the donation led to the eventual lucrative contract; it was only *circumstantial evidence.*

CISC (complex instruction set computer) [C] A part of the central processing unit in a computer that carries out a relatively large set of instructions.

civil law [L] That part of the law dealing with noncriminal acts, such as contract disputes. Civil law generally deals with disputes between people or companies, in contrast to criminal law that deals with violations of public law.

claim [HR] [I] A request made by an employee for payment of medical expenses or by a person for payment of damages from an insurance company for such situations as an auto accident or home damage.

After the accident, the Smiths made a *claim* for car repairs.

C language, also C++ [C] A high-level programming language used by professional computer programmers.

class action [L] A lawsuit filed on behalf of a group of people. One of the more well-known recent class actions involved women who had breast implants and claimed to have been harmed by them.

class A stock [A] The name given to the basic class of stock when there is another class. This indicates that there are some differences between the rights of the stockholders in each class. The other class of stock is usually called class B stock.

classes of stock [A] Most companies have only one class of stock. However, when a company wants to offer one class of stock for the public and reserve a separate class of stock, with special rights, for management or the founders, then two or more classes of stock are created. Typically, Class A stock is offered to the public, while Class B stock is held internally. Class B stock is typically given super voting rights and/or extra dividend rights over Class A stock.

classical economics [E] The economic school of thought that emphasizes free markets, competition, and small government. Economists Adam Smith, David Ricardo, and Alfred Marshall were of this school.

clearinghouse [F] A firm that facilitates the execution of trades by transferring funds, providing delivery of certificates, and guaranteeing the performance of trading obligations.

clemency [L] Often called executive clemency, it is the reduction in the sentence of a convict. The more dramatic cases may involve a governor granting pardons for inmates on death row.

clerestory window [RE] Windows placed at the top of a building for light and ventilation, frequently seen in churches and many modern buildings.

> The architect designed the wall to have a row of *clerestory windows* along the top to bring in light without loss of privacy.

click [C] Pressing down on either the right or left button on the mouse; often one click to highlight and a double click (which means pressing twice on the button) to initiate an action.

> Double *click* on the icon to open that program.

client server [C] Networks of PCs linked together by powerful computers so many users can all be served.

> Large companies are increasingly using client servers rather than the older, more costly systems that rely on mainframe computers.

clip art [C] Prepared illustrations that can be used in word-processing and desktop publishing software.

clock speed [C] The measurement of how fast a computer can think, measured in megahertz (MHz). A computer with 400 MHz will think faster than one with a clock speed of only 266 MHz.

clone [B] [C] Any product that is identical to or closely resembles another product.

> In the 1980s, IBM computer *clones* littered the market. They were popular because they were often less expensive than the computers from IBM itself, but could use all the software designed for IBM.

closed-end fund; closed-end investment company [F] A type of mutual fund with a fixed number of shares. Closed-end funds are not as common as regular or open-end mutual funds. They are traded on the stock exchanges or over-the-counter and are more like regular stocks than their counterpart, open-end funds. See *open-end fund*.

closed shop [B] A place of work where employees must be members of a specific union before they can be hired.

closely held corporation [B] A company in which the stock is divided among only a few shareholders. Often there is no market for the stock. Also, shareholders often take an active role in management of the corporation.

> One of the reasons that XYZ Corp. was able to make so many decisions so quickly was that it was a *closely held corporation*.

closing [RE] A meeting with buyer and seller, as well as any attorneys and bankers involved in the sale of real estate, at which the final transactions take place. After the closing, the buyer takes possession of the property, and the seller gets all of the net sales proceeds. This should not be confused with the contract signing. Note that closing is a noun, but the buyer or seller may use the verb "close" to talk about the meeting.

closing costs [RE] The costs associated with a closing. The closing costs include transaction fees, attorney fees, and other bank, insurance, and government (recording) fees. Many banks estimate the closing costs when the buyer applies for a mortgage so that he or she can plan for them.

The *closing costs* were not as excessive as Zippy Corp. had anticipated.

closing statement [RE] The document detailing all requirements that have to be satisfied before the real estate transaction can be concluded, such as fees and taxes to be paid.

closing the books [A] The accounting activities at the end of a period—monthly, quarterly, or annually—to finalize the accounts and prepare financial reports and statements.

clout [S] Slang for having significant influence or power, usually political. "Clout" first appeared in print in 1868, in a reference to the world of New York politics.

The real estate builder had *clout* with the local variance committee so she was always able to get her construction changes approved.

cluster zoning [RE] A type of zoning that allows houses to be grouped closely together with lots of open space around them, as opposed to more normal zoning where the houses are evenly spaced.

coaching [HR] Advice given by either a boss, peer, or member of the human resource department to improve an individual's job performance.

COBOL (Common Business Oriented Language) [C] A high-level business programming language, still widely used. This is in contrast to FORTRAN (Formula Translation), which is high-level language for mathematics, science, and engineering. COBOL language has come under criticism because of the Y2K problem. See *Y2K*.

COBRA (Consolidated Omnibus Budget Reconciliation Act of 1985) [HR] A law that enables an employee who leaves her job to continue to be covered under the company's medical plan for up to eighteen months by paying roughly the same as what it costs the company. The law stipulates several qualifying events for COBRA coverage, including termination, reduced work hours, death, and divorce.

COD (cash on delivery or collect on delivery) [B] Payment method by which a person pays for a shipment either in cash or with a certified check at the time of delivery.

Code (Internal Revenue Code) [T] See *Internal Revenue code.*

codes [RE] See *building codes.*

codicil [L] Pronounced COD-ah-sil, it's a legal amendment to a will. Changes to a will must be done with the same legal formality as the original will, not just by casually writing in the margins.

> Susan asked the lawyer to prepare a *codicil* to her will instead of rewriting the entire document.

coefficient [M] The numerical part of an algebraic expression such as $4x$. The number, or 4 in this example, is the coefficient of the expression, while x is the variable.

coefficient of determination [M] In statistics, it is also know as r^2. See r^2.

cognitive dissonance [S] A mental inconsistency between two accepted ideas. Leon Festinger, who developed this concept, postulated that a person is psychologically uncomfortable under these circumstances.

> Smithers stated, "I'm in a state of *cognitive dissonance* now that the boss has asked us to withhold our production problems from marketing."

coinsurance [HR] A benefits practice that requires the employee to pay for a portion of a benefit, such as medical insurance for which the employee must either make a small co-payment (usually from $5 to $20) per doctor's visit or pay a certain percentage of the entire bill.

cold boot [C] See *boot*.

cold call; cold canvass [B] A sales technique of calling or visiting a list of customers who have not requested the services being offered.

> The sales staff was briefed on making *cold calls*. No matter what the person contacted said, they would respond with the scripted answer.

> One of the most difficult things for the sales force at ABC Corp. was the *cold canvass*, where they went from store to store to sell their merchandise; only one store in ten was even interested in listening to the pitch.

cold water [S] A term for a negative reaction to a suggestion, idea, or plan, usually preceded by the word *throw*.

> Cruthers threw *cold water* on the project when he said, "That's the dumbest idea I've ever heard."

collateral [F] Any asset offered as a guarantee of repayment of a loan.

collateralized mortgage obligations (CMOs) [F] A security offered by the Federal Home Loan Mortgage Corp. that provides a pass-through of mortgage principal and interest to investors.

collection agency [B] An outside firm that is given accounts receivable for the purpose of collecting as much of the outstanding amount as possible.

collective bargaining [HR] Formal labor negotiations between management and unions. The word "collective" refers to the concerted action of employees through their union.

collision [I] Sudden damage to a vehicle due to an accident. Collision insurance is for the reimbursement of such damage.

column [C] The vertical presentation of data, especially in a spreadsheet. This is in contrast to a row, which is the horizontal presentation of data.

COMECON [E] The former trading bloc created by the former Soviet Union.

command [C] An instruction for a computer.

command key [C] An Apple computer key that functions with another key to shortcut through menu choices.

commercial insurance [I] Insurance for companies and other organizations as opposed to insurance for individuals.

commercial paper [F] A short-term note issued by companies. The length of issue is usually from thirty to 270 days. Money market funds are often composed largely of treasury bills and commercial paper.

commission [B] A compensation-based practice of paying a salesperson a percentage of the sales, either on a per month, or other period, or on a per sale basis. Wall Street brokers and insurance agents are often paid by this method as well; a percentage of their sales is the salesperson's gain. Thus, the more sold, the greater the compensation.

[F] The fee an investment broker charges for making an investment. Brokers and brokerage houses charge a fee or commission for buying and selling stocks or other securities. The commission is generally a percentage of the price of the investment.

[I] The percentage of a premium paid to an agent for selling an insurance policy. Often, the agent receives an amount of one-half of the first year's premium as commission and then a percentage of each subsequent yearly premium. Usually the total commission equals one year's premium.

[RE] A percentage of the price received for the sale of real estate or of the yearly rental of a property, paid to a real estate agent for selling or renting a piece of property. The sales commission is often 6 percent or negotiated lower.

commitment [RE] A promise by a bank or lending institution that a buyer will get a loan at a specified amount and interest rate. The bank's commitment is usually for a short time.

> As soon as they signed the contract on the property, the board at Spammo got a *commitment* from their bank.

committed costs [A] Long-term decisions by a company about major fixed costs, such as a plant and equipment.

commodity [F] An article of trade or commerce, usually an agricultural or mining product. Sugar, wheat, soybeans, lumber, and gasoline are examples of commodities.

[B] A type of product or service that is generally not distinguishable from a competitor's products. This is in contrast to a specialty, which has unique characteristics. Commodities compete on price, while specialties, such as luxury cars or designer fashions, generally compete on quality or design.

commodity currency [F] Currency made of either gold or silver, or currency that can be exchanged for gold or silver. Today, the United States, along with many other countries, does not have a commodity currency; its money cannot be traded for gold or silver.

Commodity Futures Trading Commission (CFTC) [F] A federal agency established in 1974 that oversees and monitors the trading of commodity options and futures.

common area [RE] Any part of a property with more than one tenant that is for use by all tenants. That area may include parking lots, lobbies, or laundry facilities. The maintenance for that area may be charged to the residents with common-area charges.

> The office was small, but the building had conference rooms available in the *common area*.

common law [L] The system of law derived from English law, which relies on judicial decisions as opposed to litigation. It is based more on principles than rules. Thus, in the absence of specific statutes, common usage and customs are considered by the courts.

common-law marriage [L] A marriage based not on a ceremony but on living together and intending to be married. Often, such an arrangement is considered a legal marriage after seven years.

common stock [F] Stocks in which the investor shares in the success of a company when it does well or suffers a loss if the company does poorly. Those who own shares of common stock have voting rights and a share of earnings when dividends are declared. Besides common stock, a company may offer preferred stock, which usually offers the investor a preference in paying dividends over common stock.

> Diane preferred to buy *common stock*; the risks were greater, but she had heard that this company was due to make a large profit.

common wall [RE] A wall shared by two buildings.

communications port [C] See *COM port*.

communications protocol [C] A standard for transmitting data between computers.

communism [E] An extreme socialist economic system based not only on the ownership of production by the government but also the central planning and controlling of the economy by the government. This system is the opposite of capitalism, in which individuals own the means of production.

community property [L] The law of property that recognizes that all property a husband and wife obtain during their marriage is owned jointly. It is an adoption of the Spanish law approach to property. Historically, there have been eight community property states: Arizona, California, Idaho, Louisiana, New Mexico, Nevada, Texas, and Washington. Wisconsin has since been added to the list, reflecting the modern notion in divorce that each spouse should have half of the property.

commutative law [M] The rule that multiplying a and b is equal to multiplying b and a. See *distributive law*.

company [B] A business entity, in general.

company contributions [HR] Refers to the payment made into a pension or 401(k)-type savings plan by the employer. This is over and above the employee's own contributions. The usual company contribution to a 401(k) plan is 50 percent of the employee's contributions up to 6 percent of his pay. Thus, the employee makes 50 percent on his money for just being an employee.

company policies [HR] Rules and standards that a company has established, such as employees' not being permitted to install personal software on company computers or fly first-class during business travel.

company politics [S] See *politics*.

comparable properties (comps) [RE] A list of recently sold properties that are similar in size and location to a property being appraised. The appraiser complies and uses the comps' sales data to establish a market price for the property being sold.

> The appraiser was lucky to have found five *comps* from recent sales records right on the block of buildings that were almost identical to the subject of the appraisal.

comparable worth [HR] The concept that men and women should be paid the same for equal, or comparable, work.

compa-ratio [HR] A ratio used for compensation analysis of where employees are in their salary grade. It is calculated by dividing an employee's salary by the midpoint of the employee's salary grade. For instance, if an employee's salary was $35,000 and the midpoint of the employee's grade was $42,000, the compa-ratio would be .8 ($35,000 divided by $42,000 equals .8). An employee at the midpoint would have a compa-ratio of 1. This ratio is used in several ways, including comparing compa-ratios with job performance ratings and comparing compa-ratios between departments.

comparative advantage [E] The concept that every country has some advantage producing some products, either by an abundance of one or more natural resources or by the skill of its population. See *Ricardo, David*.

compatibility [C] The ability of one computer to use the same software as another computer.

compatible [C] A term referring to a computer's ability to run certain types of software. A Macintosh computer is generally not compatible with an IBM machine. A DOS-based computer is not compatible with a Windows-based machine. Conversion programs, however, allow for certain word-processing and spreadsheet programs to be converted for use from one type of computer and software to another.

compensatory time [HR] See *comp time*.

competency hearing [L] An attempt to establish legal capacity by the court. When it is determined that a defendant is competent, it's called *compos mentis*, and when the defendant is found not competent to stand trial, it's called *non compos mentis*.

competition [B] Rivalry. In a healthy market, there is free competition between companies in each industry. If there is enough competition in a market, consumers will purchase the best quality product at the best price; that's how competition helps to make production more efficient.

[E] The tension between similar businesses to keep prices down and productivity up. Consumers benefit from reasonable prices for products and services. Perfect competition, as opposed to imperfect competition, or monopoly, is an economic term that describes how competition is supposed to work in an ideal capitalist society.

compiler [C] A program that takes a standard programming language, such as COBOL or C, and translates it into basic machine language.

complaint [L] The accusation in a legal case.

complex expression or number [M] A number or expression that includes an imaginary number, such as 3i. Such expressions are used in advanced mathematics.

complexity [S] A management term that stresses the need to understand and address each aspect of a project, product, or service. Trying to simplify a complex matter can lead one to miss a crucial detail and thereby forego quality. While sometimes it is necessary to simplify something to understand it, in many cases, especially where quality is involved, dealing with each detail is the best approach.

COM port [C] The communications sockets in the back of a computer to connect the mouse (usually COM1) and the modem (usually COM2).

compounding [M] The process of earning interest on interest. See *compound interest*.

compound interest [M] Interest that itself earns interest during a period. For instance, if $1,000 was invested for one year at 5 percent compounded monthly, then it would earn interest monthly not only on the initial $1,000 but on the interest generated during the year. In this case the total investment at the end of the year would be $1,051. This is in contrast to simple interest, which has no compounding during the year. If the $1,000 earned 5 percent simple interest, then the value of the investment at the end of the year would be $1,050.

comprehensive insurance [I] Insurance covering all types of possible situations. Comprehensive medical insurance combines basic health insurance with major medical insurance. Comprehensive business insurance covers any liabilities that were not specifically excluded.

> Acme Corp. was glad to have a *comprehensive insurance* policy when Sam Binky brought suit against it for his carpal-tunnel syndrome.

compressed file; compression/decompression [C] A large file compressed, or made smaller, so as to take up less space when stored and/or less time when downloaded. After a file has been downloaded, it must be decompressed. Often when a file is compressed, it will have some letters added to its file name. For example, a document titled "BOOK" may be retitled "BOOK.Z" when it is compressed.

compressed workweek [HR] A workweek of less than the standard five days. For instance, the workweek may be four 10-hour days or three 12-hour days.

comp time [HR] Extra time, or compensatory time, taken off because of previous extra hours put in.

comptroller [A] An older and outdated spelling of controller. See *controller*.

Compuserve [C] One of the commercial online services.

computer [C] A computer sits on just about everyone's desk these days with a keyboard and mouse close at hand, but defining it becomes difficult except in the general sense. Basically it calculates and manipulates data, as with spreadsheets, word processors, and graphics programs. It allows for the input of information and can provide output in a variety of forms, especially on monitors and printers. Through a modem, a computer can be connected to the internet. The ENIAC, considered one of the first computers, was developed during World War II. In the 1960s, vacuum tubes were replaced by transistors, then by integrated circuits. In the 1970s thousands of circuits were incorporated into a single chip. Nineteen seventy-seven was a momentous year as Apple, Radio Shack, and Commodore introduced the first computers for individual use. In 1981 the modern era of computers began when IBM introduced the PC, which was powered by an Intel 8088 chip and had the DOS operating system by Microsoft. Critical software for business was eventually introduced, such as *WordPerfect* in 1980, dBASE in 1981, and *Lotus 1-2-3* in 1982. Now the Pentium III chip, *Windows 98*, and the iMac are available. So, how to define computers? Well, they're moving targets because they keep on improving as more applications are found.

computer-aided design (CAD) [C] High-speed workstations that allow engineers to design products. Used extensively in engineering and architectural firms.

computer-aided instruction (CAI) [C] The use of a computer to help teach a student.

computer simulation [C] Any representation or imitation of real objects within a computer program.

> The pilots used *computer simulation* to practice with different emergency situations before they climbed into the cockpit of a real plane.

concatenate [C] To join or link together.

> In a speech recognition program, phonemes, or units of speech, are *concatenated* to form sounds.

concave and convex curves [M] In graphing, a concave curve is one that looks like the arches of McDonald's or the entrance to a cave or mine. The curve can be a pure arch or concave upward or downward. This is in contrast to a convex curve, which is shaped like a big U.

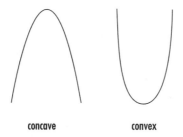

concave   convex

concealment [L] The act of hiding, or making it difficult to determine, the facts in a case.

concierge [HR] See *hoteling*.

conciliation [HR] A process used in labor disputes. The aim of conciliation is to get management and labor to sit and talk with the hope that they can work out their problems. This is in contrast to using an arbitrator who generally has the power to impose a settlement. See *arbiter; arbitrator*.

condensed type [C] A style of type where letters are pushed closer together.

condominium (condo) [RE] A type of residential property in which the buyer purchases a unit in a residential community. In a condominium, the owner has rights to the inside of his unit and common areas in the community. The owners form a condominium board that runs the operation of the common areas.

> The doctors enjoyed the *condominium* they shared: They each took care of their offices and paid fees for the maintenance of a common waiting and reception room and parking area for all their patients.

Conference Board [B] An association of business executives that exchange ideas and information on policies and practices. The Conference Board provides a number of conferences and research programs on key areas of current business concerns.

conference call [C] The linking of several office locations together by phone for a joint conversation.

confidence interval [M] In statistics, the level at which the results are acceptable. The most commonly used is the 95 percent confidence interval.

config.sys file [C] A DOS file that sets, or configures, the system for programs. It specifically loads drivers, which are routines that link peripheral devices to the operating system. See *autoexec.bat file*.

congruent [M] Two things that are exactly equal. Often used in geometry, it means coinciding exactly when superimposed. For example, if triangle A is congruent to triangle B, the sides and angles of both triangles will be exactly equal.

connectivity [S] The linking of people within a company with information and communications.

conscience fund [F] See *social investing*.

consensus building [S] Slowly building toward agreement, usually by diplomatic means, or simply by wearing down the opposition over time through determination.

consent decree; consent judgment [L] A recorded agreement between two parties to settle a case.

consideration [L] The basic element of a contract. A contract must have consideration from both parties, often with one receiving money for the promise to perform certain duties. The money and promise are each a consideration.

consignee/consignor [B] In shipping, the receiver of goods/the shipper of goods. The consignee acts as a trustee of the goods but does not have title to them. The consignor maintains the title of the goods, but not the possession of them.

> L-Mart, the *consignee*, accepted its order of 2,000 slime balls from Acme Corp.

> Acme Corp., the *consignor*, shipped 2,000 slime balls to L-Mart.

consignment [A] A system for selling goods whereby a company or individual places goods in a store but retains title to the goods. If the goods are not sold, the owner, not the store, is responsible for them.

console device [C] A piece of computer apparatus, namely a keyboard, mouse, or monitor, that allows the user to communicate with the central processing unit.

consolidated statement; consolidated financial statement [A] The combining of all business units of a company into one overall set of financial statements.

consolidation [B] The shrinking of the number of companies in a particular industry through the combining of two or more companies into a newly formed corporation.

consortium [B] A business alliance of companies formed in order to obtain more business clout than any individual company could.

conspicuous consumption [E] Ostentatious buying of goods in order to impress others. A term used by American economist Thorstein Veblen in his 1899 book *The Theory of the Leisure Class*.

conspiracy [L] The plotting by two or more individuals to break the law.

constant [M] An unchanging value. In an algebraic formula a constant is often represented with the letter k. See *variable*.

constant dollars [E] The value of the dollar in a base year. If 1990 is chosen as the base for constant dollars, any inflation or decrease in the value of the dollar after that year is adjusted so all actual purchasing power can be compared to that year.

> The economists at the government offices released figures for this year's Gross Domestic Product, as measured in *constant dollars* so that they could compare it to last year's GDP.

constructive receipt [HR] A technical tax term used especially in executive compensation referring to any benefit or compensation method where the executive has control of the money or stock. If the executive can control, or have constructive receipt of it, then taxes must be paid at that time. Often, deferred compensation arrangements avoid constructive receipt so the executive will be taxed later.

consultant [B] A business specialist who is trained in advising companies about its operations and policies.

consulting contract [HR] Term that usually refers to a person, typically an executive, who is hired as a consultant after leaving the company, using his or her expertise to perform certain work or help on specific projects.

consulting firm [B] A firm that specializes in giving advice to companies. Consulting companies can focus their expertise in just one area, such as computer operations or employee benefits, or offer expertise in a broad range of management areas.

consumer [B] The user of products and services. Appropriately this is the focus of a business, which tries to understand the needs of users and then tries to meet those needs. Sometimes purchasers are direct users of products or services, while at other times purchasers are middle-men who purchase for others to use.

> Jane bought toys for the youngest *consumers* in her household: her two- and three-year-old children.

[E] The hypothetical person that economists study. The study of the consumer is one of the basic areas of economic study, from individual consumer behavior to aggregate consumer conduct.

consumer confidence [E] A measure of how typical consumers feel about their current situation and their faith in the future. If people feel good about where they are and where they're going, consumer confidence is said to be high, and the economy will benefit. Even during an economic recovery, if consumers don't have confidence, they will be hesitant to spend. Consumer confidence surveys generally check a number of factors: how people feel about their job security, whether they will buy big-ticket items, and whether they will spend consistently on short-term purchases. There are two standard surveys, administered monthly, that measure consumer confidence. The University of Michigan's "consumer sentiment" survey, the older of the two, was begun in 1947. The Conference Board's "consumer confidence" survey, however, is more widely reported to the public. It began in the late 1960s.

consumer goods [E] Manufactured products used by consumers, not businesses. Durable goods are those that usually have a useful life of three years or more, like cars and refrigerators. Nondurable goods, like toys or games, are frequently consumed, or used, in short order.

consumer price index (CPI) [E] A monthly measure of price movements by the Bureau of Labor Statistics. A "basket of goods" is constructed of food, shelter, clothing, medical care, entertainment, and other expenditures, then priced each month. However, the basket of goods is fixed, so consumer habits are not measured, only the prices of particular items. Although it roughly measures the cost of living, the CPI doesn't take into consideration factors such as consumers shifting, say, to buy rice if the price of potatoes increases, nor does the CPI factor in consumers using discount stores. However, the fixed basket of goods is updated from time to time. The CPI is used to adjust certain government payments such as Social Security.

consumer research [B] Analysis using such tools as focus groups (small groups of representative consumers), interviews, and surveys to get information about how people use products or services, why they buy them, how they respond to marketing campaigns, etc.

> Zippy Corp. employed a prestigious marketing firm to conduct *consumer research* regarding the reaction to its new line of zippers.

consumer spending; consumption [E] Economist's label for buying goods or purchasing services. Some products, like foods, are literally consumed, while others, like toys, are just used. Economists consider both to be examples of consumption.

consumption function [E] A ratio of how much people consume to how much they earn. All things being equal, it is generally assumed that consumption will increase if income increases. More specifically, as income rises, savings rise, along with spending. As income decreases, savings decrease, along with spending.

> Economists calculate the *consumption function* as a gauge of consumer confidence.

containerization [B] The transportation of goods by ship, truck, and railroad in large sealed units that are easily transferred between these modes of transportation.

contempt of court [L] An action that interferes with or is against the court's authority.

contingency; contingency reserve [A] An event that may occur for which a company needs to set aside funds. For example, if a company has a pending lawsuit, it may create a contingency reserve for any future damages it may need to pay.

contingency fee [B] A fee paid to a consulting or law firm to hold that firm loyal to the company should the company need its services. This can be done when a company is sued and wants to hold a particular law firm known for its expertise, versus having the law firm represent the opponent.

contingent annuitant [HR] The named beneficiary of a pension plan who will continue receiving some form of an annuity payout if the employee dies. "Contingent" because it is dependent on the employee dying, and "annuitant" because the person would be receiving a form of an annuity.

contingent beneficiary [I] A second person who will be beneficiary of a life insurance policy if the main beneficiary is not alive.

> Mr. Smith received $100,000 in insurance money as the *contingent beneficiary* when his great-aunt died because the main beneficiary, his uncle, was no longer alive.

contract [L] An agreement between two people or companies that defines certain goods or services to be produced or performed and sets forth specified terms.

[RE] An agreemenr between the buyer and seller that commits the two of them to go through with a deal. The actual *closing*, when they transfer possession of the property, usually takes place a month or two later.

contracting out [B] The use of outside sources for the supplying of partially manufactured units or services that were formerly constructed or performed in-house. Often called "outsourcing."

contract work [HR] Work on a project basis.

> As a freelance accountant, Don took on *contract work* wherever he could find it.

contrarian [F] An investor who is going against popular momentum or opinions. When most investors are buying, a contrarian may be selling, and vice versa.

contributory negligence [I] Personal injury law that prevents a person from collecting damages if that person was at fault, wholly or partially, for the accident.

control key (Ctrl) [C] The key usually designated simply as Ctrl on the keyboard that works with other keys to perform a special function. For instance, in some word-processing software, the Ctrl key and the letter V will provide a whole table of special symbols that can be entered into the text document.

controllable costs [A] Costs that are deemed to be controlled by managers or at a given level of authority. Classifying costs as *controllable* and *uncontrollable* is important in responsible accounting.

controller [A] The chief accounting officer of a company, usually reporting to the chief financial officer.

conventional memory [C] The memory first accessed by a DOS-based computer. It is usually 640k of memory.

conventional mortgage [RE] A regular, non-FHA mortgage typically held for fifteen to thirty years with a fixed interest rate.

convertible bond; convertible preferred stock [A] Either a bond or preferred stock issue that allows the holder of that security to convert it for the company's common stock under prescribed conditions.

convertible mortgage [RE] A mortgage that features the option to change to a different type of mortgage at some point in its term.

> Zippy Corp. took advantage of its *convertible mortgage* when it changed its adjustable rate mortgage over to a conventional fixed-rate after five years.

convertibles [F] Securities that are a cross between bonds and stocks. Like a bond, convertibles offer a fixed rate of return but can be converted to the company's stock by a specific date. Convertibles can offer the best of both worlds in that they pay more than a stock in income, and, if the stock rises, the investor can buy the stock and participate in that rise.

convertible term [I] A term life-insurance policy that can be converted to whole life or another form of cash value life insurance.

convex [M] See *concave and convex curves*.

conveyance [RE] The written record of a real estate transaction; for example, a deed, a mortgage, or a lease.

> The *conveyances* were recorded in the county records; anyone could see how much Whammo paid for Widget's building.

cook the books; cooked books [S] To manipulate the accounting records or statements, creating a false or misleading impression to investors or other businesses.

cooperative apartment (co-op) [RE] Residential property in which the buyer purchases shares in the corporation that owns the building and also receives a special lease on an apartment.

When Alice's apartment building went *co-op*, she jumped at the chance to buy into it at a reduced price.

coordination of benefits (COB) [HR] Medical benefit rules that apply when husband and wife are covered by two separate plans, namely, when both work but for different companies. Usually the plan of the employee who is receiving the medical treatment must pay first, then the other plan may pay a benefit.

copayment [HR] A term applied to health insurance where an employee pays a percentage of the medical costs, for instance 20 percent, and the employer pays the other percentage, 80 percent.

Since Jan had a *copayment* of only $15, she wrote a check to her doctor for that amount and the rest was billed to her HMO.

copy [C] The duplication of a file.

copy protection [C] Any of several methods to prevent software from being copied and used by unauthorized users.

copyright [L] The legal rights of authors, artists, and other creative individuals to determine how and when their works should be used and to compensation for them. Under current law, copyrights granted after 1977 are protected for the author's lifetime plus fifty years. For works for hire, the period of time is seventy-five years from the date of publication or 100 years after its creation, whichever is shorter. See *intellectual property*.

[A] An asset of a company, that gives the company the exclusive right to publish specific material.

core competencies [S] The main strengths of an individual or firm. Apparently, the term began as an analysis and description of an individual's main strengths and was then applied to a business. In either case, it is a description of the main intrinsic skills and abilities. For a business it is not the actual products or services but the underlying collective learning of the organization and its people.

core values [S] The central or deep-seated beliefs of a person or organization.

> The president stated in the mission statement that responsive service was one of the company's *core values* and essential to its success.

corner office [S] The location often reserved for a top executive. It usually has the best view with windows on two sides.

corporate culture [HR] The attitudes and beliefs that guide daily behavior at a company or in the corporate world in general. Some companies encourage casualness to the point where beards, jeans, and pizza parties are the norm.

[B] The generally informal rules of the company that set behavior or attitudes for employees.

corporate income tax [T] A tax on the profits made by a corporation.

corporate-owned life insurance [HR] A somewhat complicated cash-value life-insurance arrangement between a company and its executives. The company typically pays the premiums, holds the policy, and receives the death benefit when the employee dies.

corporate raider [B] An organization or individual investor who attempts to take over particular companies, usually resisted by the management of those firms. The raider, if successful, will reshape the company and then sell it, hoping to gain a quick investment return.

corporate welfare [E] Payments to businesses either in the form of a subsidy, like farming subsidies, or tax relief for special purposes, such as a research and development tax credit.

corporation [B] The formal entity of a company that has incorporated. A company must file papers to a particular state to obtain the legal right to operate as a corporation, called *incorporation*. The corporation as a legal entity generally absolves its employees from personal liability if its products are defective or services are less than advertised. Only the corporation itself as an entity can generally be sued to make good on the company's promises. See *C corporation, S corporation,* and *limited liability corporation.*

corpus [L] The main body of money, as in a trust. Also known as the principal of the trust.

[T] The principal, or main body, of a trust.

corpus delicti [L] Pronounced COR-pus de-LIC-ti, it is the material evidence relating to a crime, such as the corpse in a murder case.

> The defending attorney asked the court to dismiss the case because although the wealthy heiress had long been missing, no *corpus delicti* was ever found.

correction [F] A term investors don't like to hear, it is a downturn in the market after a run-up in prices. Usually considered a normal adjustment to a more realistic level of prices after the market has moved upward with considerable momentum.

correlation [M] A similar relationship. For instance, if the Dow Jones average is up, chances are the S&P 500 is also up. This relationship is considered a positive correlation. A negative correlation is often referred to as an "inverse relationship." Correlation is measured between −1 for opposite correlation, 0 for no correlation, and +1 for perfect correlation. See *inverse*.

correlation coefficient [M] See *r*.

corroborating evidence [L] Further evidence supporting the main evidence presented in a case, giving it additional strength.

cosign [F] To agree to make payments if the primary borrower of a loan cannot do so. Typically, a parent cosigns an auto loan for a young adult.

[L] The act of affixing one's signature to a document to demonstrate the authenticity of the principal signature.

cost [A] The expenditure of funds for specific financial needs of a company, such as equipment, salaries, investments, or general expenses. Cost is a term used in many contexts of a company's finances, such as fixed, variable, marginal, historical, or replacement.

cost accounting [A] Accounting methods used to provide internal cost information for managerial analysis and decisions. This is in contrast to "financial accounting," which provides information for external uses, such as bankers, investors, and regulators.

cost-benefit analysis (or study) [B] An appraisal of all social as well as economic aspects of a business project or a business action.

> Market Corp.'s *cost-benefit analysis*, which weighed our loss of efficiency for three months, made us realize that the expansion was not a good idea.

cost center [A] Any part of a company about which accounting information is kept to determine the cost of that part of the organization, such as a department, business unit, region, or new product.

cost containment [HR] Efforts by a company to reduce, or at least hold down, rising medical costs.

cost of capital [A] The composite cost of all of a company's funds. In essence, it is the overall investment rate a company uses to test if a project should be approved or not; sometimes called a "hurdle rate" or "required rate of return."

cost of living adjustment (COLA) [HR] An automatic increase in compensation due to inflation or some other index. Currently Social Security is adjusted annually by a COLA, specifically by the increase in inflation as measured by the CPI (consumer price index).

cost-of-living index [E] A base year and subsequent price tabulation of living costs.

cost per thousand (CPM) [B] An advertising term referring to the marketing or advertising costs of reaching 1,000 customers.

cost-push inflation [E] The increase in inflation due to increased costs of production. Increased labor costs or raw materials, like the oil crisis of the 1970s, are said to be pushed from the cost side. This is in contrast to "demand-pull," where the demand has increased from consumers, thus pulling up prices.

cost recovery method [A] See *installment sales method.*

cost shifting [HR] The practice of transferring more of the costs of medical insurance to the employees in hopes that employees will exercise more discretion with optional health costs, thus controlling costs better.

costs of goods sold [A] The costs of materials used in the products and goods of a company.

Council of Economic Advisers [E] A group of economists officially advising the president of the United States on economic matters. The council was established in 1946.

counselor of real estate (CRE) [RE] A designation given by the American Society of Real Estate Counselors. The CRE designation is the highest offered by the organization. It recognizes the individual's professional experience and judgment.

counterclaim [L] A counter demand by a defendant to the plaintiff. It is not just an answer to the original plaintiff's charge, it is a separate action.

coupon; coupon rate [F] A bond's interest rate. The rate is given as an annual interest rate, such as an 8 percent coupon on the standard face value of $1,000, which would be $80. Bonds usually pay interest semiannually, so in this case $40 would be paid twice a year. Bearer bonds used to have coupons attached, which the investor would cut out to redeem.

covenant [L] An agreement to do something, usually formally in a contract.

coverage [HR] Term that refers to being included in certain benefits of a company, such as a medical or a 401(k) plan.

[I] The scope of what is covered by an insurance policy.

covering the short position [F] A method of buying stocks that allows the investor to make money in the stock market when stocks go down. The investor borrows a specific stock from a broker and sells them in anticipation that the stock will go down in price. When it does, the investor then buys the same number of shares back and gives them back to the broker. If the price drops, the investor has thus bought low and sold high, the mantra for investors. When the investor actually buys the stocks, he is "covering the short position."

cpi (characters per inch) [C] A measurement specifying the size of letters.

CPI (consumer price index) [E] See *consumer price index*.

cps (characters per second) [C] The measurement of printer speed.

CPU (central processing unit) [C] The heart of the computer. In other words, the computer unit that performs the processing or calculating. It's where all the real work is done by the computer.

crash [F] A sudden collapse in the value of stocks.

The crash of 1929 contributed to the Great Depression of the 1930s.

[C] That most dreaded of all computer moments: when the computer fails. Usually data, programs, and other critical information are lost, along with the user's wits. At times, the user is wise to wait several minutes and then turn the computer back on, and sometimes, just sometimes, everything is back to normal, including the user's blood pressure. Backing up files is the most sound way to prevent disasters when a crash has occurred.

creative accounting [A] A mostly casual term that refers to manipulating numbers to fit the results a company wants (within the rules of accounting, of course).

credit [A] In accounting lingo, it refers to the entries on the right side of the accounts, as in debits on the left and credits on the right. Credits indicate an increase in liabilities, revenue, or shareholder's equity.

[F] The amount of money at a company's disposal, either directly in banking or security accounts, or in the ability to borrow funds because of its financial strength.

credit card [F] The method of payment in the U.S. economy that is fast replacing cash. It allows the user to buy now but pay later. Of course, this convenience comes with a price: interest. While the American Express card requires full payment of the balance at the end of each month, cards issued by most banks allow the user to make only minimum payments, while the balance continues to accumulate interest. The bank issuing the card will usually give a limit to the amount the user is able to charge.

James had two credit cards with him so that he could charge all the items he bought while he was on vacation.

credit crunch or squeeze [E] Governmental restrictions on bank credit or the pull-back of businesses offering credit.

creditor [L] One who is owed money, versus the debtor who owes it.

credit rating [B] The financial rating given to a company so banks can determine to either extend credit or withhold it.

credit report [F] A report from an independent company of a borrower's credit history. It includes how much outstanding credit and debt the borrower is carrying and how promptly payments were made.

> After the bank received the excellent *credit report* on Zippy Corp., it decided to go through with the loan.

credits [T] Specific items that can deduct taxes directly, dollar-for-dollar, such as the child tax credit or the elderly credit.

credit shelter trust [T] See *bypass trust*.

credit terms [A] The conditions specified by a bank for money borrowed by a company, such as the amount of available credit, the percentage rate of interest, and the date by which the funds are due to be paid.

credit union [HR] A nonprofit financial organization chartered for a company or industry that provides bank activities for employees, such as car loans, savings accounts, and CDs. Credit unions often provide a slightly lower loan rate and slightly higher interest rate on deposits than commercial banks. Payroll deductions into savings accounts are usually allowed.

criminal law [L] The body of law dealing with public crimes. This is in contrast to "civil law" which in general deals with disputes between two people or companies, such as contractual entanglements.

crisis management [B] Public relations activities in which a business tries to control and minimize damages resulting from an adverse occurrence affecting its products or services.

criterion [M] A term used in spreadsheets to denote a parameter or an aspect of information.

crony capitalism [E] The form of capitalism with tight links between government officials, bankers, and favored companies, to the exclusion of others. It is felt that a number of Asian countries, such as Indonesia, have experienced recent economic troubles because they have a form of crony capitalism.

crop [C] In graphics or desktop software, the ability to eliminate parts of the document or reposition them.

cross-examination [L] The questioning or interrogation of a witness in a court case by someone other than the person who produced the witness.

cross-hatching [C] A design using opposite slanting lines to fill in graphs.

cross-merchandising [B] A method of display in a store that combines dissimilar items made by the same company. The idea is that the buyers may cross to a related product made by the same company.

> Stickey Corp. found through market research that *cross-merchandising* its brand of peanut buter with its other products, such as Stickey's Marshmallow Stuff and Stickey's Gooey Jelly, produced a high percentage of consumer crossover.

cross training [HR] The practice of training employees to perform various jobs so that if someone is absent they can fill in.

crown jewel [S] The best part of a company or deal, as in a monarchy's crown jewels.

CRT (cathode ray tube) [C] See *cathode ray tube*.

Crummey power [T] Right of a beneficiary of a trust to withdraw up to $10,000 of an annual contribution and have that withdrawal excluded from gift taxes. The right is given for only a limited time each year, typically 30 days. It is named after a Mr. Crummey who won this right in court.

crunch numbers [S] To perform numerous calculations or prepare many accounting figures.

crunch time [S] The time to get serious because important deadlines loom immediately.

cry wolf [S] To falsely call for help. From Aesop's fable of a lad who on several occasions had falsely called out that there was a wolf in the area. The villagers no longer believed him when he actually did see one and cried out for help. So, too, a person in a company who cries wolf too often without a real crisis loses credibility.

Ctrl key [C] See *control key*.

Ctrl-Alt-Del [C] In DOS operating systems, these three keys, when held down simultaneously, will restart the computer. Also known as a "soft" or "warm boot."

cube (of a number) [M] The result of multiplying a number by itself three times. For example, 27 is the cube of 3:
3 x 3 x 3 =27.

cubed root [M] The opposite of a cube of a number. As an example, 3 x 3 x 3 = 27. Three is the *cubed root* of the number 27. See *cube (of a number)*.

cubicle [B] A workspace designed to be a cross between an enclosed office and an open area. The cubicle seems to have become the norm at many companies. The space is usually surrounded on three sides with 5-foot tall partitions.

cul-de-sac [RE] A designed traffic dead end, usually in a residential neighborhood, to restrict the flow of traffic.

> Although the Smiths liked the house, they especially loved the fact it was at the end of a *cul-de-sac*.

culture shock [S] The clash of two business cultures, often the old way a company did things and the new way the company, or new boss, wants to. It could also be the result of a merger of two companies with very different ways of conducting business.

> Cruthers speculated that veteran employees would experience *culture shock* when the new management finally implemented the new policies and brought in its own people.

cumulative dividends [F] Dividends on designated preferred stock that have not been paid but will be paid when the company has the money. Also known as "accumulated dividends" and "dividends in arrears."

cumulative voting [A] A type of stockholder voting that allows one vote per share times the number of directors up for election. Stockholders can then allocate their votes however they want among the different positions, or vote for just one.

currency [F] Simply another word for paper or coin money.

current account [E] The part of the balance of payment between countries that refers to the flow of goods and services. The other part is called the "capital account," which is the actual flow of money between countries. The current account is considered the broadest measure of international trade. See *balance of payments*.

current assets [A] Short-term assets of a company, such as cash or notes that are expected to be used or converted to cash within one year.

current liabilities [A] Short-term liabilities of a company, such as accounts payable or loans that are expected to be paid to the company within one year.

current ratio [A] A ratio calculated by dividing current assets by current liabilities. It measures how well a company can meet its short-term obligations.

current value [A] A value of an asset that is determined to be generally at a true market value. Other terms that may be used interchangeably are "replacement value," "market value" or "fair market value," and "present value." This is in contrast to "historical cost," which is the original cost of the asset.

current yield [F] The current income of a bond or stock, either through interest or dividends.

cursor [C] The line on the screen that shows position; the cursor shows where the next character typed will land. Each word-processing software shows this line a little differently, either blinking or static, vertical or horizontal. The cursor can be controlled by the mouse or by the cursor keys—the left, right, up, and down arrows, and the Page Up, Page Down, Home, and End keys.

CUSIP number [F] Pronounced Q-sip, it's the security identification number that is assigned to each stock certificate. It stands for Committee on Uniform Securities Identification Procedures.

> They were able to check the *CUSIP number* to make sure that the stock was legitimate.

custodian [T] A person who manages a child's money and investments until the child is an adult, usually at age twenty-one but sometimes eighteen.

custody [L] The care and control of money, property, or children as stipulated by law. A guardian is established if parents die while their children are minors. In a divorce case, the person who is given custody is the primary caregiver.

custom-build [RE] A house ordered by a buyer before it is built, with specific amenities added on request; the opposite of a house built on speculation.

> The president of Widget insisted on a *custom-built* house so that he could have special cages built in for his exotic birds.

customer [B] The end user of a product or service. This is the focus of a business, to provide useful goods and services for individuals or other companies. A term is also used in the new quality movement that identifies each employee as a customer as well as a supplier of information or service within a company.

customer connecting [S] A term that refers to understanding one's customers and attempting to meet their needs.

customs duty [E] A duty, fee, or tax imposed on the import of goods. Often customs specifies how much a person can bring into the country without paying a tax.

> When that country raised its *customs duties*, it discouraged much of the import business.

cut and paste [C] To eliminate a piece of text or a graphic in a word-processing document and insert it elsewhere.

cut the deal [S] To conclude the deal. To reach agreement on the last terms.

cutting edge [S] A term referring to the latest, the newest, and generally the most advanced.

> Widget Corp. announced the latest widget model, which it said incorporated *cutting edge* technology.

CYA [S] Pronounced C-Y-A, it's the acronym for "cover your ass." It refers to the practice of protecting oneself in a delicate situation by writing a memo to document what happened. The writer of the memo may even send it to key people or the person who might otherwise be critical of his action. This may offer him protection if he's later accused. See *memo to file*.

cybercafe [S] A new version of a cafe in which patrons can browse on the internet while sipping café latte. In other words, a high-tech coffee house.

cyberspace [C] A term, first used by the science-fiction writer William Gibson in his 1984 novel *Neuromancer*, that refers to the common area shared by a network of computers, like the internet.

If you go online, you are wandering around in *cyberspace*.

cyclical stocks [F] Stocks that follow the general business cycle, going up at the beginning of the cycle and falling during a recession. Airlines, autos, and retail stores typically are cyclical: When the economy is floundering, people don't travel as much or buy as many cars, or they cut back on their nonessential purchases.

D

damages [L] A monetary award ordered by a court due to injury or financial loss suffered by a person or company.

data [C] Information entered into a computer, such as numbers, characters, or words, used in spreadsheets, databases, or word-processing software for tables, charts, or reports. Although it is the plural form of the singular *datum,* data is used commonly in both the singular and plural. Data seems an easier word to use, and there are few occasions when one has only a single datum of anything. But to be correct use data only in the plural sense, as:

> John said that the *data* were withheld. Furthermore, Julie says that these *data* are inconclusive.

database; database software [C] A collection of organized data and information that can be accessed, searched, and manipulated. An address book is a personal database. There are many different types of database programs available for the computer.

> John customized the business *database* to contain information about all his vendors and their orders.

data entry [C] The process of entering data into a software program.

data processing [C] The general computer activities of a company. It includes the entry, calculation, and storage of information, and the printing of computer reports. It can also include the analysis and creation of programs and systems to support the activities of other departments, such as a sales reporting system for the marketing department or a human resource database and reporting system. A company's data processing department generally oversees the installation of all company computers and usually operates any intercompany computer network. It can also be called the MIS (management information system) department.

daughter board [C] A secondary board usually attached to the motherboard, or main part of the computer. See *motherboard.*

day order [F] An order to buy or sell a security that will expire at the end of the day. An investor may wish to reconsider the transaction the next day, thus controlling the trade on a day-by-day basis.

day trader [F] An active investor who speculates on short-term trades, often in and out of a security within a day.

dBase software [C] The title of the popular database software.

DDB (double-declining balance depreciation) [A] See *double-declining balance depreciation*, and *depreciation*.

dead-cat bounce [S] A rather gruesome reference to something dropping fast and then starting to move slightly upward, giving the impression that it could bounce back upward. But indeed, it only falls down again, like a dead cat. This phrase is attributable to Wall Street, which is known for mordent humor.

dead in the water [S] Term used to describe something that is not going anywhere, such as a project, organization, or company.

deadwood [S] People who are doing their jobs in a rote and perhaps useless manner.

The boss asked the new manager to identify and get rid of the *deadwood* in the bookkeeping department.

dealers [F] Individuals or firms that buy and sell stocks for themselves rather than for someone else. This is in contrast to "brokers," who buy and sell for others. Broker-dealers do both.

death benefit [L] [HR] A general term referring to any one of several payments because of the death of a person. It could be a life-insurance payment, a pension payment, or just a lump sum paid by a company to a beneficiary.

debenture [F] A type of corporate bond that doesn't have specific assets pledged to it. Debentures are issued based on the strength of the issuer's credit.

debit [A] In accounting, an entry made on the asset or expense side of a ledger or account, usually on the left side of the ledger. Debits the obligations of a company, short-term and long-term, like accounts payable.

debit card [F] A card issued by banks that allows a customer to pay for bills with the charges automatically and immediately deducted from the customer's checking account. It's like a checking account using a card instead of checks. This is in contrast to a credit card, for which the bank sends a monthly bill to the holder of the card for payment.

debt [A] One of the two basic methods of raising capital for a company: by issuing bonds, called "debt securities." The other method of raising capital is equity, primarily of common stock. See *equity*.

[E] The amount of money that a person, business, or government owes. In 1998 the U.S. government debt was about $5.5 trillion. That is, the total of all U.S. Treasury securities equals that amount and will have to eventually be repaid (although new debt could replace it). In personal terms, think of it as the government's credit card balance. This is in contrast to the deficit, which is the amount of money added to (or subtracted from) the debt each year.

debt coverage ratio [A] Net operating income divided by annual debt service.

[RE] The ratio of the cash flow of a property compared to its outstanding loan payments.

The bank always calculated the *debt coverage ratio* to see if an income-producing property had enough income to justify a certain loan amount.

debt financing [RE] The practice of paying for part or all of a property with borrowed funds.

The Widget Corp's. new building would serve as collateral as it *debt financed* the property with a big mortgage.

debt limit [E] The official amount of government debt that is allowed. The Congress sets the limit but typically increases it as the need for additional deficit spending occurs.

debt securities [F] Investments, like bonds, in which a company or government borrows money from investors to finance long-term projects.

debt service [A] Loans and other debt payments, including interest and principal payments.

One look at Acme Corp.'s annual *debt service* led the bank to believe that the company had already overextended itself with credit.

debt-to-equity ratio [F] The relation of debt (bonds and other loans) to equity (common stock) of a company expressed as a ratio. The greater the debt the greater it is said the company is leveraged.

debugging [C] The act of locating and correcting program errors.

The programmers worked long hours *debugging* those beta programs.

decelerate [E] A slowing down of the economy. Commonly, after a number of years of sustained growth, the economy tends to decelerate. It is usually signaled by a downturn in the leading economic indicators.

decentralization [B] An organizational method in which the decision-making is delegated downward in the organization and in separate business units. This is in contrast to "centralization," where control and decision-making are reserved for a few top executives.

decimal [M] A way of expressing fractions. For example, 5 divided by 10 is .5, or "point 5."

decision tree [M] A method in management decision-making that looks at all of the options and the resultant branching options. It is so named because it looks like a tree.

declaration page [L] The front page of an insurance policy summarizing the policy benefits.

declining-balance depreciation [A] A method of accelerated depreciation in which a constant percentage of an asset's value is written off each year. See *depreciation*.

decreasing term [L] A life-insurance policy designed to protect a mortgage. The amount of life insurance decreases automatically over time to match the mortgage as it gets paid off.

decree [L] A court's formal decision in a case.

dedicate; dedication [F] The practice of designing an investment portfolio to provide the needed income or principal at some future time when specific liabilities are expected to occur. Managers of pension funds estimate when and how much money will be needed for employee retirements, then plan a portfolio that will provide the necessary money to coincide with those expected payments.

dedicated; dedicated line [C] A device or communications line meant only for a specific computer or network.

dedicated bond portfolio [F] A bond portfolio designed to meet anticipated benefit payments, such as for pension payments. The portfolio bond cash flow is thus dedicated to meet these future needs. See *immunization*.

deductible [L] The out-of-pocket amount paid before an insurer pays the rest. Typically an individual pays a deductible for medical treatment, and then the insurance company pays the remaining amount.

> When the damage to the car amounted to $1,052, Eileen decided that it wasn't worth it to make a claim since she had a *deductible* of $1,000.

deductions [T] Subtractions allowed from one's adjusted gross income. All taxpayers are entitled to a standard deduction; if one has certain expenses that exceed that amount, he can take them against his adjusted gross income. This reduces his taxable income and, thus, he pays less taxes. These expenses are mortgage interest payments (not the part of the mortgage that repays the principal), real estate taxes, certain medical expenses, and charity donations, among others.

> After all his *deductions* had been added together, James had effectively brought his taxable income down to only $20,000 from his salary of nearly $30,000.

deductive reasoning [M] The method of logic from which a conclusion follows from the premises. It is reasonsing from the general to the specific, which is the opposite of inductive reason, which reaches conclusions from particular facts or events.

deed [RE] A written document that conveys ownership in real estate.

> Zippy Corp. had a *deed* to that property; it insisted that Widget Corp. stop using it as storage for widgets.

deed description [RE] The written description in a deed of all the boundaries of the property.

> Because this was such a large and strangely shaped piece of land, the *deed description* was almost a full page long.

deed restriction [RE] A restriction on a piece of property that passes through the deed from owner to owner.

> When XYZ Developers Inc. bid on that property, it didn't know that a *deed restriction* prevented any buyer from dividing the 10 acres in any way.

deep-discount broker [F] A low-cost brokerage firm. The service is generally focused on transacting trades that investors initiate, while offering minimal research. Thus, with low expenses, they can offer active investors the lowest commissions to buy and sell stock.

> Because she was buying a large block of stock, Mary Anne used a *deep-discount broker* to minimize her transaction costs.

deep in/out of the money [F] An option in which the strike price is far above/below the price of the market price of the security. In other words, at the moment one has done either very well or very poorly. See *at the money*.

deep pockets [S] Term referring to companies with lots of money. If a subsidiary of a parent company is sued, often the parent company is also sued because of its deep pockets.

deep six [S] To get rid of something so no one can find it.

> Cruthers told Smithers to *deep six* the files, which he promptly did in the dumpster.

de facto [L] Latin for *in fact*. Term used to refer to things that exist in fact but not through any legal authority. Something that is a common practice, versus *de jure*, which is a legal practice.

> Zippy Corp. was a *de facto* corporation; the owners had never filed the legal papers to incorporate the company.

defamation [L] In general, the damaging of another person through either the written or spoken word. Libel is committed specifically through writing, and slander specifically through speech.

default [A] The failure to make a payment when due. The term generally refers to a company that is unable to meet its financial obligations.

default judgment [L] A court ruling against a defendant because of failure to show up in court or failure to perform some other action that should have been taken.

default setting [C] The standard setting a computer will implement unless told otherwise.

> Elaine had to change the *default setting for* margins in her word-processing program so she could format the report into columns.

defendant [L] The person or company that is accused of wrongdoing.

deferred annuity [L] An annuity that is anticipated to be paid some time in the future, as opposed to an immediate annuity. See *annuity*.

deferred compensation [HR] Salary or bonuses that are not paid during the year in which they are earned, but later, usually after retirement.

> The CEO of Whammo Corp. decided to take this year's bonus as *deferred compensation* so that he would not have to pay taxes on it until after he retired.

deferred maintenance [RE] Any feature of a property that should be fixed right away. Even though it sounds like it, deferred maintenance does not really mean something that should have been fixed already.

> The *deferred maintenance* on the property (primarily the need for a new roof) amounted to almost $20,000.

deficit [E] Excess of expenses over revenues. When the government spends more money than it takes in through taxes and fees, then it has a deficit and has to borrow more money.

deficit financing [E] The borrowing of money by a government to pay for expenditures that exceed taxation revenues. The U.S. government issues additional Treasury securities to finance deficits.

deficit spending [E] Any spending by the government that exceeds what it takes in as revenues.

defined benefit plan [HR] A traditional pension plan where the benefit is defined by a formula, and often based on the final years of salary.

Typical Pension Plan:

A typical pension formula could be: average final pay of the last three years *times* the years of service *times* 1.2 percent. If an employee averaged a salary of $50,000 for the final 3 years and had 20 years of service, then the pension would be $12,000

($50,000 × 20 × .012 = $12,000).

defined contribution plan [HR] The most popular investment and retirement plan in recent years, such as a 401(k) plan. It can also be a tax-deferred annuity or 403(b) plan (for certain tax-exempt organizations and public schools) or a 457 plan (for states and municipalities). It is the contribution that is defined, not the ultimate benefit, as in a defined benefit plan. One of the main features of these plans is the pretax or before-tax contributions. That is, within limits, there is no federal income tax to the employee on that portion of the contribution to the plan. The final benefit will depend on how well the investments do, which depends on which investments are selected.

Typical 401(k) Plan:

Typical contribution formula: Employees can contribute up to 6 percent of pay to be matched by the company 50 percent, with the employee also able to contribute, without company match, an additional amount up to a total of 10 percent of pay in any one year.

Typical investment selections: Plans typically offer at least three selections, but sometimes more, including a money market fund, a GIC fund often called a stable value fund, a bond fund, a stock fund, and a fund of the company's stock. Additional funds could be a balance fund (stocks and bonds) or a global or international fund.

deflation [E] A decline in prices; the opposite of inflation. It's unusual to have a sustained period of deflation. Since World War II the U.S. economy has seen steady inflation with spurts of higher inflation, but not deflation. The Great Depression saw actual deflation. See *disinflation.*

deflator [E] A price index that converts an actual number or result into a measurement relative to inflation. For instance, an increase in gross domestic product from the year before doesn't indicate precisely the actual growth in an economy without an adjustment for inflation. The amount of inflation is the deflator.

defraud [L] To deprive a person or company of property or rights through some means of deceit.

degrees of freedom [M] A statistical concept that usually refers to the number of data values in a sample. See *chi square test*.

de jure [L] Latin meaning *by right*, it refers to being lawful. For instance, if a new corporation completed all the proper forms and submitted them in the proper way, it would be a *de jure* corporation. This is in contrast to *de facto*, which implies that a company is "in practice" a corporation, but perhaps has not adhered to all the legal forms. See *de facto*.

Del key [C] See *delete key*.

Delaware-based corporation [B] A company that is incorporated in the state of Delaware and is thus governed by Delaware's laws, which are known to be favorable toward businesses.

delete key (Del) [C] The key on a computer keyboard that allows you to erase letters, symbols, or data.

Delphi technique [B] The practice of using outside experts to confirm major management decisions, especially with respect to projected trends and future events.

delta (D) [M] The mathematical notation for an incremental difference. It uses the Greek symbol (Δ) delta. In business, it has come to mean a slight change.

demand [E] Consumers desire for specific products, goods and services, tempered by their ability to pay for them. Thus the demand for goods depends on the desirability and price of them. This is one side of supply and demand. The supply side is the production of the goods. See *supply* and *supply and demand*.

demand-pull [E] The increase in prices due to an increase in consumer demand for products or services. This is in contrast to the "cost-push" pressure of increased labor costs or raw materials to increase prices.

demand-side economics [E] The economic philosophy that emphasizes the demand for goods and services, often by government spending, to stimulate economic growth. See *supply-side economics*.

Deming prize [B] A medal given annually to companies that demonstrate outstandingly high levels of quality. The prize was instituted in Japan to recognize W. Edwards Deming, an American, whose quality philosophy was critically important to Japan's growth and development.

de minimis [L] From the Latin, meaning *trifling*.

> The new tax law stated that the giving of pencils to workers was a *de minimis* gift, thus the employees owed no income taxes for them.

demographics [B] Population data by age, sex, education, location and income that is useful in market research.

denominator [M] The number or algebraic expression written below the line in a fraction. The numerator, or the number of parts to the whole, is above the line.

density [RE] The number of anything per whatever unit of size. For example, density can refer to how many people or homes or trees or cars are in a given area of property.

> The population *density* in New York is considerably higher than in Manitoba, Canada.

[C] The number of bits that can be recorded on one disk. The greater the density, the more information the disk will hold.

dental coverage [HR] Insurance coverage for dental work, such as annual checkups, filling of cavities, or more serious work. Usually there is a deductible, meaning the insured person pays an initial amount while the company pays the rest.

Department of Housing and Urban Development (HUD) [RE]
The department of the U.S. government that handles programs like low-income housing, urban renewal, urban planning, and the like.

dependents [T] Generally, one's children, one's self, and one's spouse. The taxpayer is able to reduce taxable income for each dependent, thus lowering his taxes. Sometimes others who depend on the taxpayer for support can be included, such as elderly parents.

> Because John's mother received more than 50 percent of her support from him, he was able to claim her as a *dependent*.

dependent variable [M] The variable in an algebraic formula that depends on the independent variable. It is the independent variable that "calls the shots" on the dependent variable. In an algebraic expression, the letter y is often the dependent variable, whereas the x is the independent variable.

depletion [A] The loss of a natural resource as it is used up, such as coal, timber, oil, or gas. Accountants assign a cost of that loss and record it in the accounts and financial statements of the company.

deposition [L] A pretrial interrogation of a witness or other people, usually taking place not in court but in a lawyer's office. Nevertheless, it done in a formal legal way.

depreciation [A] An accounting method of spreading the cost of an asset over its useful life. Thus, the cost of expensive new equipment doesn't adversely affect any one year's financial statements. Depreciation can be seen as the loss of value of an asset over time, and the financial statements reflect this in some way year by year.

The Many Ways to Calculate Depreciation

accelerated: A method of depreciation in which the largest amount of an asset's cost is written off in the early years.

declining-balance: A method of accelerated depreciation in which a constant percentage of an asset's value is written off each year.

double-declining balance: A method of depreciation that doubles the straight-line percentage rate until the cost is fully written off. It thus allows for a faster write-off of the asset.

sum–of–the-year's-digits: A method of accelerated depreciation in which a fraction is written off each year. That fraction is formed by the numerator being the year in question and the denominator being the sum of the asset's years of useful life. See *sum-of-the-year's-digits depreciation* for an example.

straight-line: A method of depreciation in which an equal portion of an asset's cost is written off each year.

depreciation [RE] A method of computing the "loss of value" of a real estate asset. However, real estate often increases in value over time, thus, depreciation in the case of real estate is a hypothetical loss.

depression [E] A significant and prolonged downturn in the economy. The Great Depression of the 1930s was such an event, resulting in extremely high unemployment (estimated as high as 25 percent) along with low wages and declining prices. A related economic term is "recession," which is a mild form of an economic downturn. An economy is said to be in recession after two consecutive quarters of decreasing gross domestic product. See *recession*.

deregulation [E] The process of removing government regulation in a certain industry. The idea of deregulation is to let the market determine prices and supply.

Some feel that the *deregulation* of the savings and loan industry led to the downfall of many of the savings and loan banks in the 1980s.

derivative [M] One of two calculations that form the mathematics called "calculus." The other is "integral." See *calculus*.

derivatives [F] An investment that derives its value from the price of common stock, bonds, foreign currency, or commodities. The purpose of a derivative is to manage the risk on the price of the underlying security or commodity. A simple example is a stock option based on the underlying common stock. A more sophisticated option could be an option on the S&P 500, a basket of Treasury bonds, or European euros. An option can also be of a commodity, such as oil, gold, or lumber. Because the underlying risks are difficult to understand and assess, investors, including sophisticated companies, frequently lose money when they invest in derivatives.

designated order turnaround (DOT) [F] A computerized system designed to handle smaller orders of fewer than 1,200 shares on the New York Stock Exchange. A majority of trades are handled by the DOT system.

desktop [C] The display on a computer screen that arranges program icons to make them appear as if it were the actual top of a desk.

desktop publishing (DTP) [C] A method for producing professional-looking documents using software to combine graphics and text.

> Juanita, president of the Bobby Sherman Fan Club, was able to put out her own newsletter with her *desktop publishing* program.

determinant [M] An array of numbers arranged in rows and columns that has a numerical value. It is a mathematical method to solve simultaneous equations (those with similar unknowns). A determinant is denoted with straight lines on either side of the array. A matrix has numbers as well but does not itself equal a value. See *matrix*.

devaluation [E] The reduction in the value of one currency in relation to another. This is a somewhat dramatic event under exchange rates that are fixed; but, with floating rates, weekly and daily fluctuations can occur.

developed countries or nations [E] The advanced countries of international trade. The nations considered developed today are Australia, Austria, Belgium, Canada, Denmark, Germany, Finland, France, Greece, Iceland, Ireland, Italy, Japan, Luxembourg, the Netherlands, New Zealand, Norway, Portugal, Spain, Sweden, Switzerland, the United Kingdom, and the United States. This is in contrast to "emerging countries" and "less developed countries."

device [C] Any hardware component connected to the computer, such as a disk drive, keyboard, or mouse.

devise [T] A gift of real property, namely real estate, through a will. This is in contrast to a "bequest," which is a gift of personal property.

dialog box [C] A box that pops up in a software program to allow a variety of selections as the next step in the use of the software.

diamonds [F] Traded on the American Stock Exchange, they are blocks of stock representing the Dow Jones Industrial Average. See *spiders*.

differential cost [A] The additional costs of one alternative over another.

differentiation [M] The process of calculating the derivative of the calculus. See *calculus*.

digit [M] One of the ten numbers, 0 through 9, in the current number system, which is to the base 10. The fact that the human hand has ten fingers, or digits, which are naturally used for counting, is probably what led to the decimal system. See *base* 10.

digital [C] Transmission of data by varying digits, versus analog, which varies the frequency or voltage. An example: a digital clock has only numbers, whereas an analog clock has hands.

Dilbert principle [S] The belief of rank-and-file employees that company management in general and bosses in particular are inept. Cartoonist Scott Adams's Dilbert, a worker, and Dogbert, a dog, are the central characters in his best-selling book, *The Dilbert Principle*.

dilution [F] The effect on the price of a stock by one of several actions that would decrease its price. A company could issue additional stock to the public or take a one-time charge for unusual expenses. Either way, the stock price could decrease in value because the actual value per share has been diluted.

diminishing returns [E] The law stating that after a certain point, adding more people or machinery to the production process will not yield a proportionate greater amount of production.

dingbat [C] Miscellaneous symbols, like arrows, stars, circles, and so forth, that can be used within word-processing or desktop publishing software.

DIP switch [C] Little switches built into a DIP (Dual In-line Package switch) found inside a computer chassis. Usually a techie uses a tip of a pencil or pen to flip the switches on or off.

direct cost; direct labor; direct material [A] Costs that can be directly identified and traced to specific activities such as manufacturing, labor, or materials.

direct-mail advertising [B] Advertising to specific consumers using mailings versus the mass media.

directed verdict [L] A verdict rendered by a judge in a civil trial, where the judge determines that the facts and evidence point to a definite conclusion. This is not allowed in a criminal case because of the right to a trial by jury.

direct investments [F] An investment term referring to investing directly into a business through ownership or near-ownership. This could be owning, say, 25 percent of a business, or buying a limited partnership, which is ownership without management responsibility.

director [B] An individual elected by the stockholders of a corporation to represent them in overseeing the running of the firm. Directors serve on the board of directors and meet periodically to offer their advice and to decide such financial matters as the amount and timing of a dividend of the firm's common stock.

directors & officers [L] Liability insurance for directors and officers of corporations. See *errors & omissions*.

directory [C] A hierarchical collection of files; there are main directories, sometimes called "root directories," and subdirectories.

direct reports [HR] Employees who report directly to a boss, or those who are directly supervised by someone.

direct rollover [HR] The preferred method to put a 401(k) lump sum distribution into a rollover IRA, usually when an employee leaves a company. This method allows for the money to go from the 401(k) directly into a new, or existing, IRA. The non-preferred method is taking the lump sum payout and within sixty days putting it into a rollover IRA; however, the company then must withhold 20 percent of the distribution as taxes!

disability [HR] The inability to work due to illness or accident. Companies usually have a short-term disability policy that may pay the employee's salary, or part of it, for a certain period of time, often tied to length of employment. For longer disabilities, usually over six months, companies may have a long-term disability insurance program. Social Security also covers long-term disability, but it must be a severe case.

disability insurance [L] Insurance that covers one's salary in case a disability prevents an individual from working.

> The company offered *disability insurance* so Jane was covered when the accident kept her out of work for almost a year.

disbursement [A] The payment of a bill.

disc [C] An alternate way of spelling "disk." "Disc" usually refers to a CD, or compact disc, versus "disk," which refers to a computer disk.

disclosure [B] A release of company information.

> Acme Corp. had to make a full *disclosure* to the SEC before it issued stock so potential investors would know the economic condition of the organization.

disconnect [S] A lack of continuity between two ideas.

> Cruthers observed that there was a great *disconnect* between the old insistence for wearing white shirts and ties and the new openness demanded by the changing workforce.

discount [B] A reduction in price. The amount of the discount is the difference between the full price and what is paid.

Zippy offered a 10 percent *discount* on all invoices that were paid within thirty days.

discount broker [F] A broker who primarily buys and sells securities, as opposed to a full-service broker who also provides investment advice.

Because they liked to research investments on their own, the Greens preferred to use a *discount broker*.

discounted cash flow [M] The present value of a stream of payments. An interest rate (discount rate) is used to find the present value, thus the calculation is referred to as *discounting*.

discounting [B] A price reduction in the form of cash or perhaps additional merchandise.

[M] The process of determining present value.

discount rate [E] One of two interest rates that is controlled by the Federal Reserve. The discount rate is the rate that the Federal Reserve charges member banks to borrow money. See *federal funds rate*.

[M] The rate of interest, or investment, used in a present value calculation. See *present value*.

discovery [L] The pretrial procedure through which one side gets any information held by the opposing party in the case.

discretionary account [F] An account at a brokerage firm where the investor has allowed the broker full discretion as to what securities to buy and sell and when.

discretionary cost [A] A cost that can be varied by a manager or a business unit, such as the costs of business travel and meals, training, or charitable giving.

Discriminate Function System (DIF) [T] An IRS computer program that looks through tax returns and scans for possible errors or fraudulent entries—one way the IRS identifies returns for audit.

The *DIF* pulled out the corporate tax return from Zippy Corp. for review.

discrimination [L] The unequal treatment of either an individual or a group. Some discrimination may involve age, race, or sex.

discrimination test [HR] Technical employee benefit rules that apply to 401(k) plans prohibiting such plans from allowing only higher-paid employees to contribute to them. The test determines the percentage that higher-paid employees can contribute depending on what percentage lower-paid employees contribute.

disequilibrium [E] An economic state in which forces are not in balance, altering some of the variables. This condition can occur when prices are too high or too low. Market forces then tend toward equilibrium as they sort out the price structure, bringing prices to a more normal level.

disinflation [E] The reduction or even elimination of inflation. Disinflation is thus a stabilization of inflation at a low percentage, whereas deflation is a negative inflation. See *deflation*.

disintermediation [F] An investment technique whereby individuals invest directly in securities as opposed to placing money in banks that will in turn decide where to invest that money. Banks or other financial institutions are intermediaries in that they invest money for savers. When investors bypass banks, they "*dis*" intermediate.

disk; disk drive [C] Magnetic media on which computers store information. There are two types of disks. Floppy disks are the ones that a user can pop in and out. The older version, measuring 5.25 inches, was truly floppy in that it could bend. The newer version, measuring 3.5 inches, is quite rigid. Hard disks are the ones inside a computer that cannot be removed (other than by a techie).

diskette [C] Another term for "disk." Although it is perfectly okay to use the term "disk" to refer to a floppy, some people prefer the term "diskette" to distinguish them from hard disks.

disorderly conduct [L] The general lack of reasonable conduct in public. Examples of disorderly conduct include fighting and public drunkenness.

dispersion [M] A statistical measurement of variability of data values. The standard deviation is the most common measurement of dispersion. See *standard deviation*.

display [C] The monitor of a computer.

disposable income [E] The available money consumers have after income taxes. It's the money consumers can spend on goods and services or invest in savings. Thus it is calculated by taking gross income and subtracting federal and state income taxes and FICA (Social Security taxes).

dissaving [E] The term economists use when individuals draw down their assets. It is the opposite of savings. It is said that about two-thirds of Americans save at a reasonable clip, but the other one-third often dissave, bringing down the overall savings percentage.

distributions [F] The profits a company makes that are dispersed to its investors, such as dividends. It also pertains to mutual fund dividends and capital gains that are distributed or charged to a company's investors.

distributive law [M] One of the basic mathematical rules. It states:

$$a \times (b + c) = (a \times b) + (a \times c).$$

district court [L] Established by the Constitution, a court that has legal jurisdiction over a wide geographic area.

diversification [B] A business strategy in which a company attempts to build its business in areas outside of its regular activities.

[F] An investment strategy whereby one invests a portfolio partially in stocks and partially in bonds, which is also referred to as "asset allocation."

divestiture [B] The selling of a part of a business that has not been profitable or is no longer serving the best interests of the firm.

dividend [F] The payment to stockholders, almost always quarterly, of a portion of the earnings of the company. Dividends are usually paid by established companies, in contrast to a new company, which often will not pay dividends but instead will reinvest its earnings to grow the business.

> The board of directors met to decide what the *dividends* would be for that quarter.

[I] A return of part of the premium paid for an insurance policy. This typically occurs for whole life policies.

dividend discount model [F] A standard mathematical calculation of the present value of a stock considering its future earnings. It allows an investor to determine if the stock is priced correctly based on the investor's projected estimate of earnings.

dividend in arrears [A] See *cumulative dividends.*

dividend reinvestment plan (DRIP) [F] A plan that allows investors to automatically reinvest their dividends in additional shares of a company without going through a stockbroker. To encourage stockholders to use this method, companies usually do not charge a fee.

divorce [L] The legal step to dissolve the bonds of marriage. Whereas an annulment invalidates the original marriage, divorce ends the marriage.

DNS (domain name system) [C] Software that translates the actual numerical internet address (which users never see) into the commonly used designation, such as "review.com." It's part of the technical structure of the internet that, thank goodness, users don't have to worry about. A user can just type "www.review.com" to reach The Princeton Review, and then computer software finds and makes the technical connection.

docket [L] The court calendar indicating which cases the court will hear and when.

documentation [C] The thick—and often difficult to read—book that comes with a computer or software program. It usually has the answers to users questions, if they can find them.

dog [S] A product or service that is not performing. It can also refer to an internal system or procedure.

Ten percent of the products were not selling and were considered *dogs* by the sales people.

dog and pony show [S] A set presentation that has plenty of visuals and graphs, and often fancy slides. Usually implies that the presentation will be repeated several times, or at least is a presentation ready to go when needed.

dogs of the Dow [F] An investment strategy of buying the ten stocks of the thirty Dow Jones stocks that have performed the least in the recent past in hopes that they will rebound and be the best performers in the near future. At the end of each year, all ten stocks are sold and the process starts over. The way these stocks are quickly identified is by the *highest* percentage of dividends relative to the thirty stocks. Since the company's stock price has decreased, but its earnings are often steady, it mathematically increases the percentage of dividends to stock price. Alas, the strategy doesn't always work.

dollar [E] The U.S. currency, which is in use in financial and business markets around the world.

dollar-cost averaging [F] A popular mutual fund strategy of investing a set amount of money each month to average the price at which the fund is bought. If the price drops, then more shares will be bought, and if the price rises, less shares are bought. Thus the investor hopes to buy low and sell high.

dollar is higher/lower [E] The value of U.S. currency, which fluctuates daily against other currencies. The relationship between currencies affects a number of transactions. If for instance the dollar is stronger than the French franc, then Americans who travel to France can buy more for their dollar. However, if an American invests in a France-only mutual fund, he will in turn receive less money because the French franc is lower and thus will pay them less when transferred into dollars.

domain [C] A term used in several ways in the computer field. In database software, it's the name of a field or attribute. In communications, it's all the resources within the control of the computer system.

domain name [C] See *internet address*.

domicile [T] For tax purposes, it is the location or state where a taxpayer resides, and pays taxes. If a taxpayer has homes in two states, her domicile is generally considered where her car is registered, where she does her banking, and where she is registered to vote. In some unusual cases, two states may claim a person was domiciled in their state, hoping to collect estate taxes that are due.

dominate [S] To overpower the competition by creating superior products and services and marketing them effectively.

Acme Corp.'s widgets *dominated* the widget market.

donee/donor [T] In legal talk, a person who gives a gift or contributes to a trust is a *donor*, while a person who receives the gift or trust income is a *donee*.

doormat [S] An unassertive person who lets people walk all over him.

DOS (disk operating system) [C] Pronounced *doss*, it was the main program that ran earlier versions of PCs. The more advanced Windows operating system can also run DOS programs.

dot-matrix printer [C] An older type of printer that is becoming rare with the advent of ink-jet and laser printers.

The printer has a number of pins that strike the paper as dots and form letters, numbers, and characters.

dotted-line responsibility [B] A functional responsibility between a corporate head and someone in a division or section of a company. This is in contrast to "line responsibility," the specific solid lines showing on the organization chart. In fact, some organization charts actually show this dotted-line relationship.

The corporate head of marketing had a *dotted-line responsibility* over the marketing departments in each of the divisions to maintain a consistent marketing approach throughout the company.

double-declining-balance depreciation (DDB) [A] A widely used method of depreciation that doubles the straight-line percentage rate. It allows for a faster write-off of the value of an asset. See *depreciation*.

double-density disk [C] A floppy disk that can hold twice as much information as the original floppy disk.

double-digit [S] A percentage of 10 or more; anything with two digits.

> Smith was explaining that the economists hope we do not return to the *double-digit* inflation of the late 1970s and early 1980s.

double-entry accounting [A] The common accounting system of two entries for each item, that is, a debit (on the left) and a credit (on the right). As an example, when a company pays an employee's salary, it is entered as an increase in salary expense (debit) and a decrease in available cash (credit).

double jeopardy [L] Term referring to the provision of the Fifth Amendment of the U.S. Constitution that prohibits a person from being tried more than once for the same charge if a verdict was rendered in the first trial.

double indemnity [I] Payment of twice the basic benefit in the event of loss resulting from specific causes as identified in the insurance contract.

double-sided disk [C] A floppy that uses both sides for information.

dower [T] Under common law, a surviving spouse is generally entitled to a third of the deceased's estate.

Dow Jones Industrial Average (DJIA) [F] Referred to as "The Dow," this is the most commonly used stock market indicator. It is computed by adding the stock prices of thirty major industrial companies and dividing that number by a factor that adjusts for any distortions. When a news show reports that the market has fallen by ten points, it is referring to the Dow Jones Industrial Average. See *Standard & Poor's 500 index*.

The Thirty Dow Jones Stocks (as of January 1, 1999)

AT&T	Goodyear
Allied Signal	Hewlett Packard
Alcoa	IBM
American Express	International Paper
Boeing	Johnson & Johnson
Caterpillar	McDonalds
Chevron	Merck
Citigroup	3M
Coca-Cola	Morgan (JP)
Disney	Phillip Morris
DuPont	Proctor & Gamble
Eastman Kodak	Sears Robuck
Exxon	Union Carbide
General Electric	United Technologies
General Motors	Wal-mart.

---

down [C] A term that refers to the temporary condition when a computer isn't working.

downgrade [F] The process by which a rating service for bonds drops the rating of a company.

> When the company had been *downgraded* from a AA to B rating, its investors were reticent to reinvest.

downlink [C] In satellite communications, the link from the satellite to the ground.

> The technicians felt that the communications were not going through due to a problem with the *downlink*.

download [C] The process of transferring data or programs from one computer or communications link to another computer.

downscale [B] Term referring to the selling of a less expensive, less prestigious type of merchandise. Also known as downmarket.

> The retailers in the new Snob Hill Mall were dismayed at the *downscale* merchandising of the new Clothes!Clothes!Clothes! store.

downside [S] The worst that could happen.

> Cruthers asked the task force, "What's the *downside* to recommending a new organization structure?" Smithers answered, "Your job, that's all."

downsizing [B] The process of making a company smaller by letting employees go. A famous euphemism for mass firings. See *laid off*.

> The new employees at Acme Corp. were understandably worried about their jobs when the rumor went out that, due to a bad year, Acme would be *downsizing* its workforce by 20 percent.

downstream [B] The movement of ideas or funds from a parent company to a subsidiary. The movement the other way is called *upstream*.

downtime [S] Time where little, if anything, is being done. Downtime can occur, for example, when the computer is down, there is a power outage, or there is a wait for further orders.

downzoning [RE] The process by which the zoning in an area is reduced to fewer buildings in a given area.

> After the town had suffered a glut of development, Smallville resorted to *downzoning* the residential area from quarter-acre to 2-acre minimum lots.

Dow theory [F] In 1884 Charles Dow used the closing prices of eleven stocks to represent the stock market and later established the *Wall Street Journal* with Eddie Jones. The original eleven stocks were comprised of nine railroads and two industrial companies. On December 19, 1900, he stated what was to become the Dow theory: That there were three movements going on in the market at the same time—day-to-day movements, short swings of two weeks to a month, and the main movements, lasting about four years.

drag and drop [C] The ability in graphics and desktop publishing software to click on a picture or item and move it elsewhere in the document.

draw [B] A lower regular salary that will hopefully be augmented by end-of-year bonuses, as sales quotas or profits will be realized by the end of the year. Sales people on commission, partners of professional firms, or small business owners often use this method of salary.

drill down [S] To go beyond the general, get down to the specifics. Like drilling for oil, getting to pay dirt.

driver [C] Special software commands for specific hardware devices. With DOS software it was necessary to install specific drivers for printers and other devices, whereas they are built in with Windows.

drop-dead date [S] The absolutely positively last deadline for a project or critical company activity.

drop-down menus [C] Also referred to as "pull-down menus" or "pop-up windows," they lie at the heart of making the computer user-friendly. Instead of esoteric keyboard strokes, a menu takes the user through each operation.

drop-in office [HR] An office arrangement for telecommuting employees to have a temporary office should they need to have meetings with others.

dry goods [B] Clothing, fabrics, textiles, and bedding, as distinguished from either grocery goods or machinery (called hard or durable goods).

> The shipment of *dry goods* arrived: 20 yards each of cotton, silk, and rayon.

dual listing [F] A security being traded or listed on more than one exchange, as, for example, on both the New York Stock Exchange and a regional exchange, such as the Midwest exchange.

due diligence [F] The investigation and analysis of an investment by a financial entity, such as a brokerage firm or financial advisor, as to the soundness and appropriateness of an investment for an investor. The advisor looks for such things as economic value, security law violations, accurate accounting projections, and the promoter's experience and track record.

due process [L] A phrase that implies that the government cannot take life, liberty, or property unless specific rules and procedures are followed. The concept grew out of the Fifth and Fourteenth Amendments to the U.S. Constitution.

dumping [E] The practice of selling products abroad for less than at home in hopes of expanding the market. This disrupts overseas markets; countries can and do retaliate by imposing fines for dumping.

Dun & Bradstreet report [A] A published source of credit information about companies. The information includes a credit history, any legal proceedings, current debts, and any other useful financial information.

duplex [C] The ability to send and receive information simultaneously.

durable goods [E] Manufactured goods that are generally considered to last over three years, such as cars, refrigerators, and furniture. See *consumer goods* and *dry goods*.

durable power of attorney [T] A power of attorney that remains in effect even if the person covered becomes incapacitated. This has become an issue, for instance, with elderly parents who may become incompetent. In a *general* power of attorney, an agent performs certain duties for a person but would not legally be able to continue if the person became incompetent. The durable power of attorney allows the agent to continue.

duration [F] A measurement of a bond's sensitivity to changes in interest rates. It is the mathematical calculation of the weighted average present value of the bond's stream of payments. If a bond has a duration of ten, then a 1 percent increase or decrease in interest rates will change the value by 10 percent in the opposite direction. For instance, if interest rates increase one percent, a bond with a duration of ten will decrease 10 percent in value.

duty [E] See *customs duty* and *tariff*.

DVD [C] A new consumer device for storage and playback of audio and video. It stands for "digital video disk" or "digital versatile disk." It has enormous storage capacity (twenty gigabytes) but looks deceptively like a common compact disc. Potentially this technology will be confusing to the consumer because of the associated names it has given rise to, such as DVD-ROM, Divx, DVD-R, DVD-RAM, and so forth.

Dvorak keyboard [C] An alternative keyboard with letters arranged differently than in the traditional QWERTY keyboard. It is designed for faster typing.

dyad [B] Any two people that have a close personal relationship, such as husband and wife. It is also used in reference to mentoring programs, where a mentor takes an employee under his or her wing.

E

E- [C] The ubiquitous prefix of internet activities, such as E-cash, E-commerce, E-courses, E-mail, E-money, and so forth. *E* stands for electronic. Although a lower case *e* is sometimes used, as in *e-mail*, the capital E is preferred.

e [M] A mathematical constant equaling 2.71828 . . . (nonending). It is very useful in formulas expressing growth rates, such as for population and investments, or growth in nature. The Swiss mathematician Leonhard Euler (pronounced OI-ler) saw the value of this special constant, which he named "e". It is sometimes called Euler's constant.

EAFE (Europe, Australia, Far East) [F] A commonly used index for the major financial markets outside of the United States, comprised of about 1,000 individual stocks. Morgan Stanley, an investment banking firm, created and maintains this index. The acronym is pronounced EEF-a.

early adopters [B] A marketing and business term referring to a small percentage of people who want to be first in using products or services. For instance, the new DVD format for audio and video could find a slow acceptance by the public at large, but the creators know there will always be some people willing to try it out.

early retirement [HR] Age when a person leaves an organization before being eligible for full pension benefits, often before age 65.

early withdrawal penalty [T] Penalty fee assessed when one withdraws money from certain accounts, such as an IRA or 401(k) plan, before reaching a certain age. For example, money withdrawn from an IRA (individual retirement account) is taxed as ordinary income, but if taken before age fifty-nine and a half, there is an additional 10 percent penalty. A similar penalty may apply toward employee benefit plan withdrawals like 401(k) plans, generally if withdrawn before age fifty-five. There are some exceptions to this rule, including disability and medical expenses that exceed 7.5 percent of one's adjusted gross income. Another exception allows for withdrawals without the penalty if one takes them as an annuity for at least 5 years or until he or she reaches fifty-nine and a half, whichever period of time is longer.

earned income [T] Income one earns as salary or net self-employment earnings. This is in contrast to "investment income," such as interest, dividends, or capital gains, which is called *unearned* income.

earnest money [RE] Up-front money to show seriousness in buying property.

earnings [B] A general business term usually referring to net income, versus gross sales of a company. It is recommended that the word earnings should always be qualified, such as *net earnings* or *earnings after taxes*. Earnings by itself is considered too general.

earnings per share [F] A useful investment calculation determining how much earnings a company realized for each share of outstanding stock. It is the total earnings of a company divided by the total numbers of shares outstanding.

easement [RE] Permission to use a portion of someone else's property without owning it. Towns, for example, have easements that allow them to install underground lines through private property.

> Widget gave Whammo an *easement* that allowed Whammo's trucks to use part of Widget's driveway and parking lot, which was more than useful for Whammo since it's property did not border on any road.

East-West trade [E] Trade between Asia and Russia (East) and Europe and the United States (West).

easy or loose money [E] The monetary policy of the Federal Reserve (Fed) to make more money available, usually in hopes of stimulating the economy. This is the opposite of the Fed policy of "tight money," which is used to slow down the economy.

EBIT; EBITA; EBITDA [A] These are acronyms for various forms of net income, namely: *earnings before interest and taxes; earnings before interest, taxes, and amortization;* and *earnings before interest, taxes, depreciation, and amortization.*

EC (European Community) [E] An abbreviation for European Community. See *European Union*.

E-commerce [C] Business online via the World Wide Web.

econometrics [E] Math and statistical methods in the study of economics. Usually involved in the creation of mathematical models to describe and then predict how the economy would respond given specific actions, either by individuals, companies, or governments, or all three.

economic base [B] The industries that employ people in a particular geographical area.

> The *economic base* in Smallville was severely injured when Giant Corp. Industries closed its local plant.

economic expansion or growth [E] An increase in economic activities that boosts employment and helps a country prosper.

economic indicators [E] Data, ratios, or other figures that not only describe the economy but also tend to forecast its direction. Leading indicators use information about the number of housing starts or the amount of business inventories to describe the health of the economy today and to project its short-term future.

economic life [A] The length of time assets, such as computers, equipment, machinery, or buildings, are estimated to be useful.

> Mr. Smoothie, the salesperson, assured us that the new punch-hole machine on the assembly line has an *economic life* of almost fifty years.

economic model [E] A theoretical, mathematical, or statistical relation of economic variables. Models can be simple, for example, if inflation increases then interest rates increase. Models often are quite complex with numerous equations and many variables.

economic Nobel Prize [E] See *Nobel Prize for economics.*

economic order quantity (EOQ) [A] The most efficient and economical quantity of materials or inventory for a company to purchase at one time given price and warehousing. Usually calculated by mathematical formulas.

economics [E] The study of a society's production of goods and services and their distribution and consumption. Some of the specific subjects studied by economists are how markets work, how prices and demand are related, and how to deal with problems of inflation, unemployment, and competition. Economists also examine how government actions, such as taxation, deficit spending, and regulation, affect the economy, and how countries deal with each other in foreign trade and the balance of payments. Economics is said to provide the theories for the optimization of available resources. Economics has also been called the "dismal science" (by the English historian Thomas Carlyle in the 1800s).

economies of scale [B] The reduced cost of production by virtue of higher volume. For instance, because a company can receive discounts on materials by buying in volume, it can pass those lower costs on to its customers, thereby being the low-cost producer. A company can also use more productive machinery with higher volume.

Economist, The [E] An international business publication that reports on and discusses economic issues around the world.

economy [E] The business activity of a country or region.

ECRLOT [B] A mail directory system of the U.S. Postal Service. It appears just above the name typically in junk mail. It stands for Enhanced Carrier Route Line of Travel. It allows a company to sort mailings by the actual sequence that particular mail carriers deliver the mail.

EE bonds [F] U.S. savings bonds that accumulate interest until they are cashed in. This is in contrast to "HH bonds" that pay out interest semiannually just like a regular bond, or the new "TIP bond" that pays a lower interest but increases by inflation.

EEC (European Economic Community) [E] The six western European countries—Belgium, France, Italy, Luxembourg, the Netherlands, and West Germany—that originally signed the Treaty of Rome in 1957 to form a common market. See *European Union*.

effective age [RE] Term used to describe the condition of a building. It is usually given in number of years—to contrast with the structure's actual age.

> Although Spammo's headquarters was almost twenty-five years old, the company had replaced so much of the original structure that the building had an *effective age* of only five or six years.

effective gross income multiplier [RE] The ratio of the value of a property to the effective gross income that property generates— or the income one would expect to get minus any losses or vacancies.

effective rate [M] See *annualized rate*.

effective tax rate [T] The average percentage of total income that is paid in taxes. In the example below, Marge, who is single, pays *on average* 23 percent in taxes. Her lowest bracket is zero and the highest is 31 percent. This highest bracket is called the "marginal tax rate," which is used to calculate the tax effect on additional income. Besides the federal income tax, most states also have income taxes. See *tax brackets*.

Margie's Effective Rate versus Marginal Tax Rate

Margie had a banner year with her new sales route—she earned a gross income of $97,000 in 1999.

Here's how she is taxed:

The first $7,050 is not taxed because of the standard deduction ($4,300) and one exemption ($2,750).

The next $25,750 is taxed at 15 percent: $3,862.50.

The next $36,700 is taxed at 28 percent: $10,276.

The final $27,500 is taxed at 31 percent: $8,525.

Total federal income taxes: $22,663.50

The *effective*, or average, tax rate for Margie is 23 percent (dividing total taxes of $22,663.50 by total income of $97,000 equals 23.36 percent, rounded to 23 percent).

Her *marginal* rate is 31 percent, which is the highest tax rate, or bracket, that applies to her.

---

efficient frontier [F] A mathematical calculation of the highest portfolio return with the lowest portfolio risk. It is the optimum combination of return and risk.

efficient market [F] Term used by economists to describe a market that is analyzed thoroughly and of which essentially all information is known to all investors. Economists who believe that the market is not completely efficient may claim that the market is *semiefficient* or *inefficient*.

> They were confident in their investments as it was a very *efficient market* they were in—almost all its influential factors were well known.

EGA [C] See *monitor*.

egghead [S] A somewhat pejorative term for an impractical intellectual or technical person. The term "pointy head" is sometimes used as well.

egress [RE] The path or door going out. The exit, or the opposite of the *ingress*.

80-20 rule [B] A general rule-of-thumb that says that 80 percent of the company's earnings are produced by only 20 percent of its products or services. It allows a company to focus on key products as opposed to spending time and energy equally on all of its products. It is also used in other ways, such as 80 percent of the employee problems are caused by 20 percent of employees, or 80 percent of the medical benefits are used by 20 percent of employees. The rule comes from the idea of an Italian economist, Vilfredo Pareto (1848–1923), who speculated that a few of the causes account for most of the effect.

elastic [E] A measurement of responsiveness to increased supply or demand. If a company reduces the price of a product or service and the demand for that product or service increases, then it is said that the demand for the product or service is *elastic*, because it stretches like a rubber band along with the price. A good example is the computer. As the prices of computers have come down, the demand has increased. However, if the demand doesn't change with changes in prices, then the demand for the product is said to be *inelastic*, or rigid.

elastic coefficient [E] The ratio of changes in demand as changes occur in prices.

elasticity of demand or supply [B] See elastic.

eldercare [HR] The care of older people, including the facilities and medical and social support.

elderlaw [L] The relatively new field of law that applies to the elderly, dealing with issues such as long-term care and Medicaid.

electronic commerce [C] Doing business online, via the World Wide Web. Also called "e-commerce."

electronic filing [T] The ability to file taxes electronically through computers.

electronic transfer [F] The practice of debiting and crediting money from one financial institution to another account without it actually physically passing through anyone's hands.

elevator assets [S] A slang term for a company's human resources. It refers to a company's rank-and-file employees who every day file in and out of the building and are shuttled about by elevators.

> The president reminded management to take care of our *elevator assets*, which are the core of the company.

ellipse [M] An oval or egglike geometric figure in which all points are equally distant from two points.

emancipation [L] The age at which a minor becomes an adult in the eyes of the law, usually eighteen. At that point the person is considered at the age of majority.

E-mail (electronic mail) [C] Correspondence with others via the personal computer, and the software that supports it. E-mail can be sent within a company, via a commercial online service, or through the internet. E-mail can also have files attached.

> She *E-mailed* him the new agenda for the meeting as he needed the information immediately.

embargo [E] The government prohibition of trade with or shipments to a certain country. Embargoes may occur for security, political, or economic reasons.

> The president enacted an *embargo* against Zeenomaland after the coup d'etat there.

embedded [S] Present but usually invisible.

> *Embedded* in Acme's home page on the web was a method to track those entering the site.

embezzlement [L] The illegal taking of property by someone entrusted with its possession, such as a bank employee taking money from the till.

emerging countries or markets or nations [E] Countries formerly classified as "less developed" that are creating growth economies. Such countries are Argentina, Brazil, India, Malaysia, the Philippines, Russia, and Thailand. The term "third-world" was once used, but the term *emerging* is now universally used. See *less developed countries* and *developed countries*.

eminent domain [L] The right given to the state to take private property for public use after just compensation is paid.

emoticons (or smileys) [C] Icons that provide visual cues in E-mails or postings in cyberspace. Two of the most common are the smiley face :-) and the sad face :-(. They are best viewed sideways.

Fun Emoticons

:) :-) :>	variations on the classic smiley face
:-D	big smile
8-)	smile by someone who wears glasses
:-{)	smile by someone who has mustache
:-{)}	smile, by someone who has mustache and beard
(-:	smile by someone who is left handed
;-)	wink
: -(	sad face
: -o	surprise
: -O	Uh oh!
: -p	sticking out tongue
: -X	covering mouth ("oops")
: -}	smirk
: -/	skeptical
: -#	censored
*<|:{)}	Santa Claus
<G>	grin or grinning
<L>	laughing
<J>	joking
<S>	smile or smiling
{{{}}}	hug (make large or small)

employee assistance program (EAP) [HR] A confidential counseling service provided by many companies through their human resource department. It usually provides outside trained counselors to help in drug-and-alcohol related problems and in family or financial difficulties.

employee benefits [HR] The variety of medical, life, pension, and 401(k) type of benefits offered to employees.

Employee Retirement Income Security Act (ERISA) [HR] The 1974 legislation regulating pension plans. It specifies participation rules, reporting and disclosure rules, and fiduciary standards. The acronym is pronounced er-ISS-a.

employee turnover [HR] The percentage of employees that leave a company, usually measured on an annual basis.

employer identification number [B] The number assigned to a company by the federal government and sometimes the state that identifies the company for tax and other official purposes.

employment [E] The number of people in a population who are employed. About 67 percent, or two-thirds, of the U.S. population is working. With a population totaling about 260 million people, that would mean there are about 175 million people working, full or part time.

employment agency [HR] A firm that searches for new employees for companies, especially to fill positions above the entry level.

EMU (European Economic and Monetary Union) [E] The abbreviation used to describe the close-knit economic union between European nations. See *European Union*.

emulate [C] The ability of a device or program to act like another. For instance, a cheaper word-processing software may claim that it emulates WordPerfect or Word, or that it at least works similarly.

en banc [L] A legal term referring usually to an appellate court where all the judges sit to hear the case, versus only three or more. The term is French and means *by the full court*.

encroachment [RE] Term that refers to the act of trespassing on someone else's property, or to an area that gradually changes from one type of use to another.

encryption [C] The method of coding computer communications to secure it from others, especially for financial transactions. There are various ways to scramble or have hidden keys embedded in the transmission stream. The new standard is called 128-bit encryption that is 300 septillion (30^{25}) times stronger than the 40-bit encryption found on many computers.

encumbrance [RE] A claim or lien attached to a building that affects or limits the title of the property.

end key [C] The key on the keyboard that allows the user to jump to the end of a line in a document in word-processing software or a column or row in a spreadsheet.

endorsement [I] Additional property insurance coverage over and above regular coverage, usually for specific needs such as jewelry or artwork protection.

endorsement [B] The promotional marketing of products and services by well-known individuals in entertainment or sports.

endowment [I] A life insurance policy that is a twist on a regular policy in that the policyholder receives the face value of the policy if he lives past a designated age. The most common age is sixty-five. The policyholder is then presumably ready for retirement, and the insurance amount can augment his retirement income. Another age is eighteen for a child. If the child lives to age eighteen, usually a high probability, then the policy payment is available to pay for college. These policies require higher premiums and are in a sense forced savings.

energy efficiency ratio (EER) [RE] The ratio of energy output of an appliance to its energy input. Output is expressed in BTUs, and input is expressed in wattage.

> They updated the heating and cooling system in the office space to one with a higher *EER*.

engine [C] The hard-working part of the software that operates in the background and usually performs a critical function, like the calculator in a spreadsheet.

Enrolled Actuary (EA) [T] An actuary who performs actuarial work for employee benefit plans and who can sign specific governmental pension forms that are necessary on an annual basis.

Enrolled Agent (EA) [T] A person who has completed a course of study and passed a rigorous two-day exam by the IRS, or who has worked at the IRS in a technical area for five years. Enrolled Agents, along with attorneys and accountants, can represent individuals and companies before the IRS.

enter key [C] The key on the keyboard that tells the computer to actually start the function designated.

enterprise [B] Any form of business, such as a corporation, public utility, partnership, or other business entity. It often refers specifically to a new business.

> There was a surge in *enterprise* in Smallville as new entrepreneurs came in to fill the vacant office space left when Giant Corp. Industries moved out.

enterprise resource planning (ERP) [C] A relatively new breed of software that is meant to run the whole company. That is, one computer program controls and monitors the entire process from ordering the raw materials to the time the customer pays the invoice.

enterprise zone [B] An area designated by a municipality or state to give benefits to businesses. They may offer tax credits, low financing, etc., to encourage business in depressed areas.

> Although Urban Inc. wanted to move out, the formation of an *enterprise zone* made it advantageous to stay in the depressed city of Midville.

entitlements [E] Social programs, usually directed toward the poor or the elderly. Welfare, unemployment, and Social Security are all considered entitlements.

entrapment [L] A defense by someone who was caught in a crime who claims that he or she would not have committed the crime if not induced into it by an agent of law enforcement.

entrepreneur [E] A business person who invests money in manufacturing or service industries, either to create a new company or expand an existing one. Considered the key economic player in a capitalist society, an entrepreneur is often a person who sees an opportunity in society and starts a business to fill that need. It is this risk-taking spirit that companies sometimes want to create within their own organizations and call it *intrapreneurship*. See *intrapreneur*.

Entrepreneur Magazine [B] A business magazine for small business owners.

entropy [M] A tendency or measurement of the state of disorder emerging from a state of order. The word is pronounced EN-tra-pe.

envelope [M] The confines of a problem or situation. See *push the envelope*.

environment [C] The type of hardware in a computer, such as IBM-compatible or Macintosh.

Equal Employment Opportunity Commission (EEOC); Equal Opportunity Employer [HR] These terms refer to federal legislation that prohibits discrimination based on sex, age, race, religion, or ethnic background. An Equal Opportunity Employer is one who has pledged to follow the rules of nondiscrimination.

equal protection [L] The subject of the Fourteenth Amendment, declaring that all people are to be treated equally under the law.

equation [M] Two mathematical expressions that are set equal to each other and written with an equal sign between them. For instance, a basic economic equation equates the velocity of money to the GDP divided by the supply of money. Velocity denotes how many times money turns over in a year. The equation looks like this:

$$V = \frac{GDP}{SM}$$

equilibrium; equilibrium price [E] The state of balance within an economy where no pressures are forcing changes in supply or demand. Although largely theoretical because of the complexity and dynamic nature of an economy, it explains price stability when there is no specific pressure on prices to rise or fall.

equipment [A] A major category of fixed assets for a manufacturing company.

equity; equities [B] One of two basic methods of raising capital for a company: by issuing common stock, called "equity securities." The other method is through bonds, or debt securities.

[A] Term that refers to the net worth of a business, that is, total assets minus liabilities equals the business equity.

[F] In investments it generally refers to any form of stock, such as common and preferred stock, as well as foreign stock.

The Clancys decided to invest heavily in *equities* because they had great confidence in the stock market.

[RE] The value of an owner's property after deducting all the outstanding mortgages and liens against that property, or what the owner really owns.

When Zan and Marta deducted the $150,000 mortgage they had against their property, worth almost $200,000, they had $50,000 in *equity*.

equity funds [F] Mutual funds that invest in the stock market in one way or another: Large cap, small cap, or international equities, for example.

ergonomics [C] Pronounced UR-ga-NOM-ics, it's the study of design and arrangement of equipment and furniture so that a worker can be most productive. Usually the arrangement reduces fatigue and discomfort.

ERISA (Employee Retirement Income Security Act) [HR] See *Employee Retirement Income Security Act (ERISA).*

error message [C] An on-screen message that identifies a computer-based problem.

errors & omissions [A] Liability insurance usually bought in such industries as accounting, banking, engineering, insurance, and real estate. It is protection against inadvertent actions. See *directors & officers.*

Esc key [C] See *escape key.*

escalator clause; escalation clause [RE] Part of a lease or contract that provides for an increase given certain events, such as an increase in labor costs or the price of oil or gas.

escape key (Esc) [C] A key on a computer keyboard, typically marked "Esc." In many programs, it allows the user to cancel a command or quit the program.

escheat [L] The assignment of property to the state because no heirs have been found. The word is pronounced is-CHEAT.

escrow [RE] An agreement to give money, securities, property, or a similar offering to a third party to hold until it is due to be transferred to the designated person or agency. For example, banks hold money in escrow for their customers' real estate tax payments.

> The lawyer held the down payment in *escrow* until it was set to go to the sellers of the property.

ESOP (Employee Stock Ownership Plan) [HR] A benefit plan that offers company stock as the investment. These plans are quite difficult to understand because the available plans are leveraged ESOPs, which are complex financial arrangements. Basically, if an employee has one of these plans he or she gets company stock. Pronounced EE-sop.

estate [T] The total of what a person owns at death, including investments, personal property, real estate, and any other items of value.

estate planning [T] The strategy through which a person plans the eventual distribution of assets at the time of her death. Besides preparing a will, and perhaps establishing a trust, estate planning also involves strategies that minimize estate taxes so as much of the assets as possible pass to heirs.

estate taxes [T] The amount of taxes owed at the time of one's death, often called "transfer taxes." Under federal law in 1999, if someone dies leaving an estate of greater than $650,000 to a non-spouse, there is a federal estate tax. There may also be a state estate or inheritance tax with or without a $650,000 exemption. Estates left to spouses are not taxed on the federal level, an exception referred to as the "unlimited marital deduction."

> The lawyer told the family that Great Aunt Vanessa's estate was not worth more than $500,000—thus, there would be no federal *estate taxes*.

estimated tax [T] Taxes payed on a quarterly basis by the self-employed or anyone who receives substantial income without taxes being withheld. Usually the payments are due April 15, June 15, September 15, and January 15.

> Assuming she would have a year about as successful as last year, Amy made quarterly *estimated tax* payments based on her earnings from last year.

estoppel [L] A restraint against someone who wishes to deny something he has agreed to do. The word is pronounced eh-STOP-el.

Ethernet [C] A popular local area network (LAN) protocol. It was first developed by Xerox in 1973 and then further developed by Xerox along with Digital Equipment Company and Intel. The idea originated with the concept of plugging into the "ether" wherever a computer was.

euro [F] The name of the new common currency of Europe that was inaugurated on the first business day of 1999, January 4. Its symbol is an "e" that has two parallel lines through it, as shown below. The euro began its trading at a value of $1.17 (actually $1.16675). Although European banks and stock exchanges began using euros, the current schedule calls for the euro to actually go into circulation on January 1, 2002. Then on July 1, 2002, the eleven individual currencies of each country (Austria, Belgium, Finland, France, Germany, Ireland, Italy, Luxembourg, Netherlands, Portugal, and Spain) will no longer be accepted. Good-bye marks, francs, and liras. The first common European currency proposed was named the ecu, which was hard to pronounce (E-coo). See *European Union*.

€

Eurobonds [F] Bonds that are issued and sold in a country other than the country in which the bond's currency is issued. If a bond paying in dollars is issued in another country, then it is said to be a Eurobond. Because these bonds started in Europe and are actively traded there, they are called Eurobonds even if issued and traded in other regions of the world.

Eurodollar [F] Dollars held by individuals, businesses, and governments outside the United States. Eurodollars are held in Japan, South America, and so forth, so they are not confined to Europe. But since this concept started in Europe, where it remains strong, it retains this name.

European Union (EU) [E] The latest form of an economic union in Europe. In Rome in 1957, six western European countries—Belgium, France, Italy, Luxembourg, the Netherlands, and West Germany—signed the Treaty of Rome to form a common market between them. At first it was called the European Economic Community (EEC), then the European Community (EC); currently it is called the European Union (EU). The process continues by expanding the number of countries that are part of the proposed union, and it is projected that eventually there could be a political as well as an economic union. The common currency is called the euro. See *euro*.

eviction [L] The expulsion of a person from a premises.

> The landlord finally issued an *eviction* notice to his tenants for non-payment of rent.

evidence [L] Facts and documents used to show proof in a trial.

Excel software [C] The name of the popular spreadsheet software developed by Microsoft.

exchange fee [F] In the world of mutual funds, a fee charged if an investment is shifted from one fund to another within the same company. See *mutual fund fees*.

> The *exchange fee* was 3 percent and made her decision to move less attractive.

exchange rates [E] The rate of one currency against another. If one American dollar could be exchanged for exactly four French francs, then the exchange rate would be one to four.

excise tax [T] A tax on certain consumer items, such as alcohol, tobacco, gas, guns, and airline tickets. These taxes are collected by government departments and used for special purposes, such as highway repair.

> The price on cigarettes has risen greatly due to an increase in the *excise tax* on tobacco.

exclusionary rule [L] The constitutional rule that prohibits the use of illegally obtained evidence in a case.

exclusions [I] Those specified items that are not covered by an insurance policy, typically floods or civil commotions.

exclusive; exclusive agency; exclusive right to sell [RE] Practice in which a real estate agent is given the prime right to list and sell a property. In some locales all property is automatically multilisted, meaning all brokers in the geographic area are notified of the listing and are free to sell the property.

exclusive agent [I] See *agent*.

ex-dividend [F] A traded stock that will not receive the immediately announced dividend.

executive compensation [A] Any one of a variety of special pay packages to provide incentives for the performance of the top officers of a company. Bonuses, deferred compensation, and stock options are prime examples.

executor [T] The person given the responsibility to settle an estate. That person is specified as such in the will. If the executor is not able to serve, or if there is no will (called dying "intestate"), then the court will appoint someone who is technically known as an "administrator." In past years a female executor was called an *executrix*, but the word is being phased out.

> After the *executor* of the estate, Ms. Jamison, had the property sold, she split the money among the six sisters as specified in the will.

exe file; executable file [C] A file that triggers commands to start software. The word before the suffix *.exe* in a file name can be typed in at the prompt to start the program.

exempt employee; exempt position [HR] An employee—usually a professional or manager—who is exempt from the Fair Labor Standards Act and is thus not eligible to receive overtime pay if she works more than the standard workweek. Thus, a professional's salary already has built into it the possibility of working longer hours.

exemptions [T] A tax allowance for each person in a household. For example, being married and having three children results in five exemptions. Each exemption reduces the amount of taxes. The difference between an exemption and a *deduction* is that a deduction refers to an expense. For 1999, the federal tax exemption is $2,750 per person.

Ex-Im Bank [B] See *Export-Import Bank of United States.*

exit interview [HR] An interview with a departing employee usually conducted by a human resource professional to determine why the employee is leaving. These interviews help spot the areas that need improvement.

expanded memory [C] Extra memory, useful to DOS and many DOS applications. See *extended memory.*

> Chris decided to buy an *expanded memory* program for his PC because his workload was so heavy.

expansion board [C] An electronics board that is slipped into the appropriate slot inside a computer to expand the computer's capabilities.

expansion slot [C] The internal plug, or slot, where an *expansion board* is inserted inside a computer to expand the computer's capabilities.

expat; expatriate [HR] A term referring to a citizen of one country who works in another. For instance, American citizens working overseas are called American *expats.* See *third country nationals.*

expectations [E] Outcomes that economists anticipate given specific actions in the economy. For example, if an economy grows too fast, it is expected that inflation will occur. If this happens, then interest rates are expected to increase because investors will expect to be reimbursed for a greater erosion of the value of their investment.

expenditure [A] The cost of an item for a company; payment by a company.

expense [B] A cost associated with doing business. Income minus expenses equals profits.

> When *expenses* rose so dramatically during the metal shortage, Zippy Corp. had to raise its prices.

expense account [B] An allowance given to executives and sales-people for travel and business entertainment.

> Salespeople at Zippy Corp. had to take a cut in their *expense accounts* when business was down.

expenses [A] The general category of costs for a company.

expense sheet [B] A form detailing the reimburseable expenses of a business trip.

expert system [C] A program that attempts to provide knowledge or decision-making like that of human thinking.

exponent [M] The number of times a number is multiplied by itself. It is often referred to as "raised to the power of." In the expression 5^4, the exponent is 4 (or the number 5 is raised to the power of 4), meaning the number 5 is multiplied by itself 4 times, or $5 \times 5 \times 5 \times 5 = 625$.

exponential [M] Term referring to the use of exponents or powers. See *exponent*.

Export-Import Bank of United States (Ex-Im Bank) [B] An independent bank that promotes trade with the United States through various financial supports. It was created in 1934 by the government and is financed by the U.S. Treasury. It is generally known as the Ex-Im Bank.

exports [B] Materials shipped out of a country; the opposite of imports.

> The United States is increasing its *exports* of cars to Japan.

extended memory [C] An advanced use of memory for computers using 286 chips and up, commonly used in Windows computers.

extension [C] Suffixes for DOS, Windows, and OS/2 files that indicate the type of file it is. Examples are bat, com, dev or drv, dat, doc, exe, ini, and sys, referring to batch, command, device driver, data, document, executable, initialization, and system files.

[T] An allowed delay, usually of four months, to file a tax return. This is not a delay in paying taxes, only in filing the forms. Taxpayers must pay taxes, or an estimate of what they owe, by April 15.

extortion [L] The illegal collection of money by a public official, usually by coercion or threats.

extrovert-introvert [S] An extrovert is a general classification of a person who is more outwardly social than others, whereas an introvert is more introspective. Carl Jung, who invented these terms in his 1921 book *Personality Types*, gave a more technical definition. Essentially, an extrovert uses people as a critical part of her thinking process, whereas an introvert relies mostly on his own mental network of ideas for his thinking. This is especially true in making decisions or in problem solving. People are, of course, blends of both. It generally is a mistaken notion that extroverts like people more than introverts do; extroverts are just more expressive. The word *extrovert* can also be spelled with an *a* as in extravert, but introvert is always spelled with an o.

eye contact [S] The connection established between two people when they look each other in the eye. Some people, especially extroverts, expect people always to look them in the eye when speaking to them. Others, especially technical people, have a tendency to think about a complex set of ideas as they discuss things and may not look directly into another's eyes. However, in critical discussions, eye contact tends to convey sincerity and candidness.

eyewitness [L] A person who actually saw aspects of a crime.

F

face amount [I] The amount that is paid to a beneficiary when an insured person dies. It is the amount the person was insured for.

face time [S] Time spent in face-to-face communications, as opposed to E-mail.

factorial (!) [M] The product (multiplication) of every consecutive number up to and including the specified number. Written with an exclamation point. For example, 4! = 24 or (1 × 2 × 3 × 4 = 24).

fair housing laws [RE] Federal, state, and local laws that guarantee all people freedom from discrimination when buying, renting, selling, or making any real estate transaction.

> The landlord was fined for breaking *fair housing laws* when he refused to rent to a group of women.

fair market value (FMV) [A] Used in accounting, taxation, and real estate, it refers to the market value of an asset. It is generally expressed as what an asset will sell for in a competitive market with an informed buyer and seller who are not under any duress during the sale. This is in contrast to the "original value" of the investment or real estate, or what the owner thinks the value should be.

FAIR plan [I] A governmental insurance plan (Fair Access to Insurance Requirements) that covers property for which it would otherwise be difficult to get coverage.

fair use [L] The legal use of copyrighted material, for instance a teacher making copies for classroom instruction.

fallow [RE] Land that is not used during a growing season.

> The acres and acres of *fallow* land were wasted in this farm community.

false pretenses [L] The taking of property or money through misrepresentation or fraud.

> The used car dealer made the sale through *false pretenses*: He told the customer that the shiny Camaro had been used by a little old lady when he knew it had been driven recklessly by his brother-in-law and had been in a number of accidents.

Family and Medical Leave Act (FMLA) [HR] The 1993 legislation providing up to twelve weeks a year of paid or unpaid leave for purposes of birth or adoption of a child, for one's own serious medical condition, or for illness of a family member. The person taking leave must be given either his job back or one that is substantially the same.

family limited partnership [T] An estate planning technique that converts or claims assets as part of a family business. The IRS often challenges these arrangements if it appears that it was set up just for tax purposes.

family of funds [F] The variety of funds offered by a single mutual fund company.

> The prospectus outlined the *family of funds* in equity, bonds, and money market investments offered by the investment company.

Fannie Mae (Federal National Mortgage Association or FNMA) [RE] The nickname for the Federal National Mortgage Association, which buys and packages mortgages for investors, encouraging lenders to offer more mortgages to individuals. Fannie Mae is involved in one of every four mortgages each year.

> Appraiser Co. Inc. was required to fill out a *Fannie Mae* form for any residential appraisals it did for Peach Bank.

FAQ (frequently asked questions) [C] See *frequently asked questions*.

FASB (Financial Accounting Standards Board) [A] Pronounced as FAS-bee, it's the board created by the accounting profession to set rules and standards for all accountants to follow. The primary accounting association, AICPA (American Institute of Certified Public Accountants), requires all members to comply with FASB rules or justify any variations.

fast track [HR] An accelerated method of promoting high-potential individuals up through the company ranks, allowing more responsibility earlier to test if they really have the potential.

> "That Jones is certainly on the *fast track*," commented Smithers. "He's already in charge of the department he started in."

favorites [C] See *bookmark*.

fax; facsimile [C] The transmission of a printed page or picture over telephone lines. Traditionally the transmission was between fax machines; now computers can transmit or receive faxes with a fax board.

fax board [C] See *fax; facsimile*.

fax modem [C] A combination of a fax board and modem in one unit.

F distribution or ratio [M] A statistical test between the variances or standard deviations of two distributions to see how alike or dissimilar they are. See *statistics*.

feasibility study [B] A study, often performed by an outside, impartial party such as a consulting firm, determining how well a proposed new product or a new manufacturing process would operate. Feasibility studies vary from project to project, but they include analysis of probable product demand, legal considerations, probable profits, etc.

> Before investing in automated equipment, the Acme Bookclub wanted a full *feasibility study* to see if in fact it would be workable to have a computer select, package, and invoice each book order.

featherbedding [B] The practice by a labor union of requiring an organization to keep people on the job after they are no longer needed.

Federal Deposit Insurance Corporation (FDIC) [F] The federal governmental insurance organization for banks and depositors. The FDIC will cover deposits (basically up to $100,000 per account) at any bank it insures if the bank fails or runs into financial difficulty.

> The deposits were *FDIC* insured so Mae didn't run to withdraw her money when she heard rumors about the bank's instability.

Federal Express (FedEx) [B] A private freight delivery service.

federal funds rate [E] One of two interest rates that is controlled by the Federal Reserve. The federal funds rate is the rate that banks must charge each other to loan money overnight between them. See *discount rate*.

Federal Home Loan Mortgage Corporation (FHLMC or Freddie Mac) [RE] A federal agency that buys mortgages from lenders, giving them more cash to make new mortgages, and gives aid to the FHA and Veteran's Administration-backed loans.

The Community Bank sold a block of their mortgages to *Freddie Mac.*

Federal Housing Administration (FHA) [RE] The branch of HUD (Department of Housing and Urban Development) that insures mortgages and offers low-interest guaranteed mortgages to homeowners.

Federal National Mortgage Association (FNMA or Fannie Mae) [RE] See *Fannie Mae.*

Federal Open Market Committee (FOMC) [E] Monthly meetings of the Federal Reserve (Fed).

Federal Reserve (Fed) [E] The common reference to the Federal Reserve banking system, board, or chairman that controls the supply of money and regulates banks in the United States.

Federal Reserve Bank of New York [E] The largest and most active regional Federal Reserve bank.

Federal Reserve Banking System [E] The system established in the United States in 1913 to regulate banking and money. It is usually referred to simply as "the Fed." It consists of twelve district or regional banks, and branch offices in other cities. There is a board of governors, each elected for a term of fourteen years, and the chairman, who is elected to a term of four years.

Federal Reserve Board [E] The governors of the Federal Reserve in Washington plus five presidents of the regional Federal Reserve banks. They meet monthly to decide on such monetary matters as increasing or decreasing the money supply or short-term interest rates.

Federal Reserve chairman [E] The head of the Federal Reserve (Fed) system, who is the main spokesman for the decisions of the Fed. The chairman testifies in Congress on a regular basis. The chairman usually makes very cautious and general statements to the public so as not to tip off the anticipated actions of the Fed, which could cause investors to buy or sell securities as they speculate about the actions the Fed could take.

Federal Reserve requirements [E] The ratio of reserves the Federal Reserve (Fed) requires a bank to hold against deposits. The Fed can change this ratio, which can tend to increase or decrease activity in the economy. If the Fed increases the reserve requirements, then the bank is restricted in how much money to lend, which tends to slow economic growth. If the Fed decreases the reserve requirements, then more money should expedite economic growth.

Federal Reserve system [F] The United States' national bank, made up of a group of twelve separate banks, which regulates, audits, lends, guards, controls, and administrates to its member banks. The Federal Reserve system plays a crucial role in the nation's economy as well as in the United States' international relations with the banking systems of other countries.

Federal Trade Commission (FTC) [E] The government agency directed to enforce fair competitive business practices. The agency was created in 1914 under the Federal Trade Commission Act.

fee and commission financial planner; fee-based financial planner; fee-only financial planner [F] The three basic compensation methods of financial planners. *Fee and commission* is charging a set fee for planning and then a commission for buying and selling investments. *Fee-based* is a more common method where the financial planner charges a percentage of assets of the investor, like a money manager. *Fee-only* is a small segment of financial planners who simply charge for their time, providing the maximum of objective advice because no investments or insurance are sold.

fee-for-service [HR] A term applied to health insurance where the insured is free to select whichever doctor he wishes. This is in contrast to "managed care," such as HMOs or PPOs, where there is some restriction on which doctors the insured can see. See *health insurance*.

fee simple [RE] A property owned without any outside interests or encumbrances. The fee simple represents all the rights one has in real estate—for example, the right to sell, lease, or use a property.

Most real estate is owned as *fee simple* property.

felony [L] A general category of crimes of high degree, such as arson, burglary, murder, and rape. This is opposed to minor crimes, called "misdemeanors."

fiber optics [C] Technology that uses lasers to send information through glass fibers, versus the older technology of using electricity through metal wires. Fiber optics is a more advanced and effective form of transmission.

FICA (Federal Insurance Contributions Act) [T] The Social Security taxes an employee and the company pay from each paycheck. Pronounced FI-ka. Currently that rate is 7.65 percent, up to $72,600 in 1999. An employee and his company both pay the same amount for a combined total of 15.3 percent. Those who are self-employed must pay the full 15.3 percent themselves. If they earn over that amount they still continue to pay 1.45 percent for Medicare Part A. The 7.65 percent is actually for three different purposes and three different trust funds. The retirement amount, called the "OAS fund" (Old Age and Survivors), is 5.6 percent of the total. The disability amount, called the "DI" (disability), is .6 percent of the total. The Medicare amount, called "HI" (hospital), is 1.45 percent of the total, and is for part A of Medicare.

fiduciary [L] Any person entrusted to hold or invest money or other assets for a third party; for example, a pension administrator. Depending on federal or state law, fiduciaries may be limited as to what they can do with the assets they are entrusted to hold. The word may be used as a noun to describe the person or as an adjective to describe the responsibility.

> The court appointed a *fiduciary* to help the company dispose of its assets.

> The executor's *fiduciary* responsibility included liquidating the investments so that they might be dispersed.

field [C] In cyberspace, a place to input information. In a database, it is a unit of data. For instance, in a database, a user might have the following fields that make up the record for each of her friends:

Last Name
First Name
Street Address
City
State
Zip Code
Telephone Number

FIFO (first in, first out) [A] A way of valuing an inventory and calculating taxable profit. When inventory is sold, the cost of what was bought *first* (the oldest inventory) is charged *first* against what was sold. It assumes that what was sold was the oldest inventory. This is in contrast to "LIFO," which uses the last (the newest) inventory first. It's easier to see with numbers, so check out the example below.

Dolls! Dolls! Dolls!

January: Purchased 10 dolls for inventory at a cost of $4 each.

June: Purchased 10 dolls for inventory at a cost of $6 each.

For the year: Sold 16 finished dolls at a price of $20 each.

Gross sales: $320.

In the FIFO method, 10 of the 16 dolls sold would be counted as those first bought for inventory at $4 each; the remaining 6 dolls sold would be counted as those bought for $6 each. So, our doll costs are $76 determined as follows:

$$10 \times 4 = \quad \$40$$
$$6 \times 6 = \quad \underline{\$36}$$
$$\$76$$

Total Profit: $320 − $76 = $244

Using the LIFO method, the 10 dolls bought for $6 each would be counted first, and the remaining 6 dolls would be counted as those bought for $4 each. So, our doll costs are now $84 determined as follows:

$$10 \times 6 = \quad \$60$$
$$6 \times 4 = \quad \underline{\$24}$$
$$\$84$$

Total Profit: $320 − $84 = $236

Note: In a period of high inflation, the FIFO method is more popular because profits are higher.

15 percent excess tax [T] A now defunct tax that once applied to very high amounts of withdrawals from qualified benefit plans and IRAs, and to estates. That limit was essentially applied to amounts over $150,000 per year.

file [C] A collection of electronic data. The contents of a disk file are just like those in a file cabinet and can be filled with just about anything: a word-processing document, a group of spreadsheets, and so on.

> The disk marked "Meetings 1996" had the *files* for all the minutes of the meetings held in that year.

file name [C] The specific identification of each file, such as the name of each separate word-processing or spreadsheet document that is created. Many software programs automatically put an extension on the file name that identifies the specific software. For instance, a Lotus 1–2–3 spreadsheet for DOS has an extension of wk1 or wks, a Microsoft Word document has an extension of doc. Thus, a file name of "mortgage.wk1" or "meeting.doc" helps to identify files.

file 13 [S] The trash can. It's a euphemistic way of saying "throw it away," using the normal business jargon of filing things. See *circular file*.

file transfer protocol (FTP) [C] Standard protocol used for downloading files from an internet site, called an FTP server, to a computer. Some FTP servers require a password, while others only require the user to log in as "anonymous." Often the computer takes care of these technical things and the user just presses Enter.

filing status [T] A person's tax status. It generally depends on whether they are single or married, although there are five different filing statuses. They are: single, married filing jointly, married filing separately, head of household, and qualifying widow(er).

> Jeremy marked his W-4 form's *filing status* as married, filing a joint return so that he would pay taxes at the lower married rate.

finance [B] The general activities of a company that relate to accounting, financial analysis, bank relations, and the management of its investments. It can mean the raising of money to pay for an expansion or meeting with Wall Street analysts to explain the company's financial results and prospects.

[F] "Personal finance" pertains to the management of money on an individual level.

financial accounting [A] Accounting methods used to provide information for external purposes, such as those of bankers, investors, and regulators. This is in contrast to "cost accounting," which provides internal cost information for managerial analysis and decision-making.

Financial Accounting Standards Board (FASB) [A] See *FASB*.

financial analysis [A] The examination and study of the financial statements of a company, leading to conclusions about the soundness of its management and business.

financial analyst [A] An analyst who offers opinions as to a company's financial strengths and weaknesses.

financial commodities; financial futures [F] Specific financial items sold like commodities, such as dollars, pounds sterling, francs, Treasury bonds, and S&P 500 Index. For instance, a Treasury bond future contract on the Chicago Board of Trade is worth $10,000 in Treasury bonds. Just like sugar and pork bellies, these financial items are traded and their value changes as speculators bid the value up or down.

financial planner; financial planning [F] A fairly new type of financial professional providing a wide range of financial advice, as opposed to just one main area, such as investment advice or insurance advice. As a practical matter, financial planning is an ideal that provides advice on all aspects of an individual's finances. In the past an individual would go to a broker for investment advice, an insurance agent for insurance advice, an estate planner for estate planning advice, and so forth. A financial planner is ideally a professional who is able to bring all of these aspects together into a single coherent plan for the individual. See *fee and commission financial planner*.

financial planning; financial planning seminar [HR] Sometimes offered by companies, a personal session with a planner for executives, or a seminar covering the essential topics of benefits, investments, insurance, and taxes for all employees.

financial statement [A] A report of a company's balance sheet, income statement, and net worth.

Zippy Corp. published its annual *financial statement* for investors.

finder's fee [B] A finder brings together parties for a business deal. Typically, the finder will help with the negotiations and consummation of the deal. A finder's fee is paid to that person if and when the deal is done.

> Jane was thrilled to pay a *finder's fee* to Mr. Brown when he found her some limited partners who were willing to bring in the needed capital for her expansion.

finding [L] A decision by a court about issues of fact.

fine tuning [E] The delicate process of keeping the economy on a steady growth pattern, without too much growth and without a recession. Through mainly monetary policy, the Federal Reserve tries to calibrate economic growth with the various financial tools it controls, such as adjusting the interest rates and reserve requirements. See *federal funds rate*, *discount rate*, and *Federal Reserve requirements*.

finger [C] A program that finds out information about internet users, such as names, how often they use the internet, and what they view.

finished goods [A] The stock of completed manufactured goods by a company, ready to be sold.

fired [HR] The traditional term for being terminated from a job, especially for cause. See *laid off*.

firewall [B] Protective barriers between departments for security, objectivity, or other reasons. Such barriers are usually set up between auditing and the rest of the company to keep auditing as objective as possible. See *Chinese wall*.

[C] A system of security restricting access to a network or web site to protect against hackers and/or viruses.

first in, first out [A] See *FIFO*.

first mortgage [RE] The mortgage that takes precedence over any other mortgages or liens against a property, such as a second mortgage.

> When Urban DevCo. sold its property, the owner of the *first mortgage*, Peach Bank, was paid before any of the other lenders.

first-to-die policy [I] The standard method for structuring a life insurance policy. That is, if the insured dies then the face value is paid to the beneficiary. However, a newer type of policy only pays after both parties die; it is called, appropriately, a "second-to-die policy." The idea here is that, in general, if a couple has enough money to support a surviving spouse, there may still be a need to pay the eventual estate taxes for the heirs, which the policy payout from a second-to-die policy would be available to do.

fiscal policy [E] Policies and actions taken by the federal government to stimulate the economy by increasing or decreasing government spending, or increasing or decreasing taxes. This is in contrast to "monetary policies and practices." Monetary policies have to do with increasing or decreasing the available money in the economy, a function of the Federal Reserve.

fiscal year [A] Any twelve-month period that may or may not coincide with a calendar year. A fiscal year is usually selected to include a complete season for a company. For instance, a ski resort would probably have a fiscal year from July 1 through June 30.

> The local school board's *fiscal year* began in September and ended in August so that it would coincide with the school year.

fishbone diagram [M] See *cause-and-effect diagram.*

fixed asset [A] A category of assets usually intended to be held and used for a long period of time, at least over one year.

fixed costs [A] Any cost that doesn't vary with changes in business volume. Most salaries, rents, etc., are fixed costs.

> Unfortunately for Zippy Corp., most of its major expenses were *fixed costs* so they could not withstand a long period of poor sales.

fixed disk [C] An older name for a hard disk or drive.

fixed exchange rates [E] Currency exchange rates that are fixed, as opposed to floating as they are today. Fixed rates existed among the developed nations from 1944 to 1973. See *Bretton Woods agreement.*

fixed expense [A] An expense that doesn't change, such as the cost of hiring an employee, which includes the fixed expense of employee benefits.

fixed-income securities [F] A more technical name for bonds, notes, and preferred stock. They are investments that pay a fixed amount of interest, hence their name.

F keys (function keys) [C] The group of keys on a PC keyboard from F1 through F12, which trigger preprogrammed commands.

flagship [B] A store, office, or product that is the most important, largest, best-selling, or most closely identified with its company.

> When Zippy Corp. redesigned the Zippy Zipper, its *flagship* product, most consumers were quite distraught.

> The company headquarters is located at our *flagship* offices in Memphis, Tennessee.

flame [C] Online vituperation. Flaming occurs if someone posts what someone else thinks is a stupid or offensive comment. Flames can be very nasty and may escalate to flame wars, which, like any spat, may be boring or fun to watch (and read), depending on the creativity of the venom.

flat-panel display [C] Display technology used on laptop computer screens now being adopted by regular PCs.

flat tax [T] A tax proposed by a variety of people in the past, and it is still just that—a proposal. It is a tax in which everybody pays one tax rate, such as 20 percent.

flexible spending accounts [HR] A company plan that allows tax-free money to be set aside to pay for eligible unreimbursed medical (such as eyeglasses and dental care) and dependent daycare expenses. The one hitch is that if the money is not used, it goes to the employer. Use it or lose it.

flex-time [HR] Work schedules that allow employees to choose their starting and quitting times, usually within certain limits. Employees may be able to choose either end of the designated core time. Thus, an employee may be required to work the core hours, say, from 10 A.M. to 3 P.M., and might then be allowed to select the additional three hours before or after, or both, around the core times.

flight capital [F] Foreign investments in developing countries that flee when that country experiences instability. This can be immensely disruptive for the countries.

float [A] The amount of funds represented by checks that have been deposited in a bank but not yet collected from the banks from which they are drawn.

[F] The initial public offering of a security; if investors go for it, the stock issue or bond floats.

> To raise money for improvements to its building, the Silly Corp. decided to *float* a bond for $9 million.

floater [I] A policy that covers moveable personal property, that is the policy "floats" with the property wherever it is. Typically such items are jewelry or furs.

floating exchange rates [E] Currency exchange rates that are not fixed but move on a weekly and daily basis. See *Bretton Woods agreement.*

floating mortgage rate [RE] A variable mortgage rate that moves according to some other rate, such as the Treasury bill rate. The rate is usually adjusted annually.

floating-point notation [C] A mathematical method of calculation inside a program where numbers are given a designation using binary numbers and powers, versus the standard representation of a fixed decimal point. This allows the computer to calculate faster.

floor (the floor of an exchange) [F] The actual trading area at an exchange, such as the New York Stock Exchange (NYSE). Because more and more trades are done on the computer, it will not be surprising if one day there is no actual trading on floors.

floppy disk [C] See *disk.*

flow chart [M] A detailed diagram showing the complete step-by-step process of manufacturing or any complicated process.

flush [C] The function in word-processing software that aligns words in a document evenly with either the left or right margin. If the right margin is not flush, then it is called "ragged."

focus fund [F] A relatively new mutual fund strategy where the fund manager only selects a limited number of stocks in hopes of beating the S&P 500 index performance.

focus group [B] A small group of people assembled for purposes of market research. A facilitator engages the group in a discussion that explores the merits of a consumer product being tested. Many new television shows are tested in this way before being committed to prime time.

folder [C] The designation of a file in Macintosh and Windows software.

follow up [S] To check on something after a period of time.

> The boss told Cruthers to *follow up* on the new procedures to see if they are being adhered to.

font [C] A typeface or style of text. Word-processing programs come with a variety of fonts.

Some Fun Fonts

This is called Bauhaus Font.

This is called Tekton Font.

This is called Brush Script Font.

---

font cartridge [C] A plug-in cartridge to a printer containing instructions to produce different fonts.

footer [C] The common text information printed at the bottom of each page of a word-processing or spreadsheet printout.

footprint [C] The amount of physical space taken up by a computer or other object. It can also refer to satellite coverage, specifically the geographical area a satellite can beam to.

Forbes [B] A major business news magazine, published biweekly.

Ford, Henry [B] See *mass production*.

forecasting [A] The estimating and projecting of financial trends, usually based on historical information and anticipated changes.

foreclosure [L] Usually the termination of the use of property because of unpaid obligations, such as not paying the mortgage.

foreign exchange [F] The changing of money from one country's currency to another. The foreign exchange market is not one physical place; it is a network of computers, and of course, that corner bank in Paris, or wherever one happens to be traveling. The new European currency is called the "euro."

Wanna Swap Currencies?

Country	Currency	Country	Currency
Argentina	peso	Australia	dollar
Austria	schilling	Bahrain	dinar
Belgium	franc	Brazil	real
Britain	pound	Canada	dollar
Chile	peso	China	yuan
Columbia	peso	Czech Rep	koruna
Denmark	krone	Ecuador	sucre
Finland	mark	France	franc
Germany	mark	Greece	drachma
Hong Kong	dollar	Hungary	forint
India	rupee	Indonesia	rupiah
Ireland	punt	Israel	shekel
Italy	lira	Japan	yen
Jordan	dinar	Kuwait	dinar
Lebanon	pound	Malaysia	ringgit
Malta	lira	Mexico	peso
Netherlands	guilder	New Zealand	dollar
Norway	krone	Pakistan	rupee
Peru	new sol	Philippines	peso
Poland	zloty	Portugal	escudo
Saudi Arabia	riyal	Singapore	dollar
Slovak Rep	koruna	South Africa	rand
South Korea	won	Spain	peseta
Sweden	krona	Switzerland	franc
Taiwan	dollar	Thailand	baht
Turkey	lira	United Arab E.	dirha
United States	dollar	Uruguay	new peso
Venezuela	bolivar		

foreign exchange rates [E] Currency relationships between two countries.

The new European euro had an *exchange rate* of about $1.17 (actually 1.16675) when it was first introduced.

foreign investment [E] The acquisition by businesses of assets and businesses in another country.

forfeiture [HR] The amount of money the company contributed to a plan such as a 401(k) plan that is never used by employees because the employees left before being vested in the money.

forgery [L] The making of money or documents with the intent to defraud. The government can legally print money; civilians cannot.

format [C] To prepare a disk for use with an operating system. A Mac disk needs to be formatted specifically for the Mac, while an IBM compatible disk requires an IBM format. This step prepares the disk to be usable by the computer. Disks are now frequently preformatted so this step doesn't need to be performed.

Jan *formatted* the disk before she copied the files onto it.

formula [M] An equation indicating how to do a mathematical calculation.

The formula for calculating the future value of a number is:

$$FV = PV(1 + i)^n$$

In this formula, FV stands for future value, PV for present value, i for the interest rate, and n for the number of years of compounding. Using this formula, if a person had $1,000 now, present value, and it could earn 7 percent (designated by the symbol i in the formula), and it would grow for 5 years (designated by the power of 5 in the formula), the answer would be determined as follows:

$$FV = \$1,000 \times (1 + .07)^5$$

$$FV = \$1,000 \times (1.07)^5$$

(Note: $(1.07)^5 = 1.07 \times 1.07 \times 1.07 \times 1.07 \times 1.07$.)

$$FV = \$1,000 \times 1.4$$

$$FV = \$1,400$$

That is, the $1,000 will grow to $1,400 in 5 years.

FORTRAN (Formula Translation) [C] A high-level mathematics, science, and engineering programming language still widely used. This is in contrast to COBOL (Common Business Oriented Language), which is a high-level business programming language.

Fortune [B] A major biweekly business magazine.

Fortune 500 [B] A listing of the largest 500 companies in the country by *Fortune* magazine. The listing also uses the term *Fortune* 100 for the obviously shorter listing. Other magazines now have their own listings, but this was the original one that popularized the notion of classification by size.

forward [F] A financial contract obligating one party to buy and the other to sell specific assets for a fixed-price on a specific future date.

forward slash (/) [C] See *back slash*.

401(k) plan [HR] A popular retirement-type plan offered by companies. See *defined contribution plan* and *retirement plan*.

403(k) plan [HR] A retirement plan similar to a 401(k) plan but offered to certain tax-exempt organizations and public schools. See *defined contribution plan* and *retirement plan*.

415 limits [HR] The tax code section limiting the amount of contributions that a company can provide to its employees through pensions and 401(k)-type plans.

457 plan [HR] A contribution-type employee plan for states and municipalities that doesn't have all the tax benefits of a 401(k) plan. See *defined contribution plan* and *retirement plan*.

fraction [M] A numerator divided by a denominator.

franchise; franchisee/franchiser [B] A license granted to an owner-operator of a business to use a company's name and product. The license typically binds the operator to buy only the company's products, merchandising, sales, and promotions. The owner-operator is the franchisee, the parent company is the franchiser.

> When George decided to buy a fast-food *franchise*, he investigated all the major ones that weren't already in his town: McDonald's, Dunkin' Donuts, Carvel, Roy Rogers, and KFC.

fraud [L] The intentional deceiving of others, and thereby causing harm, usually financial rather than physical.

Freddie Mac [F] See *Federal Home Loan Mortgage Corporation*.

free alongside ship (FAS) [B] Shipping policy whereby the seller is responsible for a shipment from his factory to the dock. The buyer assumes responsibility from there.

> When Acme Corp. sent its new shipment to J-Mart, they paid for shipments *FAS*.

free and clear [RE] Term that describes a property with no mortgages or liens outstanding.

> After making the final payment of their 30-year mortgage, the Manns proclaimed, "We finally own a house that's *free and clear!*"

freebie [S] An item or service given for free, such as promotional giveaways, free coffee during the day, or free pizza on Friday afternoons.

freelancer [HR] A person who picks up various jobs in a field as opposed to holding a steady job.

> Diane was a *freelance* editor working for various magazines and book publishers, an arrangement that allowed her to attend graduate school.

free on board (FOB) [B] A class of delivery charges that covers delivery only to the dock; delivery of the shipment to its final destination is extra.

free trade [E] A condition of minimal restrictions on the free flow of goods and services between countries.

freeware [C] Free software available from the internet or a user group. See *shareware*.

freight collect [B] Charges paid by the receiver of goods.

freight delivery [B] A shipment that includes delivery charges from the dock to the shipment's final destination.

> To avoid having to calculate delivery charges, Zippy Corp. always ordered its merchandise *freight delivery*.

frequently asked questions (FAQ) [C] A section in most computer and software user's guides in which many questions that are commonly asked are answered.

frictional unemployment [E] The unemployment that seems unavoidable because of adjustments that cannot be made immediately. When changing jobs, a person may be unemployed temporarily before finding a new one. If a company lays off people, those individuals will be unemployed until they find new jobs.

Friedman, Milton (1912–) [E] See *Nobel Prize for economics*.

fringe benefits [HR] Company benefits such as vacation, holidays, and pensions. During World War II these benefits were thought to be "on the fringe of wages." Since these benefits are now common, the term is clearly out of date.

front money [F] The money needed to get a project going; the money an investor needs before the financing is in place.

> They needed $20,000 in *front money* from the various interested investors to investigate the feasibility of such a project.

full employment [E] The percentage of people in an economy who are working, out of those who can work or who want to. This figure is generally held to be about 95 percent because some people can't find work they want, or some people are between jobs temporarily.

fullfillment [B] The process of completing the orders generated by direct-marketing activities. The steps usually involve processing the order, preparing the goods for shipping, and shipping the goods. A small business that generates orders sometimes uses an outside firm that specializes in fulfillment.

full-service broker [F] A broker who will not only buy and sell stocks and other securities but will also provide research and advice to customers. A full-service broker charges a higher commission than a discount broker or deep-discount broker, who do not offer investment advice.

> We went to a *full-service broker* since we weren't sure what to invest in.

functional utility [RE] Term used to describe how well a building serves its purpose; when assessing functional utility, an analyst takes into account what the market wants and how the building is designed and laid out.

> The small rooms, bad traffic flow, out-of-date architectural design, and poor layout all made the *functional utility* of that building very low.

function keys [C] See *F keys*.

fundamental analysis [F] One of two approaches to analyzing the stock market. Fundamental analysis relies primarily on economic supply and demand, business earnings, balance sheets, and economic factors of a particular company or its business sector to determine if a stock should be bought or sold. This is opposed to "technical analysis," which relies on market volume, price movements of a particular stock, or the market in general in determining the best time to buy or sell stocks. See *technical analysis*.

Fundamental Analysis–Looking at the Basics:

Economic Factors:	Individual Business Factors:
business cycles	liquidity–acid test ratio
interest rates	inventory–turnover ratio
leading indicators	profitability–earnings per share
monetary indicators	P/E ratio
	book value

---

fund manager [F] The top professional at an investment company who manages the collection of many individual stocks or bonds in a mutual fund.

funds statement; funds flow statement [A] See *statement of cash flows*.

fungible [F] Term that refers to the interchangeability of financial assets.

fuse [S] To bring two things together.

> The two companies were *fused* into one enterprise.

FUTA (Federal Unemployment Tax Act) tax [T] The mandated annual tax a company pays for unemployment insurance.

future dollars [M] A value of an investment or quantity into the future. See *future value.*

futures; futures contracts [F] Obligations to buy or sell a commodity on a specific day at a specific price. Futures contracts always expire on the third Friday of each month. Because the investor is investing in an actual commodity, it generally is considered the riskiest of all investments. They can have big payoffs, but most individual investors in futures regret having ever been bit by the futures bug.

futures exchanges; futures trading [F] Special exchanges on which futures contracts are traded. For example, the CBOT (Chicago Board of Trade) trades futures and options on agricultural commodities, such as corn, wheat, and soybeans, and on financial instruments, such as U.S. Treasuries and the DJIA (Dow Jones Industrial Average) futures.

future value (FV) [M] The value of something in the future. It could be the accumulation of a series of values, like the continual investing in a 401(k) plan, or the value of a CD in the future. The future value is calculated with an investment rate assumption. An example would be the value of investing $2,000 into an IRA each year for twenty years with the assumption of an investment rate of 8 percent. That future value is calculated to be approximately $91,500. Calculating the future value is the opposite of calculating the present value. See *present value* and, for an illustration, see *formula.*

fuzzy logic [M] A new form of algebra that uses a range of values, from true to false. It is used in decision-making with imprecise information. The outcome of fuzzy logic is the assignment of a value based on the probability that it is true.

G

GAAP (generally accepted accounting principles) [A] See *generally accepted accounting principles*.

Gainsharing [HR] A business practice of giving the employees part of the gains of the company usually through bonuses. Honeywell and Dana Corp. were early users of this approach.

Galbraith, John Kenneth (1908–) [E] An American economist and writer who is associated with strong government intervention in the economy. His 1958 book *The Affluent Society* gave a name to the remarkable economic growth after World War II.

galley proofs [B] A final mock-up of typeset materials, also referred to as "galleys." Clients, staff, and proofreaders then make a final check before printing.

Gallup organization; Gallup poll [B] An organization based in Princeton, New Jersey, that designs and conducts market research and polls for businesses.

game plan [S] A business plan or strategy that is expected to be successful.

game theory [M] The mathematical method of analyzing business situations based on games in which there is a winner and a loser. It is used in management decision-making.

gangbusters [S] Usually used with the verb *to go*, this term generally refers to a situation in which things are going extremely well.

> Sally remarked that the advertising campaign was going *gangbusters*, bringing in so many new customers.

Gantt chart [M] A work schedule chart plotted against a time scale, devised by Henry Gantt. Helpful for people who are involved with a number of simultaneous projects.

garbage in—garbage out (GIGO) [S] The common business phrase that says when a user enters in useless computer data— garbage in—the computer will produce useless results—garbage out.

garment district [B] A specific area in New York City devoted to fashion manufacturing, generally between thirty-fifth and fortieth streets and between Broadway and Seventh avenue. Because of low cost overseas manufacturing, the garment district is no longer the dominant area it once was.

garnish [HR] To withhold money from an employee's salary as required by court order. Usually the employee owes money, and this is an official way to collect the debt. The employer required to withhold the money is the *garnishee*; the court order to have the money taken out is called a *garnishment*.

> When The Yellow store won the suit against Ms. Adams, they had her wages *garnished*.

garnishment [L] A court-ordered directive to a company to take a portion of a particular employee's salary to pay for specific debts. See *garnish*.

gatekeepers [S] Those in charge of controlling who gets access to whom.

> The administrative assistants were very good *gatekeepers* for the president, keeping away all miscellaneous phone calls and unwanted visitors.

gateway [S] The point at which information is controlled or funneled.

[C] A device connecting two networks with different communication protocols, that allows the two networks to communicate. Also may refer to Gateway 2000, a large mail-order computer-maker.

> Ned used an online service as his *gateway* to the World Wide Web.

GATT (General Agreement on Tariffs and Trade) [E] A multilateral agreement reached in 1948 to prevent the 1930 debacle of trade wars between countries. See *Smoot-Hawley Tariff Act* and *Uruguay round*.

gazundering [RE] The practice of bidding down the price of a property after signing the purchasing contract but before the official closing. This is often done in a weak real estate market.

GDP (gross domestic product) [E] See *gross domestic product*.

gear up [S] To mobilize resources to get a job done.

General Accounting Office (GAO) [T] The government office that monitors the IRS and other federal financial expenditures. The GAO, established in 1921, oversees financial transactions and reports to the public.

general agent [I] A person who has been appointed by an insurance company to represent it in a given territory. The person can also be called a "captive agent." This is in contrast to an "independent agent," who will represent several insurance companies.

general contractor (GC) [RE] The person or company that supervises and is primarily responsible for completing the building or renovation of a structure.

> The *GC* on the project was responsible for hiring the subcontractors: the plumber, electrician, carpenters, and sheetrockers.

general counsel [L] The general activities of a company pertaining to legal matters, such as patents and copyrights, contracts, and filing and responding to legal suits.

general ledger [A] The record of all accounting transactions and events of a company.

general liability insurance [I] The form of insurance used to protect a company from a myriad potential liability exposures. It often includes accidents on the premises, products sold, and contract liabilities.

generally accepted accounting principles (GAAP) [A] Rules, guidelines, and standards followed by certified public accountants in the preparation of financial statements. Accountants express an opinion as part of their audit of the financial information of a company, and that opinion indicates if the financial statements were prepared in accordance with generally accepted accounting principles. The principles are generally defined by FASB (Financial Accounting Standards Board) Statements and older APB (Accounting Principles Board) Opinions.

general obligation bond (GO) [F] Generally a state-issued bond backed by the "full faith and credit" of that state. This is in contrast to "revenue bonds," which are backed by the revenue from a specific source such as a bridge, tunnel, or highway authority. General obligation bonds are less risky than revenue bonds because of the broader and more secure nature of the financial backing and usually pay a slightly lower interest rate.

general partner [B] The partner in a partnership who is in charge of the day-to-day responsibilities and usually who makes all the important decisions about the partnership. This is in contrast to a "limited partner," who has only invested money in the partnership.

generations [S] Groups of people born roughly during the same eighteen-year time periods and share common experiences and similar cultural ideas. Marketing often approaches people of different generations with different advertising campaigns seeking to appeal to the cultural uniqueness of each generation.

Generations:

World War I Born 1890 to 1908; generally characterized as having been disillusioned.

Depression/War Born 1909 to 1927; generally characterized as being frugal and having a high sense of individual responsibility.

Balance Born 1928 to 1945; generally characterized as "balancing" two forces: a sense of responsibility and having unlimited opportunities.

Baby Boomers Born 1946 to 1964; generally characterized as wanting and getting the most and the best.

Generation X; Gen X; GenXers Born 1965 to 1983; generally characterized as being realistic and aware of today's problems and challenges.

Millennium; Generation Y Born 1984 to about 2002; it's too early to determine the main characterization of this generation.

---

generation skipping [T] In large estates, the giving of money to the second or later generation, as opposed to children. This is commonly done for grandchildren. There are special rules for taxation that apply.

generic; generic brand [B] A plain, unadvertised product that is essentially the same as its counterpart.

> Bill always bought *generic* products in the supermarket; they were less expensive than regular, well-known brands.

generic drug [B] A drug that is the same as a brand name drug and that is allowed to be produced because the patent on the original drug expired. Also called a "generic equivalent."

gentrification [RE] The process of renovation that takes place as an upper- and middle-class clientele begin buying into low-income neighborhoods and upgrading them. People who lived there before gentrification are sometimes priced out of their own neighborhoods.

> In the 1980s, yuppies triggered the *gentrification* of many derelict neighborhoods in Bigville by buying buildings cheaply, fixing them up, and thus raising property values substantially.

Gen X, Generation X [S] The generation of people born after the baby boomers, also known as *Gen X* or *GenXers*. Generation X people are born generally after 1964 and up to about 1983. Although they have also been called "slackers," the term doesn't necessarily fit. Instead, they are generally characterized as realistic and aware of today's problems. The next generation after Generation X has been called the "Millennium generation," because their births will span the two centuries. See *generations*.

geometric mean [M] In financial and statistical calculations, it is the compounded rate of return over a number of years. For example, the *average* yearly return in the stock market has been about 13 percent, but the *compounded rate of return* has been about 11 percent over the last 70 years. They both represent the same data; one represents the information for an average year, the other over a number of years.

geometric progression [M] A series of numbers where each term has a constant *multiplied* to it. This is in contrast to an "arithmetic progression" where each term has a constant *added* to it. An example of a geometric progression is: 3, 6, 12, 24, 48—each term is multiplied by 2 to obtain the next number. An example of an arithmetic progression is: 3, 6, 9, 12, 1, 5—3 is added to each term to obtain the next one.

geometry [M] The mathematical study of points, lines, and shapes.

get with the program [S] An admonition to accept the new procedures, orders, policies, or game plan.

> Smithers told his staff to *get with the program* or find another job.

get your ducks lined up [S] An expression that means to put in place all the necessary authority, procedures, or approvals to get something done, presumably like ducks who swim in a straight line, one behind the other. Also seen as *get your ducks in a row.*

GIC [HR] See *guaranteed investment contract.*

GIF (graphics interchange format) [C] See *graphics interchange format.*

gift tax [T] A tax required on a monetary gift, or gifts, but usually after a specified annual amount. For federal tax purpose, that amount is generally $10,000 per recipient per year. Only a few states impose a gift tax. If a gift tax is owed, it is paid by the giver of the gift, not the receiver.

> When Marty received another $1,000 from his mother that year, he knew that she still wouldn't owe any *gift taxes* on the money she had given him.

gigabyte (G, GB) [C] A billion or so bytes. Actually, it is a little more than a billion, or precisely 1,073,741,824 bytes, or 2^{30}, that is, 2 to the 30th power. May be abbreviated as 1,024 MB (megabytes). See *byte.*

> I just updated my hard drive to one with a *gigabyte* of memory—I'm sure I'll have enough room to hold all that programming and more.

GIGO [S] See *garbage in—garbage out.*

Ginnie Mae (Government National Mortgage Association or GNMA) [RE] A nickname for the federal corporation under *HUD* that purchases FHA-insured mortgages on the secondary market and issues mortgage-backed securities that are federally insured. This encourages lenders to offer more mortgages to individuals and, in fact, is responsible for about 12 percent of the mortgages financed each year.

girder [RE] A horizontal beam that is a main support in a building.

> As the construction on the new office building downtown progressed, pedestrians could see construction workers walking along the *girders* to inspect the steel frame.

giveback [HR] A concession by a union, often a cut in wages or benefits in order to prevent or lessen workforce layoffs.

glad-hander [S] A very outgoing and cordial person. One who shakes everybody's hand. Often has a somewhat negative connotation, as to indicate someone who is trying to get ahead by being friendly in an insincere way.

glass ceiling [HR] An invisible barrier, in the form of social bias, that often keeps women and minorities from reaching the uppermost executive echelons.

glass half-full or half-empty [S] The proverbial glass that is seen as a positive, half-full, or a negative, half-empty. Thus, it refers to a person's attitude and whether he perceives a particular situation as positive or negative.

Glass-Steagall Act [B] Key banking legislation passed in 1933 that kept commercial banks separate from investment banking. Sometimes called the "Banking Act," it was intended to keep banks stable by not allowing them to engage in risky business ventures.

glitch [S] A minor problem that can affect an entire project.

global [C] A command that affects an entire program or software. For example, if a user wanted to change the column size of all cells in a spread sheet, she would enter a global command.

global business [B] The selling of products and services overseas, in addition to domestically. It involves more complex business planning and business financing. Virtually all major corporations are active in business around the world.

global fund [F] A type of mutual fund from an American perspective that invests in securities in any country *including* the United States—in other words, the entire globe. This is in contrast to an "international fund," which invests in any country *outside* the United States.

global markets; global marketing [B] Term used to describe to markets today which are no longer confined to the borders of a country. Businesses often sell products, goods, and services to other global markets and find their competition may come from overseas as well as from around the corner.

global village [S] An image of the world connected in business and in communications. Thus, businesses compete not only in their country but also around the world. One's neighborhood is now the whole world.

GNMA (Government National Mortgage Association or Ginnie Mae) [RE] See *Ginnie Mae*.

GNP (gross national product) [E] See *gross national product*.

goal setting [B] A common business practice of identifying specific objectives at the beginning of the year, revising them when necessary, and monitoring one's progress toward completion.

godfather [S] A senior management person who is looking out for a subordinate's well-being, often grooming that person for future success. Also known as a *mentor* or *rabbi*.

gofer [S] A person who runs errands, who will "go for" coffee, "go for" donuts, and so on. Sometimes spelled "gopher," after the rodent.

going concern [S] A company that is expected to continue in business for the foreseeable future.

gold [E] A metal held in high regard around the world. At one time it was a standard to which currencies had to be converted so international trade could be equated between countries. See *gold standard*.

golden handcuffs [B] Raises, bonuses, or perks given or promised to executives or key employees so that it would be difficult for these employees to leave the company.

golden handshake [B] Dismissal of an employee with generous benefits, such as severance pay.

> The special early retirement package by Acme Corp. was welcomed by many of the employees. It was the *golden handshake* they were looking for.

golden parachute [B] A special deal for executives ensuring that if they lose their jobs in the event another company buys out the firm, there will be a generous package of benefits for them, such as severance and bonuses.

> Hearing of the rumor that Zippy Corp. wanted to buy out Acme Corp., the board of directors at Acme approved a *golden parachute* for its executives.

Goldilocks market [F] An ideal stock market, "not too hot and not too cold." A market that grows steadily.

gold standard [E] A method of basing the value of currency on the value of metals such as gold and silver. The gold standard disappeared in 1971 when President Nixon stopped the convertibility of dollars into gold.

good cop-bad cop [S] A business negotiating strategy that sets two people on one team to play opposite roles, often diverting attention and being successful. One person plays the negative person, the bad cop, by indicating all the reasons why the deal shouldn't go through. Another person plays the cooperative person, the good cop, and gets on the good side of the other team. The good cop is often successful in closing the deal.

good-faith bargaining [B] A term used in labor negotiations that implies a productive and positive give-and-take in contract negotiations.

Good Housekeeping seal [B] The well-known seal of approval that signifies that a product has met a certain level of consumer satisfaction. Since 1909, the Good Housekeeping Institute tests all products that are advertised in *Good Housekeeping* magazine. Companies who are granted the seal are required to advertise in the magazine. Companies can also use the seal on their packaging and include the seal as part of their advertising in other magazines.

good-till-canceled (GTC) [F] An order with a stockbroker that stands until it is either executed or canceled. Often, however, investors make a *stop order* or a *limit order* (these will limit at what price or how much the broker will buy or sell).

goodwill [A] An intangible asset representing the reputation of a company. It can be the advantage of customer loyalty, brand names, or strategic location.

goof-proof [S] Term referring to something that can't go wrong.

googol [M] Reportedly named by an infant, the googol is a 1 with 100 zeros written behind it. In math circles, it is written as 10^{100}. It dwarfs the biggest numbers people normally think of, such as a billion or a trillion, which are only 10^9 and 10^{12}.

Gopher [C] An internet program that allows users to locate information through hierarchical menus. It was developed in 1991 at the University of Minnesota and was named after its school mascot, the gopher.

go public [S] To offer stock to the public for the first time. Often referred to more technically as an IPO (initial public offering). Can also have a slightly different meaning, referring to a company announcing something to the public that it has kept relatively secret, such as a new product.

gouge [S] To grossly overcharge for a product or service.

government bond [F] Any one of a number of U.S. Treasury bonds, especially the 30-year Treasury bond, called the "T-bond."

Government National Mortgage Association (GNMA or Ginnie Mae) [RE] See *Ginnie Mae*.

G.P.S. (global positioning system) [C] A new technology to determine a person's position anywhere in the world. It uses a network of satellites that sends out signals that can be picked up by small handheld receivers. It can pinpoint one's position by precise latitude and longitude. G.P.S. can provide locations for hikers and boaters, and even tell a golfer how far she is from the pin.

grace period [I] A specified time frame, often after a due date, in which a payment can be made without penalty.

> The insurance company gave XYZ Corp. an additional 30-day *grace period* so XYZ didn't feel it was urgent to make the payment right away.

grade [B] A term used to denote the quality of something, such as a product or service, especially a financial product. Thus, a stock or bond may be referred to as "top," "high," or "investment" grade, meaning that it represents the best of companies and is therefore a sound investment.

[RE] A general term that refers to the level or slope of a property. "Street grade" means at the level of the street. A "10 percent upgrade" means the property slopes up 10 percent from the horizon line. "Grading" a piece of land means giving it the slope and look necessary for proper drainage and appearance.

> After the bulldozers *graded* the property, they were ready to put in the roads.

graduated payment adjustable mortgage [RE] A mortgage in which payments gradually increase a set amount over a set period, and the interest rate is adjusted from time to time according to an index.

> Because they were just starting out, the owners of MelonWorks thought a *graduated payment adjustable mortgage* would be a good idea; their payments would increase as the business took off, and they were guessing that interest rates would be going down as well.

graduated vesting [HR] See *vesting*.

grandfather clause [HR] A provision, usually in connection with a company benefit plan, that allows those who are current employees to maintain some benefits that will not be offered to new hires.

grand jury [L] A jury assembled to determine if the facts of a case warrant a trial. A petit, or petty, jury is the regular jury used when a case is being tried.

grantor [T] The person who sets up and contributes to a trust. Also called "settlor," "creator," or "trustor."

grantor trust [T] A plain-vanilla trust where a person remains in control of the money or assets and can change the trust at any time.

grapevine [S] The ongoing gossip within an office. Also called the *rumor mill*.

graph or chart; graphing or charting [M] A visual presentation of data to provide clarity and understanding. The common forms of graphs or charts are line, bar, and pie. Bar charts can be vertical or horizontal or presented in 3-D form, to represent three dimensions. More complex graphs can combine line and bar charts. A pictogram uses visual pictures for impact or to make a boring chart more interesting.

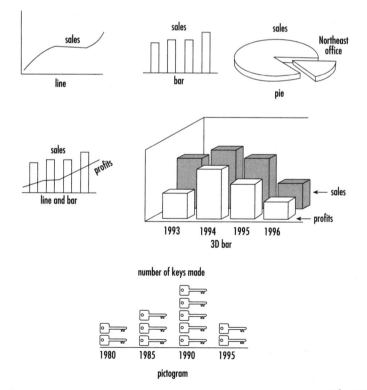

graphical user interface (GUI) [C] See *GUI*.

graphics; graphic design [C] Computer information presented as a graph or a chart, or more generally with pictures.

> Jan's boss appreciated the *graphics* in her presentation; they dramatically illustrated the drop in overhead costs over the last year.

graphics interchange format (GIF) [C] One of the popular file formats for storing pictures on a computer. A GIF file is recognized by the extension .gif, pronounced as jif. Other formats are Windows bitmap (.bmp), and joint photographic experts group format (.jpg, pronounced Jay-peg), and tagged image file format (.tif).

graphs [C] See *graph or chart*.

GRAT [T] See *GRIT*.

graveyard shift [B] The work shift that usually runs from midnight to 8 A.M. The day shift is next, usually from 8 A.M. to 4 P.M., followed by the swing shift, usually from 4 P.M. to midnight.

gray market [B] The elderly market in general. Since more people are living to an older age and more have significant money, this is an attractive market for many businesses.

gray scale [C] The series of shading from white to black.

grazing capacity [RE] The maximum number of animals that can graze in an area without doing permanent damage.

> The farmer assessed the *grazing capacity* of his land before purchasing his cattle at the auction.

Greek alphabet [M]

Letter	Name	Letter	Name	Letter	Name
A α	alpha	I ι	iota	P ρ	rho
B β	beta	K κ	kappa	Σ σ	sigma
Γ γ	gamma	Λ λ	lambda	T τ	tau
Δ δ	delta	M μ	mu	Y υ	upsilon
E ε	epsilon	N ν	nu	Φ φ	phi
Z ζ	zeta	Ξ ξ	xi	X χ	chi
H η	eta	O o	omicron	Ψ ψ	psi
Θ θ	theta	Π π	pi	Ω ω	omega

greeking [C] The practice of displaying meaningless text to represent how actual text, or illustrations, will look and flow on a page. In desktop publishing, it allows for testing the positions of text and graphics to see how they work together on a page.

green [B] A term that refers to environmental issues. Groups that advocate environmental issues are referred to as the *green* lobby. A *green* product is one that is environmentally safe.

greenback [F] Slang for dollar.

"I'll bet you twenty *greenbacks* on the game," Josh joked.

green card [HR] The visa held by resident aliens. The cards are no longer green in color, which was the case in the past.

green circle [HR] See *red circle*.

green fund [F] See *social investing*.

greenmail [B] An anti-takeover maneuver of a targeted company in which that company buys back its own stock, held by the potential takeover company, at an inflated price.

green marketing [B] The marketing of products and packaging that are environmentally sound, such as biodegradable materials. See *green*.

green shoe [F] An agreement allowing the underwriting agent of a new issue to purchase additional shares if necessary.

Gresham's law [E] A rule that says "bad money drives out good." It was expounded by Sir Thomas Gresham (1519–1579), who was a businessman and advisor to Queen Elizabeth I. In those times, coinage was uneven, with some containing more valuable metal than others. Gresham observed that when coinage was uneven, the good coins would be taken from circulation and melted down for their metal, leaving only the bad.

GRIT (grantor retained interest trust) [T] An irrevocable trust arrangement used sometimes by a wealthy person to transfer a residence (or other assets) to his children and save some estate taxes. The residence may pass to children while the parent is still living in the house. Two variations on a GRIT are a GRAT (grantor retained annuity trust) and GRUT (grantor retained unit trust). In these two versions, the person receives either an annuity or fixed (unit) amount of interest each year.

gross [B] The total amount before deducting things like taxes, expenses, etc.

> Jan's *gross* annual income was $50,000—quite a bit more than her after-tax income of about $30,000.

gross building area [RE] Total floor area, including basement and garage area, but not including unenclosed areas, such as decks.

> The *gross building area* of that property came in at 10,000 square feet.

gross domestic product (GDP) [E] A measurement of how an economy is doing. It measures the total output of goods and services within a country measured at market prices on a quarterly and annual basis. It does not count intermediate goods, only goods used for final consumption, because it is assumed that the value of intermediate goods is built into the prices of the final goods. The United States used to rely on *GNP* (gross national product), which measured the output by American businesses no matter where they were, in the United States or overseas. Starting in December 1991, the Commerce Department officially changed to reporting GDP because that is how the other major countries measure and report their economic output. The GDP measurement is only slightly lower for the United States than was the GNP (less than one-third of one percent). Some production by U.S. companies is lost since only production within a country is considered, but there are also gains: The Honda production plant in California is reported in the GDP of the United States, for example.

Here are the largest economies by GDP:

GDP in 1996 as measured in U.S. dollars, in billions:	
1. United States	$7,661
2. China	3,390
3. Japan	2,850
4. Germany	1,700
5. India	1,538
6. France	1,220
7. United Kingdom	1,190
8. Italy	1,120
9. Brazil	1,022
10. Indonesia	779
11. Mexico	777
12. Russia	767
13. Canada	721
14. South Korea	647
15. Spain	593

gross income [A] The total income from a business or property.

> Their *gross income* that year doubled, from $1 million to $2 million, when they opened a whole new chain of stores.

[T] To the IRS, gross income is gross taxable income: salary, any investment earnings, and any other income subject to income tax.

> Because the bonus was paid this year, Lora knew it had to be included in this year's *gross income*.

gross income multiplier (GIM) [RE] The ratio of the value of a property to the gross income the property generates. The GIM is a quick way to estimate the value of a property.

> The market in Snakeville supported a *GIM* of five, so when Harvey heard that Snakeville Oil Center was for sale for $5 million, he knew that it had better generate at least $1 million a year in business.

gross margin; gross profit; gross profit margin [A] Sales minus the cost of goods sold, or the amount of revenues before administrative expenses and taxes are applied.

gross markup [A] The difference between the wholesale and retail price. It is the amount of gross revenue of a retailer.

gross misconduct [HR] Any action by an employee that warrants immediate firing.

gross national product (GNP) [E] The previous standard for measuring the goods and services produced by a country each year. It measured the total production by American businesses not only in the United States but also around the world. It has been replaced with GDP because the new measurement is consistent with how other countries measure their economies. See *gross domestic product*.

gross revenues; gross sales [A] The total sales amount, without any adjustments for discounts or returns.

> JayMart gave figures for its *gross sales* for the fiscal year; the figures appeared high because none of the numerous discounts were figured in.

gross up [HR] The compensation practice that provides for a one-time payment to offset additional taxes one may owe. For instance, if a company pays for relocation to Milwaukee, the cost of the moving van and other expenses are taxable to the employee. Thus, a company will often give a commensurate one-time payment to the employee in order to offset those additional taxes.

group [I] An organization, company, or other collection of people who are covered under an insurance policy, usually at reduced rates.

Group of Seven (G-7) [E] The seven largest economic nations, who coordinate and set international trade. They are: Britain (or the United Kingdom [U.K.]), Canada, France, Germany, Italy, Japan, and the United States. When Russia is invited it is called the "Group of Eight"(G-8).

Group of Ten (G-10) [E] Sometimes called the "Paris Club," these were the ten nations in 1962 who contributed major sums to the IMF (International Money Fund) to foster international trade. They were: Belgium, Britain, (or the United Kingdom [UK]), Canada, France, Germany, Italy, Japan, the Netherlands, Sweden, and the United States.

group policy [HR] A medical or life insurance policy designed to cover a group, such as the employees of a company. Because of sheer numbers, companies can secure better medical and life insurance rates than individuals could on their own. Thus, a group rate is more attractive than an individual rate.

growth [E] An increase in business activity. This is the main subject of economics. How and why business activities increase or decrease has been the subject of a number of theories by economists and actions by governments.

growth and income fund; growth fund [F] Mutual funds that invest primarily in common stocks. Growth and income funds will stress income through higher paying income stocks, whereas growth funds stress growth only. However, during most periods, the total return of both will be similar.

growth stocks [F] Individual stocks that are primarily geared toward growth with little or no emphasis on income through dividends. Some growth stocks will pay no dividends.

growth versus value [F] A technical yet potentially important distinction between common stocks or equity mutual funds. A *growth stock* or fund has a higher than average P/E (price/earnings) ratio whereas a *value stock* or fund has a lower than average P/E ratio. Although there are other measures used, such as book value, the P/E ratio is most commonly used. The growth theory holds that if stock has a higher P/E ratio then the market has identified and recognized, that company is a good investment. The value theory holds that if a stock has a lower P/E ratio, it will have a greater potential to increase and is a better investment. Thus, the two theories and opposite approaches.

GRUT [T] See *GRIT.*

guarantee [B] A promise by a manufacturer or retailer to fix or replace a product within a certain time frame if there is a defect in the product. Some retailers offer price guarantees—a promise to refund the difference if the consumer sees a product elsewhere at a lower price.

> "You won't find better prices or service anywhere! I *guarantee* it for one year from the date of your purchase!" claimed the manager at L-Mart.

guaranteed investment contract (GIC) [HR] A common investment option in 401(k) plans that pays a relatively attractive rate of interest. The investment option is often called a stable value fund. Insurance companies often offer these investment vehicles to the plans.

guaranteed loan [E] A loan by a country or international agency to stimulate growth in a targeted country.

guaranteed mortgage [RE] A mortgage that has a second party backing up the borrower in case he or she cannot pay.

> Because of Harry's poor credit rating, Peach Bank required that he get a *guaranteed mortgage*.

guaranteed renewable [I] A life-insurance policy that allows the policy holder to renew the policy if he or she wants to.

guardian [T] The person designated by a court to be officially responsible for children when no parent is alive or available.

GUI (graphical user interface) [C] Pronounced GOO-ee, it refers to the popular and easy-to-use icons and pull-down menus that are used in conjunction with a mouse to give program commands. These graphical methods are simpler and quicker to use than the earlier method of using arrow keys and Alt and Ctrl keys for commands. This GUI methodology was first used in the early software developed at the Xerox lab in Palo Alto, California, in 1973, taken up by Apple Computer's Steve Jobs for use in the Mac, and finally by Bill Gates for use in Microsoft Windows.

guru [S] A person very knowledgeable about a specific field, often a consultant.

GW-BASIC (gee-whiz BASIC) [C] An earlier form of the BASIC computer language.

H

habeas corpus [L] The basic right of a citizen to be brought to court to determine the legality of being held in custody. Latin for *you have the body.*

hacker [C] One who illegally gains access to a private computer database.

> *Hackers* tried to get into the school records database and change all their grades from Cs to As, but they were foiled in their attempt by the newly installed computer firewall.

halftone [C] A printed image that uses very small black and white dots that appear as a continuous tone to the eye.

halo effect [HR] The effect of evaluating a product or person based on a favorable impression of one aspect of the product or one trait of a person. The term was first used in 1920 by psychologist E. L. Thorndike, who described this effect as essentially placing a "halo" over a person after one trait is judged positively, thus not allowing other traits to be judged on their own merits.

handshaking [C] The act of establishing a connection between computers, usually through the internet or through another communication connection.

hardball [S] Tough negotiations with strong, no-holds-barred tactics. Not for the weak or meek.

hard copy [C] The actual physical copy of a letter, memo, or report, as opposed to computer-saved information. Should the computer go down, the hard copy is still available.

> Did you make a *hard copy* of that document to hand out at the meeting?

hard currency [F] Gold and silver coins, also known as "specie." In the old days, people preferred hard currency to flimsy paper currency.

hard disk; hard drive [C] The long-term, main storage device for a computer.

What's the capacity of that *hard disk*?

hard dollars [B] The purchase of goods or services with cash, versus commissions, which is called "soft dollars." See *soft dollars*.

hard font [C] Styles of type used in the past that were stored in the printer itself, in contrast to "soft fonts," which were in the software. Fonts are now software based.

hard goods [B] Durable goods, such as cars, furniture, appliances, and so forth.

The price of *hard goods* had increased over the past year due to the inflation in the economy.

hard hyphen [C] In some word-processing software, it is the hyphen the user must add when a word splits at the end of a line. This is in contrast to a "soft hyphen," which is the hyphen some software automatically adds when the last word cannot completely fit onto the line.

hard numbers [S] Data or calculations that can be trusted as accurate because they were produced or reviewed by someone very reliable.

hard return [C] In word-processing software, this is the command that moves the cursor to the beginning of the next line, usually when the *Enter* or *Return* key is pressed.

hard-sell approach [B] A selling technique using a direct and immediate selling technique, sometimes called a "high-pressure approach." This is in contrast to a more subtle or indirect approach.

hardship withdrawals [HR] A provision in a 401(k) plan that allows for a special withdrawal for emergency money if the employee doesn't have other available funds.

hardware [C] Term that refers to the computer itself and connected peripherals, such as external disk drives. "Software" refers to the programming that runs on the hardware.

> She knew from the way the computer responded that it was a *hardware* problem; the word-processing program worked well on the other terminal.

hardwired [C] Hardware or software that is designed to perform a specific task and cannot be changed by the user.

Harvard Business Review (HBR) [B] A business journal, published by the Harvard Business School, which contains in-depth articles on different facets of business. It is often referred to in print as *HBR*.

hash total [A] A meaningless sum used for control purposes to determine if an item is missing. For example, if an invoice is missing from the computer records, the total of the invoice numbers will signal that the items are not complete.

Hawthorn effect or studies [HR] A series of early studies on the motivation of workers conducted at the Hawthorn, Illinois, plant of the Western Electric Company between 1924 and 1933. One of the fascinating results, called the Hawthorn effect, was that worker motivation was increased by the mere attention of the studies themselves. In general, it showed that workers act differently when they are observed.

Hayek, Friedrich (1899–1992) [E] A member of the Austrian economic school of thought, he believed in free markets. In his 1944 book, *Road to Serfdom,* he wrote about the dangers of central planning by governments.

Hayes compatible [C] Term used to describe communications software that works with the command language of the Hayes Modem. Most communications software is Hayes compatible.

Hay points [HR] A job evaluation system in which points are determined for specific levels of job responsibilities and specific job activities. The system was developed by Edward Hay.

HDTV (high-definition television) [C] A new standard for high-resolution digital television.

head [C] The part of the disk drive that actually reads data from the hard or disk drives.

head and shoulders pattern [F] In technical stock analysis, a chart formation that forms a rough shoulder-head-shoulder pattern. It generally is interpreted as a bearish sign for that stock. See *technical analysis*.

header [C] The common text information printed at the top of each page of a word-processing or spreadsheet printout.

headhunter [HR] An individual who, as a service, finds jobs for people and helps companies fill open positions. A headhunter is also referred to as an "executive recruiter."

> The executive *headhunter* charged a hefty 25 percent of the first year's salary for executives he placed—sometimes as much as $200,000.

head of household [T] A person who maintains a home for at least one dependent but is not married.

> Although she was single, Jeanne could file as *head of household* because she had two children living with her, and thus could take advantage of a lower tax rate.

heads up [S] An expression for getting someone's attention in order to alert them to sensitive information, often before it becomes public.

health insurance [HR] A general term for a variety of medical coverage at a company, such as comprehensive or major medical, and through such means as fee-for-service, managed care, HMO, or PPO. Often a monthly premium is necessary. When medical services are needed, there is often a deductible and/or a co-payment.

Some Health Insurance Terms:

managed care A general term applied to health insurance, commonly HMOs and PPOs, where there is some sort of restriction on which doctors the participant can see.

HMO (health maintenance organization) A group health insurance policy that typically emphasizes preventative medical care by covering routine examinations as well as doctor visits due to illness. HMOs employ a list of participating physicians and hospitals that must be used for coverage.

PPO (preferred provider organization) An association of doctors that offers employees a wider selection of doctors than an HMO but not complete freedom to see any doctor.

fee-for-service A term applied to traditional health insurance plans where participants are free to select their own doctors. This is in contrast to managed care.

deductible The initial payment for medical services in one year under a fee-for-service plan. Once that amount is covered by the participant, there is usually a co-payment or sharing feature thereafter.

co-payment The percentage of medical costs commonly paid by the participant after the deductible is satisfied. A typical example is that the participant pays 20 percent, and the company pays the remaining 80 percent.

stop loss A health insurance provision that pays 100 percent of the bills after a set amount of out-of-pocket expenses is paid by an employee. The eomployee's loss is stopped. Typically, a stop loss occurs after $1,000 or $2,000.

---

heavy hitter [S] A powerful person with authority.

hedge; hedging; hedgers [F] To protect oneself against an existing investment position by buying or selling other offsetting securities, such as options.

> The makers of cranberry juice *hedged* their investment by buying a future contract on cranberries for a decent price when they sensed that there could be a drought in their bogs.

hedge fund [F] A high risk fund that allows the investment manager free rein. Conservative investing styles have no place here; hedge funds involve selling short, acting on options, borrowing money, and any other particular strategies that offer very high returns with, of course, very high risks. In 1998, the hedge fund Long-Term Capital Management made headlines not only because of its failure but also because it had two Nobel Prize-winning economists on its board.

hedging [E] The practice of buying and selling in different markets to take advantage of a difference in price.

help key [C] The designated key to provide assistance within a software program.

Hertz (Hz) [C] The frequency of electrical cycles per second. One Hz is equal to one cycle per second. Named after Heinrich Hertz, who in 1883 detected electromagnetic waves.

heuristic [M] Any method that helps a person learn better or investigate problems more effectively. The word is derived from the Greek *heúreka* (eureka), supposedly shouted by Archimedes (c 287–212 B.C.) when he was taking a bath and realized how to determine if the king's crown was made of gold.

hexadecimal [M] Term refering to the number 16. The hexadecimal system of numbers uses 0 through 9 and then the letters A through F to represent the numbers 10 through 15. Computer programmers use the hexadecimal system because numbers can be written more compactly. The number 12 is 1100 in the binary system but simply the letter C in the hexadecimal system.

HH bonds [F] U.S. savings bonds that pay interest semi-annually as does a regular bond. Currently, one can only obtain HH bonds by the redemption from EE bonds, which is a tax-free exchange. HH bonds are in contrast to EE bonds, which accumulate interest until cashed in.

hidden assets [A] Assets of a company that are undervalued or ignored, such as real estate holdings or the overfunding of a pension plan.

hidden file [C] A file prevented from being accessed, sometimes to prevent unauthorized use by others.

hidden persuader [B] A term used to describe a marketing and advertising technique that is used to motivate people to buy products. The term was popularized by Vance Packard in the 1950s.

hierarchical [B] An adjective used to describe the structure of authority in a business. It can also describe the structure a business puts in place to limit the access one has to certain computerized information.

hierarchy of needs [HR] See *Maslow's hierarchy of needs*.

high-definition television (HDTV) [C] See *HDTV (high-definition television)*.

high flyer [F] A heavily traded stock that has had a dramatic rise in price.

high resolution [C] A term to describe the high-quality images on a monitor screen.

high-wage strategy [E] An economic policy by a country to emphasize and encourage high wages for its workers, either through wages alone or a combination of wages and benefits.

high-yield bonds; high-yield fund [F] Bonds or mutual funds that invest in bonds that pay a higher rate of interest than normal because they are rated lower than average. They are also called "junk bonds" because they are rated so low. They are rated below triple-B. Although they are the riskiest of bonds, they may potentially provide investors with high income.

> Marcel only invested a small portion of his bond portfolio in *high-yield bonds* because they are so risky.

hiring freeze [HR] The halting of additional hiring, usually for a temporary period of time, to control costs.

hiring hall [HR] A union-operated employment office where workers—especially in construction—are notified of jobs on a daily basis.

histogram (frequency diagram) [M] In statistics, a bar-chart diagram that represents the frequency of data values, often roughly bell-shaped. It is a basic way to represent statistical data. The name *histogram* derives from the Greek word *histos* for mast, thus it is a mast- or column-like bar chart.

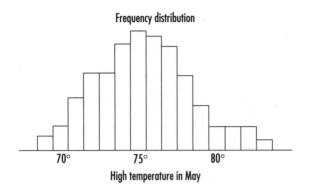

Frequency distribution

70°   75°   80°

High temperature in May

historical costs [A] An accounting method using the original cost of an item, in contrast to "inflation accounting," in which current market costs are used with the effects of inflation built-in.

hi-tech [A] A term applied to any number of newer technologies. It is a contraction of "high technology."

hit the bricks [S] A union term meaning to go on strike.

HMO (health maintenance organization) [HR] See *health insurance*.

Hobson's choice [S] A take-it-or-leave-it proposition, which means one has no choice at all. The term came from a Mr. Hobson, an Englishman who owned a prized stable of horses. When a person came to buy one of his steeds, Mr. Hobson would only allow him to buy the one next to the door.

holder of record [F] A stockholder who holds stock at the time a dividend is announced and who will receive it.

hold harmless clause [L] A contractual clause that stipulates that a party will not hold another liable for damages in the course of conducting the specified work.

holding company [B] A firm that controls directly or indirectly other companies by virtue of owning enough shares of stock in each of the companies. Although typically a firm needs to own more than 50 percent to control another company, sometimes it may own less than 50 percent but still actually control it. A holding company often doesn't actively involve itself in the management of those companies. Also, the companies it controls usually continue to retain their own identities.

holding period return [F] A quick calculation, and not a very meaningful one, that determines how much an investor has made on an investment over the time it was held. The profit plus any interest or dividends is divided by the original price.

holographic will [T] A will written by a person by hand.

home key [C] The key on a keyboard that allows the user to return to the beginning of the document or spreadsheet.

home office [B] The main headquarters of a company.

home page [C] The initial screen on a World Wide Web site. It usually has general information about the organization. Pages beyond the home page usually have more detailed information.

home shopping [B] The increasingly popular method of shopping for items at home through toll-free telephone numbers, through catalogs, television shopping programs, and the computer.

homicide [L] The unlawful killing of a person by another, which, of course, almost all killing is.

horizontal analysis [B] The analysis of companies in the same business. This contrasts with "vertical analysis," which looks at the various businesses and suppliers from raw goods to customers. See *vertical analysis* and *integration*.

[A] The comparison of a company's financial statements over two or more periods.

horizontal move or promotion [HR] A move by an employee to a similar level, as opposed to an increase in level. Also known as a "lateral move."

hospice care [I] Care for the terminally ill in their own homes or at a special facility meant to create a homelike atmosphere.

host [C] Any computer system with a distinct address. Each host on the internet has a name and a numeric network address called its IP (internet protocol) address.

hostile takeover [B] An unfriendly takeover of a company, usually through buying enough shares of stock to control the company.

hoteling [HR] A term to describe a relatively new office arrangement where sales people and telecommuters can use a general office area operated by the company. General offices are equipped with a standard desk, telephone, and computer. Some large companies even have a person called a "concierge" to coordinate who is using what office and to make plane and restaurant reservations. E-mail and voice mail can be easily accessed from any of these offices.

hot key [C] A designated key used to call up a program, such as a calculator or calendar, to check data or text for reference while using another program.

hot link [C] A link between programs that automatically updates data or information in one program as it is entered in another. For example, if a word-processing document is hot-linked to a spreadsheet program that captures regional sales data and calculates the overall sales totals, then the sales totals in the word-processing document will be automatically updated as sales data is entered in the spreadsheet.

hotlist [C] See *bookmark*.

housecleaning [S] Term referring to the reorganizing and generally replacing of some people after a new boss or owner arrives. The new boss or owner may want to place their own stamp on the operations. It is sometimes referred to as "getting rid of dead wood."

household [E] Defined by the census as a single person living alone or a family living together under one roof. To economists, this is an important economic unit, which is analyzed and used in their statistics.

housing starts [E] A figure representing the number of new homes started in the construction field. The housing starts figure is a leading economic indicator.

> The *Wall Street Journal* reported that new *housing starts* were up for the third consecutive quarter—an important indicator that the country is coming out of its period of recession.

housing stock [RE] The total number of housing units.

> The *housing stock* in our area was inadequate for the influx of people that Papco was bringing in for its new factory.

HP-compatible printer [C] A printer compatible with the standards set by Hewlett-Packard, the manufacturer that dominated the early printer market. Just as IBM dominated the early personal computers and set the standards, Hewlett Packard has set the standards for laser printers. Thus other printer manufacturers have adopted those standards.

H.R. 10 plan [HR] See *Keogh plan*.

HTML (hypertext markup language) [C] The formatting language of the World Wide Web. It determines the appearance of web pages, and it defines the links in the web site.

HTTP (hypertext transport protocol) [C] The basic technical standards for the World Wide Web. Web addresses begin with the prefix: http://. It is this standard that has allowed the rapid growth of the web.

HUD [RE] The acronym for the Department of Housing and Urban Development.

human capital [E] Workers seen as an asset in the economy. Increasing employee training or education increases human capital.

human engineering [B] The method of designing machines and work operations not only for worker efficiency but also for comfort and ease of operation so as to reduce job fatigue and increase motivation. See *ergonomics*.

human relations [HR] A management technique that stresses employee motivation in the workplace.

After Mr. Brown took a course in *human relations*, he made an effort to reward employees, recognize their achievements, and give incentives for good work.

human resources (HR) [HR] The people resources of a company and the department that oversees the policies and procedures of these resources. It is the general term for the activities of recruitment, compensation, benefits, training, labor relations, and manpower planning. Traditionally, the department was called "personnel," but that has given way in most companies to the term *human resources*.

human resource accounting [A] The recognition or accounting of specific skills and attitudes of a company's employees, such as the level of training, quality of leadership, morale, and decision-making.

Hume, David (1711–1776) [E] Scottish economist and historian who is known in particular for his ideas on international trade. He wrote about how the balance of payments between countries were self-correcting.

hung jury [L] A jury that is unable to reach a verdict in a trial. Either a new trial is ordered or the matter is dropped.

hurdle rate [F] A desired rate of return for a business or project. Thus, all planning is based on this rate to measure proposals.

hybrid pension plans [HR] Pension plans that have features of both defined contribution and defined benefit plans. Two such plans are called "money purchase" and "target benefit" plans.

Hybrid Pension Plans:

money purchase plan A pension plan in which the company agrees to contribute a specified amount to the plan on behalf of each employee. The amount available at any time will be determined by the contributions and how well the investments do.

target benefit plan A pension plan in which the company agrees to contribute a specified amount to the plan with a formula that sets up a "target" benefit for each employee. It is similar to a defined benefit plan, without the actual guarantee of the final benefit. The final benefit is ultimately determined by how well the investments do.

---

hyperbola [M] A mathematical curve.

hyperinflation [E] A very rapid increase in inflation, sometimes called "galloping inflation." It may be hard to imagine in the United States, but some countries have experienced inflation rates as high as 50 percent–100 percent per year. After World War I, a number of European countries experienced such hyperinflation.

hypertext; hyperlink [C] Text linkages within computer documents. A hypertext document has highlighted words, called *hyperlinks*, which, when clicked on, will direct the user to more information about that word. Think of hypertext as layered documents with pathways that lead the user from one to another.

hypothecate [F] To pledge securities for a margin account as a form of collateral without giving up ownership of the securities. Pronounced as Hi-POTH-e-cate.

hypothesis [M] A tentative explanation or theory that requires further investigation.

I

IBM (International Business Machines Corp.) [C]
The world's largest computer company. It started in 1911 in New York in the tabulating and punch card business. IBM launched its computer business in 1953 with the 701 computer. In 1981, it introduced the PC and set the standard for personal computers. In 1983, the PC was *Time* magazine's "man of the year."

IBM-compatible [C] The main class of personal computers that are based on the original IBM PC standards.

I bonds [F] A new type of U.S. savings bond that increases in value by a rate of inflation, thus its name: I for inflation. The first issue of this new bond was a ten-year bond in January 1997 and was called TIPS (Treasury Inflation Protection Securities) but has become known by the more user-friendly term *I bond*. The rate of interest starts out lower than a regular EE bond and stays at that level; however, the value of the bond, which starts at $1,000, can increase as inflation increases. When the bond increases in value, the actual interest paid increases as well because the fixed rate of interest is then calculated on the higher value of the bond. See *savings bonds*.

icon [C] A small graphical computer image or symbol used in place of words or commands. Icons are clicked on to open different programs, which is easier than in DOS, where the user has to type in a command.

> My favorite *icon* is the one for Quicken—a big dollar sign with the logo across it.

idiot proof [S] An adjective describing procedures that are so simple nobody can make a mistake, not even an idiot.

idle time [B] Time that is not usefully engaged. Also known as "downtime."

if it's not broken, don't fix it [S] A cautionary phrase for those who want to meddle in just about everything. Basically it means if something is working well, one should leave it alone, or he could end up breaking it.

imaginary number [M] The square root of a negative, shown as *i*. Although this expression doesn't exist in normal numbers because a number squared is always positive, in advanced math a convention has developed to account for such nonexistent numbers. It is written with the radical or square root sign as: $i = \sqrt{-1}$

IMF (International Monetary Fund) [E] See *International Monetary Fund*.

immediate annuity [I] An annuity to be started immediately, as opposed to a "deferred annuity," which will be paid at some point in the future. See *annuity*, as well as *pension payouts*.

immunity [L] The exemption from prosecution of a witness, even if an illegal act is involved, in exchange for information that will help a case.

immunization [F] An investing technique used by institutional firms to protect their bond portfolio against interest rate fluctuations. Short- and long-term bonds are combined to provide a predictable rate of return regardless of interest rate movements. See *dedicated bond portfolio*.

impanel [L] To select a jury.

imports [B] Goods that are shipped into a country for consumption.

> Those televisions were *imported* from Korea; I purchased them in downtown Atlanta.

imputed income [HR] Income derived from certain benefits, usually life insurance, that a company provides for its employees and that the IRS considers compensation even though it is not direct pay. Income tax must be paid on some of these benefits.

imputed income tax [HR] The income tax liability that is unrelated to a person's direct earnings. As an example, any life insurance a company provides to an employee over a face value of $50,000 will be taxed.

in basket exercise or technique [HR] A method of evaluating a candidate for employment by presenting the kind of materials that would be found in an in-box (or in-basket) and evaluating how the person handles each item. Also used as a training exercise.

inc. [B] See *incorporated*.

Inc. [B] A magazine for small business owners. It focuses on issues of entrepreneurship.

in camera [L] Latin for *in chambers*, it is a judicial proceeding closed to the public, usually in the judge's office. The judge typically examines sensitive or confidential documents *in camera* before deciding if a jury or the public should see them.

incentive bonus; incentive compensation [HR] The compensation practice providing incentives and rewards to executives for improving the company's performance. If the results are met, compensation is given, often in the form of cash bonuses and stock options.

incentive stock option (ISO) [HR] See *stock options*.

income [A] The revenue of a business. Income minus expenses equals profits.

income dividends; income distributions [F] The distribution of dividends and capital gains paid by a mutual fund to its equity investors. Dividends earned by stocks are usually accumulated and paid to investors during the year according to a schedule.

income in respect of a decedent (IRD) [T] Any one of several income items that would have been taxed to the decedent when alive that is instead taxed to the beneficiary or heir, such as installment sales payments, deferred compensation, pension, and IRA payments. The beneficiary or heir must include all received income items in his gross income.

income shifting [T] The technique of moving reported income into another year or to another person (for example, as a gift to a child), or arranging investments so that taxes are paid on less income in the current year.

> By receiving the last payment on his book in January 1999 rather than December 1998, Mark used *income shifting* to even out the tax burden—he didn't expect to make much money in 1999.

income statement [A] A key financial statement that shows a company's revenues (sales), expenses, and net income (profits) during a period of time, at least annually and often quarterly. It is sometimes called the "statement of earnings" or the "profit and loss statement." Whereas a balance sheet shows the financial condition of a company at a particular point in time, the income statement shows the results of the company's operations over a time period, such as from January 1st through December 31st. The following is an example of an income statement:

Income Statement

MacSoftware, Inc.
For the year ending December 31, 1998
(in thousands of dollars)

Total Revenues	$ 30,000
Cost of goods sold	5,000
Gross Profit	25,000
Expenses:	
Salaries	12,000
Benefits	3,000
Administrative Expenses	5,500
Office Rent	1,500
Total Expenses	22,000
Net Profit before Taxes	3,000
Taxes	1,300
Net Income	$ 1,700

income stocks [F] Stocks that pay regular dividends, such as those from blue-chip companies.

Maisie preferred *income stocks* so that she would receive regular dividends from her equity investments.

income tax [T] A tax imposed on personal or business income. In the United States, income tax is "progressive"—the more a person makes, the higher the percentage of the income is taxed. Some taxes are "regressive," such as sales taxes, where the rate is the same for everyone.

incorporated (inc.) [B] Term applied to a company that has organized and been granted the legal status of a corporation. The abbreviation *Inc.* or *Corp.* after a name indicates that a company is a corporation, such as Westbrook Financial Advisers, Inc. Each country has its own designation. In Britain, for instance, the letters *PLC* stand for "public limited company."

> MacSoftware, Inc. was *incorporated* in the state of Delaware.

incubator [B] Low-rent office space with low-cost services organized for start-up businesses, often on a university campus. Once a business becomes a going concern, it leaves to establish itself permanently.

indemnity [I] Protection or insurance against loss.

> The company had *indemnity* against the fire through its casualty insurance policy.

indenture [L] A term meaning either a contract detailing the obligation of an issuer of a bond or a deed conveying real estate and detailing obligations by both the seller and buyer.

independent agent [I] See *agent*.

independent contractor [T] A person who is in business for himself and works on a by-project basis with various companies. If he works exclusively for one company, the IRS may deem him an employee of the company rather than an independent contractor, and he will lose certain tax benefits.

independent variable [M] The variable that calls the shots, so to speak, in algebraic formulas. It is the dependent variable that *depends* on the independent variable. In an algebraic expression, the letter x is often the independent variable, whereas y is the dependent variable.

indexation [E] An automatic linkage between a benefit paid and inflation. For instance, Social Security benefits are indexed to the CPI (Consumer Price Index).

indexes or indices [F] An index is a device that serves to indicate a value or quantity. The most famous index is the Dow Jones Industrial Index, which includes thirty major stocks that are considered to be a bellwether of the overall market. The most used index by finance professionals is the S&P 500 index, which includes the 500 largest capitalized stocks in the country. The S&P 500 is considered more useful because it is broader based and thus a better representation of the overall economy.

A Number of Market Indexes:

Dow Jones Industrial Average (DJIA) 30 major industrial stocks. There is also a transportation index of 20 airline, trucking, and railroad firms, and a utility index of 15 gas, electric, and power companies. The three averages form the Dow Jones 65 Composite Average.

S&P 500 500 of the largest companies based on capitalization (share price times the number of outstanding shares). The S&P 500 is comprised of 400 industrials, 40 utilities, 40 financial, and 20 transportation companies. This index represents about 70 percent of the stock market (New York, American, and NASDAQ).

Russell 2000 Considered a good index for smaller capitalized stocks, it consists of 2,000 stocks of the larger Russell 3000 (which is an index of the largest publicly held companies and represents about 98 percent of the stock market). The Russell 2000 generally represents companies with a market value of $250 million or less.

Extended Market The remaining stocks outside of the S&P 500 that are regularly traded. Since there are about 5,000 regularly traded stocks, the extended market consists of about 4,500 stocks.

EAFE (Europe, Australia, and the Far East) This Morgan Stanley index represents the major stock markets outside of the United States. It is comprised of about 1,000 stocks.

Salomon Brothers Investment Bond A useful index of Treasury, corporate, U.S. agency, and mortgage-backed securities. It is considered a good combination of income and price fluctuation.

---

index fund [F] A mutual fund that matches an index, such as the S&P 500 index, to provide a return that duplicates the overall market. Because mutual fund managers have a hard time beating the market averages, index funds have become very popular. Index funds also match other market averages, such as small cap stocks and international stocks.

indexing [RE] A method of changing the rate on an adjustable rate loan according to a set index—the Eleventh District of the Federal Reserve rate, for example. A loan that is indexed may be called an "indexed mortgage."

> The bank was *indexing* all the current loans to its best customers to three points above the prime rate.

index lease [RE] A lease that allows rent to move up or down, according to a set index.

> The Musico Corp. preferred *an index lease* in which its rent would change based upon the cost of living index.

index option [F] A right to buy or sell an option on an index, such as the S&P 500, at a set price on a set day. It is a bet that a certain market index will rise or fall at a certain time.

indictment [L] A formal accusation issued by a grand jury. An indictment is a charge that must be proven at a trial.

indirect costs; indirect labor; indirect materials [A] Costs that are difficult to identify and charge to a particular product and thus are lumped together as factory overhead.

individual retirement account (IRA) [T] The contribution of up to $2,000 per year of salary into a special account with a bank, mutual fund, or brokerage account, for an employee's retirement. If an employee is covered at work with a pension or 401(k)-type plan and is earning too much, his contribution will not be tax-deductible, although he may still make the contribution. A "rollover IRA" is a tax-free transfer typically from a 401(k)-type plan. A "self-directed IRA" is a brokerage account. A "conduit IRA" is a somewhat temporary IRA where money has been rolled over from a 401(k) or other qualified plan when a person leaves an employer. He may eventually roll that money into a plan of a new employer. A newer version of an IRA is called the "Roth IRA" after Senator William Roth of Delaware. See *rollover IRA* and *Roth IRA*.

industrial [B] An adjective that describes the production of goods and services. Financial services, transportation services, and utilities are not categorized as industrial businesses. Industrial goods are goods used by other businesses in the production of goods and services. Manufacturers make up one of the largest segments of the industrial sector in business.

> The shortage of *industrial* goods, such as heavy machinery and raw materials, accounted for much of the poor output in this quarter.

industrial espionage [L] The stealing of confidential materials or secrets of a company, such as product formulas, research data, or business plans.

industrial park [RE] A separate area set aside in a city where traffic and utilities are designed specifically for industrial use. Local governments create these zones to keep such use of land away from residential areas.

industrial psychology [HR] The study of worker motivation and behavior.

industrial revolution [E] The slow but significant change from an agrarian society to a manufacturing society. Before the 1800s, most people throughout the world, including Asians, Europeans, and Americans, lived an agrarian life.

inefficient markets [F] This can either refer to securities markets that are not widely analyzed or markets that are well researched with some investors having more useful information than others, such as insider information. In either case, inefficient markets are primarily of interest to speculators because the risks are hard to quantify.

inelastic [E] Term used to describe the demand or supply of a product or service that changes very little with changes in price. As the price of gas goes up, there may be little change in demand because truck drivers still need to deliver their goods, and people still have to drive to work. See *elastic*.

inequality [M] A mathematical relationship in which one side of an equation is greater than or less than another. The symbol > is greater than, and the symbol < is less than. An example of an inequality expression is $2x > y$, meaning that twice the value of x is always greater than y. An inequality can include the equal sign as well, such as the expression $4x \geq y$, meaning that four times the value of x is always greater than or equal to y.

in escrow [F] Money or other assets left in an account or in the care of someone until certain conditions or obligations are due. For instance, as part of a mortgage arrangement, banks often collect real estate taxes on a monthly basis in an *escrow* account and then pay once or twice a year to the municipality.

infinity (∞) [M] The mathematical concept of boundlessness or endlessness. It is a concept mathematicians use, but it is beyond comprehension.

inflation [E] A general rise in prices. An unexpected rise in inflation often will be detrimental to the stock market. Inflation is measured by the CPI (consumer price index). See the *consumer price index*.

> Increased consumer spending can result in periods of increasing, or at least mild, *inflation*.

inflation-indexed treasuries [F] See *I bonds*.

inflection point [M] A point on a graph where the curve, or line, changes direction.

infomercial [B] A program-length television show that is an advertisement. It is designed to look like regular programming but intended to promote a specific product or service.

information highway [C] Otherwise known as the "electronic highway" or "cyberspace," it is just another name for the internet. Has also been called the "Infobahn" or "Iway".

information technology [C] The use of a computer for storing, retrieving, and manipulating text, sound, and video.

infringement [L] A violation of a law, a contract, or a person's rights.

ingress [RE] The entrance, or the path, or door coming in, which is the opposite of *egress*.

inheritance tax [T] A general concept of a tax levied on assets in an estate when a person dies. More specifically, it is a tax imposed by some states by calculating the tax according to who receives the estate assets, as opposed to a tax simply by the amount in the estate. Commonly under an inheritance tax system, if a spouse or child receives assets, there is generally less tax imposed than for other more distant relatives, and the highest tax is imposed when a nonrelative receives the assets. The idea is that those who are closest to the deceased will have less tax imposed on the assets, and therefore more assets. Even though a distinction is made by recipient, the executor of the estate is still responsible for paying the inheritance taxes before distributions are made to the heirs. An inheritance tax is in contrast to an "estate tax," which, if there is a tax, is simply based on the total estate, regardless of who receives it. All states have either an inheritance or estate tax. Besides a potential tax levied by a state, there is also a potential federal tax, which is an estate tax concept. See *estate tax.*

in-house [B] Any job done within a business, as opposed to hiring an outside consultant or another company to do the work.

> Smithers preferred to have all the art work done *in-house*. It was less expensive, and he certainly had enough talented people on his staff to handle it.

initial margin requirement [F] The deposit an investor puts down on a new securities transaction before borrowing the rest from the brokerage firm. The Federal Reserve determines the minimum margin as a way to curb overspeculation in the market.

initial public offering (IPO) [F] A company's first stock offering to the public. Some IPOs cause a stir because many investors believe it's a time to make a killing, whereas experience has shown that IPOs often drop in price after an initial flurry of interest, and reality sets in.

injunction [L] A court order preventing an individual or a company from performing an act, such as a union from striking or a company from enacting a lockout.

injury [L] Any wrong or damage done to another.

> The woman spilled her coffee on her lap and sued the restaurant owner for *injuries* sustained from the scalding-hot beverage.

ink-jet printer [C] A printer with technology that allows one or more color inks to spray onto paper for high-quality printing. This is different from a laser printer, which, with a laser, paints dots of light onto an electrically charged drum and then places toner powder onto paper.

inner circle [S] The group of people in a company who are part of the key decision- or policy-makers.

in play [S] Term refering to a company that is generally performing poorly and ready for a takeover.

input device [C] A computer device to put information or data into the computer, such as a keyboard, a mouse, a scanner, or a modem.

inquest [L] A coroner's investigation into the cause of death.

insanity [L] The legal definition of a state of mental illness. If a person is declared insane, he is considered incompetent to stand trial.

insert key [C] The computer key that allows a user to insert words into a sentence without overwriting the existing words.

insider [HR] A term used with respect to executives who have limitations on when they may exercise stock options because they have inside information about the company.

insider trading [F] Trading based on inside information, a practice that is usually illegal. Since executives of a company have specific information about the company and company actions that could affect its stock price, they are restricted in trading in their stock. The Securities and Exchange Commission (SEC) monitors insider trading closely to preserve the integrity of the market. See *technical analysis*.

inside the Beltway [S] A term refering to the center of Washington, D.C., and to political influence. The interstate highways of I-95 and I-495 completely encircle the city. It is also called the Capitol beltway.

insolvency [L] The inability to meet financial obligations, which can result in bankruptcy.

> After a severe drop in sales, ZYX Corp. had to declare its *insolvency* and seek protection under Chapter 11 bankruptcy.

insolvent [B] Term used to describe a company that is no longer able to meet its financial obligations.

insourcing [B] A new word meaning the use of people and re-sources "in" the company, versus "outsourcing," which uses outside resources. It can also refer to internal services set up as semi-in-dependent units to sell their services to departments in competition with outside sources.

installment sale [RE] A sale in which payment is made over time in a series of installments, often annually. Taxes are generally due when payments are made.

installment sales method [A] An accounting method used for installment sales in which part of each payment is considered as cost and part is considered as profit. This is in contrast to "cost recovery method," in which all costs are recovered first, then profit is realized.

Institute of Real Estate Management (IREM) [RE] A professional organization for real estate managers, which offers the CPM and AMO designations.

institutional investors [F] Firms or organizations that invest large sums of money in investments. Insurance companies and pension systems are examples of institutional investors.

instruction [C] A command. If a user gives a command to her computer, such as pressing the Enter key, she has instructed it to accept the information.

instrument [L] A written formal document that provides an agreement and evidence of that agreement.

> The mortgage *instrument* had clearly outlined all the conditions for indexing the mortgage.

insurable interest [I] A company or individual that can identify a specific loss to be insured. For example Luciano Pavarotti, the opera star, could probably get insurance on his performance at a particular concert, but an average person could not. For the average person, missing a neighborhood concert would result in no specific monetary loss.

insurance [I] The business of offering financial protection due to specific losses or risks, such as life, property, auto, or health insurance.

insurance commissioner [I] The state official overseeing a state insurance's laws.

insured [I] A person or company who is covered for specific risks by insurance. The insurance company is called the *insurer*.

insured bonds [F] Municipal bonds, primarily state revenue bonds, that have purchased insurance against nonpayment of interest or principal. The insurance results in a less risky bond and a lower interest rate paid to the investor.

insurer [I] The insurance company that sells policies and insures against a variety of risks. The person or company who is covered is called the insured.

As *insurer*, the State Insurance Corp., reviewed all the claims made for the tornado.

intangible asset [A] An asset that has no physical substance but is still valuable to a company, such as a trademark, a patent, reputation, or goodwill.

integer [M] A whole number as opposed to a decimal or fraction.

integral [M] One of two calculations in calculus. The other is the "derivative." See *calculus*.

integrated circuit [C] The heart of a computer chip. It is the myriad tiny transistors and resistors etched onto semiconductor material that form the complete and complex circuit of logic for a computer.

integration [B] Combining or bringing different aspects of the production process together.

As the company began to show consistently high profits, the CEO began to think about possibilities for *integration.*

Four Ways to Integrate

forward integration The expansion of a business to be closer to the consumer. For example, a doll manufacturer buys toy retail outlets.

backward integration The expansion of a business back toward the tools of production. For example, a doll manufacturer buys a cotton mill for the fabric used in production.

horizontal integration The expansion of a business by purchasing another like company. For example, a doll manufacturer to buys its competitor's action-figure manufacturing facility.

vertical integration The expansion of a business forward and backward to be involved in all stages of production, distribution, and retailing. For example a doll manufacturer purchases the plastics company and the retail outlets.

integration [M] The process of calculating one of the two calculations of the calculus. The other process is "differentiation." See *calculus.*

integrity [C] Term usually used to refer to quality, accuracy, reliability, and timeliness of a sysyem or its date.

System *integrity* was violated due to error.

Intel [C] The leading manufacturer of integrated circuits in the world. It was founded in 1968 and developed the first microprocessor in 1971. It has produced a series of highly successful microprocessors, including the 286, 386, 486, Pentium, Pentium II, and Pentium III.

intellectual property [B] Material that is copyrighted, patented, or trademarked.

Protections for Intellectual Property (see entries under each term):

copyright©	such as: Copyright© 1999 by Princeton Review Publishing, L.L.C.
patent	such as a Bose audio speaker
service mark ˢᵐ	such as Financial Profilesˢᵐ
trademark™	such as Apple Computer's apple with a bite out of it
trade name	such as Intel Inside
trade secret	such as the formula for Coca-Cola

Intel microprocessors [C] The integrated circuits made by the Intel Corp. that are the standard for personal computers.

interest [F] Most commonly the term refers to money paid on the use of money. Loans, bank accounts, bonds, and other interest-bearing investments are all examples of interest. *Interest* can also refer to an investor's equity in a business; for example, an investor might buy a 10 percent interest in a business.

[M] In financial math, the amount of interest is usually calculated on the principal of the money invested and usually quoted as a yearly amount. Interest on $1,000 at 5 percent is $50 per year. This is known as "simple interest," in contrast to "compound interest," which accumulates interest during the year and earns interest on the accumulating interest as well as the principal.

interest-only loan [RE] A special loan in which the borrower pays back the interest for a set time and then the principal in one lump sum at the end of the loan period.

> Because its resources were scarce, Zippy Corp. was forced to take out an *interest-only* loan for capital expenditures.

interest rates [E] Rates of payments from bonds, notes, money market funds, CDs, savings accounts, or other interest-bearing investments. See *interest*.

interest rate curve [F] See *yield curve*.

interface [S] A term that generally means to interact with others but can also mean computer interaction with a user, as in the term "user interface."

interim financing [RE] A temporary loan that is usually paid off as soon as the full financing for a project comes through.

> To get the project going, ABC Co. was able to secure some *interim financing*.

intermediate bonds [F] Bonds or notes that have a maturity generally between two and ten years. They are considered less risky than long-term bonds, which have maturities of twenty to thirty years. Short-term bonds usually have a maturity of one to two years

internal audit; internal auditor [A] An employee of a company, usually in an independent department, who is responsible for auditing various aspects of the company. The job includes assessing accounting procedures, checking for fraud, and promoting efficient operations.

internal controls [A] Methods and policies to minimize errors and fraud and to promote efficient operations.

internal rate of return (IRR) [A] The effective rate of return on an investment over the life of a project. It can also refer to an internal rate of return used as a hurdle rate for accepting or rejecting proposed projects.

[M] The rate of return that discounts an even stream of payments to a present value. This is commonly used in real estate projects. The net present value is the actual present value of the uneven cash flow, whereas the interest rate is the IRR.

> The appraisers, accountants, and bankers all calculated the *internal rate of return* for the ten-year period that Zippy Corp. intended to own the factory before deciding if it was a good investment.

Internal Revenue Code (Code) [T] The body of tax laws in the United States. There are also tax rules and regulations that are more specific applications of the actual laws. The IRS is responsible for administering taxes according to the Internal Revenue Code.

> The author believes that it is called the *Internal Revenue Code* because it is written in such cryptic language.

Internal Revenue Service (IRS) [T] A branch of the U.S. Treasury Department that collects income tax and enforces the tax code. It can impose penalties, seize property, or take action if it is necessary to collect taxes.

> Petra called the *IRS's* toll-free 800 number (800-TAX-1040) to get a set of tax forms.

international fund [F] A type of mutual fund that invests in securities in countries outside the United States. This is in contrast to a "global fund," which invests in countries including the United States.

International Monetary Fund (IMF) [E] Created by the Bretton Woods agreement in 1944, it encourags international cooperation in monetary matters, including the fixing of exchange rates within a narrow range. It also provides economic advice to developing countries. The IMF is generally charged with stabilizing international currencies, versus the World Bank, which is charged generally to fight poverty and develop the economies of poor nations. In 1967, the IMF created Special Drawing Rights (SDR), which was intended to be an international currency but which has been of very limited value. In 1990, the IMF had 152 member countries, while in 1996, there were 181 members. See *Bretton Woods agreement*.

International Standard Book Number (ISBN); International Standard Serial Number (ISSN) [B] The number assigned by the Library of Congress to books or serial publications such as magazines, newspapers, and newsletters. ISBNs and ISSNs are used to identify and track these publications.

International Trade Commission (ITC) [E] A U.S. agency organized in 1974 to investigate and make recommendations about damage to the U.S. domestic industry by foreign businesses. Dumping is one of the practices the commission considers seriously. See *dumping*.

International Trade Organization (ITO) [E] An international body proposed in 1947 with the UN Organization, but never fully ratified. GATT now performs the functions envisioned for the ITO.

internet [C] A worldwide network of computer networks. It all began as a network of computers for the U.S. Defense Department called the Defense Advanced Research Projects Agency Network (DARPANET). It has since expanded to an ungovernable network of networks not managed by any one group. It is the source of an almost unimaginable amount of information, allowing access to thousands of user groups, files at many universities, and even video clips from the latest movies. Those who spend time on the net are even said to have become "netizens."

internet address [C] The actual full address for a user's internet or World Wide Web location. For example, the full internet address for The Princeton Review is: http://www.review.com. The "at" symbol (@) is often used as well. The last three letters indicate the type of organization; for instance ".com" means a business, ".org" maens a nonprofit organization, and so forth, as shown below:

.com and so forth:

.com	commerical
.edu	educational
.gov	governmental
.mil	military
.net	internet service provider
.org	nonprofit organization

internet relay chat (IRC) [C] Computer conferencing on the Internet. The system allows more than one user to participate at a time. A user can enter into a party line of sorts (usually arranged around a specific subject) and join in or just "listen" in by watching the typed communications on the screen.

interstate/intrastate [B] Business activities across state lines is *interstate* commerce, while business within one state is *intrastate* commerce.

interval [M] In statistics, the determination of how to separate data values into ordered and sequenced data.

inter vivos trust [T] A trust taking effect while the person is still alive. It is Latin for "between the living" and pronounced in-ter-VEE-vos.

intestate [T] Term that refers to dying without a will. The state laws determine who gets what; usually everything goes to spouses and children. Pronounced in-TES-tate.

in the ballpark [S] A phrase that indicates a person is generally in the right area but not necessarily precise. If an estimate is calculated, it is said to be *in the ballpark*, although it may not be 100 percent accurate.

in the black [S] Profitable. This is in contrast to the phrase *in the red*, which means less than profitable. See *in the red*.

in the money [F] See *at the money*.

in the red [S] Unprofitable. Presumably, red ink was used to denote negative figures so it would stand out. See phrase *in the black*.

in toto [L] Latin, meaning "in total."

intranets [C] In-house company networks.

intrapreneur [B] An employee of a large company that is given the flexibility and financial support to create new products or services and to provide the kind of close relationships with customers that a small entrepreneur usually develops.

inventory [A] The current stock of finished merchandise, goods in progress, raw materials, and supplies such as packing and shipping material. The two main ways of valuing inventory are first in, first out (FIFO) and last in, first out (LIFO). See *FIFO*.

> XYZ Corp. preferred to use the LIFO method of *inventory* valuation so it would show lower profits this year.

inventory control [A] Methods and procedures designed to minimize the costs of inventory, such as the economic order quantity, reorder point, and safety stock techniques.

inventory-to-sales ratio [A] A ratio comparing the amount of current inventory against sales of specific goods. It's a measure of how long it would take to sell existing inventory.

inverse [M] An opposite relationship. An example of an inverse relationship is the relationship between interest rates and the value of bonds. If interest rates increase, then the value of bonds decrease. See *correlation*.

investment [E] The economic use of capital to increase the production of goods and services.

investment advisor [F] See *ADV form*.

investment bank [F] A firm specializing in underwriting and advising firms in issuing new or additional securities to the general public, such as Goldman, Sachs & Co. and Lehman Brothers. In Britain it is called a "merchant bank." However, in the United States, a merchant bank usually refers to a select number of investment firms that buy companies, usually selling them later for a profit after turning them around to profitability.

investment club [F] A small group of average investors pooling their money and deciding on what stocks to invest in. It has been assumed that a well-run investment club could provide better than average investment returns; however, that is now called into question based on the recent controversy with the most famous of investment clubs, the Beardstown Ladies. In 1998 it was discovered by an outside journalist, and confirmed by an accounting firm, that instead of the 23.4 percent return the ladies advertised, they hadn't even beaten the overall market at 15 percent, but instead had only achieved a lowly 9.1 percent return.

investment grade [F] Bonds with a top rating of AAA, AA, A, or BBB by Moody's or Standard & Poor's.

> Mr. Smith advised his children to put their money in *investment grade* bonds only; he felt that junk bonds were silly and risky.

investment income [T] Income received from various investments and taxed as unearned income.

> The additional *investment income* Linda had realized from a short-term gain in the stock she sold put her into a higher tax bracket.

investment tax credit [A] A reduction of taxes permitted when a firm invests in certain assets. The Tax Reform Act of 1986 generally repealed this credit.

Investor's Daily [F] A daily newspaper for active investors.

investor sentiment [F] A measurement of investor advisers who are bullish or bearish. Too high a bullish sentiment is interpreted as a danger sign for the market.

invisible hand [E] A term used by Adam Smith to describe how individuals work for the greater good through their individual actions. He said that as an individual pursues his own ends he is "led by an invisible hand to promote an end which was no part of his intention."

invoice [A] A document sent to a purchaser showing the sale, delivery date, and the incurred fee.

I/O [C] Input/output. The way a computer works: A user puts data in, and the computer puts data out.

IP (Internet protocol) [C] See *TCP/IP*.

IRA [T] See *individual retirement account*.

IRD (income in respect of a decedent) [T] See *income in respect of a decedent*.

IRMA board [C] A connection allowing communications between a personal computer and a mainframe computer.

IRR (internal rate of return [A] See *internal rate of return*.

irrational number [M] A number that cannot be created by a fraction, such as the square root of 2. See *rational number*.

irrevocable life-insurance trust [I] A trust set up to receive the proceeds of a life-insurance policy.

irrevocable trust [T] A trust that cannot be changed once it's set up. Sometimes people who are not sure about irrevocable trusts set up a trust as revocable first and only after several years decide to make it irrevocable.

IRS Code [T] See *Internal Revenue Code.*

IRS Regulations [T] Specific and detailed instructions that have been formulated by the Internal Revenue Service that interpret the broad language of the tax laws called the "Code."

ISDN (Integrated Services Digital Network) [C] A fast and efficient digital network that can transmit voice, data, and video. It replaces the slow and inefficient analog telephone system.

ISO, ISO 9000, ISO 14000 [B] A series of quality standards originating in Europe in 1987 and adopted worldwide. ISO stands for the International Organization for Standardization. The 9000 is the block of numbers set aside for manufacturing quality standards, and 14000, for environmental management standards.

isolationism [E] The favoring of business activity only in one's own country, to the exclusion of other countries. Because today's economy is an increasingly global one, it is a narrow and potentially damaging outlook.

ISOs (incentive stock options) [HR] See *stock options.*

italics [C] A type style used to emphasize letters, numbers, or symbols by slanting the font of the characters.

iteration [M] The process of repeating a calculation, usually with one variable changing each time.

J

January effect [F] The tendency for the stock market to do well in the month of January. See *Super Bowl predictor*.

Japanese business terms [B] There are several words in the Japanese world of business that are becoming part of American business language as well, such as *kaizen* and *keiretsu*.

Know Your Japanese:

bunsha   The management philosophy of breaking up a company into smaller and more manageable business units.

kaizen   The word for continuous improvement.

kanban   The Japanese word for just-in-time inventory or manufacturing.

kanbrain   The just-in-time arrival of brain power.

karoshi   The Japanese term meaning death from overwork.

keiretsu   The cozy network within Japanese financial and business circles that work together.

JAVA software [C] Created by Sun Microsystems, it is an object-based, interactive, general-purpose programming language, commonly used in the creation of World Wide Web sites. A major advantage is that it can run on almost any computer or operating system.

jawboning [E] The exhortations of the president in particular to business, unions, or consumers, as opposed to specific legislation.

jeopardy assessment [RE] A procedure in which the Internal Revenue Service may seize property immediately if it thinks the property is about to be hidden to escape taxation.

> To prevent the president of Slimy Corp. from hiding those properties, the IRS moved quickly and used *jeopardy assessment* to seize them.

jet lag [S] The sluggishness a traveler feels after flying across several different time zones, especially to Europe or Asia. Some people are more affected than others.

JETRO (Japan External Trade Organization) [B] A Japanese organization that was ostensibly designed to help American small business sell its products in Japan, but has been accused of trying to better understand American innovation to help its own companies back in Japan.

JIT (just-in-time) [B] See *just-in-time inventory and manufacturing.*

jobber [B] A middleman in the sales process who buys goods from a wholesaler and sells them to a retailer.

> Zippy Corp. sold to a number of *jobbers*, who purchased quantities of finished zippers from Zippy and sold them to the small retail sewing supply stores around the country.

job-cost sheet [A] A record of the costs of a unit or batch of goods, usually including the direct materials and labor costs, and the allocation of factory overhead.

job description [HR] A listing of an employee's job duties and what is expected in terms of performance. A junior accountant's job description may include the responsibility of posting accurate information into the company's double-entry accounting software system, for example. The job description is often the basis for a performance evaluation and a merit salary increase. It can also be referred to as a "job specification."

job elimination [HR] The determination that a particular job is no longer necessary, usually part of a downsizing process at a company.

job enrichment [HR] An increase in a person's responsibility and/or authority, giving the person a bigger job.

job ranking [HR] A compensation department task to determine the relative value of various jobs within a company. Often there are subjective aspects, besides objective ones, in determining the ranking, such as how important or difficult the tasks of one job are compared to another.

job satisfaction [HR] The overall or specific contentment people enjoy from their job. This can arise from actual job responsibilities, pay and benefits received, interaction with other workers, and working within a company culture that provides personal satisfaction.

job security [S] A term often meaning that a person has a certain job protection because of specific job skills or knowledge. It can also mean a specific union agreement that protects the jobs of workers.

> Zim thought he had *job security* because of his knowledge of the mainframe computer, but the company decided to get rid of the large computer and Zim when it switched to PCs.

job sharing [HR] Term referring to two people sharing the same job but at different times. Thus two people are doing one full-time job. The two people may, for instance, work alternate weeks and keep each other informed of happenings on their watch.

job skills [HR] The specific knowledge and abilities that can make one person more valuable than another. Operating computer software, performing statistical calculations, making great presentations, and writing compelling proposals are all examples of job skills.

job specification [HR] See *job description.*

Johari window [HR] A model showing four equally divided parts of a square representing four key interactions between people. The four segments are (1) those things about a person that both she and others know, (2) those things a person dosen't know about herself but others do (such as personality idiosyncrasies), (3) those things a person knows about herself but others will probably never know (such as personal and professional secrets), and (4) those talents and possibilities about a person that she and others do not know about (her potential). It was created by Joe Huft and Harry Lagham, creating the word Joe-Harry or Johari, and is commonly used in management development programs.

joint and survivor (J&S) annuity or option [HR] The pension plan option providing for a survivor payment when an employee dies. Most commonly a 50 percent J&S option is selected by a married employee. Although there is a reduction in the pension, it provides 50 percent of the pension to the surviving spouse. See *pension plan*.

joint liability [L] The responsibility of two or more parties, or partners, for the actions of the others, usually in connection with a specific project or business activity.

joint life expectancy [I] Life expectancy of two people as opposed to one person. Joint life expectancy of a couple both at age seventy is about twenty years, even though the life expectancy of each person may be only about sixteen years. This means that there is a 50 percent probability that one of the two spouses will live about twenty more years.

joint return [T] The type of tax return married couples usually file. If separated, a person may elect to file a separate return so he or she is not responsible for the other person's taxes.

joint rotation [HR] The movement of employees to different jobs so a company has a better trained workforce and the potential to keep employees motivated.

joint tenancy [L] The legal term that applies to the ownership of a financial account or real estate property by more than one party. It is usually specified, or assumed by the amount each has invested, what percentage each party owns. For instance, a brother may have paid 75 percent toward the vacation home and his sister 25 percent. The rights of each party are usually transferred through a will. See *tenancy*.

joint tenancy with rights of survivorship (JTWROS) [T] The legal term that applies to the ownership of a financial account or real estate property where the surviving party will automatically own 100 percent at the death of the other party. Technically, both people own 100 percent. Typically spouses own financial accounts and real estate this way, as well as parents and children. Sometimes the full term is not written, but only the abbreviation JTWROS. See *tenancy*.

> As husband and wife, they had *joint tenancy with rights of survivorship* in their home.

joint venture [B] An agreement between two or more businesses to perform a task together or produce a product neither wants to do on it's own.

> Biggie Oil and Largesse Gas formed a *joint venture* to explore for oil and gas in the remote region of Alabascar.

journal; journal entry [A] The method of entering the detail of a transaction into a company's accounting system. Journal entries are then posted to a ledger, usually called the "general ledger."

journeyman [B] A skilled union worker who has successfully mastered a trade or specialty, such as plumbing, carpentry, or electrical work.

> General Building Corp. only hired *journeymen* for its different subcontracting positions.

JPEG (joint photographic experts group) [C] A popular standard for the compression of color pictures because of the detail that results. Pronounced JAY-peg.

judgment [L] A final decision by a court.

Jughead [C] An internet utility to search for key words within gopher menus.

junior partner [B] Someone who, to a limited degree, shares in the profits and decision-making of an organization.

> When Brown was made a *junior partner* at LMNO after only two years, she knew that it was simply a matter of time before she became a full partner.

junk bonds [F] See *high-yield bonds*.

jurisdiction [L] The authority given to a court or judge to handle a particular case.

jurisprudence [L] The study of law, including the principles underlying the system and the decisions rendered by the system.

jurist [L] A legal scholar.

jury [L] A group of people chosen randomly from the community who determine the facts and verdict in a case. Usually twelve people serve on a jury. A petit jury hears ordinary civil and criminal cases, whereas a grand jury hears cases to determine facts and accusations presented by a prosecutor for potential indictment.

just compensation [L] The full payment for property. The term usually applies to cases in which the state, through the power of eminent domain, takes over property for its use. This is commonly done when a highway is built, and property owners are due payment.

just-in-time inventory (JIT) [B] An inventory strategy of ordering from suppliers so that no storage is necessary; it arrives just when the inventory is needed. It supports just-in-time manufacturing operations.

just-in-time manufacturing (JIT) [B] A manufacturing strategy that only makes products when they are ordered instead of ahead of time. Dell Computer, for example, employs this technique. It requires swiftness and coordination of operations, inventory, and delivery.

K

kaizen [B] See *Japanese business words.*

kanban [B] See *Japanese business words.*

kanbrain [B] See *Japanese business words.*

kangaroo court [L] A court that has no legal authority. It is a slang term for a court that purportedly rendered an unfair verdict. The term dates from the 1850s, when it referred to irregular legal proceedings that jumped around like a kangaroo .

karoshi [B] See *Japanese business words.*

keep a lid on it [S] A expression to suggest that one shouldn't talk about a certain subject.

keiretsu [B] See *Japanese business words.*

Kennedy round [E] One of the so-called "rounds" or negotiations of international trade between the major countries of the world. The Kennedy round was held from 1964 to 1967. The last round, concluded in 1993, was called the Uruguay round. See *Uruguay round* and *GATT.*

Keogh plan [HR] Pronounced KEY-oh, it's a pension plan for the self-employed and partnerships. Keogh plans can take different forms, such as a defined benefit plan, a defined contribution plan, or a hybrid plan. These plans are often called H.R. 10 (House of Representives bill number 10) plans.

kerning [C] The adjusting of the space between letters so they look evenly spaced. Certain letter combinations look better if placed closer together, such as a "V" and an "A" as in VAT.

keyboard [C] The part of a computer that looks like a typewriter.

> Vic got a new ergonomic *keyboard* specially designed to reduce wrist strain.

Keynes, John Maynard (1883–1946) [E] Widely influential British economist and author. His ideas were published in his 1936 book *General Theory of Employment, Interest, and Money*. He stressed the important role of government in the economy, ideas that were behind President Franklin D. Roosevelt's actions during the Great Depression. His last name is pronounced KANES.

Keynesian economics [E] Economic theory based on the ideas of John Keynes, the British economist. One of the most distinguishing features is the emphasis on the active government role in an economy. Pronounced KAN-ze-en. See *Keynes, John Maynard.*

keypad [C] A small keyboard or a separate area of keys usually on the right side of a computer keyboard.

key-person insurance [I] Insurance for companies against the death of key management members. The insurance would pay the estimated amount, needed to keep the company going until a replacement could be hired. Companies could suffer or go out of business if key management, particularly owners, were lost by the company.

keypunch [C] An obsolete method of punching precise square holes into dollar-bill-size cards, usually called IBM cards, for processing first in a mechanical way and more recently by computer. The Hollerith machine used these cards in what is considered the first data-processing system, for the 1890 census. Herman Hollerith, a statistician who had worked at the U.S. Census Bureau, formed the Tabulating Machine Company, which merged into what is now IBM in 1911.

kickback [B] A rebate, usually given to a supplier or retailer in return for shelf space or services. The practice can be considered legal, unethical, or illegal, depending on the type of business and the secrecy of the payments. For instance, in retailing this is a standard practice, especially to secure shelf space. In the awarding of government contracts, this is illegal, especially when contractors secretly pay officials to secure a contract or deal.

> The city inspector was fired for receiving *kickbacks* from contractors in return for giving them city contracts.

kicked upstairs [S] A term referring to the management practice of removing an executive who was not performing adequately to a more senior position, usually one in which the executive is out of the way.

kicker [RE] An incentive or bonus for an investment. A kicker may be required by a lender to increase its potential return on the loan it's making.

> Peachy Bank took a chance with Zippy Corp.'s new venture, so in return the bank asked for a 10 percent *kicker* on the loan. If Zippy made the million-dollar profit it claimed it would owe Peachy Bank an additional $100,000 bonus.

kiddie tax [T] The tax for a minor under the age of 14 on investment income over a certain amount.

kidnapping [L] The forcible or fraudulent taking of a person illegally.

killer app or application [C] A software program that is very useful and exciting and has the potential to make its developers very rich. Early killer apps were word processors and spreadsheet programs.

kill fee [B] A fee, in media and publishing, to pay a writer or other creative person for a commissioned article, art work, or creative work that is rejected.

killing [S] A big profit.

kilobyte (K, KB, or Kbyte) [C] About 1,000 bytes. Actually it's 1,024 bytes, or precisely 2^{10}, that is, 2 to the 10th power. See *byte*.

kinetic energy [M] The energy an object generates because of its speed.

kiosk [C] A self-standing computer station or display area. Some companies use kiosks for benefit information where employees can get updates on their 401(k) plans. Pronounced KEY-osk.

KISS [S] An acronym for Keep It Simple, Stupid, meaning simpler is better.

kiting [A] Various illegal practices of creating false bank account balances by altering the account books, issuing checks in excess of existing balances, or altering the checks themselves.

kludge or kluge [C] A crude and inelegant computer program. Usually it is a first attempt and temporary solution to a problem. Pronounced KLOOJ.

knock down [RE] Construction material that arrives unassembled but totally ready to be assembled and installed.

Kondratieff cycle [E] Named after the Russian economist Nikolai Kondratieff, who postulated that capitalist economies follow long-duration cycles, namely fifty-four- or fifty-six-year cycles of peaks and valleys. It is sometimes referred to as the "K cycle."

krugerrand [F] A South African gold coin.

kurtosis [M] A statistical measurement of how well data values bunch around the center of a distribution. It is also referred to as "peakedness."

L

labor [E] In economic terms, a factor of production. It includes not only the physical number of employees but also their skills and experience.

labor costs [E] The total expenditure on payroll, taxes, benefits, and other costs associated with maintaining a workforce. Traditionally, there are three economic cost factors affecting business: labor, land, and capital.

labor demand [E] The aggregate of individuals needed to fill current job openings. As one of the factors of production, it is a force that can cause prices to increase or decrease. As the demand for labor increases in a growth economy, wages, salaries, and benefits tend to rise.

labor force [E] The aggregate of individuals who either hold existing jobs or who are available for work. By the U.S. Bureau of Labor Statistic's definition, the labor force consists of employed people over the age of sixteen.

> The *labor force* increased greatly the year that the first baby boomers hit age sixteen.

labor intensive [E] Industries that require more labor than average to either start or sustain a company, such as the automotive industry. This is in contrast to "capital-intensive" industries, such as oil refineries or chemical plants.

labor market [E] The economic market where wages, salaries, and the conditions of employment are determined by market forces.

labor unions [B] Organizations authorized by employees of trades or sectors of the economy to represent employee interests in bargaining for wages, work rules, and employee benefits. Unions may negotiate contracts or call for employee strikes. The AFL-CIO (American Federation of Labor-Congress of Industrial Organizations) is the largest union in the United States, representing employees from many different trades.

ladder portfolio [F] A bond investment portfolio comprised of a range of bond maturities, such as from two to ten years.

lading [B] A shipping term referring to the actual cargo. The bill of lading is a list of the contents of the cargo.

Laffer curve [E] The theory, popularized and named after American economist Arthur Laffer, that if tax rates increase too much, the total amount of tax revenues tends to level off. People adjust to the higher rates by finding ways around them. Then, if tax rates rise even further, perceived as confiscatory, then the tax revenues actually start to fall. According to the theory, tax receipts will eventually fall all the way back to zero if the rates are extraordinarily high. It is reported that Laffer first drew this relationship on a napkin during a luncheon.

lagging economic indicators [E] Data, ratios, or other figures that tend to come later, or lag, in an economic cycle, such as a build-up of inventories and rising prices. See *leading economic indicators*.

laid off [HR] Fired because a position has been eliminated, not because of poor performance. The phrase may be used as in, "Sally was laid off," or "There are lay offs at Widget Manufacturing."

Rose-Marie Stock, a New York recruiter and consultant, points out the euphemisms that abound for the traditional *laid off*. Here's an unlucky list of 13:

Corporate aligned, de-layered, downsized, fired, got the axe, given the boot, pink slipped, reduced-in-force, re-engineered, restructured, rightsized, terminated, and the latest heard on the internet—uninstalled.

---

laissez-faire [E] An economic theory stating that business is better off without government interference. In economic lingo, it allows for free markets with a minimum of government interference, thus producing the best allocation of a nation's resources. Pronounced Lays-a-FAIR. It originates from the French verbs *laisser* (to allow) and *faire* (to do).

> The president inaugurated a new era of *laissez-faire* economics when he announced that the government would be deregulating business.

lally column [RE] A steel support column.

> There weren't enough *lally columns* planned in the building's basement to meet the city's building code so the engineers had to redraw the plans.

LAN (local area network) [C] See *local area network*.

land [E] In economics, all natural resources, including the sea and outer space. Also considered one of the three factors in production, namely, labor, capital, and land.

land contract [RE] Real estate bought on an installment plan. In this specific type of contract, the buyer pays the seller in installments and uses the land but doesn't receive the deed or title until the final sales price has been paid.

> ABC Corp. decided to sell its property using a *land contract* rather than give Acme Corp. a mortgage; that way it could hold the deed and foreclose easily if Acme didn't perform.

land planner [RE] A consultant who studies an area and gives reports on traffic, amenities, appropriate use of natural and manmade resources, quality of life, etc. Land planners typically work for municipalities to develop a master plan for a community.

> Mr. Brown, *land planner* for the town board of Smallville, realized that the plan for an industrial park on the waterfront was not an appropriate use—the canal leading to it was virtually impassable.

landscape [C] A page orientation in which the page is wider than it is tall, just like a painted landscape. This is in contrast to the normal business letter orientation, called "portrait," which is taller than it is wide.

landscaping [RE] The verb, "landscape" means to add trees and shrubs and ornamental plantings to a site. The noun, "landscaping" refers to the actual plantings.

> As it was so dry, the company *landscaped* the area with cacti and rock gardens. However, the affect of this *landscaping* was so horrid that it made the property undesirable.

language [C] A set of characters that allows a computer to perform commands. BASIC, C, COBOL, and FORTRAN are names for some widely used computer languages.

lapse [I] The termination of an insurance policy because the insured did not pay the premium on time.

laptop [C] A very small computer that, can fit on one's lap and be easily transported.

> As Michele sat in the waiting area for her flight, she found herself surrounded by a sea of *laptop* computers, each perched on the laps of busy businesspeople.

larceny [L] The illicit taking of property, such as money. When violence or intimidation is used, it's called "robbery." "Grand larceny" is the taking of property worth over a certain dollar amount; taking property of a lesser value is called "petit" or "petty larceny."

large-cap fund; large-cap stock [F] The term "cap" stands for "capitalization," meaning the number of outstanding shares of a company multiplied by the price of one share of stock. A large cap stock can be defined differently but is generally considered a company with a capitalization, or cap, somewhere over $1 billion to $5 billion. A large-cap mutual fund is one comprised of large cap stocks. See *small-cap fund/stocks.*

laser [C] A device that creates a narrow, intense, and precise beam of light. The word is an acronym for Light Amplification from the Stimulated Emission of Radiation. It has found many uses from high quality printing to CD-ROMs (compact disc-read only memory). It was conceived at about the same time—1957—by Gordon Gould, a graduate student in physics at Columbia University, and Charles Townes and Arthur Schawlow of Bell Labs.

LaserJet [C] A Hewlett-Packard series of laser printers used for IBM-compatible computers.

laser printer [C] A printer technology that, with a laser and an electrically charged drum, places a black powder toner material onto paper. This is in contrast to an ink-jet printer, which sprays a jet of ink onto paper.

LaserWriter [C] A series of laser printers used for Macintosh-based computers.

last in, first out [A] See *LIFO*.

late charge [RE] A penalty a borrower must pay for not making a payment on time.

> Because his mortgage payment was due by the tenth of each month and he never paid until the twelfth, Whizzy incurred hundreds of dollars in *late charges*.

laundering [L] The illegal movement of money, from an illegal activity such as drugs, through a legitimate company so it looks clean.

law [L] The general activities of a company pertaining to legal matters. See *general counsel*.

LAWN (local area wireless network) [C] A LAN (local area network) connected by radio rather than actual wires.

lawsuit [L] Proceedings of a person or company in pursuing a remedy in a court of law. Often just the word *suit* is used. See *class action*.

lawyer [L] The professional that provides legal advice and representation for a company. Lawyers can be part of an organization (general counsel's office) or outside (law firm). See *general counsel*.

layout [C] In desktop publishing, the art of positioning artwork, graphics, and text for the most effective arrangement.

[RE] The arrangement of the rooms themselves in a building and the of space and details in each room.

> The *layout* of that house, designed by the famous Igoguchi Design Team, was so simple and useful that the house sold immediately.

LCD [C] See *liquid-crystal display*.

lead charitable trust [T] A trust to provide income for a specific charity while the person who sets it up is alive. When the person dies, the money, or principal, goes generally to a family member. It allows an ongoing donation to a charity through income from the trust while the principal is retained for the family.

leadership [B] A basic management concept for providing direction and initiative to accomplish business tasks. It refers to individuals but can also refer to a business as well. For instance, Microsoft has been considered to have taken leadership in software development.

leading economic indicators [E] Data, ratios, or other figures that tend to come early in an economic cycle. Each month the government announces a set of leading economic information, or indicators, such as housing starts or the amount of overtime pay earned by workers, which, if high, tends to predict a healthy economy. See *lagging economic indicators*.

leading question [L] A legal tactic allowed during cross-examination in a trial but not during direct examination. It is a question that presumes certain facts.

> During the cross examination, Smith was asked a series of *leading questions* including, "Isn't it true you saw Jones take the money from the till?"

lead time [B] In production, it is the time from initial startup to the completed product. In management, it is the time from the start of a project to its completion.

lean and mean [S] An organization that has the fewest number of people to conduct its business (the lean part). It also describes an organization where people are very motivated (the mean part). It is also called a real "corporate machine."

learning curve [S] The time it takes to learn something new.

lease [L] The written legal document for a rental agreement.

> The terms of the *lease* specified that the lessee was liable for any damage to the property.

leased fee estate [RE] The ownership interest of a person who owns property and leases out some or all of it. The leased fee estate entitles the owner to collect rents and other potential income from the property, and to repossess the property when the lease ends.

leasehold estate [RE] The ownership interest of a person or company renting a property, usually for a specific number of years. The leasehold estate includes the rights to use and occupy the property but not the right to sell.

> Mr. Brown realized that his *leasehold estate* was valuable when he sublet the factory he'd rented for $1,000 a month from ABC Corp. to XYZ Corp. for $2,000 a month.

leasehold improvement [A] An improvement made to leased property such as buildings, landscaping, and parking lots. The improvements are considered long-term assets.

least-squares method [M] A statistical calculation to determine how one variable is correlated to another. It is the method of summing the squared differences to a minimum.

LED [C] See *light-emitting diode*.

ledger [A] See *general ledger*.

left brain–right brain [S] Term refering to the two halves of the brain, left for logic and language, and right for art and visual patterns. It is felt that each half is responsible for, or at least concentrates on, different functions. Thinking can thus be referred to as "left-brain thinking" if analytical, logical, and reasonable, and as "right-brain thinking" if artistic, emotional, imaginative, and intuitive.

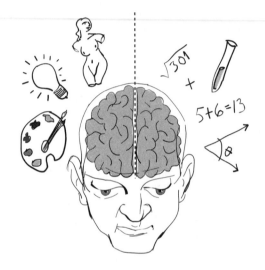

left/right justify [C] In word-processing software, the even flush of text on either the left or right margin. In business correspondence the text is always left justified, but most commonly not right justified. If a margin is not justified it is often called "ragged."

legacy [T] The same as a "bequest," which is the disposition of *personal* property through a will. This is opposed to "devise," which is the disposition of *real* property, or real estate.

legal description [RE] The section, block, and lot numbers of a property that identify it on a tax map, or a "metes and bounds description" in a deed or legal document that identifies the boundaries of the property.

> When Robert went to the county records to investigate the Hammer Headquarters building, he had the section, block, and lot numbers for the property, as that was how the *legal description* was filed.

legal matters [L] The general activities of a company to address areas of legal concern. See *general counsel*.

legal tender [F] Money that, by law, must be accepted as payment. On the United States dollar, and other denominations, these words appear: "This note is legal tender for all debts, public and private."

Lehman Brothers bond index [F] A widely used corporate bond index that measures the total return of a diversified portfolio of corporate bonds. See *Salomon Brothers investment bond index*.

lemma [M] A subpart of a theory.

less developed country (LDC) [E] A country whose economy is poorly developed. Sometimes these countries are termed "under-developed" or "undeveloped," but it is more common to refer to them as less developed countries, or LDC for short. Examples of countries that are classified as less developed are Cambodia, Mongolia, and Uganda. See *emerging countries*.

lessee/lessor [RE] In legal talk, the tenant/the landlord.

less than carload (LTC) [B] A shipping term referring to the expense without the discount associated with a full carload of freight.

> Because it was shipping such small amounts, Zippy Corp. had to pay the *LTC* rate.

let's do lunch [S] A common casual business phrase for "how about having lunch?"

letter of credit [F] A bank promise to pay once certain conditions are met, usually the shipment of goods.

letter of instruction [T] A document sometimes provided along with a will to specify in lay terms what a person wants done or to emphasize the intentions of the deceased person.

letter of intent [L] A preliminary agreement.

letter quality [C] A description of a printed page that is good enough to send out as a business letter. One of the great advantages of the laser and ink-jet printers over the old dot-matrix printers is that they are able to produce letter-quality documents, making the typewriter virtually obsolete.

leverage [F] The use of a high percentage of borrowed capital in an investment. Thus, investors use very little of their own money. Remember those levers from physics class? They enable a small amount of force to produce a larger amount of work. Leverage in financial terms is the same idea: It's using a small amount of one's own money to make a large investment. Highly leveraged companies have a lot of debt in relation to the amount of their equity.

> We bought a futures contract worth $10,000 for $1,000 by *leveraging* $9,000 of our investment.

leveraged buyout (LBO) [F] The takeover of a company using borrowed money. Investors typically make LBOs by pledging the assets of the company they are taking over and repaying the loans from company profits after the takeover is complete.

> The sharks at Zippy Corp. performed an *LBO* at Metal Corp. by borrowing huge amounts of money pledged against Metal Corp.'s assets.

liabilities [A] The money and obligations owed by a company.

> Acme Corp.'s *liabilities* were balanced by its assets and equity.

liability [L] A legal term that refers to the extent to which people or companies are legally bound to make good on a loss or damage resulting from their actions.

> The lawyers for Zippy Corp. gave the bad news that the company had a great deal of *liability* for its faulty zippers.

liability insurance [I] Protection against any claims made if someone is injured or property is damaged on one's premises.

> When their neighbor slipped and broke her arm on their front step, the Browns were relieved to have *liability insurance* to cover her claim against them.

liable [L] Term meaning legally responsible.

> The XYZ Network was held *liable* for fraud in reporting the unsanitary processing of meat in a food market chain because the reporters used fake resumes in getting jobs there.

libel [L] See *defamation*.

LIBOR (London Interbank Offer Rate) [F] A short-term interest rate in the Eurodollar market.

licensing [B] Getting legal permission to use something or do something that another person or company owns.

> The Intel Corp. *licenses* the use of the phrase "Intel Inside" to computer manufacturers.

lien [L] A legal claim on property.

> Because the homeowners would not pay their bills, the company was able to get a *lien* against their house.

life estate [RE] The use of a property and all the rights associated with it for one's lifetime.

> When the Bumsteads let their son buy their house, they retained a *life estate* so that they could continue to live in it until they died.

life expectancy [I] The average remaining life of a person. Today, at age sixty-five, individuals have about sixteen more years of life expectancy if male and twenty-one if female.

life insurance [I] Insurance against the premature death of a person.

Term versus Whole Life:

Term life insurance: Insurance that is pure life insurance in that it does not contain any investment build-up, only insurance. Typically, the annual premium rises as the insured gets older, and the insurance is in force for a specific term, hence its name. However, most term insurance policies allow the policyholder to renew the policy year-by-year but with higher rates. It is primarily for people who want insurance for only a period of time, such as the time it takes for their children to grow up. Term life insurance is considerably less expensive than whole life insurance because there is no investment component.

Whole life insurance: Insurance that is not only life insurance but also contains a cash value of investments. It will remain in force as long as the policy premiums are paid. The policy accrues value over time, and, if surrendered, the policyholder receives the cash value. The annual premium is usually set and does not rise, although it is considerably more expensive than term insurance. The traditional whole life policy now has a number of variations.

Variations On Whole Life Insurance:

Universal life insurance: Insurance in which the insurance company invests the cash value in interest-rate sensitive instruments, such as money market funds. Importantly, the insured is allowed to change the amount of life insurance, with a corresponding premium increase or decrease.

Variable life insurance: Insurance in which the insured person selects how the cash value is invested. The insurance company offers a number of choices, such as equity, bond, or money market investments.

Universal variable life insurance: Insurance that allows the insured to change the amount of the insurance as well as the selection of how the cash value is to be invested.

LIFO (last in, first out) [A] A way of valuing company inventory and calculating taxable profits. When inventory is sold, the cost of the inventory bought *last* (most recently) is charged first against what was sold. This is in contrast to FIFO, which uses the first inventory first. See *FIFO*.

light-emitting diode (LED) [C] A semiconductor diode display technology that emits a glow when charged. The light is usually red or green, but other colors can be generated.

light pen [C] A stylus-type pen that can "draw" on a computer screen by touching the screen and moving lines and objects.

lights-out factory [B] An idealized, fully automated (computerized) factory of the future that will require no people, thus no lights.

like-kind exchange [T] See *tax-free exchange*.

limited liability corporation (LLC) [B] A corporate form in which the business entity may be considered as a partnership for federal tax purposes and that has limited liability for the owners on the state level. The abbreviation LLC is used after the business name.

limited liability partnership (LLP) [B] A partnership arrangement in which the partners are only liable for their own actions, not for the other partners. The abbreviation LLP is increasingly appearing behind most accounting and law firm names.

limited partner [B] An investor with essentially no liability in an enterprise other than his or her investment. Limited partners generally have no say in the operation of the business. See *limited partnership*.

> GenCo. had a dozen or so *limited partners* who helped to finance the business but who did not interfere in the day-to-day operation of the business.

limited partnership [F] An investment in which investors provide the money for a business enterprise and "participate" in the profits, losses, or tax credits but not in the operation of the business. The general partner manages the business. These investments are essentially ill-liquid; they cannot be bought and sold freely. Typically a partnership purchases property (real estate), or items (equipment leasing), or mineral rights (oil and gas) for specific periods of time, usually five to seven years, and then intends to sell the property and rights hopefully realizing profits and passing them on to the investors. These investments have fallen out of favor because of their past poor performance. See *limited partner*.

limit order [F] Instructing a stock broker to buy a stock only when the stock falls to a specific price or to sell when the stock rises to a specific price. The order may be good until canceled (GTC) or a day order. This is in contrast to a "market order," which directs the broker to buy or sell immediately at whatever the market is. See *day order*.

> We gave the broker a *limit order* to buy the shares when the price dropped to $2.

line [B] Term that refers to the selection of products a company offers. It can also refer to the production line where products are assembled.

linear [M] A mathematical expression resulting in a straight line when graphed.

linear programming [M] A mathematical method of finding the optimum or best solution to a complex problem. On a technical level, linear programming is the solving of linear equations. Business applications include distribution systems, manufacture scheduling, and the mix of products a company offers.

linear thinking [S] Incremental step-by-step logic, as opposed to conceptual thinking.

line authority [B] The management authority to control and make decisions that affect people in the chain of authority.

line graph [M] A common graph showing a line connecting the important points. See *graph*.

line responsibility [HR] Direct responsibility of a department head for employees who report to him or her. This contrasts with a functional or "dotted-line responsibility" that sometimes exists in a company. See *dotted-line responsibility*.

linkage [S] The connection and synergy between business units within a company.

liquid [F] Any asset that can be immediately converted into cash. A checking account is a liquid asset because it can be used in the same basic way as cash. The process of converting assets into cash is called "liquidating."

liquid asset [A] Any asset in the form of cash or one that can easily be converted to cash.

XYZ had very few *liquid assets*; it wasn't able to make any major purchases until it received a loan from the bank.

liquidate [L] To sell assets, usually to pay debts.

Acme Corp. had to *liquidate* its business to pay off its creditors.

liquidating value [A] An estimated amount of money an asset would sell for if a company was liquidated, or closed down. Also called *"break-up value."*

liquidation [A] The process of closing down a company, including selling the assets of the company and paying creditors.

liquidation price [RE] A price below market value, usually occurring when there is not enough time to let a property stay on the market and get the best price. The price the seller ends up taking is called the "liquidation value" of the property.

When Zippy Corp. went bankrupt, it had to sell off many of its real estate holdings at a *liquidation price*.

liquid-crystal display (LCD) [C] A display technology used on calculators and especially laptop computer screens, originally just black and white until color technology was developed. The LCD was developed in 1963 at the RCA Sarnoff Research Center in Princeton, New Jersey.

liquidity [E] The ability to convert assets into ready cash to meet financial obligations.

liquidity trap [E] The situation wherein interest rates have been reduced so low that monetary policy no longer can work. Monetary policy tries to stimulate the economy by pushing interest rates down.

lis pendens [L] The legal notice that a suit is pending. Pronounced les-PEN-dens.

litigation [L] The engagement of the legal process.

littoral [RE] The shore area of property. It can also refer to property that borders on water.

living trust [T] A trust that is funded with assets while a person is alive, just as its name implies.

living will [T] A document that specifies how one is to be treated for medical purposes if incapacitated. Also, the document can specify if organs are to be donated. This is in contrast to a "will," which specifies how financial assets are to be distributed after death.

Lloyd's; Lloyd's of London [I] A consortium of insurance companies based in London that are known to insure unusual risks. It is not a single insurance company as many people suppose but a group of companies.

LLP [B] See *limited liability partnership*.

load [C] To put a program into a computer's memory from a device, such as a disk.

> I just *loaded* that new version of Doom on my computer—let's play it!

[F] The amount of the upfront commission charged when investing in a mutual fund. See *load funds*.

load-bearing wall [RE] See *bearing wall*.

load funds [F] In mutual funds, the upfront commission charged to the buyer of the fund. A "front-end load fund" is one in which the commission is paid up front when the fund is purchased. A "back-end load fund" is one in which the commission is paid when the fund is sold. A "no-load" means that there's no commission on the purchase of the fund. A "low load fund" has a low commission.

> The offer price on that fund was higher than its net asset value, so Fred figured out that it must be a *load fund*.

loading [I] The part of an insurance premium that pays for the normal operating expenses of the insurance company, such as staff and administrative costs.

loan [E] Money borrowed by individuals, businesses, or governments to finance activities.

loan-to-value ratio [RE] Ratio of the amount of money a bank will lend for a mortgage to the value of the property that is being mortgaged.

> Because the bank needed a *loan-to-value ratio* of less than 80 percent, the Smothers Company could not take out a mortgage of more than $800,000 on its property appraised at $1,000,000.

lobbying [B] The efforts of businesses or business groups to influence actions in Congress or the president, or locally at the state or city level.

local area network (LAN) [C] A group of computers connected directly to each other by cable. It's common for a company to link its computers together.

> The philosophy department has its own *LAN*, which is hooked up to other departments by a WAN (wide area network).

local taxes [T] Taxes collected through local municipalities; they are in addition to state and federal taxes. These taxes, often called real estate taxes, are for police, schools, and libraries.

> After paying the federal and state taxes, Sharon was aware that other taxes were owed: sales, excise, and *local taxes*.

location-location-location [RE] A common phrase in real estate meaning that the location of a property is the one and only thing that is important. Other factors are also important, depending on the property or the purpose the owner has for it, such as how it is financed or whether it has any water rights.

lock box [A] The use of a post office box number that is actually within a bank for the quick depositing of checks. For instance, when one sends a check to cover an American Express monthly bill, the post office box number on the envelope is not the crditor's headquarters but in fact a local bank. First, it's within the person's state so the check clears quickly, and second, it's actually within a bank so the money gets deposited immediately. It's part of an effective cash management program.

[RE] A locked box that contains keys to a property so brokers can show it. Usually written without the space between the words as lockbox.

lockout [B] The closing of a plant or business by an employer as a means to force employees to accept management's labor contract proposals. The 1998-1999 NBA (National Basketball Association) lockout of the players is a noteworthy example. This is in contrast to a "strike," where workers refuse to work to try to force management to accept labor's contract offer.

loft [RE] Attic space or one of the upper floors of a warehouse or factory.

> In the 1980s, many artists rented inexpensive *loft* space in the warehouses in lower Manhattan because they liked the wide, tall, and open rooms.

logarithm [M] The power, or exponent, of a mathematical expression. In the equation $100 = 10^2$, 2 is the logarithm of 100, to the base 10. It is written as $\text{Log } 100_{10} = 2$. Most people normally think of logarithms, when they think of them at all, to the base of 10. However, in mathematics, the base can be any number, including e, which is called the natural logarithm. (See e.) It's called natural because it describes relationships often found in nature, such as the growth of bacteria.

logarithmic curve [M] A nonlinear curve that uses logarithms.

login [C] The same as log on. See *log on/off*.

logo [B] A symbol or representation associated with a company or organization. For instance, The Princeton Review uses a bold red arrow pointing upward on a slant, and Random House uses it's famous house symbol.

log on/off [C] To start up or shut off computers, or to enter/exit a network or internet service provider. Most often a user ID is necessary to log on. This is the verb form. The noun form is usually written with no space between the words as "logon" and "logoff."

long bond [F] A bond with a maturity usually longer than ten years. The popular thirty-year Treasury bond is often quoted as the "long" interest rate. An investor who buys these bonds is said to be "going long." The U.S. Treasury issues twenty- and thirty-year bonds.

long-term capital gain or loss [T] A gain, or loss, on an investment or asset held for over one year. Any asset held for a shorter period is called a "short-term capital gain" or "loss." The holding period for a long-term capital gain has varied as the law changed, but beginning in 1998 the period of a year-and-a-day was restored.

long-term care [HR] Comprehensive medical and nonmedical treatment in the care of the disabled, especially the elderly.

long-term debt [A] Notes or bonds issued by a company, usually longer than one year or longer than current liabilities.

lookup [C] A data search in spreadsheet software. It is used within a macro, where a user wants to reference a table and find a specific value within that table.

loophole [T] See *tax loophole*.

loose cannon [S] A dangerous person without supervision. A person who generally gets into trouble or causes trouble and needs to be kept on a short leash. The term originated from ships of yore when a cannon got loose from its position and rolled freely on deck—a dangerous prospect.

loose money [E] See *easy money*.

lose-lose [S] See *win-win*.

loss [A] The lack of a profit during a specific period of time.

   [I] Damages to individuals or companies due to injury or destruction of property.

loss leader [B] The strategy of selling a popular product at a low price to attract customers, who hopefully, once attracted, will buy other merchandise.

Lotus Notes [C] A useful computer groupware that allows for E-mail, fax, data transfer, and other communications between employees.

Lotus 1-2-3 [C] A popular spreadsheet software program introduced in 1982. See *spreadsheet*.

lowballing [S] The practice of setting low standards or goals so they can be easily met. It can also mean giving a low bid on a job to ensure getting it. Sometimes a consulting firm will lowball a project bid so it can put some idle people to work.

lowest common denominator [M] The smallest number to which all other numbers in a group can be changed.

low-grade [B] Term used to describe an item of poor quality.

> Don't purchase anything from that store—they only sell *low-grade* parts.

Luddites [S] People who are averse to technology. It all started with a man named Ned Ludd, who in 1779 broke into a house and smashed hosiery knitting machines. Then in the early 1800s, British workers who destroyed other labor-saving textile machines to stop progress were referred to as "Luddites." The term is now used for people against technological progress.

lump-sum distribution [T] The distribution of all money in a pension or 401(k) plan as a single sum. Because these types of plans are considered "qualified," which means they meet certain tax criteria, or qualification, they are eligible to be put into a Rollover IRA or have special tax considerations.

> When Mr. Banko received a *lump-sum* payment upon his retirement, he had to either pay a substantial income tax on the amount or put it into a rollover IRA.

lump-sum purchase [B] A purchase of several items or assets for a single amount, usually at a discount.

> The owners at XYZ Corp. were able to make a *lump-sum purchase* of all of ABC Corp.'s inventory when ABC went out of business.

luxury tax [T] An excise tax on specific expensive items. Luxury cars, very expensive jewelry, and large boats are examples of items that may incur a luxury tax. These taxes can end up reaping little revenue because wealthy taxpayers either defer their purchases or buy used items.

The *luxury boat tax* caused such high unemployment within the U.S. boat industry that it was repealed.

M

Maastricht Treaty [E] A European agreement reached in 1991 that called for a closely knit economic community. It has led to the recent economic unification of Europe. The name comes from the Dutch town where the conference was held.

MAC; Macintosh [C] A series of computers introduced by Apple Computer in 1984.

Machiavellian [S] An unscrupulous business person. The term comes from the Italian writer Niccolò Machiavelli (1469–1527) who wrote *The Prince* in 1513. In it, he describes methods by which a strong ruler can gain and keep power, including cruelty and deceit. He also said that to be feared gives a ruler more security than being loved.

machine tools [B] Power-driven and occasionally computer-controlled equipment used to cut and shape metal, such as drill presses, grinders, lathes, and milling machines. The production and sale of these sophisticated machines are considered gauges of economic activity.

MAC OS [C] The Apple operating system that runs the computers of the MAC (Macintosh) series.

macro [C] A short program inside a regular program that is designed to carry out a specific command or function. A macro can automate a boring, repetitive, or difficult task so the user doesn't need to go through all the steps each time.

macroeconomics [E] The branch of economics dealing with aggregate aspects of the economy, such as supply and demand, how markets work, and the interrelations between countries and economies. Some of the subjects it covers are inflation, unemployment, fiscal and monetary policies, and the balance of payments. It is the study of the whole economy, in contrast to "microeconomics," which studies how individual people or companies operate within the economy.

Madison Avenue [B] A symbol of the advertising center where ideas for promoting products and services originate. Named for the actual street in New York where many of the major advertising firms were based; many have now gravitated to other locations.

magistrate [L] A public official who performs a low-level judicial function, such as a justice of the peace who performs marriages.

magnetic ink character recognition (MICR) [C] A machine-readable code used in the banking industry. Those numbers at the bottom of a check are read by computers to direct where the check is going and from whence it came. All banks in the United States and banks in many foreign countries use MICR readers to process their checks.

mailing list [B] The names and addresses of potential customers.

[C] On the internet, a service to which one can subscribe to get E-mail about a certain topic. Some mailing lists are just like newsgroups, except the information comes right to the subscriber's mailbox. Some are moderated, meaning that someone out there decides which posts to send out to which members.

mail merge [C] The word-processing method of combining a form letter file with a file consisting of names and addresses to produce and print individualized letters.

mainframe [C] A very large, powerful computer and system capable of manipulating and storing most of the data of large corporations. The PC (personal computer) has become so powerful that it can run applications that previously required a mainframe.

major medical [HR] Health insurance primarily for large medical expenses such as surgery and hospitalization.

Malcolm Baldrige Quality Award [B] Established by Congress in 1987, it is a major award to those companies that demonstrate outstanding quality in their products, services, and customer satisfaction. The award is named after the late Secretary of Commerce Malcolm Baldrige, a proponent of quality management.

malfeasance [L] A wrongful act, usually by a public official. *Misfeasance* is the improper execution of a lawful act. *Nonfeasance* is the failure to perform duties a person was officially sworn to do.

malice aforethought [L] Malice is a general term for a state of mind that accompanies a wrongful act. Malice aforethought is the state of mind in connection with a predetermination to commit a crime such as homicide.

malpractice [L] Wrongful conduct in a profession or field. A doctor who does not perform a medical procedure as generally accepted can be liable for a charge of malpractice.

Malthus, Thomas (1766–1834) [E] A British economist who predicted that the eventual growth of the population would outstrip the means to produce enough food. These ideas were written in his 1798 *Essay on the Principle of Population*. Although this calamity did not come to pass, there are still Malthusians who predict such dire events in the future.

managed care [HR] A term applied to health insurance, specifically HMOs and PPOs, in which there is some restriction on the doctors a person can see. This is in contrast to the traditional fee-for-service, where one is free to select whichever doctor she or he wishes. See *health insurance*.

management [B] A term that can either mean the group of people who run a particular business, or the general art of how to run a business. Management as a general art encompasses planning, organizing, staffing, controlling, and leading.

> When *management* and labor didn't agree on the terms of the new labor contract, labor threatened to strike.

management by objectives (MBO) [B] A method of management in which specific company objectives are set that can be quantified and measured. Compensation and bonuses are then rewarded based on the accomplishment of those objectives. See *total quality management*.

management by walking around (MBWA) [B] A method of staying in touch with employees and problems by being present from time-to-time at production locations.

management consultant [B] A professional firm or individual who offers management advice to companies.

management fee [RE] The fee, usually monthly, paid to the company that operates a building on a day-to-day basis.

The co-op charges included a monthly *management fee*, sent to the co-op management company.

[F] The fee paid to the managers of a mutual fund, usually one-half to one percent of the total money invested. See *mutual fund fees*.

management information system (MIS) [B] See *data processing*.

management style [B] The general orientation of an executive or company toward the business or employees. Companies may be said to be employee-oriented, bottom-line-oriented, or community-oriented, depending on the attitude and philosophy of the company.

management training [HR] Courses and seminars given to increase the knowledge of the employees in a company. Topics often include presentation skills, time management, and how to be a better manager.

manager [B] A person who has been given responsibility over a department or activity.

M&A [B] See *mergers and acquisitions*.

mandamus [L] A directive of a court that a public official perform some act, usually when time is of the essence.

mandatory minimum withdrawal age $70\frac{1}{2}$ [T] For IRAs (individual retirement accounts) withdrawals must begin at age seventy-and-a-half. These mandatory withdrawals are minimum amounts, often only about 5 percent. If these minimum amounts are not met, a penalty of 50 percent of what should have been taken out can be levied. This rule was intended to make sure income taxes are eventually paid, even if a person did not need the income.

manic-depression [HR] A severe psychological disorder causing a person to swing between mania (excessively intense) and depression (sadness).

manslaughter [L] Homicide without malice aforethought. See *malice aforethought*.

manual labor [B] Labor that involves the use of one's hands. Carpentry, assembly, and digging are examples of manual labor.

> The road crews insisted that no *manual labor* be done on days when the temperature rose above ninety-five degrees.

manufacturer's agent or representative [B] Sometimes known simply as a "rep," it refers to a person outside a company who officially sells the company's products. A rep may represent a number of companies or just one.

manufacturing [B] The general term for a company's activities in the fabrication and assembly of raw materials into finished products. This can involve large-scale automated machines, assembly lines with combination of workers and some automation, or simple manual labor. See *mass production*.

manufacturing sector [E] The business sector based on manufacturing, versus the service sector. Manufacturing is the production of consumer items.

margin [A] The difference between the cost and selling price of a product, which is profit. Comes from the phrases "margin of profit" or "profit margin." See *gross margin*.

[C] The distance from printed material to the edge of the paper.

margin account; margin call [F] A line of credit with a stockbroker. With a margin account, an investor can leverage, or borrow, up to a certain percent of the price of a stock from a broker. If the value of a stock that has been bought on margin falls, the broker may make a margin call: either the investor puts more money into the margin account or the stock will be sold. It's the broker's way of minimizing the risk in the investment. Although the basic Federal Reserve rules require that an investor puts up at least 50 percent of the price of an original transaction, only 25 percent generally needs to be put up with an ongoing account. A number of brokerage houses increase this amount to 35 or 40 percent.

> Claudia wanted to invest $10,000 in SPAM Corp. but because she had a *margin account*, she had to put up only $5,000, and her broker covered the rest.

marginal analysis [E] The study of how a small change affects an economic outcome. That is, how things are affected at the edge or margin. It tries to answer practical problems such as how profit is affected by producing one more item, how the demand is affected by increasing the cost by a small amount. This has become a fundamental study of economics. This study within economics is often called marginalism. The mathematics of "one more" is part of the calculus. See *marginalism* and *utility*.

marginal cost [E] The cost of producing "one more." The greater the quantity produced, the lower the cost of each item. Because a company wants to make a profit, it is important to produce a quantity high enough to make a satisfactory profit.

> The accountant of Zippy Corp. had assessed the *marginal cost* of each type of zipper so she knew which were worth making more of and which were not.

marginalism [E] The economic concept of decreasing (or increasing) interest in products or services as a person uses them. For instance, a person may be excited to go on Space Mountain in Disney World, but after each run he probably gets less and less excited about the ride. The desirability of this service is said to decrease the *utility* for him at the margin. Some services, such as traveling first class, increase desirability at the margin. See *marginal analysis* and *utility*

marginal revenue [E] The revenue received by selling "one more." The more quantity a company wants to sell, the more the price will have to drop in order to attract more consumers.

marginal tax rate [T] The rate paid on the last dollar of income earned—the highest tax rate paid. See *effective tax rate* and *tax bracket*.

marginal utility [E] See *utility*.

marital deduction [T] See *unlimited marital deduction*.

market [E] Term referring to either the potential customers or the geographic area where customers reside. In general, it means the place where buyers and sellers of a good, product, or service meet.

The *market* for Zippy Zippers has increased steadily since zippered jackets came back into style. The *market* area for their sale is Atlanta—the center of the zippered-jacket phenomenon.

market analysis; market study [RE] The study or analysis of a particular market, including such factors as economic resources, levels of unemployment, and current and historical market trends in the area. The marketability study analyzes how well a particular product may be sold in an area.

The XYZ Corp. ordered a *market analysis* before it started its 500-unit residential development. It wanted to see what the chances were of selling all the units within two years.

market area [B] The geographic area of expected demand for a product or service. See *SMSA (Standard Metropolitan Statistical Area)*.

market basket [B] The list of household items that comprise the "basket" used to measure increases in the CPI (consumer price index). The CPI is the main measurement of inflation.

market breadth [F] The proportion of stocks rising in an upward market or falling in a declining market. If many different sectors and sizes of stocks rise together, it is said to be a broad market participation. If only one sector rises, it is said to be a narrow market participation. Investors look for a broad market movement for the best investment environment. See *technical analysis*.

market correction [F] See *correction*.

market cycles [F] Up and down shifts in the market as economic and business activities shift. The market goes up in a bull market and backs down in a bear market. See *business cycle*.

market economy [E] An economy in which the free market system operates.

market forces [E] The dynamics of supply and demand and price movements.

marketing [B] The general term for all activities of a company that occur after the manufacturing of its products. It usually includes distribution, storage, advertising, and selling of products. The term is also commonly used to refer to the advertising and promotion of a product or service.

market momentum [F] Generally, the number of stocks hitting new highs. If a high percentage of stocks is increasing its value, it's indicative of *market momentum*. See *technical analysis*.

market order [F] An instruction for a broker to immediately buy or sell a stock. The investor is thus willing to accept what the market offers. This is in contrast to a "limit order" which specifies at what price the broker is to execute the investor's order.

> We called our broker and placed a *market order* to sell our shares in XYZ Corp. when we heard of its impending financial problems.

market research [B] The compiling and analysis of consumer information so as to project future consumer interest in specific products or services.

market share [B] The percentage of the market a particular company or product has.

> Zippy Zippers reported that it has 22 percent of the plastic zipper *market share*.

market timing [F] An ideal investing strategy of switching into or out of stocks just before they rise or decline.

market value [A] Generally, the price at which a product or asset can be sold. Also called "fair market value."

[RE] The term used to define the most probable price a property will sell for in a competitive market with an informed buyer and seller who are not under any duress during the sale.

> The real estate appraisal, assuming all fair market conditions, gave the *market value* for the subject property as of October 4, 1996.

Markov analysis [M] A mathematical method of analyzing current movements to predict future movements. It is used for marketing analysis, among other applications. It is named for the Russian mathematician Andrei Andreevich Markov (1856–1922).

Markowitz, Harry (1927–) [F] An American winner of the Nobel Economics Prize for his early work on investment portfolio optimization. He pioneered this approach beginning in 1952 when he postulated that one's individual holdings do not matter as much as one's overall asset allocation.

mark to the market [F] The process of tallying all futures accounts at the end of each business day by crediting or debiting them even though they were not sold. This is done because futures contracts move up and down during the day, and it enables brokers to check margin requirements for their customers.

markup [B] The difference between what a retailer pays for a product and what it charges its customers.

> The *markup* on those dresses is nearly 100 percent—the store pays $50 for them and charges $99.95.

marriage penalty [T] A fact of U.S. tax laws by which a married couple will generally pay more by filing a joint tax return than if their incomes were split and they were taxed as two single people. This problem was minimized somewhat by changes in the tax laws in 1981, though some couples are still penalized.

married put [F] A hedge position by purchasing a stock and its put option at the same time, that is, marrying them together. This strategy allows for an unlimited upside potential through the stock, while providing some insurance for a downturn with the put. A put is an option to sell the stock at a certain price.

Marshall, Alfred (1842–1924) [E] A British economist trained as a mathematician who brought numerical precision to the field of economics. He is known for an explanation of the concept of utility, which states that the more a person buys a particular product, the less utility it provides, until it has no utility and the person no longer buys it. He coined the term "elasticity" to describe changes in demand for changes in price. See *elastic* and *utility*.

Marshall Plan [E] A critically important American effort to rebuild Europe after World War II. General George Marshall was in charge of formulating the plan.

Martindale-Hubble [L] A handy reference that lists all lawyers in the country and their specialties. It comes in several volumes and is found in most business and general libraries.

Marx, Karl (1818–1883) [E] A controversial German economist. In 1848, he wrote the *Communist Manifesto* with Friedrich Engels. Later, in 1867, he wrote *Das Kapital*. He postulated that capitalism would self-destruct and evolve into communism, where private property would be eliminated, and there would be only one class of people.

Maslow's hierarchy of needs [S] A list of individual needs organized from low to high priority that was postulated by Abraham Maslow (1908–1970). At the bottom are physiological needs such as food and water, then safety needs of security and stability, then belonging needs of affiliation and love, then the need for self-esteem, ego, and finally the need for self-actualization. His theory that lower needs must be satisfied before attaining the higher needs and his sequence of needs have been challenged.

mass marketing [B] A marketing strategy of selling products or services throughout the United States with one strategy, ignoring regional or segment differences.

mass media [B] Television, radio, magazines, and newspapers that reach a large segment of the population.

mass production [B] The manufacturing of products in quantity through assembly lines, automation, and high-speed machinery. The first mass production was demonstrated and developed by Eli Whitney (inventor of the cotton gin) in 1798. He contracted with the U.S. government to produce 10,000 muskets. Until then, each was made individually. He developed a new gun and all the machinery to make it with an assembly line. Over a hundred years later, Henry Ford, in 1913, established the assembly line for automobiles with the help of Frederick Taylor, a leading efficiency and scientific management expert. Today, computers automate production through CAM (controlled automating machinery) and design the products and parts with CAD (computer-aided design).

master limited partnerships (MLPs) [F] A limited partnership that passes its profits (and losses) on to investors; however, they resemble stocks in some ways. Unlike limited partnerships that are ill-liquid, no ready market MLPs are traded on stock exchanges.

master plan [RE] An overall plan for land use by a community or city.

masthead [B] The section of a publication that lists the owners, publishers, editors, and staff.

matching gifts program [HR] An arrangement offered by some companies that will pay a charity or educational institution a sum that matches an employee's contribution.

materiality [A] A basic accounting concept stating that only those events that are relatively important to the business need to be recorded in the accounting records.

material witness [L] A person whose testimony is central to a case.

math coprocessor [C] A special computer circuit that performs high-speed mathematical calculations.

matrix [M] In mathematics, a rectangular array of numbers, usually in large parentheses. The horizontal numbers are referred to as rows and the vertical numbers as columns. A similar-looking but very different array of numbers is called a "determinant," which is bracketed by straight lines. A determinant equates to a value, whereas a matrix does not. See *determinant*.

matrix algebra (or matrix math) [M] The specific order of arithmetic operations involving matrices, such as addition, subtraction, and multiplication. See *matrix*.

matrix management [B] The method of management in which a manager of a project uses services and people from several functional areas of the company. Often, these are temporary projects. Employees assigned to a project have dual responsibilities, to the project and to their own functional area.

maverick [S] A person who takes bold steps.

May Day [F] May 1, 1975, a monumental day on Wall Street when fixed commissions were eliminated, ushering in considerable competition for investors' business. See *Big Bang*.

MBA [B] An abbreviation for Masters of Business Administration, which is a graduate degree from a B-school (business school).

MBO [B] The acronym can stand for one of two management activities. It can refer to the popular management technique, Management By Objectives. Objectives are mutually set by management and workers with performance of the organization measured against these objectives. The acronym can also stand for Management Buy Out, which is a company bought by its management.

mean (average) [M] Sometimes called the "arithmetic mean" or the "average," it is the value obtained by adding the values and dividing that number by the number of values. It is the most common of all statistical measurements. The mean is often represented in statistical formulas by x-bar, or a bar over a capitalized x: mean = $\overline{X}$.

media [B] The common channels of communication in which advertising is placed, such as magazines, newspapers, radio, television, cable, and billboards.

median [M] The midpoint of the data values. It's the number in the middle when three or more numbers are in sequential order. If there is an *even* number of data values, then the average of the two numbers in the middle is the median. For instance, the median of the four numbers 4, 8, 17, and 23 is 12.5: (8 + 17 = 25 and 25 ÷ 2 = 12.5). See *mean* and *mode*.

medical savings account (MSA) [HR] A new form of medical insurance that is still in the experimental stage in which a company deposits money into an account for an employee at the beginning of the year. If he or she doesn't use it, the employee gets to keep the money.

Medicare Part A and Part B [HR] The basic medical plan for retirees that is part of a person's Social Security benefits. Part A covers hospitalization, while Part B covers doctor's bills. Medicare generally starts at age sixty-five, whereas Social Security retirement benefits could begin as early as age sixty-two. Medigap is the additional insurance that spans the time gap in coverage.

medigap coverage [HR] See *Medicare Part A and Part B*.

meeting the margin [F] The act of putting in extra money to keep an investment should the value of the investor's stock investments drop. The broker makes a margin call (asks the investor to put more money in the account), and the investor must either meet the margin by putting in that extra money to keep the investment, or the broker will sell the stock.

mega [S] A term meaning "big."

megabyte (M, MB, meg) [C] About one million bytes. Actually, it's 1,048,576 bytes, or precisely 2^{20}, that is, 2 to the 20th power. See *byte* and *gigabyte*.

megahertz (mhz) [C] The measurement of the speed of transmission of a computer's electronic devices. A megahertz is one million cycles per second. It measures the speed of the computer's CPU, or central processing unit.

Member, Appraisal Institute (MAI) [RE] A professional designation given by the American Institute of Real Estate Appraisers.

> The bank would only accept an appraisal report that had been reviewed and signed by an *MAI*.

memory [C] The place where a computer stores the information it's processing. RAM is short-term memory that is erased when a computer is turned off. Memory can also be permanently stored on a hard drive.

memo to file [S] A memo that is written to document what happened in an incident or to express a person's knowledge of an incident. It is generally kept in a person's private files. If at a later time a person comes under fire for an incident, he can consult the memo to file to refresh his memory, or to show others why he took the action he did. See *CYA*.

mental health [HR] The mental well being of an employee. The phrase "mental health benefit" refers to the payment of a bill incurred for psychological counseling

mental-health day [S] A day off taken by a person who is physically well but who's mind needs a rest.

mentor [S] A senior management person who is looking out for a subordinate's well-being, often grooming that person for future success. Also known as a "godfather" or "rabbi."

menu [C] A list of commands and options in a computer program.

menu bar [C] A series of options in a computer program usually represented in a row by words such as: File, Edit, View, Insert, Format, Tools, Table, Window, and Help.

menu driven [C] A software program in which each command choice is provided for the user. This is a lot easier than the older keyboard function commands that used the Alt, Ctrl, and F keys.

mercantile [B] An adjective for anything pertaining to trade or commerce.

mercantilism; mercantilists [E] The system of trade predating the industrial revolution in which merchants formed the main market economy.

merchandise [B] Items sold at the retail level. *Merchandising* refers to all the steps involved in selling at the retail level—purchasing, advertising, promoting, etc.

merger [B] When two or more companies join to form one; it may or may not involve dissolution of the individual companies.

The *merger* of Zippy Corp. and Whammy Corp. would make the two relatively small companies into one powerful company in their industry.

mergers and acquisitions (M&A) [B] The activity of merging or acquiring companies, usually by investment banking and law firms.

merit increase [HR] An increase in salary, often given periodically, to reward successful job performance.

metes and bounds description [RE] A type of legal description that gives the boundaries of a property as defined by different landmarks on it.

> The Metes and Bounds Description of the Zippy Industrial Complex
>
> Beginning at a point 100 feet south of Main Street, running thence south 81 degrees, 3 minutes 0 seconds west, 700 feet thence...

metropolitan statistical area (MSA) [B] See *standard metropolitan statistical area (SMSA).*

Mickey Mouse [S] An adjective describing nonsensical project or procedures. The term is taken from the famous Disney character.

microcomputer [C] Another name for the PC (personal computer).

microeconomics [E] The study of how individuals or companies behave in the economy, versus the entire economy as a whole, which is the study of macroeconomics. See *macroeconomics.*

microelectromechanics [C] The class of tiny mechanical devices, often microscopic in size.

micromanage; micromanagement [S] An overly meticulous style of management, in which a manager checks on each step of a project and requires approval to go on to the next step. This style tends to irritate employees by not giving them credit for being able to handle certain aspects of their work.

> Employees soon began complaining about the new department head's *micromanaging*; it seemed she didn't trust them to carry out the tasks they had performed flawlessly for years.

microprocessor [C] The brain of the computer. Also called the "CPU" (central processing unit), or the processor. CPUs are given names such as 286, 386, 486, Pentium, Pentium II, or Pentium III, which refer to how quickly the brain can think.

Microsoft Corp. [C] The largest software firm in the computer industry, providing basic PC operating software—DOS and Windows—and many applications, such as *Word* and *Excel.*

Microsoft Network (MSN) [C] One of the major commercial online services. It is operated by the Microsoft Corp.

mid-caps [F] Stocks that are a cross between large-cap and small-cap stocks. Although the size of a company that is defined as a mid-cap can vary, it is most often valued between $750 million and $4 billion in capitalization. See *large-cap fund or stocks.*

middle class [E] A general term loosely applied by economists and politicians. It is the class of people above the poverty line and below the wealthy population. It is said to consist of people earning from about $20,000 to $75,000 a year.

middle management [B] Administrative managers who are neither the heads of departments nor the individuals who interact with customers. They are the general group of employees who carry out senior management objectives through others, thus the name "middle" managers. It is the level of management that is often targeted in layoffs.

mile [RE] A unit of length of 5,280 feet; 1,760 yards; or 1,609.34 meters.

mill [M] One-tenth of one cent. Used in some areas to compute real estate taxes.

Mill, John Stuart (1806–1873) [E] A Scottish economist and philosopher who in 1848 wrote a widely read book entitled *Principles of Political Economy,* which was a comprehensive review of the economics of the time.

mindshare [C] A term in the computer industry referring to the attention of software developers. For example, the internet has mindshare in that it is so popular, many software developers are focusing their attention on it.

minimum wage [E] The lowest wage that can be legally paid to an employee by a business. In September 1997, it was raised to $5.15 per hour from $4.25.

minor [T] A child, or generally, a person under the age of eighteen. A minor cannot transact financial business, and thus a parent or custodian must take care of any investments or taxes owed.

minority [HR] A protected class of employees, including African Americans, Hispanics, and others.

minority interest [A] An interest in a company, usually through shares of stock, owned by a company other than the parent company.

mint [E] The actual manufacture of coins and paper money, as authorized by the government. The process of making coins is called minting. In the United States, coins are minted in one of the three government mints: Denver, Philadelphia, or San Francisco.

MIPS (million instructions per second) [C] The speed at which the computer executes functions. For example, 2.5 MIPS is 2,500,000 instructions per second.

Miranda rule [L] The rule stating that a person's rights must be read to him at the time of an arrest. The U.S. Supreme Court decreed in *Miranda v. Arizona* (1966) that a person in custody is vulnerable and therefore must be told that he may remain silent and that he has the right to legal counsel.

mirror site [C] An internet server where duplicate files are maintained, or mirrored. A user can choose to connect to the closest site for access speed. For instance, a popular German site may be mirrored in the United States.

MIS (management information system) [B] See *data processing*.

miscellaneous deductions [T] A category of itemized deductions that must exceed 2 percent of the taxpayer's adjusted gross income in order to be deducted.

misdemeanor [L] See *felony*.

misfeasance [L] See *malfeasance*.

misery index [E] A combination of high unemployment and high inflation, in other words, high misery. In the 1976 presidential race, candidate Jimmy Carter blamed President Gerald Ford for a high misery index. In 1980 during the next election, Ronald Reagan in turn attributed the high misery index to Carter.

mission statement [B] A formal declaration by senior management of the goals and objectives of its business.

> In its *mission statement*, McSoftware Inc. stated that it wanted to offer easy-to-use software for the home user and to provide a place of work where talented employees would be rewarded.

Mississippi Scheme [F] See *bubble*.

mistrial [L] The ending of a trial because of a lack of a verdict, often because of a hung jury.

mitigating circumstances [L] Conditions that tend to lessen the charges.

mixed economy [E] An economy that has features of capitalism (free markets) and socialism (government control).

mixed number [M] A number made up of an integer and a fraction, such as $5\frac{1}{2}$.

mixed-use zoning [RE] Zoning that allows different types of buildings in the same area, such as a mix of residential, office, and commercial space in one district.

> The developer wanted to take advantage of the *mixed-use zoning* by building up a whole section of downtown with residential apartments, convenience stores, and office space.

MMX [C] An Intel computer technology that increases graphics and audio performance.

mode [M] The most frequent data value that appears in a set of numbers. See *mean* and *median*.

model [M] A mathematical representation of a real process. If the model is valid, it will represent and project useful values. Inherent in a model are assumptions and their relationships. A model allows the running of *what ifs*, technically called "sensitivity analysis."

modem [C] A device used to transmit data over a telephone line by turning it into signals. A computer user needs a modem to go online. Some modems are external, hooking up outside a computer, but most are now internal. The word *modem* is a contraction of the words modulator and demodulator.

moderator [C] The person who is responsible for overseeing a chat session.

modern portfolio theory (MPT) [F] The prevailing overall theory of investing, consisting of several key tenets. These are: that investors are more concerned with risk than return (that is, investors are risk averse), that capital markets are efficient (that is, most information that can be known is known), and that asset allocation is the most important strategy (versus individual stock or mutual fund selection).

Modigliani, Franco (1918–) [E] See *Nobel Prize for economics*.

mogul [B] A powerful person in the business world.

> The *moguls* from the oil cartel gathered together in the World Financial Office to discuss policies that would affect the worldwide economy.

mom-and-pop operation [B] Any small, primarily family-owned company.

> Even though Smith's Ice Cream Parlor had expanded from a *mom-and-pop operation* run by Mr. and Mrs. Smith into a worldwide franchise, they still had the best ice cream around.

momentum [F] See *market momentum*.

momentum investing [F] A recent approach to investing that encourages buying the stocks that have risen the most and therefore have the most momentum.

mommy track [HR] A less-than-advantageous career path sometimes foisted upon a woman who has had a child. When a woman has a child, there may be an attitude within a company that she is not serious about her career. Such an attitude can lead to missed opportunities for the woman, who may indeed be very career-minded. A woman on a mommy track may get pay increases but generally not the opportunities for advancement other employees get.

M1, M2, M3 [E] See *money supply*.

monetarism [E] The economic school of thought that believes that changes in the supply of money are the main determinant in the economy. Too much money in the economy leads to increases in prices (inflation), resulting in an economic boom. Booms, however, lead to recessions. Too little money in the economy levels or decreases prices and potentially causes an economic recession. Since the Federal Reserve (Fed) controls the money supply, the Fed should gauge the optimum money supply to continually sustain growth without much inflation. Since early 1980s, the U.S. economy has been largely controlled by monetary policy.

monetary aggregates (M1, M2, M3) [E] See *money supply*.

monetary policy [E] Policies and actions taken usually by the Federal Reserve to increase or decrease the amount of money available in the economy. This is meant to either stimulate or slow down the economy. These policies are in contrast to "fiscal policy," which consists of actions by the president and Congress to increase spending and decrease taxes.

money [E] An official medium of exchange for goods and services officially designated for use by a country.

Money [F] A popular magazine for individual investors.

money market; money market instruments [F] Short-term investments, either money market mutual funds or individual short-term investments such as Treasury bills, commercial paper, or bankers' acceptances.

money market fund [F] A very liquid mutual fund that earns short-term interest rates that usually allows the investor to write checks against it.

> We kept a *money market fund* so that we would earn some interest and still have the option to use the money if we needed it.

money purchase plan [HR] See *hybrid pension plan*.

money supply [E] The amount of money a population has to spend at any given time. The money supply includes cash and checking accounts, but it also includes assets that can be sold and turned into cash. The money supply is measured by the monetary aggregates M1, M2, and M3:

> **M1** All demand deposits at banks by individuals and businesses, and coins and currency circulating in the economy.

> **M2** All M1 deposits plus all time deposits, savings accounts, and money market funds.

> **M3** All M1 and M2 amounts, plus large deposits at banks and institutional money market funds.

monitor [C] The computer screen.

Computer Monitor Standards

CGA (color graphics adapter) The first video system that offered both color text and graphics. It was soon replaced by the **EGA (enhanced graphics adapter)** that had many more colors than the CGA, plus text that was easier to read. Soon, however, it was toppled by the **VGA (video graphic array)**, which had great graphics, high resolution, and superior text. It, however, was topped by the **SVGA (super video graphics array)**, which is like the VGA, only better. Many of the super-graphic CD-ROM titles need SVGA in order to run.

---

monopoly [E] Any market controlled by one company that, as a result, can set the price of a good. Microsoft has been accused of having a monopoly in computer operating systems.

> After Zippy and Whammy merged, they drove their competitors out and had a *monopoly* on the zipper market.

monopsony [E] An economic term for a market with one buyer, as opposed to a monopoly, which is a market with one seller. Pronounced Ma-NOP-sa-ne.

Monte Carlo simulation [M] A trial and error method of random sampling used in market research and other business applications. It's name is derived from the famed place of gambling, or chance, along the French Riviera.

moonlighting [B] The term for holding down a second job to make extra money.

> Company policy expressly forbids *moonlighting*—Zippy Corp. wants its workers rested and ready for work each day.

Moore's law [C] The law describing the dramatic march of progress in integrated circuits, codified by Gordon Moore, one of Intel's founders. He originally said that the number of transistors on a chip will double every eighteen months and more recently said that the cost of a semiconducting manufacturing plant doubles with each generation of microprocessor.

morale [S] The general mood of the people in an organization or company, either positive or negative.

moral hazard [E] Incentives for individuals, companies, or countries to act in ways that incur costs that they do not have to bear. It is not always easy to determine if an action is really a moral hazard issue in every case. A common textbook example would be a woman who wears her expensive diamond necklace in public because she has it insured. The necklace now has a greater chance of being stolen, thus making it a greater risk to the insurance company and also presenting a greater risk to the woman herself of being attacked. In 1998, when the IMF (International Monetary Fund) provided loans to Russia to help in its financial difficulties, some economists said that giving these loans was a moral hazard because it only communicated to countries that if they messed up they would be bailed out. Instead, these economists promoted the idea that if countries knew they would not be helped, then they would make sure not to mess up in the first place.

moral turpitude [L] Antisocial behavior of a high degree, such as depravity.

moratorium [RE] A time period during which an activity is stopped for a specific reason.

> The town of Smallville placed a two-year *moratorium* on commercial building to assess the environmental impact on the water supply.

morbidity [I] A word that sounds as bad as it is. It means the number of cases of specific diseases, such as tuberculosis. A "morbidity table" refers to the number of people who have a specific disease.

Morningstar mutual fund service [F] A popular mutual fund reporting service for individual investors.

morph; morphing [C] A computer technique of animation in which a person or object is made to change shape before the viewer's eyes. The transformation is made in a liquid motion. This technique is used in advertising and in movies. The word is derived from the word "metamorphosis."

mortality charges; mortality table [I] The charge for pure insurance in an insurance policy. Using actuarial tables, the insurance company determines the probability of death given age, sex, and other factors such as smoking habits. This is translated into the premium charged to a particular person.

mortgage [RE] A long-term loan, typically thirty years, for buying real estate. The loan is pledged against the real estate. Mortgages can be for shorter periods, such as twenty or fifteen years. For a fixed-rate mortgage, the monthly payments are equal, although the amount of interest declines and the amount of principal increases during the life of the mortgage. This is technically called "amortization." For a variable-rate mortgage, the amount of monthly payments is altered when the rate of interest changes. The word *mortgage* comes from Old French and literally means *dead pledge.* The idea is that if the payments are not made, then the real estate pledged is lost (or dead).

> Before it could close on its new office complex, Widgets Inc. had to obtain a *mortgage* in the amount of almost a million dollars.

mortgage-backed securities [F] Pooled mortgages that pass through the interest and principal payments to investors. These bond-like investments are issued by several organizations, but primarily Ginnie Mae (Government National Mortgage Association) or Fannie Mae (Federal National Mortgage Association).

mortgage banker/broker/company [RE] A person or organization specializing in providing mortgages to buyers of real estate. A broker will match a buyer to a mortgage lender, whereas a banker or company will actually receive monthly payments.

Ames Construction Corp. hired a *mortgage broker* to find the best financing available for its new development.

mortgagee/mortgagor [RE] In legal talk, the mortgagee is the lending institution that provides the mortgage (the bank), while the mortgagor is the person who has the obligation to pay back the borrowed money.

mortgage term [RE] The amount of time within which the mortgage loan is scheduled to be paid back.

Sminkley Consulting preferred a *mortgage term* of only five years, rather than a longer fifteen-, twenty-, or even thirty-year term.

Mosaic [C] The first widely used internet browser. It was introduced in 1993 by the University of Illinois National Center for Supercomputing Applications. It was the application that caused internet use to explode. Some of the developers went on to work on Netscape Navigator, which is one of the two most popular browsers today. Microsoft Explorer is the other.

most favored nation (MFN) [E] The traditional term for countries that are granted the best trading conditions given to any country. This term has recently been replaced by the Senate with the new term "normal trade relations."

motherboard [C] The main circuitry board of a computer. It houses the CPU, the memory, and other important electronics.

I thought I'd put some extra RAM into the *motherboard* rather than buy a whole new computer.

motion [L] A legal request of one party made to the court.

motivation [HR] The desire and drive to achieve a goal. Since setting and accomplishing goals is a fundamental aspect of management, it is studied by management specialists and business schools.

mouse [C] A small pointing device used to control the cursor on a computer screen. It was developed in 1964 by Douglas Engelbart, a professor working at the Stanford Research Institute in Menlo Park, California.

mouse pad [C] A small pad designed to allow smooth navigation of a mouse.

moving average [F] A rolling average of the stock market, or other performance, that is adjusted as time moves on. For instance, a frequently used period is 200 days, in which one more day is added and one subtracted, so the last 200 days is averaged. It is helpful in showing a general trend. See *technical analysis*.

MPEG (motion picture experts group) [C] A popular internet compression standard and file format for computer video.

Mr. Market [F] A fictitious person who metaphorically represents the stock market. It is said that each day the investor meets Mr. Market, who, like a chameleon, is never the same.

Mr. Nice Guy [S] A person who tries to be overly nice to people in the office.

MS-DOS [C] The Microsoft Corp.'s name for DOS (disk operating system), which was the original popular PC operating system introduced in 1980. The MS stands for Microsoft. The IBM version is called PC-DOS.

MSN [C] See *Mircrosoft Network*.

multiemployer plan [HR] A pension or other benefit plan in which a number of companies have pooled their plans together. This is used primarily with union employees who work at various companies, such as carpenters or electricians.

multilateral trade [E] An agreement between many countries on international trade issues. This is in contrast to "bilateralism," which is an agreement between just two countries. See *GATT*.

multimedia [C] A combination program of text, graphics, audio, and video, usually used to convey an idea or story.

multinational [B] Adjective describing companies that do substantial business in many countries. Interconnecting suppliers, production, management, and strategic plans around the world is now not only commonplace but also considered a necessity in larger companies.

multiple correlation or regression [M] In statistics, comparing or correlating many variables to find which are correlated, if any.

multiple listing service (MLS) [RE] A computerized service of real estate sales listings distributed among different real estate agents so that many real estate offices and brokers attempt to sell a property.

> Jan thought it would be best to list with a broker who had *MLS* so that her home would be shown by as many agents as possible.

multiplier [E] Term usually referring to the ripple or multiplying effect of monetary policy when action is taken by the Federal Reserve, and the supply of money in the economy is increased or decreased. Since bank deposits spur borrowing, which spurs economic activity, the effect of one deposit is said to have a *multiplier* effect on the economy.

multiprogramming/multitasking [C] Term referring to an operating system that allows more than one program to be run simultaneously. Windows, OS/2, and Macintosh are examples of multiprogramming or multitasking operating systems.

multi-user [C] Term referring to a program or computer shared by more than one user at the same time.

municipal bonds (munis) [F] Bonds issued by municipalities—cities, towns, states, counties—usually for public improvement or operating budgets.

murder [L] The act of killing another person with premeditation or malice aforethought.

Murphy's law [S] The premise that if something can go wrong, it will. Murphy was a fictitious private in the Army who always screwed up.

> Charlie thought of *Murphy's law* as he gave his presentation: The slides were out of order; he spilled coffee on the overhead projector; his clients kept interrupting with phone calls; and his staff forgot to make the correction to the client's misspelled name on the report he handed out.

mushroom, I feel like a [S] A saying generally meant to express frustration when a person doesn't know what's going on, but should. "I feel like a mushroom, kept in the dark and fed s—t," which is how mushrooms are grown.

mutual fund [F] A collection of investments managed by a professional investment firm. Mutual funds have become very popular, as opposed to buying individual stocks. The three main types of mutual funds are stock, bond, and money market funds.

Types of Mutual Funds:

Aggressive growth funds are the riskiest of equity funds, and seek maximum capital appreciation and provide little current income. Typically, the funds invest in new companies or new industries. Some may also use options and short-term trading strategies.

Growth funds usually invest in common stock of established companies. These funds are considered less risky than aggressive growth funds because the funds invest in well-seasoned companies that may also pay dividends.

Growth and income funds invest in well-seasoned companies with a track record of paying dividends. This type of fund is less risky than growth funds because it only invests in larger capitalized companies with higher income and higher paying dividends. Dividends can cushion the blow in the event of a market decline.

Balanced funds focus on a combination of growth and preservation of principal. A balanced fund invests in a mixed portfolio of stocks (frequently about 65 percent), preferred stocks, and bonds. Investors hope to receive a combination of income and growth.

Income funds seek a high level of current income by investing in high dividend-paying common stock, and government and corporate bonds. They are less sensitive to the stock market but more sensitive to changes in interest rates.

Bond funds invest primarily in bonds for current income. Bond funds can hold a variety of bond types or can specialize in corporate, Treasury, or tax-free municipal bonds. They can also specialize in the term of the maturity, such as long-term, intermediate, or short-term. They can also specialize in high-grade or high-yield (junk) bonds.

Sector funds are stock funds that specialize in a specific industrial sector such as health care, banking, technology, precious metals, or chemicals.

International funds invest in stocks outside of the United States.

Global funds invest in stocks inside and outside of the United States.

---

mutual fund fees [F] The variety of fees charged by mutual funds, such as front-end, back-end, exchange, management, redemption, and 12b-1 fees.

mutual life company [I] A form of an insurance company that is owned by the policyholders. Policyholders have a dual relationship with the insurance company, as customer and owner. Company profits are mostly paid to policyholders as dividends. Although some major life insurance companies are mutuals, only about 100 of the 1,200 insurance companies are structured this way. In more recent times, some mutuals have petitioned states to allow them to change to a corporate form that issues stock to the public.

my people will talk to your people [S] A somewhat humorous phrase often meant in jest, suggesting that a person is so important that they have a staff of people to do all their detail work, such as setting up appointments or taking care of paperwork.

N

NAFTA (North American Free-Trade Agreement) [E]
A three-country trade agreement between Canada, Mexico, and the United States that was concluded in 1993 and went into effect January 1994. It has been a controversial agreement, particularly in the United States, where critics charge that jobs have been lost to lower-wage workers in Mexico. This agreement follows the 1988 agreement between Canada and the United States in a similar free-trade agreement.

NAIRU (nonaccelerating inflation rate of unemployment) [E]
Pronounced NEH-ru. It is the lowest theoretical rate of unemployment that will not increase inflation. It was thought to be about 6 percent, but at the beginning of 1999 the rate of unemployment was about 4.5 percent and inflation remains at a very low rate. The general theory is that if unemployment is too low, then organizations needing employees will bid up the price of salaries to attract new employees, thus increasing inflation.

naked option [F] The buying of an option when the underlying stock, or commodity, is not owned, thus naked of the underlying asset. Options are frequently bought when the stock is also owned, called a "covered option." With a naked option, the investor is either buying or selling an option of a stock that he or she dosen't yet own. With a commodity option, the investor may have to buy shares of the commodity at the agreed upon price to fill the contract.

nanny tax [T] The taxes—including FICA (Social Security taxes)—that are required to be paid on the compensation of people hired to care for children. The nanny tax has been controversial and complicated to determine.

nanosecond [C] A nanosecond is a very short time. One nanosecond is one billionth of a second. It's how fast computers execute functions.

NASD (National Association of Security Dealers) [F] The association of the over-the-counter (OTC) brokers and parent of the actual computerized system called NASDAQ. The association was established in 1939 to regulate the OTC market. In 1998, NASD acquired the American Stock Exchange and the Philadelphia Stock Exchanges to expand its market reach, although those exchanges will operate as separate entities. See *NASDAQ*.

NASDAQ; NASDAQ issues; NASDAQ system [F] The computerized system known as the over-the-counter (OTC) stock market. The name is an acronym for National Association of Securities Dealers Automated Quotation System. It's pronounced NAZ-dak. The system handles almost 5,000 companies' stock prices on a daily basis. The NASDAQ handles smaller companies, in contrast to the New York Stock Exchange, which, in general, handles larger companies. Some large companies are traded on the NASDAQ, such as Microsoft, Intel, and Federal Express. See *over-the-counter (OTC) market*.

national account [B] A sales term referring to the sales responsibility for a major company, versus the responsibility for the usual sales area, for instance the New Jersey territory.

National Association of Insurance Commissioners (NAIC) [I] An organization of state insurance commissioners formed to achieve some uniformity between the states.

National Association of Manufacturers (NAM) [B] A major national organization of business that promotes the interests of manufacturing.

National Association of Realtors (NAR) [RE] The main trade and professional organization for the real estate industry; it includes such professional organizations as the American Institute of Real Estate Appraisers (AIREA), American Society of Real Estate Counselors, Institute of Real Estate Management, and Realtors National Marketing Institute, among many others.

national debt [E] The money that the federal government owes, usually in the form of Treasury bills, Treasury notes, and Treasury bonds. See *debt*.

> The interest on our huge *national debt* is one of the major expenses the government must pay each year.

National Futures Association (NFA) [F] A regulating and enforcement agency for the futures exchanges established in 1982.

National Labor Relations Act [HR] Also called the "Wagner Act," it requires employers to bargain in good faith with duly elected unions. The 1935 legislation prohibited blacklisting (lists of union activists employers avoided hiring), yellow dog contracts (a worker's promise not to join a union if hired), and other tactics against the formation of unions.

National Labor Relations Board(NLRB) [HR] The Federal agency that oversees labor laws in the United States, in particular the National Labor Relations Act of 1935, also known as the "Wager Act."

National Register of Historic Places [RE] A listing of historic sites that are considered worthy of preservation. Homes and buildings that are registered must be maintained according to strict guidelines.

> Once the headquarters of Spiffo had been put in the *National Register of Historic Places*, the company had to get approval for any renovation to the structure, especially the facade of the building.

natural logarithm [M] See *e*.

NAV [F] See *net asset value*.

n.b. (note well) [B] A notation at the end of a memo to bring attention to the reader. The initials are for the Italian term *nota bene*, which means *note well*.

negative cash flow [A] The term for losing money. When expenses are subtracted from income and a negative number results. Also said to be *in the red*.

> Although Zippy Corp. had a *negative cash flow* from a combination of major purchases for the factory and decreased sales, company executives felt that next year the new equipment would start paying for itself.

negligence [L] The failure to exercise due care in the performing of one's duties.

Nellie Mae [F] The nation's largest nonprofit student loan provider. See *Sallie Mae*.

nepotism [HR] The practice of hiring someone related to another employee. It may be company policy not to have two related people in the same department, in particular, a boss and subordinate. It is felt that the relationship may encourage favoritism and prevent full exercise of authority.

net [S] The bottom line. See *net net.*

> Charlotte calmly explained to her group, "The *net* of this directive is that if we don't produce this product on time, we'll catch all hell from headquarters."

net asset value (NAV) [F] The price of one mutual fund share. At the end of each trading day, mutual funds calculate the total value of all the stocks or bonds in their fund. This is divided by the total number of shares to arrive at the NAV.

net earnings [A] The resultant earnings after deducting all expenses and taxes from gross earnings.

net income multiplier [RE] The ratio of the value of a property to the net income the property generates. It is similar to "gross income multiplier," but it utilizes the net income rather than the gross income.

net income ratio [RE] The ratio of the net operating income to the effective gross income multiplier.

> The bank calculated the *net income ratio* for Zippy Corp. to estimate how well the company was managing its property.

netiquette [C] Good manners on the internet or an online service.

net net [S] The absolute bottom line, or end result. It's even more bottom line than just *net.* See *net.*

> "The *net net* of this project," Ted explained, "is that we either are in business, or we find other jobs."

net operating income (NOI) [A] A business's income after deducting its operating expenses from its gross income but before deducting income taxes and any debt service.

> From its *net operating income*, it looked as if Zippy Corp. would do well this year, but the giant tax bill would wipe out most of its profit.

net present value (NPV) [M] The present value of an uneven stream of payments. This calculation occurs typically in an analysis of new business projects or ventures. For instance, in commercial real estate a new building is projected to show varying annual cash flows, at first negative when startup costs are high and rentals are low, to eventually mostly positive. To find the net present value of this uneven series, the present value of each payment must be individually calculated and then all of those present values are *netted*, or added together. In this process, negative as well as positive present values are combined. NPV is in contrast to determining the present value of a series of *equal* payments, such as annuities or pensions, where there are neat formulas to determine the entire present value in one calculation.

Netscape Navigator [C] One of the popular web browsers.

net 30 [B] The general business payment standard or understanding, meaning a bill is due in full in 30 days.

network [C] A group of computers that are hooked together. If a user is part of a network, she can send a file directly from one computer to another.

> The internet is the largest *network* of computers.

network or cable [B] An advertising purchase on national media, particularly on the major networks or on cable television.

networking [B] The practice of meeting, greeting, and shaking hands; networking involves making and using professional contacts to get work. Popular in business where the exchange of information and establishing contacts are an important part of expanding a business. It also means one's personal contacts in business.

> Cruther's *networking* among his business contacts landed him a new job.

net working capital [A] The excess of current assets over current liabilities. Also called "working capital."

Network Solutions [C] The private company that the government has granted the authority to give internet domain names and addresses for the United States.

net worth [A] One's assets minus one's liabilities.

After adding up the value of his real estate—worth over $500,000—and subtracting the mortgages—only $100,000—Michael realized that his *net worth* was well over $400,000.

neural network [C] A computer program that attempts to model itself on the operation of the human brain. It does this by trying to simulate how the neurons in the brain work.

never got the message [S] A phrase used to characterize a person, or group of people, who were not told of something important or who misinterpreted the message given.

Smith who always left at 5 P.M. *never got the message* that people were encouraged to stay late to finish the project.

new age [S] The general cultural idea of spirituality, which advertising sometimes attempts to tap into.

newbies [C] Those who are new to the online world.

"Don't give her a hard time; she's a *newbie,*" said one techie after many of the previous entries made fun of Mary's inability to fathom internet lingo.

new issue [F] A new stock or bond. Often referred to as an IPO (initial public offering).

new math [S] A new way to look at or to calculate something.

Smithers told the investor that with the *new math*, unlimited internet stock P/E ratios were okay.

new media [C] The internet news and advertising media. Although it is relatively new, it already has a number of established positions, such as content provider, online researcher, technology manager, and web site programmer.

new paradigm [S] A somewhat pretentious phrase meant to indicate that "I have a new idea." It is usually not a valid new way of viewing the world, however.

newsgroup [C] A discussion group on the internet revolving around specific topics and consisting of articles or postings made by different users. If a user makes a contribution, he is posting to the newsgroup. There are literally thousands of newsgroups covering any topic imaginable, from support groups for sufferers of obscure diseases to humorous stories to careers.

newsletter [F] Any one of a number of short publications that offers news and advice in a particular field.

news release [B] A promotional communication to the press from businesses or individuals to promote their products and services.

New York Stock Exchange (NYSE) [F] The first, and foremost, stock exchange in the country, founded in 1792. It's considered to be the center of U.S. stock market action. Results of trades conducted on the NYSE are published every business day.

New York Stock Exchange Composite Index [F] An index of all stocks listed on the New York Stock Exchange. It is weighted by capitalization, meaning the price of each stock is multiplied by the number of shares outstanding. There are also four specialized indexes for industrial, transportation, finance, and utilities.

nexus [S] A connection between two things. "Nexus" is also the name of a popular database used in various businesses.

> Cruthers told the economists that there did not seem to be a *nexus* between increased foreign competition and the increased strength of the dollar.

niche market; niche marketing [B] The marketing strategy that targets a narrow market segment, usually a market not served by larger companies. Pronounced NICH.

Nielsen ratings; Nielsens [B] The number of people viewing a particular television show, as measured by the A. C. Nielsen Company.

NIMBY syndrome [S] The acronym for Not In My Back Yard, which refers to community action against new business buildings and structures. For instance, the construction of cellular antennas have come under attack in some communities even though many of those activists, use cellular telephones.

9-to-5; 9-to-5er [HR] The normal work day, from 9 A.M. to 5 P.M. A person who just works those hours versus one who comes in early and stays late.

NLQ (near letter quality) [C] With a dot-matrix printer, a print mode that is close to letter quality but not quite. Dot matrix technology, while good for its time, is no match for ink-jet and laser technology that produces letter quality—meaning quality equal to a typewriter.

Nobel Prize for economics [E] The Nobel Prizes are awards given to those the Royal Swedish Academy of Sciences deems to have made significant achievements in the fields of science. It was founded by a bequest by Swedish chemist and inventor of dynamite, Alfred Nobel. The first prize was awarded in 1901, but it was not until 1969 that a prize was designated for economics. American economists have dominated the prizes. The following are the Americans who are past recipients. Since the Prize is only given to people who are alive, Fischer Black did not win in 1997 for his work with Scholes and Merton on pricing financial options (he died in 1995).

1970 Paul Samuelson *"For the scientific work through which he has developed static and dynamic economic theory and actively contributed to raising the level of analysis in economic science."*

1971 Simon Kuznets *"For his empirically founded interpretation of economic growth, which has led to new and deepened insight into the economic and social structure and process of development."*

1972 Kenneth Arrow (and British economist John Hicks) *"For their pioneering contributions to general economic equilibrium theory and welfare theory."*

1973 Wassily Leontief *"For the development of the input-output method and for its application to important economic problems."*

1975 Tjalling Koopmans and Leonid Kantorovich *"For their contributions to the theory of optimum allocation of resources."*

1976 Milton Friedman *"For his achievements in the fields of consumption analysis, monetary history, and theory, and for his demonstration of the complexity of stabilization policy."*

1978 Herbert Simon *"For his pioneering research into the decision-making process within economic organizations."*

1979 Theodore Schultz (and British economist Arthur Lewis) *"For their pioneering research into economic development research with particular consideration of the problems of developing countries."*

1980 Lawrence Klein *"For the creation of economic models and their application to the analysis of economic fluctuations and economic policies."*

1981 James Tobin *"For his analysis of financial markets and their relations to expenditure decisions, employment, production, and prices."*

1982 George Stigler *"For his seminal studies of industrial structures, functioning of markets, and causes and effects of public regulation."*

1983 Gerard Debreu *"For having incorporated new analytical methods into economic theory and for his rigorous reformulation of the theory of general equilibrium."*

1985 Franco Modigliani *"For his pioneering analyses of saving and of financial markets."*

1986 James Buchanan, Jr. *"For his development of the contractual and constitutional bases for the theory of economic and political decision-making."*

1987 Robert Solow *"For his contributions to the theory of economic growth."*

1990 Harry Markowitz "For his Portfolio Theory"; Merton Miller for his work on "Miller-Modigliani Theory"; and William Sharpe *"for his Capital Asset Pricing Model."* Taken together, their work revolutionized the financial and business industries.

1992 Gary Becker *"For having extended the domain of economic theory of aspects of human behavior ... including crime, family life, and racial bias."*

1993 Robert Fogel and Douglass North *"For applying economic theory and quarantine methods to historical puzzles."* Fogel's work on slavery as an efficient economic system is controversial.

1994 John Nash and John Harsanyl (and German economist Reinhard Selten) *"For their separate contributions to the field of game theory, which is used to predict how information and competition affect economic outcomes."*

1995 Robert Lucas *"For the economist who has had the greatest influence on macroeconomic research since 1970."* He has challenged the notion that the government is able to fine-tune the economy.

1996 William Vickrey (and Scottish economist James Mirrlees) *"For their fundamental contributions to the economic theory of incentives."*

1997 Robert Merton and Myron Scholes *"For their work (with the late Fischer Black) in developing option valuation formulas."* Their work has led to the development of derivatives that attempt to provide more efficient risk management of investments.

no brainer [S] An obvious or simple solution.

no-fault insurance [I] Auto insurance payments made regardless of who was at fault.

no-load; no-load fund [F] Mutual funds that charge no commissions for buying or selling shares of a fund.

> Mike always bought *no-load funds* as it rankled him to pay any sort of commission.

no-load insurance [I] Newer types of insurance sold by banks or mutual fund investment companies without agents and thus without commissions or loads.

nolo contendere [L] A statement that a defendant will not contest the charges. In Latin it means *I will not contend.* Pronounced No-low con-TEN-dah-ree.

no-lose; no-win [S] See *win-win.*

nominal [M] The actual or named rate of interest. This is in contrast to the "real" interest rate, which is adjusted for inflation. See *real.*

nominal GDP [E] The total domestic output in actual current dollars, or what they are worth today. This is in contrast to "real GDP," which measures domestic output adjusted for inflation. See *gross domestic product.*

nonbearing wall [RE] A wall that is not important to a building's integrity.

> When the architect made plans to tear down walls on the first floor to open the rooms into one large space, she made sure they were *nonbearing walls*.

nonconforming [RE] Term refering to a building or part of a building that no longer conforms to current zoning ordinances because the zoning came into effect after the structure was built. Nonconforming structures are legal because they were conforming at the time they were built. Also called "legally nonconforming."

> That extension compleated last year is a *nonconforming* use because the new zoning ordinance stipulates that there must be a minimum of 20 feet between it and the property line.

nondurable goods [E] Sometimes called "consumer goods," like toys or games, these are goods that are expected to be "consumed" in short order, usually within one year. See *consumer goods*.

nonexempt employee; nonexempt position [HR] An employee, usually an office worker, who is nonexempt from receiving overtime pay if she works more than the standard workweek. It's a double negative, meaning employee gets overtime if she works more than 40 hours a week. A manager or professional is an *exempt* position, meaning overtime work is expected, and extra pay is not given for it.

nonfeasance [L] See *malfeasance*.

nonguaranteed term [I] The cheapest term life insurance with an important catch: There is no guarantee that it can be renewed year by year.

nonprofit organization [B] An organization, under law, that doesn't pay taxes. Nonprofits—things like churches, hospitals, and charities—may also receive tax-deductible contributions.

> When you purchase something for a *nonprofit organization*, you don't need to pay sales tax on that item.

nonqualified compensation or plan [HR] An arrangement that does not meet IRS rules for pension or other tax-qualified plans. It is commonly a deferred compensation plan by a company. Because there are no tax benefits to a company, a company is free to devise whatever special compensation arrangement it believes is appropriate for its executives.

nonresident alien [HR] A foreign national who does not meet permanent resident status which requires a green card.

no par value [A] See *par value*.

normal curve; normal distribution [M] The graph of a typical bell-shaped curve where the mean, mode, and median are all the same. See *bell-shaped curve*.

normal retirement [HR] A somewhat misleading term that has a technical pension definition. It means the age at which a person will have no reduction in a pension payment. It appears often in an annual benefit statement and does not mean when employees "normally" retire.

normal trade relations [E] The new term for most favored nation. See *most favored nation*.

notary public [L] A person who is authorized by the government to certify affidavits and acknowledgments, called "notarizing."

> Before she signed that legal document, Jan had to find a *notary public* to notarize her signature so that it would stand up in court.

note [A] A written promise to pay a certain sum by a certain date, often specified in a legal document that outlines the terms of the loan, including the amount borrowed, the interest rate, and the time in which it must be repaid.

notebook [C] A portable computer that is smaller than a laptop.

notes [A] The footnotes to financial statements where all the important details are buried.

notes payable; notes receivable [A] Accounting entries showing either the amounts due or the amounts to be paid by a company.

Notes software [C] See *Lotus Notes*.

notice [L] An official legal notification by one party or company to another that a lawsuit has been filed against them.

Notice of Tax Due and Demand for Payment [T] Notice the capital letters? This is serious. This is the official notice that the IRS sends a person if she hasn't paid up in full, and there's no more discussion on the subject. This is the beginning of a collection.

> After Charles had been audited and was found to owe an additional $2,000, he received a *Notice of Tax Due and Demand for Payment*.

NOW account (negotiable order of withdrawal) [F] A bank checking/savings account earning slightly higher interest. Although the term was common in the 1980s, most banks have their own name for a combination checking and savings account.

NQSOs (nonqualified stock options) [HR] See *stock options.*

ns (nanosecond) [C] See *nanosecond.*

nth degree [S] A term that refers to something taken to an extreme.

nuisance [RE] Something that takes away from the enjoyment of a property.

> That garbage dump emits such a toxic odor; it is a public *nuisance.*

null hypothesis [M] An assumption made at the beginning of a statistical experiment that the results obtained are by chance only. The object of most statistical experiments is to find a reason for the results other than chance, and thus reject the null hypothesis. This *nullifies* the hypothesis of chance by proving that there is a cause or reason for the results. At first this appears to be a confusing double-negative to statistical newcomers, but it becomes understandable after working with specific problems. In math formulas, the null hypothesis is usually written as H_0, and the alternative nonchance hypothesis is written as H_1.

number cruncher [S] A sometimes unflattering, sometimes flattering, reference to a person who primarily does calculations, computer work, or accounting all day. It is sometimes implied that the person doesn't have a sense of the big picture. It can also refer to someone who is admired because of a very good ability with numbers.

numerator [M] The number or algebraic expression written above the line in a fraction. The number below the line is called the "denominator."

Num lock key [C] A key on the keyboard that switches on and off the use of the numeric keys, grouped together and usually found on the right side of the keyboard.

O

object-oriented interface [C] The use of icons and dialog boxes with a mouse to give commands within a software program, common with Macintosh and Windows programs.

obsolescence [A] The decline in the value of an asset due to changing technology rather than to wear and tear.

occupancy rate [RE] The percentage of units in a building that are occupied or rented.

> Because of the recession, the main office building downtown has an *occupancy rate* of only about 50 percent.

occupational hazard [I] The potentially harmful condition of a work environment. Occupational hazards can cause headaches, sickness, or accidents.

OCR (optical character recognition) [C] The software behind the use of a scanner to read text. The software is able to recognize text and convert it for use in a word-processing or desktop software program.

OD (organizational development) [HR] See *organizational development*.

odd lot [F] An order to purchase common stock shares that is not a multiple of 100. Brokers charge extra for odd lot purchases and sales.

off-budget [E] Term refering toexpenditures that are kept off-the-budget so as to preserve the original budget estimates.

offense is the best defense [S] The business strategy of taking the initiative, as opposed to waiting until competitors try new approaches or introduce new products and services. See *best defense is a good offense*.

offer [RE] A price and any special terms that a potential buyer makes to a seller.

> The ABC Corp. made an *offer* of $3 million for the purchase of the XYZ Building.

offering price [F] The price at which a stock or mutual fund is offered to the public. The difference between the offer price and the net asset value of a fund is the commission charged.

Office of Management and Budget (OMB) [T] A presidential advisory office that helps develop the federal budget.

officer [B] A person given specific company authority. Often the title of vice president is given to officers.

> As a bank *officer*, Joan had authority to approve business loans up to $250,000.

offset [F] A pension plan that offsets (subtracts) from a pension an amount a person would receive from Social Security. The offset is usually up to one-half, because the company pays one-half of the Social Security taxes..

> The majority of futures contracts are *offset* by other contracts.

offset plan [HR] A pension plan that offsets (subtracts) from a pension an amount a person would receive from Social Security. The offset is usually up to one-half, because the company pays one-half of the Social Security taxes.

offshore banking [B] Banking operations that are in small nonregulated, or low-regulated, countries, mainly islands. These are places where the small economies are geared to be business friendly to encourage such banking.

off the books [A] An expense or payment that is not formally recorded. A transaction that is off the books is usually hidden from taxation and in general is illegal.

> Marvin was willing to take such low pay because he would be paid *off the books* and therefore wouldn't pay any income taxes on the amount.

off the charts [S] Spectacular performance. Something that is off the charts is surprising and unusual, and generally positive.

> Smithers was excited as he told production that the new line was generating numbers *off the charts*. "You'll probably need a second shift if this keeps up," he sputtered.

off the hook [S] Term that refers to being spared further suspicion or concern. If one is *off the hook* it indicates that they were once on the hook, meaning they were considered thought to be involved in something that the company, or boss, was concerned about.

off the shelf [S] A standard solution. A product or service already prepared and ready to go.

> Smithers told the purchasing agent not to reinvent the wheel but to use *off-the-shelf* software.

old boy network [S] Generally the traditional favoritism in business toward male friends of relatives or business connections. Since men held the positions of power, women appropriately felt left out of this favoritism.

old math [S] An outdated method to calculate something or figure something out.

> Cruthers told his client not to use the *old math*, but rather, the new math of internet unlimited P/E ratios.

oligopoly [E] A market characterized by a few large producers. Pronounced ol-a-GOP-a-lee.

> There were only two zipper manufacturers in all of Alabascar, but then again, most Alabascarans used buttons. Thus, the two firms had an *oligopoly* in Alabascar and could dictate the market price of zippers.

oligopsony [E] An economic term for a market structure in which few companies are buyers, versus *oligopoly* in which few companies are sellers. Pronounced ol-a-GOP-sa-nee.

ombudsman [S] Generally an independent person who investigates a complaint, files a report of the situation, and mediates a solution to a problem.

on board [S] Term that refers to being attuned to and motivated toward a particular strategy or management team. With "the program."

> Smith felt he had to get *on board* with the new management approach or find himself without a job.

on consignment [B] A retailing method where vendors provide retail stores with goods for sale without the store paying for them until sold. If the items are not sold, then the retailer returns the goods.

online [C] To be connected by modem to the internet or a commercial service, such as America Online. If one is talking about a piece of equipment, online means being connected properly and ready to go.

> Marie did an *online* search for that information and accessed the archives at Podunk University.

on spec [B] Work done in "speculation" of a possible contract or deal. The term is used especially in advertising.

on-the-job training (OJT) [HR] The practice of learning while working rather than taking a training course to learn a job. Although on-the-job training can be frustrating for both boss and employee, it can be the quickest way to learn a job.

on the merits [L] A judicial ruling based on the facts of the matter rather than on a legal technicality.

on the same page [S] A term referring to being together or being of one mind about a policy, procedure, or project.

> Cruthers reacted to Smithers, "Let's get *on the same page* here. We need more connectors, or we won't be able to produce enough product."

on the same wavelength [S] Term refering to being attuned to the boss, the company, or just someone's ideas.

> Smith was shunted aside because he was not *on the same wavelength* as the management team.

OPEC (Organization of Petroleum Exporting Countries) [E] A cartel of mainly Middle Eastern countries (Venezuela and Indonesia are also included) that produce oil. OPEC has engaged in price fixing activities, which in the mid-1970s led to dramatic increases in the price of oil. The cartel in recent years has not been overly effective in controlling the price of oil.

open architecture [C] A computer system that can be used by third-party designers to develop programs for its use. The IBM-PC system is such an architecture, allowing many add-ons and software programs.

open court [L] Public court proceedings.

open door policy [HR] A standard practice that allows employees to see the boss with just about any problem or question. The boss's door is always open, so to speak.

open-end agreement or contract [B] An agreement in which the supplier of a good or service will continue to provide the buyer's requirements in general, whatever they may be.

> The law firm of Smith & Smith maintained an *open-end agreement* with XYZ Corp. to provide a variety of legal services.

open-ended question [S] The asking of a very general question to elicit a thoughtful answer. This is in contrast to a yes-no question.

> The interviewer asked Donna a typical *open-ended question*, "Why is the human resources function in a company so important?"

open interest [F] The number of particular futures contracts that are still outstanding and are not offset. The more open interest, the more activity in that contract.

open market operations (of the Fed) [E] The buying or selling of government securities by the Federal Reserve (Fed), in general to influence money supply, growth in the economy, and inflation. By buying securities, the Fed distributes money to banks, which in turn release most of it in the form of loans. The action increases the supply of money and hopefully increases the growth in the economy.

open outcry [F] Orders on futures exchanges that are called out publicly in a system where he or she who yells loudest will probably do best. This probably rings to mind those scenes where traders are in an area yelling out their orders for the best bid.

open shop [B] A place of work where employees are given the right to decide whether they want to join the union. This is in contrast to a "closed shop" in which employees must be members of a specific union either before or when they are hired.

operating budget [A] The financial plan, or budget, for revenue and expenses of a company.

operating expenses [A] Expenses a company incurs in the normal operations of a business. These are in contrast to "capital expenses," which are long-term investments.

> Although the electric bill and property taxes were included in the monthly *operating expenses*, income tax and asset depreciation were not.

operating income [A] The excess of revenue over expenses. It's the income from normal business activities before the additions or subtractions of nonoperating income, such as investment and interest income.

operating system [C] A program that manages the operations of a computer. The operating system is the interface between the different applications and the hardware. Some of the different operating systems on the market are Windows, DOS, OS/2 for IBM-type computers, and System 8.5 for the Mac. Windows NT and UNIX are operating systems for networks.

operations [B] The crucial part of a business that actually manufacturers the product, or the department that actually performs the service.

operations research (OR) [M] The application of mathematical methods to a variety of business problems. Originated during World War II, a number of mathematical methods were developed that later were applied to business. Some problems OR deals with are the analyses and improvements of production, inventory, distribution, transportation, scheduling, and marketing.

opinion [A] See *auditor's opinion*.

opportunity costs [A] An alternative investment or project that is given up for another. It's a basic concept in business that all investment or business options have some risk, even those that seem the safest. The safest option risks losing the opportunity of greater gains elsewhere. With limited funds available to a business, investing in one project means a business cannot invest in another that could prove to be more profitable.

optical scanner [C] A device that captures text in a document, like a copy machine, so it can be use in word-processing or desktop publishing software.

optimization [M] A term used in investment mathematics to find the right balance between the different asset classes, given an amount of risk desired.

optimize [S] To find the best result given the circumstances. If the best result is not pursued, one will suboptimize.

option [F] The right to buy or sell a stock, or a commodity, for a set price up until a specific end date. An option to buy a security is called a *call* option. An option to sell a security is called a *put option*.

option key [C] A key on the Macintosh keyboard that, in concert with other keys, can generate special characters or special commands.

OR [M] See *operations research*.

oral contract [L] A contract that is not in writing. An oral contract, usually consisting of a spoken agreement, may be enforceable in court.

> The dress designer felt that she had obtained an *oral contract* with Zippy Corp. when the vice president assured her that he would supply all the materials for the new zipper model.

order entry [B] The procedures involved with handling and processing incoming orders for the products or services of a business. Usually it involves a systematic or computerized method to capture and track an order.

order taker [S] An employee who simply does what he or she is told. The term probably originated in sales to describe a person who was unassertive and just took orders from customers.

ordinal number [M] A number that represents the order in a series as well as the magnitude of a quantity. This is in contrast to a "cardinal number," which only represents its magnitude but not order. For instance, AOL has 13 million (cardinal number) customers and is the number one (ordinal number) internet service. An ordinal gives the position, or order, such as first, second, third, and so forth.

ordinance [L] A local law that pertains to citizens and businesses, such as jaywalking (crossing the street illegally) or panhandling (begging for money in public).

ordinary income [T] A term used in taxes meaning income on which the full amount of taxes is due without any special deduction or reduced rate such as capital gains taxation, which at the beginning of 1999 has a maximum rate of 20 percent.

ordinate [M] In graphing, the vertical distance from the x-axis to a point. See *abscissa*.

organizational development (OD) [HR] The use of a variety of techniques, such as team building, group dynamics, and sensitivity training, all designed to make an organization function more productively. The consultant who conducts OD activities is often called a "change agent" because there are attitudinal and behavioral changes that often are needed to be made.

organizational goals [B] The business plans and projects for the immediate future of a company.

organization chart [B] A graphic diagram of who reports to whom in a company. The overall company chart usually shows the senior executives as well as functional heads of departments. Each department then has its organization diagrammed in more detail.

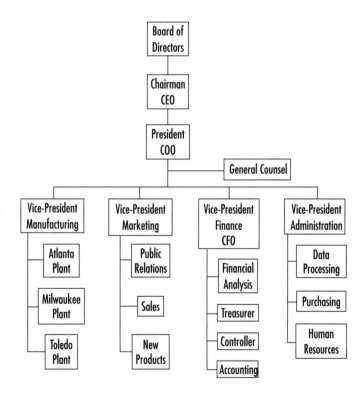

organization man [S] An employee who adopts completely the organizational goals of a company. The term was made popular by the 1956 best-selling book of the same name by William Whyte.

Organization for Economic Cooperation and Development (OECD) [E] An international organization that encourages economic growth, high employment, and financial stability among its members. It was an outgrowth of an organization to help Western Europe after World War II. In 1961, it started to extend membership to other nations, and today most of the major nations are members.

organized labor [B] Unions authorized by employees of trades or sectors of the economy to represent employee interests in bargaining for wages, work rules, and employee benefits. Unions may negotiate contracts or call for employee strikes.

origin [M] In graphing it is the zero point. It is that point at the center or where the x-axis and y-axis meet.

original equipment manufacturer (OEM) [B] A company that makes products that are used in other products as components. Such items may include computer monitors or speakers that may be sold along with the basic computer because the name brand or special features of the monitors or speakers are desired by the customer.

orphans and widows [C] In word-processing software, an orphan is the first line of a paragraph that appears alone on the last line on a page. A widow is the last line of a paragraph that appears alone at the top of the next page. Word-processing software allows the user to eliminate widows and orphans so that all the lines of a paragraph fall on the same page.

OSHA (Occupational Safety and Health Act) [HR] The 1970 legislation that set standards for worker safety not only in the factory but also in the office. Pronounced O-sha.

OS/2 [C] An operating system for IBM PCs that has the ability to run more than one program at the same time.

other people's money (OPM) [B] A phrase referring to business ventures founded with the capital of other people's money as opposed to the business owner's own money. It may be banks or venture capital that provide the seed money for the business, but generally little or no money is put up by the owner of the business. Since many start-up businesses need financing, OPM is a critically important element of that financing.

outdoor advertising [B] The various forms of ads that appear "out of doors." Most commonly, the billboard is used and is located at high-traffic areas.

outlet [B] A retail store that is operated by a manufacturer or has direct manufacturer goods. Outlet stores are usually for the purpose of selling off overstock and irregular or damaged goods.

> The Smiths always made a yearly trek to the *outlets* to get the best bargain on school clothes and supplies.

outlier [M] In statistics, a data value that is far outside the normal range.

out-of-pocket [S] Not available during a certain time.

> "I'll be *out-of-pocket* for about two days in Brussels," said Cruthers.

out-of-pocket costs [S] Nonreimbursable expenditures, especially medical costs that are borne by an employee.

out of the loop [S] Not part of the regular chain of communications or rumor mill.

out of the money [F] See *at the money.*

outplacement service [HR] A service to employees who have lost their jobs, generally due to downsizing. The service is usually performed by outplacement firms that provide counseling, assistance in writing resumes, interviewing skills, and help in networking for jobs.

outside directors [B] Nonemployees/officers who serve on the board of directors of a company. Sometimes all directors of the board are outside directors, but often there are certain officers of the company that are appointed, such as the president, executive vice president, and vice president of operations, among others.

outside-the-box thinking [S] Nonconformist thinking. Thinking of new ways, new products, new services, new procedures, new approaches to advertising and marketing a product, and so forth. That is, to think outside the usual way of thinking about something.

outsourcing [B] The practice of purchasing either parts or services from outside the company as opposed to producing or performing those services in-house. For instance, in manufacturing, a company could either produce many of the parts or buy them, usually cheaper, from outside sources. In services, a company could either have a staff of in-house lawyers or buy those legal services from an outside law firm. Also, a company could outsource employment recruiters, hiring on a temporary basis experienced recruiters to hire for a particular department where immediate and highly dedicated hiring is necessary.

out to lunch [S] Someone who is not with it.

overage [B] Excess supply. Overage may also refer to a provision in some leases to collect a certain percentage of a retail store's sales above the rental. Yet another usage can refer to the amount of money a company is over budget in a certain area.

> There was an *overage* of sheet metal this month, so next month's supply had to be adjusted.

overdraft [A] A check drawn on a checking account in which there are insufficient funds to cover the check. Sometimes referred to as an "NSF check" or a "not-sufficient-funds check." Basically, it means a bad or bounced check.

overhead [A] Costs that cannot be specifically charged to a product or project but instead are lumped together and charged to all units of the company. These costs can include rent, taxes, and general office expenses.

[S] Term that collectively describes the useless people in an organization.

> Cruthers whispered that the two accountants from Head Office were just *overhead* and not to be taken seriously.

overnight [B] To rush a letter, report, or material, using an overnight delivery express service.

> Williams suggested that the only way to get the samples to the vendor was to *overnight* it.

overrun [B] A quantity of publications printed beyond the number actually needed. Some catalog businesses, for instance, print an overrun of catalogs as a contingency in case some get lost, or for additional mailings.

over-the-counter (OTC) [F] A stock traded on the NASDAQ, which is in contrast to the New York Stock Exchange. Brokers are connected to the OTC and trade electronically with each other. The OTC market is mainly comprised of smaller companies, although some larger firms not yet registered on the Big Board (The New York Stock Exchange) are traded. See *NASD* and *NASDAQ*.

over the top [S] A spectacular result, even higher than high.

over the transom [S] Surprise work that came in, generally unsolicited. Commonly used in the book publishing business to refer to unsolicited manuscripts.

overtime [HR] Work that is done beyond standard hours that may call for additional compensation, particularly for nonexempt employees. Employees sometimes have the choice of taking time off in lieu of money. See *nonexempt employee*.

overwrite mode [C] In word-processing software, the replacing of letters by typing over the existing ones.

owner's equity [A] See *stockholder's equity*.

own the eyeballs; own the user's eyeballs [S] Generally a software term for trying to dominate users so as to monopolize them.

P

Pacific Rim [E] The countries that surround the Pacific Ocean. Some of these countries, such as Indonesia, Japan, Korea, and Malaysia, have enjoyed booming economic growth in recent times. However, in 1998 these countries experienced a severe slowdown.

Pac-Man defense [B] Just like the popular 1980s video game, this term describes the strategy in which a business tries to take over a company that initially tried to take it over.

padding [B] This term describes the act of adding unnecessary or irrelevant material or costs.

> Jones was fired for constantly *padding* his hours on his time sheet; he frequently billed the company for time he hadn't spent working.

page break [C] This term describes the separation of one page from another in word-processing software.

page up/down key (PgUp/PgDn) [C] The keys on a computer keyboard that move the cursor up or down one page at a time.

pagination [C] A word describing the numbering of pages in a document.

palette [C] The selection of colors that are available to be displayed by a computer monitor.

palmtop [C] A computer so small that it fits in the user's hand or palm. It is also referred to as a personal digital assistant (PDA).

P&L (profit and loss statement) [A] See income statement.

paperless office [B] The idealized concept that no paper will be needed in the office of the future as all work will be done on computers.

paper profits [A] A gain in capital that is theoretical because of an increase in the price of a stock or investment but that remains unrealized until the stock or investment is actually sold.

paper shuffler [S] A person who does his job in a clerk-like manner and always follows procedures.

parabola [M] A mathematical curve in which all oncoming parallel lines reflect to a single point.

paradigm; paradigm shift [S] A model or theory of business practices. When this theory changes drastically and suddenly, a paradigm shift occurs. This was the case in the 1980s when business turned away from the concept of hiring for lifetime employment to downsizing their workforce and seeking out fresh, young employees.

parallel port [C] A twenty-five-pin socket on a computer used to connect a printer or other device. The parallel port allows for more than one bit of data to be transmitted at one time.

parallel processing [C] The ability of a computer to carry out multiple tasks simultaneously.

parameter [S] An aspect or constraint on a problem or situation.
   [M] See *statistic*.

paranoid [HR] Adjective describing a person who is mistrusting and suspicious of the actions of others.

pardon [L] An executive privilege to relieve a person of further punishment for a crime. See *clemency*.

parent company [B] A company that owns one or more smaller companies. Although a parent company is a separate legal entity, it may tightly oversee and manage the companies it controls. However, even if a parent company takes a hands-off approach to its controlled companies, it may be held responsible along with the subsidiary in a lawsuit.

Pareto's optimality [E] A theory that no one can become better off without someone else becoming worse off. It was postulated by the Italian economist Vilfredo Pareto (1848–1923). His last name is pronounced pa-RAY-to.

Pareto's rule (law or diagram) [M] The "80–20" rule suggests that 80 percent of a company's business comes from 20 percent of its customers, or that 80 percent of a company's problems come from 20 percent of its activities. It appears to be a common occurrence in business. It is named for Vilfredo Pareto, (1848–1923) an Italian economist.

Parkinson's law [S] A law that observes that the amount of work to be done expands to fill the time available for its completion. It is named for the English historian C. Northcote Parkinson.

parole [L] The release of a person from prison after he has served part of his sentence under certain conditions of lawful behavior. "Probation" is the release of someone convicted of a crime without imprisonment, usually under conditions set by the court.

partnership [B] The situation in which two or more people join in association to form a business and do not operate under a corporate form of business. Limited partners contribute only money to the venture, not input or expertise. General partners, however, have the responsibility of running the firm. A silent partner remains in the background, contributing money and perhaps expertise.

par value [A] An arbitrary value set as the face amount on the stock certificate, often $1.

[F] The face value of a bond, usually $1,000. Municipal bonds usually have a face value of $5,000. Treasury issues have varying par values.

Pascal [C] A popular computer programming language. It was created by the Swiss professor Niklaus Wirth in the 1970s and named after the famous French mathematician Blaise Pascal.

Pascal's triangle [M] A specific order of numbers in a triangular array devised by the French mathematician Blaise Pascal (1602–1674).

passive-aggressive [S] A behavior typified by attempts to undermine the credibility or authority of another person while disguising any obvious negative or hostile feelings toward them. It is an indirect way of getting even with someone.

passive income; passive losses [T] Sources of income (or losses) that result from a businesses in which one is not an active participant.

> Abby noted the *passive income* generated from the rental of her investment property in Alabama on her tax forms.

password [C] A security method used to keep unauthorized people from obtaining sensitive information. A private word, phrase, or number is usually required before a user can gain access to information, be it a computer network or voice-mail system.

patent [L] Legal right to hold sole ownership of an invention for a period of twenty years from the date of application. If a company uses an invention that is not its own without authorization, it can be charged with patent infringement. After the twenty-year period, the invention falls into the public domain. See *intellectual property*.

path/pathname [C] The text that maps out the location of a file within the complex of files and directories in a computer.

payback period [A] The period of time it takes to recover the initial cost of an investment.

[F] The amount of time it takes for the money an investor put into an investment to come back in interest, income, or appreciation.

paycheck withholding [HR] Various items that are deducted from gross pay, such as medical and life insurance, 401(k) deductions, FICA taxes for Social Security, and state and federal income tax withholding. Sometimes refers to income tax withholding only.

payload [B] Any cargo that will produce income. Payload is typically expressed in weight.

> That shipment of peaches was 200 pounds of *payload* for the peach growers.

payoffs [B] An illegal payment or bribe to third parties or to middlemen who perform some service for a company.

payout ratio [F] The percentage of net earnings that a company pays to its investors in the form of dividends. The higher a payout ratio, the less a company has to invest in equipment and other technology.

payroll [A] The total of all the salaries paid out to a company's employees. Salaries are usually paid to professionals, while wages are usually paid to factory workers.

PBX (private branch exchange) [C] A telephone company-like system that functions within a company. Each extension within a company can be dialed directly without having to call out of the office.

PC (personal computer) [C] The name IBM gave its microcomputer and what all IBM clones are called. Although the term refers to all microcomputers, it is generally used to refer to IBM-type computers as opposed to Macintoshes, or Macs. See *computer*.

PC-DOS [C] The specific DOS for IBM-type computers. It stands for "personal computer disk operating system."

PCS (personal communications services) [C] A term describing a variety of wireless communication devices.

PDA (personal digital assistant) [C] A hand-held computer with a variety of features including wireless communication to phones or computers.

peer group; peers [S] A term describing people at the same level in an organization.

> The three managers who reported to the vice president were all required to complete *peer* reviews of each other.

peer review [HR] A performance review of a worker written by another worker at the same level in a company. This is sometimes done at companies to obtain comments from those who work side-by-side. These comments are then funneled to the boss who completes the review. Business psychology studies show that comments from peers are often very perceptive and accurate.

penalty [T] An additional amount of money due because of omission or correction.

pencil in [S] The act of making a tentative plan in a schedule book. It is in contrast to inking in a more permanent plan.

> Cruthers told the staff to *pencil in* Saturday work if the project wasn't done by Friday.

pen computer [C] A computer that lets the user write directly on a small monitor with a special stylus to capture a signature or note for future reference.

penny stock [F] A low priced stock. Although inexpensive, these stocks rarely cost a penny. Usually more than $1, these stocks are traded on the over-the-counter market and other smaller exchanges.

> Pension Benefit Guarantee Corp. (PBGC) [HR] A government agency that protects pension plans. If a pension plan does not contain enough money to pay benefits, the PBGC will pay up to $30,000 per retiree per year. Each pension plan must pay premiums into the PBGC, which is used to establish the fund to pay benefits if necessary.

pension plan [HR] A retirement fund that pays a benefit at a specific retirement age, usually as a monthly payment. The employer is often the only contributor. The usual form of payment is an annuity payment, but some companies offer a lump sum. Typically, a reduced benefit is paid if the employee retires before a certain age. See *retirement plan*.

Common Pension Plan Payouts

Single-life annuity Payment to only the employee, with no payment to a beneficiary.

50 percent joint and survivor annuity A reduced payment plan for the employee, in which a payment of 50 percent of what the employee received is paid to the spouse for life in the incidence of the death of the employee.

100 percent joint and survivor annuity A reduced payment plan for the employee in which a payment of 100 percent of what the employee received is paid to the spouse for life in the incidence of the death of the employee.

Period certain option An annuity form of payment that promises to pay a preset number of payments even if the retiree doesn't survive to receive them all. For instance, if an employee selects a ten-year period certain, benefits would be payable for as long as the employee was alive. However, if the employee dies within the first ten years, the remaining payments are payable to a named beneficiary or estate.

Social Security leveling option An annuity form providing a greater pension benefit before age sixty-two, or whenever the employee starts Social Security, and then a lower pension payment thereafter. A person may wish to level the combination of pension and Social Security payments. It tends to keep retirement income level before and after Social Security.

Lump-sum payment A one-time payment that usually can be put into a Rollover IRA that may have some special tax advantages.

Pentium chip [C] The name Intel has given to its 586 microprocessor. The Intel Pentium chip is several times faster than the old 486 microprocessor. The more advanced Pentium II is even faster, running at a speed of 450 mhz.

PEO (professional employer organization) [B] A new development in business, it is the company that is responsible for the human resources function of a company that chooses to outsource that department. A PEO can recruit and hire employees and set up 401(k) plans.

P/E ratio (price/earnings ratio) [F] See *price/earnings ratio.*

per capita [A] A Latin word meaning *per head*. A per capita expense is one that a company has to pay for each person it employs. Pronounced per-CAP-a-ta

> Instituting this new health plan would incur a *per capita* annual expense of $900.

per capita; per stirpes [T] The two methods of distributing assets outlined in a will, either to specific people (per capita) or to family lineage (per stirpes). Pronounced per-CAP-a-ta and per-STIR-pees.

percent [M] One part in a hundred.

percent yield [F] The income or dividend return of an investment, such as a stock or bond. If a bond has a par value of $1,000 (as is the standard) and it pays $80 during the year, then the yield is 8 percent per year ($80 divided by $1,000 equals .08 or 8 percent).

per diem [A] Latin word meaning *per day*. Expense accounts in business are often calculated per diem, meaning that an employee is given a daily allowance for her expenses.

> Before Brown went on his business trip, the company cut him a check for $700, a *per diem* allowance of $100 for each of the seven days he'd be at the conference.

perfect competition [E] See *competition*.

perfectionist [S] One who strives to get everything right the first time, every time.

performance appraisal [HR] A formal review of how well an employee has done over the past year that is used to determine the amount of a merit increase he will receive.

performance bond [RE] A bond usually given by a builder or developer to the local municipality to guarantee that all improvements it was contracted to complete will be completed.

> Smallville always required a hefty *performance bond* to insure that local developers would fix all roads and install proper utilities before they were finished with their jobs.

peril [I] A possible cause of loss, such as fire, accident, or premature death. Technically, there is a distinction between the terms *peril* and *hazard*. A peril is the cause of a loss; a hazard is the condition that caused the loss. For instance, an accident is the peril, whereas a slippery floor is the hazard.

period certain option [HR] See *pension plan.*

peripheral [C] Any hardware device that is connected to a computer, such as a monitor, mouse, keyboard, or printer.

perjury [L] The act of lying in court while under oath.

perk; perquisite [HR] Extra compensation a company offers in addition to salary, such as country club memberships and free coffee. It sometimes also refers to fringe benefits such as 401(k) plans.

> The salary wasn't great at Zippy Corp., but the *perks*—from a company car to a lifetime supply of zippers—were great.

permutations [M] All of the possible arrangements of items in a specific order.

perpendicular [M] Lines that cross at right angles.

personal computer (PC) [C] See *PC.*

personal digital assistant (PDA) [C] See *palmtop.*

personal property [T] Non-real estate assets, such as furniture, jewelry, and cars.

personalty [L] A technical term for personal property; something moveable, such as furniture. Pronounced PER-sa-nel-tee.

personnel [HR] The traditional name for the company function of overseeing hiring, training, compensation, benefits, and other related activities. Now, the department is more commonly referred to as "human resources," or "HR." See *human resources.*

personnel file [HR] The file a company keeps on individual employees, which includes their job application, resume, performance reviews, and related items.

PERT diagram [M] An acronym for Program Evaluation Review Technique. It is a scheduling method that shows the sequence of the various activities that need to be completed before accomplishing a project.

Peter Principle [S] A theory that employees in a company will be promoted until they reach a job that they are incapable of completing. It was the title of a 1969 book, *The Peter Principle*, by Laurence Peter.

> Mr. Green was promoted because he excelled at all the bookkeeping jobs. This resulted in the loss of a good bookkeeper and the making of a lousy boss, a perfect example of the *Peter Principle* at work.

petty cash [A] A small amount of cash kept on hand at a company for immediate and miscellaneous expenses.

phantom stock plan [B] A form of an incentive stock option in which no actual stock is used. An employee is rewarded as if real stock was used.

Phillips curve [E] A diagram describing the relationship between inflation and unemployment developed by economist W.H. Phillips (1914–1975). Philips postulated that when unemployment is high, inflation is low, and vice versa. However, there have been times where both have been high or low. In the 1970s, inflation soared and unemployment was high. In the 1990s, inflation and unemployment were both low.

pi [M] A repeating mathematical constant that equals 3.14159. It is extremely useful in geometry and equals the circumference of a circle divided by its diameter. It is represented by the Greek letter for p, which is π. Although the constant was known as early as about 2000 B.C., the actual symbol π was not used for this constant until A.D. 1700s.

PIC file [C] A file extension for graphic files. PIC is short for picture.

pictogram [M] A graph that uses pictures to represent figures. See *graph*.

piece work; piece workers [B] Factory work that is paid for by the piece. The more pieces a worker completes, the more he earns.

> Acme Corp. had its new line of slime ball covers sewn by *piece workers* for fifty cents per piece.

pie chart or graph [M] A circular graph that shows divisions of items according to their frequencies. See *graph*.

pie in the sky [S] An unattainable goal that is often dreamed of.

piercing the corporate veil [L] The process of placing responsibility for wrongdoing on a corporate entity that is seemingly unrelated to it. This occurs when a subsidiary of a parent company is a separate legal entity, but the parent company is held responsible along with the subsidiary.

Pigou effect [E] A theory that price and wage flexibility could be managed to obtain full employment. British economist Arthur Pigou (1877–1959) postulated that if the supply of money was increased enough, individuals would increase their spending, which would lead to full employment.

PIN (personal identification number) [C] A numerical password used for identification.

pin head [S] An adjective used to describe a person who is unimaginative and small in his thinking.

pink-collar jobs [HR] The term used for traditional office work such as administrative and receptionist work, where women held most of the jobs. The term came into vogue in the 1920s.

pink sheets [F] Daily reports giving the prices of thousands of stocks that are traded on the over-the-counter market.

pink slip [HR] A notice of termination of employment. The term first came into being in the 1920s when a pink slip with a discharge notice was inserted in the last pay envelope. When a company is sending out pink slips, it is firing employees. May also be used as a verb, as in "Jones was *pink-slipped* on Friday." See *laid off*.

> The cutbacks at Zippy Corp. led to the issue of 300 *pink slips* last
> week; it had to let a substantial part of its work force go.

pixel [C] The smallest element making up an image on a computer screen. The word pixel is formed from pix (picture) and el (element).

Pkzip/Pkunzip [C] A shareware software program that compresses and decompresses files. PK stands for Phil Katz, of Pkware Inc. Pronounced P-K-zip and P-K-unzip.

plaintiff [L] A person who initiates a lawsuit against another person or company.

plan A; plan B [S] The main plan of action is plan A. If it doesn't work out, the fall-back plan is plan B.

planned economy [E] An economy that is controlled mostly by the government, as opposed to a "free market economy," in which individuals and businesses make most of the economic decisions.

plasma display [C] A flat-screen technology that contains inert ionized gas.

play politics [S] See *politics*.

plea [L] The broad category of responses of a defendant in a criminal case.

plea bargaining [L] A legal arrangement through which a person pleads guilty to a lesser charge in return for a lighter sentence. Individuals who plea bargain are usually required to provide valuable information in a case.

plotter [C] A large-scale graphics printer.

PMS colors [B] The standard within the graphic arts and printing industry to identify the exact shade of a color. PMS stands for Pantone Matching System.

point [RE] An amount representing 1 percent of a mortgage amount. One or two points are often charged by lenders to cover the costs of processing mortgage applications.

> To provide an incentive for borrowers, American-European Bank was offering a mortgage with no *points*.

point and click [C] The process of moving the cursor on the screen with a mouse and clicking to select an option.

point of purchase display or promotion or sale (POP) [B] The displays that sit on or next to the check-out counter in a store. They are designed to cause impulse or unplanned purchases. Any sale made at the point of sale is called a point of purchase sale.

point-to-point protocol (PPP) [C] A communications protocol that allows computers to connect to the internet through a phone line or high-speed connection.

pointy head [S] A pejorative term for an impractical intellectual or technical person. It comes from the term "egghead."

poison pill [B] A strategy used by a company to prevent or thwart a threatened takeover. The strategy commonly involves paying lucrative bonuses to executives to create debt. These maneuvers may be too costly to allow the threatening company to pursue the takeover.

policy [I] An insurance contract. A life insurance policy specifies who is insured, the beneficiary, and the various terms of the insurance. A property insurance policy specifies what property is covered, which perils are covered, and how much will be paid under what conditions.

policy loan [I] The amount of loan that is allowed under a life insurance policy, if any.

policy owner [I] The company or individual who has the right to exercise control over an insurance policy.

politics [S] A term describing actions performed to get ahead not only by just doing a good job but also by being nice to the boss and doing things to get noticed. This is opposed to getting ahead through "teamwork" or by doing one's best and hoping to get noticed. A person who commonly engages in politics is called one who "plays politics." There is another, more broad meaning to the term as well. When one says that there are *politics* involved in a business deal, she is referring to touchiness surrounding the situation.

polling the jury [L] The act of a judge asking each jury member for his or her individual verdict.

polynomial [M] See *binomial*.

Ponzi scheme [S] An illegal investment pyramid scam in which money from new investors is not invested but spent by those running the scheme. Some of the money is used to pay off complaining investors to keep them quiet. It is named after Charles Ponzi, who was in and out of jails most of his life. In Boston in 1920, his was convicted of selling foreign postal coupons that were worthless. Thousands of people lost their money and six banks failed. He died in a charity ward in Rio de Janeiro in 1949. See *bubble* and *pyramid scheme*.

population [M] A specific term in statistics that refers to the whole range of whatever is being studied, as opposed to a sample, which is only a part of the whole group being studied.

pop-up window [C] A menu of options that appears on a computer screen within a software program.

port [C] The place on the back of a computer into which various peripheral devices are plugged. There are two main types of ports, parallel for a printer and serial for a mouse.

portability of pensions [HR] A feature not currently available with pension plans that would allow a person to take his accrued pension money with him upon leaving a company. In contrast, a 401(k) plan does have portability in that a person can take that money when she leaves a company.

portfolio [F] An investor's total investments.

portfolio of skills [HR] The variety of job skills that a person has that makes her more valuable to a company or that makes it easier for her to move from one job to another. These are skills such as knowledge of a variety of computer software programs, communication skills including the ability to write effective letters and reports, presentation skills, and in-depth technical know-how about a field.

portrait [C] A page orientation in which the page is taller than it is wide. This is in contrast to "landscape orientation," which is wider than it is tall.

positioning [B] A business strategy of presenting and packaging products or services in a certain way so as to influence customers.

> Acme Perfume decided to sell its fragrance under the new name of "Essence" instead of its traditional name, "Plain Jane," in hopes that this *positioning* would attract a more upscale buyer.

post; posting [C] A contribution to a newsgroup. One user's post may be responded to by other posts. A newsgroup is much like a giant community bulletin boards, and a post is like the little card one person pins up.

post date (a check) [B] To make a check valid at some future date, usually within a short period of time. When the check is made out, the date when the check can be cashed is put in the date section.

post office; Postal Service, U.S. [B] The quasi-governmental enterprise that is the main delivery service for mail. Its huge operation includes about 800,000 employees and processes about 200 billion pieces of mail each year. It has the legal obligation of universal mail delivery and is self-sustaining.

potential gross income multiplier (PGIM) [RE] The ratio of the value of a property to the amount of income that property is presently (or potentially could) generate.

pound; pound sterling [E] The currency of the United Kingdom that was the key international currency standard as early as the 1800s. It still remains a key currency but has been supplanted by the U.S. dollar and the European euro.

poverty [E] The lowest category of individual earnings and assets in a country. It is determined either by a general percentage or by a specific level of earnings per size of households.

power [M] The number of times a number is multiplied by itself. It is often referred to as "raised to the power of." It is also referred to as the "exponent." In the expression 5^4, the power (or exponent) is 4, meaning the number 5 is multiplied by itself 4 times, or $5 \times 5 \times 5 \times 5 = 625$.

PowerBook [C] A family of portable computers made by Apple Computer.

power breakfast; power lunch [S] A meeting of powerful or influential people that takes place while dining.

power of attorney [L] The legal authority to perform financial or personal duties for another person. The authorization is usually in writing.

> Karla was out of the country for three months on an archaeological dig and had given Paul the *power of attorney* to pay her rent from her checking account.

power users [C] A casual term applied to techies: math-, engineering-, or science-oriented computer users who use high-speed computers for their applications.

PPO (preferred provider organization) [HR] See *health insurance*.

PPP (point-to-point protocol) [C] See *point-to-point protocol*.

PR [B] See *public relations*.

practice of law [L] The professional conduct of a lawyer according to rules of the legal profession.

pre-admission testing [HR] A cost-saving approach to elective surgery in which a patient goes for mandatory pro-operative testing before being admitted. This saves money in that the patient is not charged by the hospital for occupying a room while having tests done.

precious metals [F] Gold, silver, and other metals of high value. Mutual funds of precious metals are invested in mining stocks and gold bullion.

predatory pricing [B] The strategy of reducing prices of products to drive competitors from the marketplace.

preemptive rights [A] A stockholder's right to keep a constant percentage of outstanding stock. When more stock is offered to the public, and there is a preemptive right, stockholders can purchase additional shares before they are sold to others.

pre-existing condition [HR] A medical condition that could make it difficult to obtain health insurance. Typically, a health insurance plan excludes payment for the treatment of health problems one already has, at least for a period of time.

prefabricated house (prefab) [RE] A house that is constructed in parts in a factory and then put together at a site.

preference item [T] See *alternative minimum tax.*

preferred stock [F] A class of stock in which the dividend is fixed, like a bond. Typically, preferred stock is more desirable than common shares if a company is liquidated.

preliminary hearing [L] A court proceeding to determine whether there is enough evidence to hold a person for trial.

premeditation [L] Forethought and deliberation about a crime.

premium [B] An additional amount paid above the market value, or a free gift given to a customer to entice them to make a purchase.

> That figure represents a *premium* over recent market sales, due to the great demand.

[I] The charge for insurance. Premiums are commonly paid annually, semi-annually, or quarterly.

> The annual *premium* for Mary's term life insurance rose this year from $100 to $120.

[F] The amount of a bond's price that is greater than par value. When interest rates decline, the market value of a bond goes up and is valued at a premium.

prepaid expenses [A] An expense paid in advance, such as rent. A company may have the extra cash, or it may want to add to expenses at the end of the accounting period as a way of decreasing its immediate taxes.

prepayment clause; prepayment penalty [RE] That part of a loan contract that indicates what penalties if any are due if part of the loan is paid early.

> XYZ Corp. had thought about paying off the balance of the loan, but the *prepayment penalty* made it wiser to wait and pay it off on schedule.

prepayment of principal [RE] The process of paying additional principal ahead of schedule, usually to shorten the loan period, especially with a fixed-rate mortgage. For a variable rate mortgage, prepayment of principal usually decreases the monthly payment amount, leaving the term the same.

preponderance of evidence [L] The degree of proof required in a civil trial. A civil trial can be decided by the presence of a significant amount, or preponderance, of evidence. This is in contrast to a criminal case, in which the evidence must prove guilt beyond a reasonable doubt.

pre-qualified for mortgage [RE] The process by which a buyer of property obtains pre-approval from a bank or mortgage company for a loan whose amount is based on the buyer's income and assets. This allows the buyer to quickly buy a property as soon as it is found.

prescription drugs [HR] Drugs that are prescribed by a physician for a specific medical condition, usually paid for in part by company medical plans. Medicare, however, does not include the cost of drugs.

present-day dollars [M] See *today's dollars.*

present value (PV) [M] The worth of something in the future, valued in the present. An example is a zero-coupon bond, in which the value in the future is set at $1,000 (its maturity value). What is the value today, or present value? Well, if the interest rate is 7 percent and the bond matures in ten years, then the present value is about $500, or about one-half. If an investor invests $500 today and the investment earns 7 percent interest, in ten years she will have $1,000. To calculate a present value, an interest rate called the "discount rate" is needed along with the number of years the money will be invested. See *future value*.

president [B] Typically the chief operating officer of a company. In many cases, the chairman is the top executive responsible for policy and the overall direction of the company, whereas the president, who reports to the chairman, is responsible for day-to-day operations.

pretax [T] The ability to contribute to an investment such as a 401(k) from gross pay, reducing the amount of wages that will be taxed.

price [B] The amount a company gets for its products. Retail price is the full price a consumer pays. Wholesale price is the price the distributor pays, especially if buying in bulk.

[E] The amount a consumer is willing to pay, and the amount a producer is willing to sell it to you for. See *supply and demand*.

price/earnings ratio (P/E ratio) [F] An important investment calculation, it is the ratio of the current price of a company's stock divided by the company's earnings per share. It is a tool investors can use to see if a stock has been evaluated by the market at higher or lower price than other stocks in the same industry.

pricing [M] The analysis of setting prices in the marketplace.

prima facie [L] A case that does not require further facts, for instance when a person is caught with stolen money. It is Latin for *at first view*, or *on its face*. Pronounced PRE-ma FAY-shee.

primary care physician [HR] A term describing the first doctor a person sees before visiting a specialist, or the one doctor who is responsible for a person's overall medical treatment in an HMO (health maintenance organization).

primary metropolitan statistical area (PMSA) [B] A specific designation by the U.S. Census Bureau of a metropolitan area of over 1 million people. When two PMSAs overlap they are known as a "consolidated metropolitan statistical area (CMSA)." See *standard metropolitan statistical area (SMSA)*.

prime (number) [M] A whole number only divisible by itself and 1. The number 1 is not considered a prime number. The numbers 2, 3, 5, and 7 are examples of prime numbers.

prime rate [F] The most favorable rate of business loan a bank offers. It's reserved for its preferred customers.

PRIME/SCORE [F] A PRIME is a unit of investment containing only the income part of the stock, whereas a SCORE is the unit containing the growth or appreciation of the same stock. Therefore, a stock has been divided into two so an investor can, if she so chooses, receive only one element of that stock. They are limited in number and are traded on the American Stock Exchange. Both acronyms are a bit of a reach with PRIME standing for Prescribed Right to Income and Maximum Equity and SCORE being Special Claim on Residual Equity.

principal [F] The amount of money borrowed or invested. Principal is distinguished from the interest, dividend, or growth on the original investment.

> In the first few years of mortgage payments, you are paying almost all interest; very little of the *principal* is paid back.

prioritize; prioritizing [S] The act of ranking activities or goals in order of importance.

> The boss was *prioritizing* our department goals, putting service first and coffee breaks last.

private letter ruling [T] An individual letter from the IRS that formally answers an important tax question initiated by a taxpayer.

privately held company [B] A company that is owned by a family or small number of investors and does not issue publicly traded stock. Some large companies that are privately held are Cargill, Koch, and United Parcel Service.

private sector [E] That part of the economy made up of businesses and individuals, as opposed to the government.

privatization [E] The process of moving government functions into the private sector. Many cities have privatized the removal of garbage, among other services. The proposed idea of having individuals deposit a part of their Social Security payments into their own private account is also called privatization.

proactive [S] The strategy of taking action; being on the offense.

probability [M] A mathematical method that determines the likelihood of something happening. For example, the probability of getting heads when flipping a coin is 50 percent.

probable cause [L] The possession of some facts or evidence that point to a person or company's wrongdoing.

probate [L] The legal process of proving that a will is valid, establishing the competency of the executor, completing the transfer of assets, and paying any federal and state estate taxes.

probate court [L] The court that settles wills, estates, and trusts. Can also be called surrogate court. Adoption is also occasionally settled by these courts.

probation [HR] The initial period of time in which a new employee must prove his or her worth, or else be terminated.

   [L] The release of someone convicted of a crime without imprisonment, usually with conditions set by the court. Parole is the term used for the conditional release from jail.

pro bono publico [L] A lawyer who is doing public good works, such as taking a case without compensation. The lawyer is then said to work *pro bono*. The *publico* part of the term is not used in speech. Pronounced pro-BO-no PUB-ly-ko.

process [L] A formal decree of a court exercising jurisdiction in a case that frequently compels an individual or company to appear in court.

Prodigy [C] One of the commercial internet access services.

producer price index (PPI) [E] An economic index of commonly used raw materials. It is generally thought to be a good leading indicator of inflation because it will eventually affect consumer prices.

product [B] A good or service offered by a company. Usually thought of as only manufactured goods, it is also used to mean a line of services at a firm.

> The accounting firm of Smith, Smith, and Smith offered three *products*: audit services, tax services, and offshore tax-haven services.

[M] The result of multiplication. Multiplying 4 by 5 results in the product of 20.

production [B] The assembling and manufacturing of goods.

productivity [E] The ability of a company to more efficiently make goods or perform services. It is usually measured by the amount of output compared to an amount of input.

product life cycle [B] A certain amount of time that a product may be viable, especially those that may be faddish or seasonal. For instance, a new toy or computer game may have a life cycle of only a few years before the public gets bored of it and moves onto something new. The product life cycle often follows the sequence of introduction, growth, maturity, and then decline.

profit [A] The difference between what it costs to produce something and what income is received for selling it. Income minus expenses equals profits.

[E] In economics, it is the incentive to price products and services high enough to make it worthwhile for producers but low enough to be afforded by consumers.

profit and loss statement (P&L) [A] See *income statement*.

profit center [B] A part of a company that is responsible for its revenue and expenses, or profits. It is usually a separate business unit.

profit-sharing plan [HR] A program in which employees receive a portion of company profits in one way or another. It can be an end-of-year bonus paid to employees, or it can be a contribution to a 401(k)-type savings plan. For a self-employed person, a profit-sharing plan can take the form of a SEP (simplified employee pension) or a Keogh (H.R. 10) plan.

pro forma statement [A] A financial statement projecting revenues and expenses, either as a normal business planning tool or for a hypothetical situation. Sometimes done when a company is considering buying another company or merging with another, or showing anticipated expansion. The term *pro forma* means *for the sake of form* in Latin. A company is "giving form to" a possible event.

program; programmer [C] A program is a set of instructions that tells a computer how to process the information it gets. A programmer is the person who designs the program.

program budgeting [A] The practice of creating a separate budget for a unit within a government agency. It allows separate government programs to have their own budgets.

program trading [F] A sophisticated investment strategy of taking an opposite position in futures contracts to one's investments. This is primarily a strategy for a large investor or institutional investment firm who employ computer systems to automatically transact these trades. Program trading was blamed for much of the fall in stock prices in October 1987.

progressive tax [E] An income tax system where the percentage of tax on an individual's income increases as that individual's income increases. For instance, as of 1999 the first federal tax rate is 15 percent, followed by 28 percent, then 31 percent, 36 percent, and eventually 39.6 percent as income exceeds $283,150. This is in contrast to a "flat tax," in which everyone pays the same tax rate. The FICA tax for Social Security is a flat tax. See *regressive tax*.

project budgeting [A] The practice of creating a separate budget for a specific project within a company.

projection [M] A mathematical or quantitative extension of known information into the future. For instance, if the inflation rate is currently 3 percent, a projection for inflation could be 3 percent, higher, or lower, depending on how conservative one wanted to make the assumptions.

promissory note [RE] A legal obligation to pay back a mortgage according to a schedule or specific time. Technically, the mortgage is the pledge of the property as security of a loan, whereas the promissory note is the actual loan payment schedule.

promotion [B] The presentation, communication, or advertising of a product or service that spurs interest in the product or service.

> As head of marketing, Jane proposed getting a national sports figure to *promote* the company's new line of underwear.

[HR] An elevation in responsibility, usually accompanied by an increase in salary.

prompt [C] An instruction that appears on the computer screen that asks the user to perform some task or give some information. The most recognized prompt of the past was the DOS "c" prompt, which looked like this: C:>. It tells the user to type in some sort of command right there.

property tax [T] A tax on the value of real estate. In some states, cars and other personal property are subject to property tax as well.

proprietary information [B] The private information of a company. This includes company strategies as well as proprietary formulas, such as the formula for Coca-Cola.

proprietary lease [RE] The lease a co-op corporation gives to a co-op apartment owner to allow the owner to live in a specific apartment. The owner's payments cover operating costs and any debt on the complex.

> When Debbie bought a co-op apartment to live in, she signed a *proprietary lease* with the co-op board to pay the monthly expenses.

prorate [A] To divide costs and allocate them proportionally. For example, overhead is often prorated across company divisions.

prosecutor [L] A public official who prepares and presents cases in court on behalf of the government.

prospectus [F] A legal document made available to potential investors that provides financial information about the company or mutual fund.

Before Andrew invested in the mutual fund, the fund manager sent him a *prospectus* for review.

protectionism [E] Various steps taken by a country to preserve its jobs, wages, and businesses.

protégé; protégée [S] A young person who is promoted by an influential boss or executive. The extra e appears when the word is used to describe a female. Both are pronounced pro-ta-ZHAY.

protocol [C] An agreed standard language that allows for compatibility between computers.

prototype [S] A model of a new product or invention.

proxy [A] A person who is authorized to act in place of another. A company usually solicits proxies from stockholders who do not expect to attend the annual stockholder's meeting.

proxy dispute or fight [B] A battle between two or more rivals in a corporate struggle for control. Often it is between company officers and outside investors who want to take over control of the company. The battle involves trying to win the right to individual stockholder proxies for votes.

proxy statement [F] An absentee ballot that allows stockholders, who have the right to vote on major company decisions, to cast a vote even if they aren't able to make the annual shareholder meeting in person, which almost no one does.

prudent man rule [L] A legal standard of conduct usually dealing with money. It requires that a person who has custody of money for another act as a *prudent man* would.

psych pay [S] Psychological benefits of a job, versus the actual pay. It may be a sense of accomplishment, status, or self-esteem.

public (going public) [F] The process by which a company puts shares in the corporation up for public sale. See *initial public offering*.

> After years of private ownership, the expanding WHIZ Toy Corp. decided to *go public* to raise money for future growth.

public affairs [B] See *public relations*.

public defender [L] A lawyer who is assigned to the criminal case of a person who does not have money to hire a lawyer.

public domain [L] Intellectual property that has exceeded the length of a copyright and are thus available for anyone to use. For instance, Shakespeare's works are part of the public domain.

public domain software [C] Software that has been given over to the public for anyone's use.

public relations (PR) [B] The general activities of a company that communicate a positive image of itself. This activity is often simply referred to as PR. "Public affairs," a part of a company's PR activities, are activities directed toward governmental agencies, elected officials, and special interest groups.

> Jane, head of the *public relations* department, proposed that the company sponsor the local theater group to improve its corporate image in the community.

public sector [E] Government activities at the federal, state, and local level. This is in contrast to the private sector, which is the economic activities of businesses and individuals.

public spending [E] Government spending at the federal, state, and local levels.

punitive award; punitive damages [L] Monetary compensation awarded to a person in a case, often for their pain and suffering.

purchasing power parity (PPP) [E] The general hypothesis that consumers equally situated in different countries have roughly the same purchasing power.

push/pull [S] The ability of a web site user to pull information from a site as well as telegraph his interests through software so companies can *push* specific information towards him.

push the envelope [S] To broaden the scope of the solutions to a problem. The term came into usage in 1978 when a NASA aircraft was being tested for a higher altitude. It was said that the aircraft's altitude envelope had to be expanded, or pushed. The term "envelope" had been used in aviation for many years as a boundary for the normal performance of aircraft.

put option [F] An option to sell a stock at a set price. The investor in a put option is betting that the price of the stock will decline, and consequently, he will be able to buy the stock at a lower price than the option to sell it, thus making money. A "call option" is an option to buy a stock at a set price.

pyramid scheme [F] A classic illegal investment scheme in which an operator hires distributors and receives sales commissions from them, who in turn hire distributors for commissions, and so on. Each level receives a percent of the hired sales. The scheme is illegal because the original operator's motive is just to receive commissions, not to really operate a bona fide business. The pyramiding usually falls under its own weight because the cumulative commissions make whatever product is sold too expensive. See *Ponzi scheme* and *bubble*.

Pythagorean theorem [M] The formula that specifies that the square of the hypotenuse (the long side of a triangle) equals the sum of the squares of each other side: $c^2 = a^2 + b^2$.

Q

Q&A [S] The common abbreviation for questions and answers. At the end of a presentation there is often a time for Q&A.

QDRO [T] [A] See *qualified domestic relations order*.

Q rating or score [B] A public relations type rating as to the public awareness of a personality. The higher the rating, the more favorable awareness a personality has.

Q ratio [F] A ratio of stock prices to their replacement value. It is often used to determine if the market is too high or low and therefore may signal a market upturn or downturn.

Q-TIP trust [T] A particular trust that allows a spouse to transfer assets to a surviving spouse but directs that any remaining assets after the death of the surviving spouse go to specific beneficiaries. It is used primarily when a spouse has children from a previous marriage. There is only a potential estate tax on the assets after the surviving spouse dies. The name is derived from *qualified terminable interest property*. Pronounced Q-tip.

quadratic equation [M] A common mathematical expression that has the form:

$$ax^2 + bx + c = 0.$$

quadratic formula [M] The general mathematical expression used to solve any quadratic equation.

qualified benefit plan [HR] A specific employee benefit plan qualified by the IRS to receive special tax advantages. Typical plans are pension, 401(k), and 403(b) plans. Lesser known plans are also qualified, such as ESOP (employee stock ownership plan), SEP (simplified employee plan), and Keogh (H.R.I.O. plan). These plans, in general, are tax-deferred in that the earnings are deferred to a later date. At retirement the plans, if paid in a lump sum, can generally be put tax-free into a rollover IRA.

qualified domestic relations order (QDRO) [T] A court order that requires a payment, in particular a benefit plan, in connection with a divorce. It can often mean the splitting of a 401(k) or pension plan into two, so that the other spouse is allowed to put his or her half into an IRA. For tax purposes, these transfers of assets are usually without tax consequence. A QDRO can also be a court order regarding child support or alimony. Pronounced QUAD-row.

qualified lead; qualifying lead [B] A sales prospect that is evaluated as an interested buyer. The process of evaluation is called **qualifying** the lead, whereas the actual prospect is the qualified lead. The purpose of qualifying a prospect is to determine if time and effort should be extended or if it would be a waste of time.

qualified opinion [A] See *auditor's opinion*.

quality benchmarking [B] The measuring of a company's products or services against the best quality products or services in the field. The goal is to meet or exceed the best available.

quality circle [B] A group of workers who are designated to meet regularly, usually in a small group, to discuss and implement specific improvements in the production and quality of their products. See *TQM*.

quality control [B] Any process a company uses to ensure that its product or service has a consistently high quality. Inspections and consumer feedback are examples of quality control tools.

> After instituting a whole program of *quality control*—from spot-check inspections to new computer evaluation programs—Zippy Corp. was able to lower the number of defective zippers produced.

quality of life (issues) [HR] Any of several issues that are perceived by people as improving their lives. Also called "lifestyle issues." Issues such as time off or childcare are prime examples.

quant [S] A person with strong mathematical, computer, or engineering abilities.

quantity discounts [M] Discounts that are usually available by buying in bulk or volume.

quantum jump or leap [S] A dramatic change or increase in action. The internet can be said to have experienced a *quantum leap* in users. The term comes from the physics' study of particle behavior versus the study of wave behavior.

questionnaire [B] A common market research tool used to determine customer attitudes about products and services. Devising the questionnaire is critical; it must include not only standard questions about age and income level but also questions posed so as to get objective, useful opinions. See *focus group*.

queuing theory [M] A mathematical analysis of things that happen in a single line, such as in a queue (the British word for "line"). Business applications are in manufacturing, customer service, and fast-food restaurants, among others. Sometimes called "waiting-line theory."

quick and dirty [S] A short and quick analysis to a problem, frequently concerning numbers.

> Smithers said that the *quick and dirty* way to estimate the defined benefit formula was to multiply by 1.2 percent. It was close enough to give a ballpark answer.

quick assets [A] The amount of cash, receivables, and marketable securities that can be converted quickly into cash.

quick ratio [A] See *acid test*.

quid pro quo [S] An equal exchange of things. Latin for **something for something**. Pronounced QUID-pro-kwo.

> Jim referred several clients to Jane as a *quid pro quo* for Jane helping him win an important municipal contract.

quitclaim deed [RE] A deed that passes any rights or interests in a property from one person to another without warranty as to other rights that someone else may have. Typically, IRS auctions carry a quitclaim deed.

> As all the town records had been lost in the great flood of 1926, the purchasers of the Bumstead estate got all the possible heirs to sign *quitclaim deeds* so that they could get free title.

quota [B] A specific manufacturing or sales mark that a department strives to meet. A quota may either be a number of items a department wants to produce or sell, or a certain increase over the last period.

> All the departments met their monthly *quotas* of selling 10 percent more than the previous month.

quotas [E] Limits placed on the import of certain goods.

> Alabascar placed strict *quotas* on textiles imported, allowing only one standard bale of wool per foreign country. This was done to protect its only viable industry.

quote [F] A market price at a given time.

quotient [M] The result of division. For example, when the number 14 (the dividend) is divided by 2 (the divisor), the quotient is 7.

Qwerty keyboard [C] The traditional keyboard on computers and typewriters. The name is derived from the sequence of keys in the upper left corner of the keyboard. A newer arrangement of the keyboard that has not caught on is called the Dvorak keyboard, which some claim allows for faster typing.

R

r (correlation coefficient) [M] A measurement of how closely two variables are related to each other. An *r* value of 1 would mean a perfect fit, or correlation; a value of 0 would indicate no correlation; and −1 an opposite, or inverse, relationship. Thus, *r* could be any number between +1 and −1. For instance, how related is watching TV sitcoms and doing well in statistics? If the answer is .8, or some high number toward 1, then it would mean the more sitcoms watched, the higher the stat grade. If the answer is .2, or a number close to 0, there would be little relation between the number of sitcoms watched and the grade. Finally, if −.9, or a number close to −1, the more sitcoms, the lower the stat grade.

r^2 (r squared) [M] A measurement of how closely the regression line fits the actual data, usually as shown on a scatter diagram (sometimes called scattergrams or scatterplots). Also see *coefficient of determination*.

rabbi [S] A senior management person who is looking out for a subordinate's well-being, often grooming that person for future success. Also see *godfather* or *mentor*.

rabbi trust [HR] A trust for executives set up in connection with deferred compensation plans. It allows money targeted for the eventual payment of the compensation to be safe because it is in a trust. However, if the company goes bankrupt, creditors are able to get at the money. It is named "rabbi" because one of the first created was for a rabbi. This is in contrast to a "secular trust," in which the assets are not subject to creditors. Because money is immediately vested to the executive in a secular trust, it is taxed when contributed. A rabbi trust avoids immediate taxation because the money is not guaranteed to the executive but is taxed when the compensation is eventually received.

rack jobber [B] A wholesaler that supplies and stocks retail displays. A jobber generally means a middleman who buys from manufacturers and sells to retailers.

radical sign ($\sqrt{}$) [M] A mathematical sign indicating a root of a number. It typically shows the square.

radio button [C] See *button.*

radio call letters [S] Letters used to designate the name of a radio station. It is not a well known fact that many of the call letters of radio stations are acronyms. For example, WGN in Chicago stands for World's Greatest Newspaper (owned by the *Chicago Tribune*), WOR in New York stands for Wonders (or World) of Radio, and KTTV in Los Angeles stands for Times Television (once owned by *The Los Angeles Times*).

ragged right [C] In word processing, a noneven right margin. This is the preferred margin for general business correspondence. In more formal writing or printing, an even, or flush alignment, right margin is used. The left margin is always even.

raider [B] An aggressive investor who tries to take over companies, usually by buying up enough of the companies' stock. Some recent notorious examples are Carl Icahn, Irwin Jacobs, and T. Boone Pickens.

rails [B] An abbreviated term for railroads.

rainmaker [S] Often used in a law or consulting firm, a term referring to a person who has wide contacts and is effective in bringing in new business. In other words, the rainmaker causes money to rain down on the firm.

RAM (random access memory) [C] A computer's main memory. It represents how much information a computer can hold and manipulate.

ramp up [S] The advance time to get up to speed, or introduce a product or service, just like a ramp to a highway.

R&D [B] See *research and development.*

random [M] A unorganized or nonsequential order or number. See *random number.*

random number [M] A number selected in an unordered way. Statistics uses random numbers and random sampling to arbitrarily select people for a survey. Computers or tables can generate random numbers for such experiments.

random walk [E] The path of business or economic variables that seem to be unpredictable, or random, just as people are as they walk aimlessly. The price of stocks on the stock market is often said to follow a random walk. Sometimes referred to as the "random walk hypothesis" or the "random walk theory."

R&R [S] Stands for rest and recreation. Derived from the army, term used when soldiers were sent temporarily away from the battlefield to relax before being sent back.

> Jane explained to her boss, "When this project is done, I want some R&R."

range [M] A simple statistical measurement of how wide a distribution is dispersed. It is the difference between the maximum and minimum data values.

rate [I] The cost of a unit of insurance, which thereby determines the amount of the premium.

rate of return [F] Although a general term, it usually means the annual percentage return of an investment. It can mean just the interest or dividend of a security, or it can mean the total return, which is the increase or decrease of the investment plus the interest or dividend.

rating bureau [I] An organization that provides rates and other services to insurance companies.

rating services [F] See *AAA, AA, A ratings.*

ratio [M] A fraction or relationship between two numbers. The P/E ratio (price/earnings) is the fraction of price divided by earnings. Business and investments use many ratios. Some accounting ratios are the current ratio, the acid ratio, book-to-bill ratio, and inventory-to-sales ratio.

rational expectations [E] The economic idea that consumer behavior follows a certain logic. For instance, if inflation starts to fall, consumers will not immediately adjust to it because they have come to expect higher inflation. Their expectations are based on their rational experience.

rational number [M] A number obtained by dividing one whole number by another. For example, 3 divided by 4, written as 3/4, is a rational number. Numbers that cannot be created by a fraction are called irrational, such as π.

raw materials [E] Basic minerals and materials usually mined and used in most manufactured goods. Iron, aluminum, and sand are all raw materials used in many products.

razor blades [B] A business and marketing approach that assumes there is more money to be made on the replacement parts than the item that uses them, such as razor blades, film, and more recently, high-volume computer disks.

readme file [C] A text file attached to software programs that contains last-minute changes that didn't make it into the instruction booklet.

read-only file [C] A file that cannot be changed. It can be read but not changed or erased.

Reaganomics [E] The general economic policies employed by the Reagan administration, of which cutting taxes was a central tenet. According to Reaganomics, paying less in taxes would enable businesses to produce more, thereby increasing economic growth and creating more jobs.

real [M] In finance, a number adjusted for inflation. This is in contrast to a "nominal" value, which is the actual, or named, value. For instance, if an investment earns 5 percent (nominal) interest but inflation takes away 3 percent, then the real interest rate is only 2 percent (and after taxes even less).

real estate taxes [T] See *property taxes*.

real GDP [E] The total domestic output adjusted for inflation. This is in contrast to nominal GDP, which is domestic output in actual dollars. See *gross domestic product*.

real income [E] Income adjusted for inflation. This is in contrast to "nominal income," which is in actual dollars.

> When prices rose 10 percent that year, Smithers informed his boss that he wanted a 10 percent raise so that his *real income* would remain the same.

real interest rates [E] Interest rates with inflation subtracted out. Thus if short-term rates were 5 percent and inflation was 2 percent, then the real interest rates would be 3 percent.

reality check [S] A prompt return to realistic expectations after a period of fanciful thinking.

real property [T] A term generally meaning real estate.

real time [C] The calculation of data as fast as it's inputted.

realtor [RE] An individual who specializes in the buying or selling of real estate.

realty [RE] Another name for real estate.

reasonable doubt [L] The degree of certainty required of a juror to decide a criminal case.

reassessment [RE] The process of giving a property or group of properties a new assessed value.

rebate [B] Money that is refunded to the purchaser of a product from the manufacturer. Rebates are often given as incentives to buy.

recapitalization [A] A major change or restructuring of the long-term financing mix of a company. Recapitalization can frequently occur during bankruptcy proceedings.

recapture [T] Additional tax due when an asset is sold for tax breaks previously given, most commonly depreciation. Depreciation can reduce taxes for a number of years but it lowers the tax basis of the asset, which results in a recapture of additional taxes when sold.

> When David sold his rental property, because its value was depreciated, he was forced to *recapture* some of the value and pay taxes on it.

recession [E] A temporary decline in economic activity, usually characterized by greater unemployment and decreased consumer spending. Technically, a recession is defined as two consecutive quarters of decreasing gross domestic product. A recession can last from several months to a year or more. Since World War II recessions have occurred about every four years (coinciding with four-year business cycles), but since 1980, after the application of monetary policy, there have been three recessions, as of this writing. The first two were almost back-to-back from January 1980 through July 1980 and July 1981 through November 1981. The third was from July 1990 until March 1991. Because there is a lag in compiling economic data, it is usually several months after the fact before economists know when a recession began or ended. A related term is "depression," which is a significant and prolonged downturn in the economy, the last one being the Great Depression of the 1930s. See *depression*.

reciprocal [M] The opposite, inverse, or reverse of a fraction. The reciprocal of 4 is $\frac{1}{4}$ (1 divided by 4). In algebraic terms, the reciprocal of *a* is $\frac{1}{a}$ (1 divided by *a*).

reciprocity [E] The practice of countries giving each other the same trade concessions or restrictions.

reconciliation [A] An accounting calculation that accounts for all relevant transactions between two periods, such as month to month. It provides a check that the numbers are correct.

record [C] In database software, one complete set of information. For example, for a mail-order catalog company, a record is all the information on one customer.

rectangle [M] A four-sided geometric figure with opposite sides equal and square corners. A four-sided figure without equal opposite sides is a trapezoid.

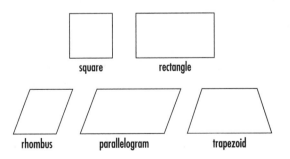

square   rectangle

rhombus   parallelogram   trapezoid

red circle [HR] A salary that exceeds the maximum for its salary grade. This can occur when an employee is performing extremely well, or when a person has been demoted to a lower salary grade, but her salary remains the same. A less common term is "green circle," meaning a salary that is below grade.

redemption fee [F] A mutual fund fee charged when shares of the fund are sold. Also called "deferred sales charge," "back-end load," or "exit fee."

red eye [S] That late night flight from the West Coast to the East. When a traveler gets to the East Coast very early in the morning, she could be sleepy and have red eyes.

red flag [S] An immediate signal for attention.

> Cruthers was told that if he put the expense through as a dinner it would be a *red flag* to accounting; therefore, he was to classify it as a conference meeting.

red herring [S] A distraction from the real issue or issues.

> Smithers told the staff that the new headquarter's directive to cut back on paper clips was a *red herring.* The real issue was who had the power over their division—their own divisional management or headquarters.

red-herring prospectus [F] A preliminary prospectus offered to investors before the price is set and before the SEC (Securities and Exchange Commission) has ruled on the prospectus.

red ink [S] Debt or financial losses, or both. The term undoubtedly comes from the use of the color red to show a loss on a financial statement because it stands out.

> The chairman directed the president to stop the flow of *red ink,* or he would be history.

redlining [B] The illegal practice of banks or insurance companies discriminating against people in poorer communities, such as limiting the amount of loans in those communities or refusing to offer homeowner policies.

red tape [S] Excessive paperwork and procedures causing cumbersome steps and administrative delays. The term comes from the use of a red ribbon, or tape, to secure official papers. The practice dates at least from the 1700s in England.

> The new government agency was attempting to cut down on bureaucratic *red tape*; applicants needed to fill out only a short one-page application to get a loan.

reduction in force (RIF) [HR] The more formal term for downsizing or rightsizing, that is, when the company has reduced its number of employees. See *laid off*.

re-engineering [HR] A technical-sounding term for downsizing. It usually means the company has reexamined how it has been doing business and has formulated a plan to change it. See *laid off*.

refund [T] A tax amount returned after overpayment.

> Fred was thrilled to discover that not only did he not owe any taxes but he would also be receiving a *refund* of $500.

regional exchanges [F] Smaller versions of the NYSE and AMEX exchanges. Regional exchanges are located around the country and trade the same stocks as those listed on the NYSE and AMEX. Results of the five regional exchanges are combined with results from the NYSE and AMEX to get a composite trading listing.

registered bonds [F] Term that refers to the fact that bonds that are now issued have to be registered in the investor's name, versus the past practice of bearer bonds. See *bearer bond*.

registrar [A] The firm that updates stock certificate records for a company.

registration [F] The process of preparing securities for public sale, with the underwriter providing detailed information to the SEC (the Securities and Exchange Commission).

regression analysis [M] The analysis of how closely the data of two variables in a statistical experiment or study is related, or correlated. For instance, in a business study there may be a positive relationship between the stock market and cars sold, that is, a rise in the sale of cars follows an increase in the stock market. See *r*.

regression line (least-squares line) [M] The straight line that best fits or passes through the scatter diagram. The line then not only represents the data but also predicts it as the line is extended farther. See r^2.

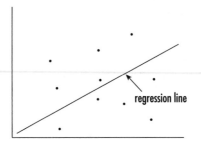

regression line

regression to the mean [M] In statistics, a statement that the sample data will be similar to the whole population when the sample size is large enough. For example, when tossing a coin, a person might start with getting mostly heads or tails by chance, but if he keeps tossing the coin he will eventually get close to an equal number of heads and tails. This is called regressing to the mean, meaning that after a while the aggregate of the tossing will approach the mean, or the average, of the population.

regressive tax [T] Any tax in which everyone is taxed at the same rate. The FICA tax for Social Security and state sales taxes are regressive. More recently, proposals to treat income taxes this same way have been called the *flat tax*, which is a more descriptive term. The current U.S. tax system is called "progressive:" the higher the income, the higher the tax rates. See *progressive tax*.

regs [T] The abbreviated word for tax or other government regulations.

> Paul asked Larry to check the *regs* on the IRA distribution rules and pass them on to Bill.

regular part-time [HR] Term describing an employee who regularly works less than a full-time employee. If a company permits this practice it often is for less than thirty hours per week. If an employee works more than 30 hours, the company may be required to pay certain employee benefits.

regulation [E] Government rules and supervision, usually through legislation, of various business and financial activities.

Alabascar's *regulations* forbade the use of electrical shears to produce wool; only mechanical ones were allowed on the sheep.

reinsurance [I] Insurance protection for insurance companies. For large risks, insurance companies buy reinsurance for extra protection for themselves. A large loss could seriously affect or wipe out a smaller insurance company.

reinvent the wheel [S] To start something from scratch, even though the work has been done before.

reinvestment [F] Process by which shareholders of mutual funds can reinvest the money they earn, take it in cash, or do a little of each.

James checked his *reinvestment* options and decided to put his earnings back into the mutual fund.

REIT (real estate investment trust) [F] A mutual fund of real estate investments. Some only invest in actual real estate while some only invest in mortgages. Some are hybrid, investing in both.

release [L] The legal giving up of something, usually in writing.

Acme Corp. obtained a *release* from the contract because XYZ Corp. did not uphold its side of the bargain.

release on one's own recognizance [L] To allow a person to be released without bail on the promise he will show up for trial. See *bail*.

relocation expense [HR] The expense incurred when moving to another job in another city. This usually includes the moving van, transportation to the new location, and often real estate expenses. If a company requests the relocation, it usually pays most, if not all, of the expenses.

remainderman [T] A person or organization that is to receive a trust's assets, generally when the person who set up the trust dies.

renewable term [I] Term life insurance that is guaranteed to be renewed if desired by the policy holder.

rent [RE] Money paid for the use of real estate or other property.

Bradley and Co. charged *rent* of $20 per square foot for the office space in its building.

[E] In economics, rent can be earnings from land, labor, or capital.

rental income [T] Income received from the rental of real estate; it is taxable income offset by specific expenses incurred and depreciation.

The *rental income* from their upstairs apartment brought Masie and Phil another $2,000 a year in taxable income.

reorder point [A] A point in time when new inventory needs to be ordered, generally when a certain low level of inventory is reached. It is also a term for ananalysis that determines the reorder date for manufacturing materials that will result in the least amount of storage.

reorganization [L] Court permission to restructure a company, usually so as to continue operations to pay creditors.

rep [B] See *manufacturer's agent*.

replacement cost [I] Property or homeowner's insurance that will reimburse the value of replacing the property if destroyed or damaged. This is in contrast to offering to only reimburse the "current value." For instance, if a person had to replace a sofa it may cost $300, whereas the actual value of the eight-year-old used sofa may be only about $50.

replacement ratio [HR] A retirement planning term referring to the percentage of gross income that would be needed in retirement relative to the gross income required while working, in order to maintain the same financial life style. Because of several items that will generally be less, a retired person won't need the same gross income to maintain his after-tax income. For example, once retired one will not owe FICA taxes. Social Security benefits may be either tax-free or only partially taxed, commuting and clothes expenses decrease, and often there are state income tax exclusions for retirees. Replacement ratios are often quoted from 65 percent to 75 percent.

repos [F] See *repurchase agreement*.

repriced stock option [HR] A new twist on a stock option, the repricing of an option when the stock has declined in value, sometimes precipitously. High tech companies feel that if they don't reprice options at a lower price, their workforce will lose morale and may leave. On the other hand, shareholders of the stock feel that it dilutes the value of stock price. See *stock options*.

repurchase agreement [F] Also called "repos," it is a financial arrangement, usually involving banks, that holds government securities for a short period of time and pays a current interest rate. The investor must "repurchase" the securities at the end of the agreement. Essentially, an investor "sells" the securities to a bank as collateral for a loan.

required rate of return [A] See *cost of capital*.

requisition [A] A form filled out to request something.

> Brown filled out a purchase *requisition* for 200 notebooks and sent it to the stock department.

rescind [L] To void a contract or other agreement, usually when both parties agree to do so.

rescission [L] Cancellation of a contract or other agreement.

research and development (R&D) [B] The process of developing new products and improving those a company already has. It also refers to the department responsible for this creative process. In chemical or pharmaceutical companies there are extensive laboratories that work on developing new uses for products or new drugs. In many companies there is a distinction between pure research, if a company can afford it, and applications research, which works on specific practical products.

> Zippy Corp.'s *R&D* department came up with a full marketing proposal for the new Spiffy Zipper it developed.

reserves [A] Funds retained by a company for anticipated specific needs, such as a pending lawsuit or anticipated bad debts.

[I] Money set aside by insurance companies to provide for an estimated amount of potential liabilities under their insurance policies.

residential property [RE] Property used for homes, as opposed to commercial or office space. Single-family homes, apartment buildings, and co-ops all fall in this category.

> Teenyville was almost all zoned *as residential property*; the residents didn't want much commercial use in their small village.

residual value [A] An asset's remaining value after it has been fully depreciated. Sometimes called "disposal value."

> The *residual value* of that machinery was so low, it wasn't worth selling.

residuary clause [T] A provision in a will that disposes of everything not specified to be distributed.

resolution [C] The number of pixels on the screen. The higher the number, the greater the clarity and sharpness of the image.

response time [C] The amount of time it takes for a computer to respond to a command.

responsibility accounting [A] A system within a company where costs are assigned to the business unit that has the responsibility for the control of costs.

restraining order [L] A court order preventing an action, usually until a court hearing can be conducted.

restricted stock [HR] Stock given to an executive that does not become fully owned usually until a later date. Dividends, however, may be distributed to the executive in the meantime. It is given as an incentive for the executive to stay and to continue to perform at a high level. It is called *restricted* because the executive cannot immediately treat it fully as his or her own.

restructuring [HR] Sometimes referred to as "corporate restructuring," in any language it means change at work. The change could be a simple one, as when a department begins reporting to a new executive, leaving the work process and employees the same. It could also mean the elimination of positions, with the existing work responsibilities parceled out among those who remain. See *laid off.*

resumé [HR] A summary account of one's accomplishments and jobs held. For scholars, the term *curriculum vitae* is sometimes used, although it is old-fashioned.

retail [B] Goods and services sold directly to the consumer. This is versus wholesale goods, which are sold to retailers.

retail prices [B] Prices paid by consumers at regular stores. This is in contrast to "wholesale prices," which usually represent the price distributors pay to manufacturers before products are shipped to retail stores.

retained earnings; retained income [A] The amount of earnings left in a company to be invested in growing the company, versus earnings paid out in the form of dividends to stockholders.

retainer [B] A fee often paid to a law or consulting firm to keep those services available if needed. Often it is the initial payment to a consulting firm by a company to start work on a project.

retiree [HR] One who has achieved that exalted status of not working but receiving a pension and living the good life. Actually refers to just about anyone who leaves a company after from about age fifty-five to sixty-five, whether they receive a pension or not.

retiree medical [HR] A usual way of referring to the medical plan a company has for its retired employees. At age sixty-five, company medical plans usually dovetail with Medicare.

retirement counseling [HR] A session with a company benefits specialist to complete forms and make benefit decisions at the time an employee is retiring.

retirement plan [HR] Any one of a number of financial plans de-signed to provide income to a person after he or she retires from work. The government allows an employee and/or the company to contribute a certain amount of income toward retirement plans. This income is usually exempt from taxes until paid out as a pension. There are myriad rules governing these plans, and there are various forms that these plans take. Because of the potential tax advantages, these plans are very popular. See *pension plan*.

How Shall I Retire? A User's Guide to Retirement Plans:

Company plan Pension and profit-sharing plans, usually funded almost completely by a company. Employees may be allowed to add to them.

401(k) plan A popular company plan in which employees are able to contribute (up to a certain amount) on a pretax basis. That means they don't pay any taxes on any income that goes into the plan. Often a company will match part of the contribution.

403(b) plan Similar to the 401(k) but for teachers and employees of nonprofit institutions. Often called a "tax-deferred annuity."

457 plan A deferred compensation plan for municipal workers.

Individual retirement accounts (IRA) An account one may set up on his own. Most people who are covered under a company plan cannot deduct the contribution, but the contribution can still be made. If one does not have a company retirement plan, IRA contributions of up to $2,000 per year are deductible from income.

SIMPLE plan A plan for small businesses, created in 1996. It stands for Savings Incentive Match Plans for Employees.

Simplified employee pension (SEP) An IRA-like account for employees of small companies that have no formal company plan. SEPs are simpler than pension plans because the paperwork is minimal.

Keogh (H.R. 10) plan A retirement plan (pronounced KEY-oh) for the self-employed, employees of small unincorporated businesses, and people in a partnership form of business. Maximum contribution is figured as a percentage of income. Although there are a variety of Keogh plans, the more complex ones may require a consultation with a professional specializing in these plans.

---

retirement planning seminar [HR] Sometimes offered by companies for employees over a certain age. The seminar can cover such topics as benefit options, the potential taxes on those benefits, Social Security benefits, investments, insurance, and estate planning.

retrieve [C] To call up data stored in the computer or disk.

retro; retrofit [S] A recently voguish term that is used with a sense of nostalgia. That is, like retrofit, to redo or restore something to its original condition or look.

> The old hotel was *retrofitted* with the original furniture and given a new coat of paint in the original color.

retroactive tax [T] A new tax bill that reaches back to collect additional taxes on a period before the tax was actually passed. For instance, a tax is retroactive if it is passed in August but the taxes apply all the way back to January of that year.

return [F] A very general term, usually meaning the profit made from an investment.

Return key [C] The key on the keyboard that enters or confirms a command.

return on assets [A] See *return on investment.*

return on equity [A] A calculation determined by dividing the net income, after taxes, by equity. It is considered an important performance measurement of a company's management.

return on investment (ROI) [A] A traditional and important calculation determined by dividing the net profits, after taxes, by the total assets of a company. It is sometimes called the "profitability ratio" because it shows the ability of the company's assets to generate profits. It is sometimes also called "return on assets."

returns [B] Items that are brought back to a store for either credit or exchange.

> Green receives a profit from the sales we make, less the *returns*.

returns and allowances [A] The costs associated with items that are brought back to a store for either credit or exchange.

revenue [A] A general term that refers to the income produced from investments or production. Revenue also refers to the taxes the government collects.

The increases in *revenue* at XYZ Corp. were directly attributed to a more efficient management.

The *revenue* raised by the increase in taxes was enough to pay for some of the government's new programs.

revenue bonds [F] State bonds backed by the revenue, or income, from a specific source, such as tolls on bridges, tunnels, or roads. They are considered riskier than general obligation bonds and therefore often have insurance to back up the risk. See *general obligation bond.*

reverse annuity mortgage (RAM) [RE] A mortgage specifically designed for an older homeowner who has little income but an asset, her house, that can be used to provide income. The homeowner gets to stay in her house and receives an income toward the value of it. When the owner dies the bank sells the house and recoups its investment. Although these mortgages have been talked about for many years, they have not been used with any popularity.

To supplement her income, Sophie took out a *reverse annuity mortgage:* She received a monthly check from the bank, and they would deduct the amount from the sale of her house after she died.

reverse split [F] The opposite of a stock split. A reverse split results in fewer shares than the investor had. Although not common, the strategy is usually intended to increase the price of each share.

revocable trust [T] A trust that can be changed or eliminated during one's life. See *living trust.*

RFP [S] Stands for Request For Proposal and is a call for a proposal from a company, often a consulting firm.

RGB monitor [C] A monitor that creates color by three signals, one red, one green, and one blue, which also creates the acronym RGB.

Ricardo, David (1772–1823) [E] The British economist who laid the theoretical foundation for Adam Smith's observations, particularly in the area of trade. He first used the term "comparative advantage," meaning that one country usually has an advantage producing certain goods. Portugal had an advantage producing wine, and England, textiles; thus together, the two had a basis for international trade.

rider [I] Additional coverage on a life, health, or property insurance policy, over and above normal coverage. For instance, a property policy could have a rider covering specifically named pieces of jewelry.

right [A] See *stock right*.

right angle or triangle [M] A 90° angle or a triangle having one angle at 90°.

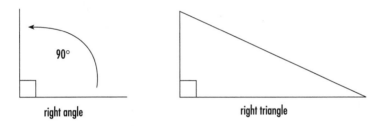

right angle   right triangle

right brain [S] See *left brain–right brain*.

right-of-way [RE] A right to cross over someone else's property for some reason.

> The B&O Railroad had a *right-of-way* through Marvin Place for its train tracks.

rightsizing [B] The process of rearranging the work process to get the right number of people doing the right jobs. Often means making a company smaller. See *laid off*.

right-to-work law or state [B] Laws that prevent a company from requiring workers to automatically join a union when hired.

rigmarole [S] Nonsensical procedures or double talk.

> Smithers cautioned those new in the department that the forms were just a headquarters *rigmarole* and not to spend too much time on them.

riparian rights [RE] The rights of owners of river beds and ocean fronts, as well as fishing rights. See *water rights*.

risk [F] A widely used and important concept of investments that speaks to the uncertainty of income and growth present in many investments. Commonly, professional investors use the statistical measure of one standard deviation as the measurement of risk in the stock market. The basic idea in the world of finance and investment is: The greater the risk, the greater the potential gain of an investment (or loss). High-risk investments may be a big gamble, but they lure investors with a possible high return.

[I] The basic business of insurance companies. Through insurance actuaries, the costs of risks are determined and priced through premiums to policyholders.

risk management [I] The general term for the business activity that assesses the various risks a company faces and that develops a plan for the potential coverage or payment of those risks.

risk of forfeiture [HR] A technical term referring to the possibility that an executive may not receive a specific benefit.

road kill [S] The crude phrase used to indicate that a person, or company, has been wiped out by an event or circumstances. The phrase is borrowed from the highway, where animals are killed by traffic.

> Larry became *road kill* when his proposal was rejected and he was left without a job.

robbery [L] The crime of taking property by violence or intimation of harm.

robotics [B] Computer controlled devices and machines, usually on manufacturing production lines. Auto manufacturing, for example, has adopted the use of robotics in spot welding frames.

robust [S] Very strong, as in robust sales.

rock and a hard place, between a [S] A seemingly impossible situation, which is where one would be between two immovable objects.

rocket science; rocket scientists [S] Terms referring to the most technical of subjects and people who specialize in them. Such people are sometimes referred to as "quants" because they use complicated math to study and solve financial problems.

The boss said, "I'm no *rocket scientist*, but I know that one plus one equals two."

rollout [B] A term referring to the formal introduction of a new product or service.

rollover mortgage [RE] A mortgage in which every few years—or whatever time specified—the mortgage amount is technically due, yet the lender carries over the amount to a new mortgage with a new interest rate. May also be called a "renewable mortgage."

Zippy Corp. liked to have a *rollover mortgage* so it could take advantage of better interest rates every few years.

rollover IRA [HR] An IRA to receive the lump sum distribution from a 401(k) plan or pension plan.

ROM (read only memory) [C] As the name implies, memory that can only be read, not changed in any way. ROM chips in the computer's hard drive typically contain the instructions that are written when the computer is manufactured. The data in ROM memory stays there even after the computer is turned off. The computer's basic input/output system is stored on a ROM chip.

Roman numerals [M]

Number	Symbol	Number	Symbol	Number	Symbol
1	I	15	XV	150	CL
2	II	20	XX	200	CC
3	III	25	XXV	400	CD
4	IV	30	XXX	500	D
5	V	40	XL	600	DC
6	VI	50	L	900	CM
7	VII	60	LX	1,000	M
8	VIII	70	LXX	1,500	MD
9	IX	80	LXXX	1,900	MCM or MDCCCC
10	X	90	XC	1,930	MCMXXX
		100	C	1,963	MCMLXIII
				1,996	MCMXCVI
				2,000	MM

Rome Treaty (Treaty of Rome) [E] Six Western European countries that signed the Treaty of Rome in 1957 to form a common market between them: Belgium, France, Italy, Luxembourg, the Netherlands, and West Germany. It was the first step toward a close economic union that has culminated in the introduction of the euro in January 1999 as a common European currency. See *euro*.

root directory [C] The most central of directories in a computer. All other directories branch from it.

rosy scenario [S] An overly optimistic outlook. It is sometimes said that a person is looking through "rose-colored glasses."

rotation [F] The phenomenon of different business sectors doing well in the stock market at different times. Thus an investor can rotate out of a sector, such as airline stocks, and rotate into a sector, such as manufacturing stocks.

Roth IRA [T] A newer form of an IRA (individual retirement account) introduced in 1998 by Senate Finance Chairman William Roth of Delaware. It doesn't provide a tax deduction for the contribution, but it allows a tax free distribution if held for at least five years and past age $59\frac{1}{2}$. See *individual retirement account*.

round file [S] Another name for *file 13*, the trash can.

> Smith told the administrative assistant to toss the useless documents into the *round file*.

rounding [M] The practice of eliminating the preciseness of a number. The number $151,284 could be rounded to $151,000 or $150,000 depending on the application. It allows the focus to be on the magnitude not the preciseness of the number. A number can be rounded up or down to the nearest number desired.

round lot [F] A group of stock shares sold in a multiple of 100. A round lot is usually less expensive to purchase than an odd lot.

row [C] The horizontal presentation of data, especially in a spreadsheet. This is in contrast to a column, which is the vertical presentation of data.

royalty [A] Compensation paid to an owner of an asset or publication, usually on a percentage basis. An oil company can pay a royalty to the owner of the land from which oil is being pumped, or a publisher can pay a royalty to a writer who has written a book or other publication.

rule of 72 [M] A useful mathematical rule that gives the years it will take for an investment to double. Simply divide the rate of return into the number 72, and the result is the number of years. For example, if the rate of return is 7 percent, then it will take about 10 years for the investment to double ($72 \div 7 = 10.285$). Thus, if an investor starts with $1,000 and it can earn 7 percent, then in about 10 years she'll have $2,000.

rule of 78 [M] A rather complex method by which a lender can calculate how much interest to refund a borrower if a loan is paid early. Each month is assigned a fraction, beginning with 12/78, 11/78, and so on for each month of the year. If a loan is paid off in only two months, for instance, then 23/78 of the interest is refunded. The 12 and 11 of the first two months are added together.

rumor mill [S] The ongoing gossip within an office. See *grapevine*.

run chart [M] A simple time graph of points showing a trend, if any, in a series of events. For instance, the run chart of days people are absent shows that Monday is the most frequent day.

run it by me [S] A phrase bosses use instructing subordinates to keep them informed of critical information.

> Cruthers barked at his staff, "Keep me informed of what will be in the report. In fact, *run it by me* before it's sent out to headquarters."

run it up the flagpole [S] To suggest an idea knowing it may meet with opposition. The full phrase is: Run it up the flagpole and see if anyone salutes. Presumably, if saluted, so to speak, then the idea has a chance.

run the numbers [S] To do a complete calculation of the problem.

> Cruthers directed the accounting department to *run the numbers* so he could see if any profit could be made.

Russell 2000/3000 [F] Two useful indexes of smaller cap stocks. The Russell 2000 consists of smaller capitalization stocks. It generally represents companies with a market value of $250 million or less. The Russell 3000 consists of the 3,000 largest publicly traded stocks of U.S. domiciled corporations and includes both large, medium, and small capitalization stocks. It represents about 98 percent of the total capitalization of the New York, American, and NASDAQ markets.

rust belt [B] A term that is itself rusty, it refers to sections of the Midwest in which unproductive factories were abandoned in the 1980s and left to rust. These factories, which produced basic products such as steel and autos, were outproduced and outpriced by foreign competition. They were also referred to as "smokestack industries" because of their tall smokestacks. However, since then there has been a remarkable modernization, with the new plants being some of the most efficient in the world.

S

sabbatical leave [HR] Authorized leave, paid or unpaid, for either community service or personal time off.

safety stock [A] That extra or reserve inventory kept on hand for above normal production.

salary [HR] The compensation received for work. The term "salary" originally comes from the Latin word for *salt*, which is what Roman soldiers were paid with as it was so scarce and valuable at the time.

salary grade [HR] The normal compensation practice of having a series of grades that have ranges, minimums, midpoints, and maximums. Each employee is placed in a specific grade, depending on the level of job responsibility. See *broad-banding*.

salary reduction plans [T] Plans such as 401(k) and 403(b) that allow pretax contributions. An employee's taxable salary is thus *reduced* by the amount of money contributed to the plan. This means that the employee doesn't pay federal income taxes on the money that is contributed, thus lowering her taxes.

salary review [HR] That once a year, or less frequent, event where a boss reviews his employees' job performances and determines if a salary increase is warranted.

salary survey [HR] A compensation department activity that determines what average salaries other companies are paying for similar jobs. Companies exchange information on a confidential basis so that no one participating in the survey knows which company has reported specified information.

sale [B] Any receipt of cash, check, or credit card in exchange for goods or services. A sale may also refer to a discount.

> L-Mart made over 2,000 *sales* that weekend because of the big sale they were having—20 percent off every item in the store.

sale and leaseback [B] A financing technique involving the sale of an asset that is then leased back to the seller. It allows the seller to realize the money in an asset without giving up the use of it.

sales forecast [B] A projected amount of sales for a specific period of time, such as monthly, quarterly, or yearly.

sales promotion [B] The practice of using specially designed advertising and other promotions to push certain products or services.

sales quota [B] A performance standard or goal for a sales person or persons during a particular period of time.

sales representative or rep [B] The person who has the actual contact with the customer. Often referred to informally as a *sales rep*.

sales tax [T] A state tax on certain purchases; a percentage of the total price of taxable items. States often exclude certain items, such as food and drugs, from the tax. A few cities also have a sales tax.

> Bob bought a new suit for $500, but with the 5 percent *sales tax*, the bill came to $525.

sales territory [B] A geographic area assigned to a particular salesperson or persons.

Sallie Mae [B] The government sponsored Student Loan Marketing Association that was created in 1973 to buy student loans from banks. The quasi-public organization promotes student bank loans.

Salomon Brothers bond index [F] An overall index of fixed-income securities that combines U.S. treasury and agency securities, corporate bonds, and mortgage-backed securities. This combination is considered a good overall bond index considering both income and price fluctuation. The index is approximately 55 percent U.S. treasuries, 20 percent corporate bonds, and 25 percent mortgage-backed securities.

sample; sample distribution [M] A statistical term that refers to a part of the whole population of what is being studied, as opposed to the entire population.

Samuelson, Paul (1915–) [E] See *Nobel Prize for economics*.

samurai bonds [F] Yen denominated bonds issued in Tokyo by U.S. and other foreign companies. This eliminates the uncertainty of currency fluctuations for the Japanese investor.

sandbag [S] To deceive or attack from behind. The derivation of this term is uncertain, but it's guessed that it arose in olden days when a seemingly honest person offered a bag of money that turned out to be just sand.

> Cruthers returned to the office dejected, explaining to his staff, "We've been *sandbagged* by the marketing people. They told us that we didn't have to prepare for the meeting, but, in fact, the president expected us to give a detailed presentation."

S&L (savings and loan) [F] See *bank failure*.

S&P 500 [F] See *Standard & Poor's 500*.

sans serif [C] See *serif*.

same store sales [B] The reporting of sales of only those stores that were up and running during the last period. This allows a better comparison in industries especially where companies are opening new stores rapidly, and increases in sales can be masked by what is happening to the basic concept of the store. Stores that have a strong increase in same store sales are perceived as having a strong and successful business concept.

satellite office [B] Generally a secondary office of a company.

save [C] To transfer computer data from temporary memory to permanent storage.

savings [E] Amounts of money that individuals set aside to build up their financial reserves. Savings are the amount left over after taxes and expenses.

savings and loan [E] See *bank failure*.

savings bonds (EE, HH, and I bonds) [F] The several different types of savings bonds issued by the federal government. The traditional *EE bond* accumulates interest until cashed in; the *HH bond* pays interest semiannually like a regular bond; and the new *I bond* (or TIPS) pays a lower fixed-interest rate but increases the value of the bond by inflation. See *EE* and *HH* and *I bonds*.

Say's law [E] A theory that states, "Supply creates its own demand." It means that what is produced (supply) will be bought (demand). There is some controversy about what Say really meant. It was postulated in 1803 by the French economist Jean Baptiste Say (1767–1832).

scalable font [C] A particular font style that can be made larger or smaller by a software program.

scalage [A] A deduction given for an item that is likely to shrink or leak during shipping.

> There would be a 2 percent *scalage* discount for the grain shipment.

scalars [M] In science and engineering, quantities that have magnitude (size) but not direction. An example of a scalar is the degrees of temperature. This is in contrast to a "vector," such as wind velocity toward the northeast, which has magnitude and direction.

scanner [C] A device that captures text in a document, much like a copy machine, so it can be use in word-processing or desktop publishing software. Sometimes called an "optical scanner."

scatter diagram (scattergram or scatterplot) [M] A graph or plot of data, usually in the form of dots. This data in the aggregate can take on shapes, meaning there is a correlation, or the data can be randomly scattered, meaning there is no correlation. See r^2 and *regression line*.

scientific notation [M] A method of representing large numbers, or very small numbers, as a power of 10. For instance, the number 2,500,000,000 in scientific notation is 2.5×10^9.

SCORES/PRIMES [F] See *PRIMES/SCORES*.

S corporation (subchapter S corporation) [B] A legal corporate form of a company where the profits or losses can pass through to the individual owner. See *C corporation* and *corporation*.

screen saver [C] Designs, often with movement, that appear on computer screens when the computers are still on but not in use. Although some are intriguing, they're just for show. In the early days of monitors, images could be burned in the screen, but this is no longer the case.

scroll; scroll key [C] To move the lines displayed on a screen up or down.

> We had to *scroll* through three pages of text before we found the line that needed to be edited.

seamless [S] Perhaps an overused word today, referring to how closely things work or fit together.

> Samantha remarked at how *seamless* the two computer software programs worked together.

search [C] To look for a file, information, or a program. Using the internet, the right search engine (Yahoo, Excite, Alta Vista—web search tools) will make a search more efficient.

> He conducted a *search* for an article on *Jane Eyre*.

search and seizure [L] The legal right of police officers to search a premises with a proper warrant and take the evidence found.

search engine [C] Software tools used to find information on the internet. Some of these sites have become not only search tools but also popular sites for information.

Popular Search Engines on the Web:

Alta Vista www.altavista.com

Excite www.excite.com

Hot bot www.hotbot.com

Infoseek www.infoseek.com

Lycos www.lycos.com

Metacrawler www.metacrawler.com

Yahoo www.yahoo.com

---

search warrant [L] An order from a court to allow police officers to search a premises. The warrant often stipulates where the police may search and what they are looking for.

seasonal adjustment; seasonal variation [E] Known variation during the year based on experience, used to correct economic data and information. For example, the use of gasoline normally increases in the summer as people take vacations, and that increase is assumed in calculations for the months of June, July, and August.

SEC [F] See *Securities and Exchange Commission*.

secondary market [F] Stocks and bonds traded after they are initially offered. Even though the New York Stock Exchange and other exchanges provide for initial offerings called IPOs (initial public offerings), the exchanges are primarily a place to trade these shares on a continual basis, called the secondary market.

secondary mortgage market [RE] The market in which banks sell their mortgages to government and private agencies in order to have more cash on hand to extend new mortgages.

> The ABC Company found out that its loan with Peachy-Keen Bank had been sold on the *secondary mortgage market* to Ginnie Mae.

secondary offering [F] An additional chunk of stock offered by a public company that wants to raise additional money.

> After Cheapo Electronics issued a *secondary offering*, the price per share of its stock went down.

second career [HR] A shift to a new career, either because of personal interest or practical circumstances.

second mortgage [RE] The mortgage that takes second place behind a main or first mortgage. It is an additional mortgage on a property, often a credit-line home loan.

second-to-die policy [I] See *first-to-die policy*

secretary's office [B] A name sometimes given to the department that handles official stockholder business of a company. This does not generally refer to the clerical assistant to an executive, once referred to as a secretary but now called an administrative assistant.

sector fund [F] A mutual fund that focuses on a particular sector or industry, such as biotechnology, energy, or precious metals. It can also focus on a geographic region or single country, such as the Pacific Rim, Japan, South America, Argentina, Europe, or Spain.

secular trend [E] A persistent long-term change based on fundamental factors, such as continuing increase in the standard of living, basic consumption habits, or gradual changes in technology. This is in contrast to "seasonal trends" which last only part of a year, or "cyclical trends" which last only as long as a fad lasts. Hula hoops were part of a cyclical trend, whereas the use of computers is a secular trend, a long-term use of technology. The word secular comes from Latin, meaning *of the age*.

secular trust [HR] A trust similar to a rabbi trust except that the money is not subject to bankruptcy creditors, and executives are taxed on the money when it is deposited into the trust. These trusts can be used in conjunction with executive deferred compensation. See *rabbi trust*.

securities [F] Stocks or bonds.

Securities and Exchange Commission (SEC) [F] A government watchdog agency that regulates the investment industry. Created in 1934, the SEC makes sure that investors are properly informed about their investments and that transactions are fair and free from fraud. It also investigates alleged wrong doing, such as illegal insider trading.

securitization [F] The forming of secondary securities from existing bonds and other fixed-income securities. In other words, it creates a security from a security.

seed capital; seed money [B] The initial money and assets needed to start a business.

> The BIG Development Corp. estimated it would need close to $200,000 in *seed money* to purchase the property, obtain all the permits, and study the market.

self-defense [L] A legal defense by a person for actions taken during a crime, such as fighting off an attacker.

self-directed [HR] Self-motivated. Able to initiate action without being told what to do.

self-directed IRA [F] An IRA that is a brokerage account.

self-employment [B] The act of being in business for oneself, generally without incorporating the business. A self-employed person simply completes schedule C as part of his federal tax return.

self-incrimination [L] A statement in a court case in which a person says something that implicates him in a crime. Under the Fifth Amendment, a person cannot be forced to incriminate himself.

self-insured [HR] An insurance method whereby a company assumes the risk and payment of certain types of insurance, as opposed to buying insurance for that purpose, such as a medical plan or property insurance.

self-regulation [B] Procedures adopted by businesses in a particular industry to monitor and promote standards of professional behavior and business practices.

sellers' market [S] The market condition in which sellers have the upper hand. Prices are usually higher, and sellers can negotiate on their terms. This is opposed to the "buyers' market," in which the prices are low and buyers control the market.

selling short [F] See *short selling.*

selling short against the box [F] A maneuver by an investor who owns shares of a particular stock and wants to keep them but worries that the price of the stock may drop. The investor could sell the shares but would incur immediate capital gains on those shares. The investor could also sell borrowed ones, called "short selling," or selling short. That way, if the stock does go down, the investor could buy shares at the lower price to replace the borrowed shares she sold. The investor bought low and sold high, although in reverse order. If the stock does go up, the investor has the original shares to replace the borrowed shares that she sold. See *naked option* and *short selling.*

semiconductor [C] Solid substances, in particular silicon, that can be altered electronically in an on and off state. The most important semiconductor is the transistor.

semifixed costs [A] Costs that are calculated to rise in steps with increased levels of production. They can also be referred to, appropriately, as "stepped costs."

semilogarithmic graph [M] Graphs that are logarithmic on one axis only, usually the y-axis. This is usually a better way to show data that grows exponentially, such as the growth in the stock market.

semivariable costs [A] Costs that vary with production amounts, but not proportionately.

> Our utilities are a *semivariable* cost. If we produce less, we use less electricity, but not a lot less; we run machines less often, but the lights and computers are still running.

senior issue [A] A security of a company that has priority over another security issued by the same company. Preferred stock is senior to common stock; bonds are senior to debentures. This is the opposite of a "subordinated security."

seniority [HR] Term referring to the length of time a person has been employed by a company. In a unionized plant, seniority usually plays a major role in promotions and layoffs.

> He had the benefit of *seniority*: He'd been with the firm longer than anyone else, and when others were let go, he was able to stay on.

senior partner [B] Generally refers to a senior member of an accounting, law, or consulting firm. Senior partners may receive special compensation and bonuses.

sensitivity analysis [M] See *model*.

sensitivity training [HR] A popular 1970s training technique designed to increase the awareness of other people's and one's own feelings. These groups were also called "T-groups," for training groups, because they were under the direction of a trainer.

SEP (simplified employee pension) [HR] An IRA-type plan generally for smaller companies because of its simplicity and ease to set-up and administer. These plans are sometimes referred to as SEP-IRAs. See *retirement plan*.

sequester [L] To keep a jury in isolation, not allowing them to go home or have public contact.

serial port [C] Typically a 9-pin computer port primarily for communications devices such as a mouse or an external modem. On a Mac a serial port is used for the printer too. This is in contrast to the "parallel port," which takes a 25-pin connection that can pass more information simultaneously.

serif [C] The fine line or curve that finishes off the main strokes that form a letter, to give it style. Typefaces without these finishing touches are called "sans serif."

SERP (supplementary executive retirement plan) [HR] An additional pension amount for executives to make up for the pensions disallowed because of government regulations. The plans are allowed but do not have any favored tax treatment, such as special forward averaging or rollover to IRAs. All payments are simply ordinary income.

server [C] The main control computer that runs a network of desktop computers. The server controls software, communications, and printers.

service [B] The intangible thing a business might sell, such as assistance, consultation, or advice. Service also refers to the help a manufacturer gives to a purchaser after the product is brought home.

> XYZ Corp. also offered a consultation *service* for its clients—it would conduct market research and offer strategies.

> Mike had to call the manufacturer for *service* when his new dishwasher broke down.

service of process [L] The legal notice given to people or companies to make sure they are aware of the charges brought against them.

service mark [L] A trademark of an intangible service. This is noted with the letters "sm" in superscript. A typical trademark is for a tangible item that one can touch or see and is noted with the letters "tm." See *trademark* and *intellectual property*.

service providers [C] Companies that give online access; there are commercial service providers and internet service providers.

services [B] Nonmanufacturing businesses, such as airlines, car rental agencies, and hotels. Many businesses today are service businesses where success in dealing with the public is a key ingredient to profits.

service sector [E] The business sector based on services, not manufacturing. Services are such businesses as airline travel, investment services, water parks, movies, and, of course, Disneyland.

set [M] A mathematical expression including all elements in a group.

settlement options [I] The variety of payment forms to settle life insurance claims, such as lump sum or annuity forms.

7-pay life [I] A form of paying for a life-insurance policy over only seven years to meet certain legal requirements before cash values can grow tax-deferred.

seven sisters [B] The original seven oil and gas companies that controlled most of the production, distribution, and sale of gas and oil in the world. The seven were BP, Exxon, Gulf, Mobil, Shell, Socal, and Texaco.

severance package [HR] A potential variety of services offered when a person is laid off. The package can include outplacement, a temporary office with a phone, and additional compensation called severance pay.

severance pay [HR] Pay offered to an employee after he or she has been terminated, usually through downsizing.

> Zippy Corp. had to let some employees go, but it offered them a generous *severance pay* of one week's salary for each year they had been with the company.

shakeout [B] A dynamic period in a business sector that results in one or only a few companies dominating the field and the rest of the field becoming weaker competitors. When a business sector is deregulated, there could be a shakeout of companies.

shakeup [B] A major change in the structure, organization, or employment of a company.

> After a disastrous year, there was a major *shakeup* at Acme Corp.— all the offices were reorganized and a new CEO was hired.

share [F] One unit of company ownership through a stock certificate.

shared services [S] Two companies combining their abilities to perform a service or parts of a service.

shareholder [F] See *stockholder*.

share of wallet [S] A company's share of a customer's dollars. A related term, especially with respect to software or the internet, is "own the eyeballs."

shareware [C] Software that is distributed (usually by modem) on the honor system. Users can try out the software, and if they like it, the people who wrote it ask that the user send them a donation or specified fee. Thus, contrary to common misconception, shareware is not free.

shark repellent [B] Business jargon for any one of several strategies for thwarting takeover bids from outside companies or investors. Buying up shares of one's own stock or paying high bonuses to company executives could be such strategies.

Sharpe, William (1934–) [F] American winner of the Nobel Economics Prize who has promoted the use of risk in evaluating investments, especially including the measurement of beta. See *beta* and *Sharpe ratio.*

Sharpe ratio [F] A measurement of the riskiness of a stock or mutual fund developed by William Sharpe. It is a somewhat crude measurement of the expected or past return above treasury interest divided by the standard deviation of the stock or mutual fund. The greater the standard deviation, or risk, the lower the Sharpe ratio.

shelf life [B] The amount of time a product can safely stay on a retail shelf before it spoils.

shelf space [B] The physical space at stores to display goods and merchandise, such as at grocery or bookstores.

Sherman Antitrust Act [B] Federal legislation in 1890 prohibiting monopolies in businesses.

shift key [C] A basic key on the keyboard that allows the user to access uppercase letters, symbols, and other functions. In the old days with typewriters, the keys actually "shifted" so capitals could be typed.

short selling [F] An investment strategy that at first seems either illegal or contorted, although it's perfectly legal, albeit confusing. First one borrows shares from a broker and sells them. Then it is hoped that the price will drop. When it does, the shares are bought at a lower price and then returned back to the broker. It's a backward way to make money; sell first, then buy. Of course this strategy doesn't work if the price of the shares goes up. See *uptick rule* and *technical analysis.*

short-term capital gain or loss [T] A gain, or loss, on an investment or asset usually held for one year or less. Any asset held for longer than one year is called a "long-term" capital gain or loss.

show cause order [L] A court order requested by one party that requires another party to convince the court that a certain action should not be carried out.

> The ABC Company petitioned the court to allow it to mention the technology it licensed from XYZ Corp. in its advertising. Although XYZ protested fiercely, the judge agreed with ABC and ordered XYZ to *show cause* why this would violate the existing licensing agreement.

shrinkage [A] The difference between the amount of inventory a company actually has and what it should have. Shrinkage can occur through employee pilfering, customer shoplifting, or lost shipments.

> The accountants at Zippy Corp. were happy after inventory had been completed—they had less than 1 percent *shrinkage*.

sick days [HR] The number of paid days during the year that an employee may take off due to illness.

sidebar [B] Boxed information, often shaded, that appears as part of a magazine story or in a book. It gives additional or background information.

sigma [M] In statistics, the symbol for standard deviation. One sigma is one standard deviation. The small Greek letter sigma (Σ) is used in statistical formulas to represent standard deviation. See *six sigma* and *standard deviation*.

significance level or test [M] In statistics, the standard level of acceptance of correlations. That level of significance is usually .05 or .01, or either 95 percent or 99 percent accurate.

silent partner [B] A partner in a business who provides financial backing but does not take part in the active management of a firm.

Silicon Valley [C] The area just south of San Francisco that is home to many high-tech firms. Ground zero is considered Palo Alto and Stanford University.

silos [S] Noncoordinated business strategies between separate business units within the same company. The opposite of *synergy*. Just as silos stand separately on the midwestern plains, so do separate company units that each pursue their own direction, often to the detriment of the whole company.

silver bullet [S] The one solution or idea that will solve a problem or situation. Just as the Lone Ranger left the silver bullet to represent the best solution, so too the term is used to mean the best way out of a situation.

> The marketing group had a brainstorming session to find the *silver bullet* to counter its competition.

silver certificates [F] U.S. dollars that were printed before 1963 and were backed by silver reserves. Silver certificates are collector's items today, even though they can no longer be traded for silver.

simple correlation or regression [M] A comparison or regression between just two variables. Multiple correlation or regression analysis compares many variables to find which, if any, are correlated.

simple interest [M] Interest rates that do not compound, or earn interest on interest during a period. See *compound interest*.

SIMPLE plan [HR] A new type of self-employed pension plan. See *retirement plan*.

simplex method [M] A specific linear programming method that allows the solving of complex problems. It involves computational routines in an iterative process. See *linear programming*.

simplify [M] An algebraic operation that combines similar terms to condense an equation as much as possible.

simulation [M] A modeling technique used to represent a process or calculation.

single-country fund [F] A sector mutual fund that invests only in a single country, such as Japan or Spain. Investors who believe that special circumstances prevail in a country can try to take advantage of it through a fund that specializes in it.

single life annuity [HR] See *pension plan*.

single premium [I] Life-insurance policies paid for in one lump sum.

sinking fund [A] An accumulation of funds in anticipation of some need at a specific time in the future, such as when the par value of bonds are due.

sin tax [T] A slang term for taxes on cigarettes or alcohol, so called because they are products that have a negative connotation in society.

> Raising the *sin tax* had two benefits: increased revenue and an incentive for people to quit smoking and stop drinking.

SIPC (Securities Investor Protection Corp.) [F] A governmental agency created in 1970 to shield investors from brokerage house failures.

six sigma [M] A statistical measurement of six standard deviations from the mean. Deviation in statistics is represented by the Greek letter sigma (Σ). It is considered the ultimate goal in the new push toward manufacturing quality. The standard of six sigma specifies that there should only be 3.4 errors per million. Six standard deviations is 99.99976 percent of all the data values. Four sigma specifies 621 errors per million, or 99.9521 percent of all data values.

skewed distribution [M] A statistical distribution that is not centered, as is the typical bell-shaped curve or normal distribution. It is sometimes called asymmetrical because it tilts to one side or another. If the distribution is completely symmetrical then the mean, mode, and median are the same, and the skew is zero. The distribution is said to be skewed to the right when the mean is to the right, or greater, than the mode. That is, the peak of the distribution is toward the left (which may seem counterintuitive). The distribution is skewed to the left when the mean is to the left, or less than, the mode and appears to lean to the right.

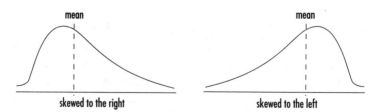

skewed to the right   skewed to the left

skilled labor [B] Employees who have more than just a minimum level of education and training.

skill sets [S] Useful business skills, such as presentation skills, negotiating skills, people skills, verbal skills, writing skills, mathematical skills, and so forth.

SKU [B] An acronym that stands for "stock-keeping unit" and refers to a specific identifying stock number for each separate product carried by a store. Pronounced SKEW.

slamming [C] The illegal practice of having one's long-distance carrier changed without one's approval or knowledge.

slander [L] See *defamation*.

slash key [C] Actually there are two slash keys: the forward slash, which is a vertical line leaning to the right, and the backward slash, which is a vertical line leaning to the left.

slice and dice [S] To perform all kinds of calculations on a set of numbers or a problem.

SLIP (serial line internet protocol) [C] Similar to PPP (point-to-point protocol), only an older version. See *point-to-point protocol*.

slogan [B] An advertising phrase that is meant to be highly memorable and favorable for consumers. Slogan examples are: GE—"We bring good things to life"; Prudential—"A piece of the rock"; and Buick—"Wouldn't you really rather have a Buick?"

slope [M] The steepness of a graphed line. It is measured by the *rise over the run*, meaning the vertical distance divided by the horizontal distance.

slowdown [B] A protest method in which employees at a plant purposely slow down production.

> Although they did not strike, employees at Acme Corp. instituted a *slowdown* to protest the measly wage increases offered in the new contract.

small-cap fund; small-cap stocks [F] The term "cap" stands for capitalization, or share price times the number of outstanding shares. A small-cap stock is usually defined as belonging to a company worth less than $750 million to $1 billion. See *large-cap fund/stocks.*

small claims court [L] A specific court to deal with minor amounts of money.

smart cards [F] Plastic cards that contain a computer chip that stores information about the user and that doesn't need to communicate with a central computer.

> The University issued a *smart card* called MediCard to each student; it contained the complete medical history of that student, so a doctor could instantly see the student's medical history by swiping it in the computer.

smart terminal [C] A terminal connected to a network that can run programs from a central host computer.

Smith, Adam (1723–1790) [E] The author of *The Wealth of Nations* (1776), which provided the basis for modern capitalist ideas. He suggested that individuals should be able to pursue their own economic interests in a free market.

smoke and mirrors [S] The technique of creating an illusion by using whatever means available, such as fancy graphs, impressive figure heads, glossy-prepared reports, whatever can impress while deceiving.

smokestack industry [B] A term referring to past large industries such as steel mills that had decaying and less productive factories. See *rust belt.*

Smoot-Hawley Tariff Act [E] Struggling with the beginnings of the Depression in 1930, President Herbert Hoover signed this bill, which raised tariffs by over 50 percent. European countries retaliated and raised theirs. By closing their own markets to the other, the countries caused world trade to fall two-thirds and deepened the Depression.

smoothing [M] A statistical process of rounding values so that a clearer pattern of the data values may emerge.

snail mail [C] The regular, old, envelope-and-stamp U.S. Postal mail system.

SOB [S] Acronym for Son of a Bitch, meaning a not-so-nice person.

socialism [E] A social and economic system where the production of goods and delivery of services are owned by the government. This is in contrast to "capitalism," in which individuals own the means of production.

social investing; socially responsible investing [F] Also called "conscience" or "green funds," these investments are designed for investors who want to invest with a social conscience. They generally shun companies that are not "politically correct" or that have poor environmental records.

> Marissa and Dal were only interested in *socially responsible investing*—it was part of their campaign to improve the planet.

Social Security [HR] The basic government pension plan and other benefits. Payments are made into the system while one works through the Social Security tax, called FICA (Federal Insurance Contribution Act). The system includes not only a basic pension but also disability and Medicare. The technical trust funds are OAS (Old Age and Survivors) for the pension benefits, DI (Disability Insurance) for disability payments, and HI (Hospital Insurance) for Medicare part A. Part B of Medicare, which pays a portion of doctor's bills, is paid for in part by premiums to retirees (25 percent) and by general government revenues (75 percent). Together these trust funds comprise the entire Social Security system and are technically known as OASDHI.

Social Security leveling option [HR] See *pension plan*.

Social Security number [HR] The nine-digit identification number assigned to each person. The first three digits are the geographic area where the recipient lives when applying for number; the middle two digits have no significant value; the last four digits are straight numerical.

Social Security tax [T] See *FICA tax*.

soft boot [C] See *boot*.

soft dollars [B] Indirect payments for services. For instance, a consulting company may be paid for its consulting services by receiving commissions from selling insurance policies to its clients. In other words, it is paid in soft dollars for its consulting, actually getting its revenue from something else and in reality doing its consulting services for free.

soft font [C] Fonts or styles of type that are stored in a computer or software. This is contrasted to "hard fonts," which are stored in the printer.

soft goods [B] Just as the name implies, manufactured goods that are soft, such as clothing, linens, and bedding.

soft hyphen [C] In word-processing software, the automatic adding of a hyphen when the last word cannot completely fit onto the line. This is in contrast to a "hard hyphen," which requires the user to enter the actual hyphen.

soft market [B] A market characterized by the oversupply of an item.

> Due to an excess of zippers this year, it was a *soft market*.

soft return [C] In word-processing software, the automatic movement of the cursor to the beginning of the next line.

soft-sell approach [B] A selling technique using a more subtle or indirect approach, versus the hard sell or high pressure ad.

software [C] Any of the application programs that provide word processing, spreadsheet, database, or communications.

> The computer system they purchased came with a whole array of *software*, from word-processing applications to online services.

sole proprietorship [B] The simplest form of business, where the owner simply starts a business without a formal corporation or partnership. In general, the business owner simply completes the tax Schedule C with his or her personal tax return.

solicitor [L] See *barrister*.

SOP [S] Acronym for Standard Operating Procedure. It refers to the standard way things are done in an organization.

South Sea bubble [F] See *bubble.*

space bar [C] The bar at the bottom of the keyboard that moves the cursor one position at a time.

spam [C] Internet junk mail. It's an acronym for Stupid Person's AdvertiseMent. The person or company who sends it is called a spammer.

special drawing rights (SDRs) [E] See *International Monetary Fund (IMF).*

special interest group (SIG) [C] A group of people who share a particular interest with each other through a bulletin board within an online service or on the internet.

specialist [F] A member of the stock exchange who maintains an orderly market for specific stocks. He "specializes" in those stocks. He can buy and sell those stocks within his own portfolio to maintain an orderly market.

specialty [B] A business that offers products or services that are either unique in the marketplace or are in limited supply. This is in contrast to a "commodity," which is a product or service that is not distinguishable from its competitors. Whereas specialties compete on quality or design, such as with luxury goods, a commodity generally competes solely on price.

specialty shop [B] Any retailer that sells a small range of items or items that focus on one general theme. Called a "boutique shop" if the specialties are gifts, accessories, or fashionable clothes.

> That mall had only small *specialty shops*, stores such as Light Bulbs R Us, Only Jeans, and House of Zippers.

specie [F] Another word for coins. Pronounced SPE-she.

speculation building (spec) [RE] A building constructed before it has a buyer. This is in contrast to a "custom" building, which is ordered by a client.

speculator [F] One who invests in risky financial transactions, not just average stocks and bonds. Investments may take the form of highly risky stock or unusual transactions like speculating in interest rate movements or currency devaluations.

speech recognition [C] See *voice recognition*.

spell checker [C] A handy word-processing software feature that allows for the checking of words for spelling errors.

spiders (Standard & Poor's Depositary Receipts) [F] Traded on the American Stock Exchange, spiders are blocks of stock representing S&P 500 components. See *diamonds*.

spin-off [B] To sell a business unit or a part of the business and reestablish the new entity as a separate company.

split [F] See *stock split*.

split-dollar insurance [I] A way of buying life insurance whereby an executive and the company split the cost of a whole life-insurance policy. It is a method of providing insurance at low cost for the executive and a share in the eventual death-benefit payout for the company.

split screen [C] A feature of some software programs that can show two documents at one time with a horizontal or vertical split.

spoilage [A] Manufactured goods that are not high quality and thus must be junked or sold at a reduced price.

spooling [C] The process by which information that is sent to a printer waits to be printed. A computer is faster than a printer, so by sending the information to the printer's spooler, the computer can continue its operations. The word *spool* is an acronym for Simultaneous Peripheral Operations OnLine.

spot market [F] Another name for a cash market, in which things are bought and sold right there, for cash "on the spot."

spot radio and TV ads [B] Radio or TV ads in specific markets, versus network ads.

spread [F] In stock markets, the difference between the bid and ask price on a stock. In the futures market, the spread is the difference between a sell contract and a buy contract on a commodity. In both of these cases, the spread will dictate how much money an investor makes in a deal.

spreadsheet [C] One of the four popular applications of software programs: spreadsheets, word processing, desktop publishing, and database management. Spreadsheets allow for the input of data or a table of data that can be manipulated. Inputs are made to cells, which can be referenced by other cells. Rows are the horizontal entries; columns are vertical. The rows are usually numbers and the columns alphabetized. For instance, cell C7 is the C column and the seventh row. Formulas in cells can reference, manipulate, and calculate data from other cells. The business applications of spread-sheet programs are numerous, such as in accounting, finance, sales, and marketing. The original spreadsheet, created by Dan Bricklin in 1979, was called VisiCalc. Lotus 1-2-3 followed in 1982. The two most popular spreadsheets programs are *Excel* and *Lotus 1-2-3*.

square (of a number) [M] The result of multiplying a number by itself. For example, 2 squared equals 4 $(2 \times 2 = 4)$. It is written as $2^2 = 4$.

square peg in a round hole [S] Someone who is ill-suited for a job. The term comes from the simple test young toddlers are given to put round, square, and triangular pegs each in their proper holes. The toddler sometimes will try to force a peg in the wrong hole, with considerable frustration. Similarly, trying to force a person into the wrong job will usually fail.

square root [M] A factor of a number that, when squared, equals the number. For instance, 4 is the square root of 16. It is written as: $\sqrt{16} = 4$.

s-shaped curve [M] A curve that represents an event or a series of events, usually in a real-life situation, that is diagrammed like a rough-shaped S. It could represent the sales of a new breakfast cereal that increased dramatically at first but then leveled off.

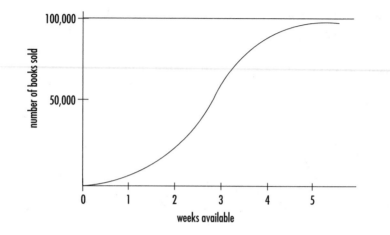

stable value fund [HR] An investment choice in a 401(k) plan that pays higher than average interest, often called a "GIC" (guaranteed investment contract).

staff [B] Departments or employees who perform administrative duties as opposed to manufacturing or activities directly affecting the customers of the business. Such departments as accounting, data processing, human resources, law, or marketing are departments often referred to as staff.

stagflation [E] The combination of economic stagnation and inflation, thus the combined word: stag (for stagnation) and inflation. It was thought that these two could not exist together for more than a brief period of time. Either there would be inflation or stagnation of the economy, but not both. However, in the 1970s, both were experienced in the United States—a stagnant economy with high inflation.

staggered ladder of maturities [F] An interest rate strategy of buying Treasury notes at different, staggered maturities to obtain the average of the interest rates available. As a note comes due, the money is used to purchase a long note to keep the ladder always intact.

Standard & Poor's [F] An investment advisory service that publishes a variety of financial information. It is perhaps mostly known for its S&P 500 index, which is the widely used index by professional investors as a gauge of the stock market as a whole. See *Standard & Poor's 500*.

Standard & Poor's 500 [F] One of the most widely used indexes by professional investors as a gauge of the stock market as a whole. It contains the 500 largest stocks in the United States by capitalization. Capitalization is the share price of a company times the number of outstanding shares. Because the index contains so many companies, it is considered the best overall measurement of the stock market, versus the Dow Jones Industrial Average, which consists of only 30 stocks. The reason people pay so much attention to the Dow average is its familiarity—it's been around since 1884. See *Dow Jones Industrial Average*.

standard deduction [T] An amount of federal tax deduction given to a taxpayer, that varies according to one's tax filing status, single or married. One receives either the standard deduction or itemized deductions, whichever is higher. For 1999, the standard deductions are: $4,300 if single, $7,200 if married, and $6,350 if head of household.

standard deviation [M] One of the most common statistical measurements, measuring how data values are spread around the mean, or average, of the data. It is represented by the Greek letter sigma (Σ). One standard deviation is the measurement of approximately 68 percent (about two-thirds) of the data values. Or, put another way, one can expect that two-thirds of the data will fall within one standard deviation in a normal distribution of data values. Two standard deviations capture approximately 95 percent of the data, and three standard deviations approximately 99 percent. See *bell-shaped curve* and *six sigma*.

standard error [M] A statistical calculation determining how imperfect the sample is relative to the population. It's also called the "standard error of estimate" and is equal to the standard deviation divided by the square root of the number of observations.

standard metropolitan statistical area (SMSA) [B] A specific designation by the U.S. Census Bureau of a geographic area helpful to business, particularly for advertising. In particular, it identifies a metropolitan area of over 50,000 people. Also called an "MSA" (metropolitan statistical area). See *primary metropolitan statistical area (PMSA)*.

standard opinion [A] See *auditor's opinion*.

state of the art [S] The most current knowledge in any field, especially in technology.

statement of cash flows [A] A key financial report that shows the sources and uses of the company's cash flows over a specific period of time. It can also be called "statement of sources and applications of funds," or "statement of changes in net working capital." Sometimes it is simply called the "funds statement." Here is an example of a statement of cash flows:

Statement of Cash Flows

MacSoftware, Inc.
For the year ending December 31, 1998
(in thousands of dollars)

Cash flows from operating activity	
Net Income	$ 1,700
Increase in accounts payable	500
Decrease in accounts receivable	(200)
	2,000
Cash flows from investment activity	
Sales of marketable securities	200
Payment of long term debt	(100)
	100
Net increase in cash	2,100
Cash at begining of year	2,900
Cash at end of year	$ 5,000

statistic [M] A technical element that describes some aspect of a sample of the population, such as the *mean* or the *standard deviation*. This is in contrast to the term "parameter," which describes some aspect of the entire population of a distribution.

statistician [M] A mathematician who studies the particular specialty of statistics, such as averages, standard deviations, and correlations.

statistics [M] Mathematical methods that analyze, represent, and interpret numerical data. The mean, mode, and median measure the central tendencies of the distributions; the range, variance, and standard deviation measure the variability of a distribution. The mathematics of statistics appears to have started in the late 1700s in London and was referred to with the word *statist,* an old word for statesman or politician. There are many mathematical, or statistical, methods that have been developed. To determine if two samples, or a sample and the population, are similar, there are several tests: The t test measures the difference between the means; the F ratio measures the difference between the variances or standard deviations; the chi square test measures differences of the frequencies; and the z score measures the standard deviations from the mean.

status quo [L] A Latin term meaning *the position now,* it refers to things as they are now or the current conditions.

> Although California voters passed the proposition, a temporary restraining order was issued forcing the *status quo* to continue until the hearing.

status report [S] A brief written summary of where one is on a project. Keeping people, especially bosses, informed is important in business, thus the status report.

status symbol [B] Some possession or activity that ostensibly represents one's social or economic status.

statute of limitations [L] The length of time a person or company has to bring legal action against another party for wrongdoing. Once that time has passed, there is no legal right to bring an action.

stay [L] A court order preventing some action until specific conditions are met. A stay of execution is an order preventing some action for a period of time.

> Jamie received a *stay* of eviction from her apartment until she could find a suitable place to live.

stepped costs [A] See *semifixed costs.*

stepped-up basis [T] The valuation of assets and investments at the time an estate is probated. Because the assets are valued at the current market price and an estate tax is assessed at that value, if any is due, the new tax basis is this higher tax basis. Thus, if a person receives an asset through an estate, it also comes with this higher or stepped-up basis, which lessens any capital gain owed later when the asset is sold.

sticky wicket [S] An awkward or difficult situation. The term has its origins in cricket, where it refers to a playing field made sloppy or "sticky" from rain.

stipulate [L] To agree to or to concede something in a legal matter.

stochastic [M] Term referring to random variance. Stochastic modeling means using random numbers, within limits, to project results. Thus, if cash balances fluctuated across a specific range, then one could use stochastic models to account for all the possible values. Pronounced sto-CAS-tic.

stock [F] One unit of ownership in a company. Selling stocks is the means by which a company raises capital. Stock also refers to the certificate that shows ownership of shares. The terms *stock* and *share* are essentially interchangeable.

stock buyback [A] A company's buying of its own stock on the open market. There are several reasons why a company would do this: Sometimes to make it harder for the company to be taken over by another company, sometimes to increase the price of the remaining stock, and sometimes because a company has excess cash and feels there is no better alternative use for the money.

stock dividends [A] Dividends paid as additional common stock rather than in cash.

stock exchange [F] A place where stocks and securities are bought and sold, such as the New York Stock Exchange (NYSE) and the American Stock Exchange (AMEX).

stock exchange index [F] An index of stocks that represent the stock exchange, such as the Dow Jones Industrial Average (DJIA) as a representation of the U.S. stock market.

The Stock Exchange Indexes of the World:

Where:	Common Reporting Index:
Australia	All Ordinaries
Britain	London FT 100, FT 250
Canada	Toronto 300 composite
Europe (euro)	DJ Stoxx, DJ Stoxx 50
France	CAC 40
Germany	Frankfort DAX, Xetra DAX
Hong Kong	Hang Seng
Italy	Milan MIBtel
Japan	Nikkei 225, 300, Topix
Mexico	I.P.C. All Share
Singapore	Straits Times
United States	Dow Jones Industrial Average, S&P 500

stockholder [F] An investor who owns stock in a company. *Stockholder* and *shareholder* are used interchangeably.

stockholder's equity [A] What the owner's of a company own. That is, the sum total of all outstanding stock, common and preferred shares, and retained earnings. It's what the accountants determine is left over after liabilities.

stock market [F] The general term for the market of common stock on various stock exchanges.

stock options [HR] A common compensation plan for employees that offers company stock at a current market price to be bought at that price, usually anytime within ten years. If the stock goes up, then the employee can exercise those options at the lower set price and receive the gain. There are generally two types of options, ISOs (incentive stock options) and NQSOs (nonqualified stock options). Taxes are not due on ISOs until the stock is sold, whereas taxes are due on an NQSO when exercised. If the stock price has declined below the option price, it is said to be "underwater." If the stock price has fallen precipitously, the company may reprice it to provide continuing incentive to its executives. Some companies, especially high-tech firms, offer stock options to a wide range of employees.

stock right [A] A right given to a stockholder to purchase a prescribed number of shares, or a fractional share, at a predetermined price.

stock split [F] The practice of splitting, or dividing, a share of stock into more than one share if the price of a share gets too high. A common split is two for one, that is an investor would now have twice as many shares, each at one-half the price. This doesn't result in any increase for the investor, but it allows the company to put the stock back in what the company believes to be its normal trading range after a run-up in price.

stop loss [HR] See *health insurance.*

stop-loss order [F] An order to a broker to sell a stock if it falls to a certain price. An order is usually placed by an investor who suspects that the price may drop. A stop-loss order may be good till canceled (GTC) or a day order.

stop payment [A] The request by a bank customer to refuse payment on a particular check issued by the customer.

storyboard [B] A series of drawings that lays out the step-by-step frames of a proposed TV commercial.

straddle [F] The investment strategy of buying a combination of put and call options. Investors look for volatile stock and try straddles to make money whether the stock goes up or down.

straight arrow [S] A person who does his job and doesn't make waves. Someone who does what he is told and doesn't ask why. Presumably the term comes from archery, where a straight arrow will always fly straight, but a crooked arrow will be unpredictable.

straight-life annuity [I] An annuity payment option that pays just for the owner. It is the highest payment of an annuity. See *pension plan.*

straight-line depreciation [A] A method of depreciation in which an equal portion of an asset's cost is written off each year. See *depreciation*.

strangle [F] An investment strategy involving both "out-of-the-money" calls and puts.

strategic planning [B] Business planning that specifies what it wants to accomplish in terms of its products or services and how it intends to carry out those plans.

> At Acme Corp., Jane was responsible for the company's *strategic planning*, which she did after discussions with the heads of the major business units and the president of the firm.

Street, the [F] The financial center of the nation: Wall Street.

street name [F] Securities deposited at and registered by a brokerage firm rather than with the individual investor, even though the investor has full rights to the security. It allows investors to quickly and easily sell the securities.

stretch [S] An attempt to get more out of people; having people stretch their efforts to accomplish the tasks at hand.

strike [B] A complete stoppage of work by employees as a protest, usually about work conditions or wages. Strikes are often used as a final bargaining tool by a union during negotiations.

> When the workers and management could not reach a settlement on cost of living increases, workers had no choice but to go out on *strike*.

strike price [F] The price of an option at which the owner of a call option can purchase the underlying stock or the owner of a put option can sell the underlying stock.

string [C] Any group of characters. If a computer asks for a string of text, it simply means a line of text.

> The *string* she entered was eight characters long.

string formula [C] A formula in a spreadsheet that contains text as well as numerical values.

strip development; strip mall [RE] A commercial area that is a strip of stores along the road, as opposed to single stores or a large mall.

Strips (Separate Trading Registered Interest and Principal of Securities) [F] Treasury securities that have their interest and principal "stripped" from the original bond to provide for essentially a zero-coupon Treasury bond.

strong dollar [E] See *dollar is higher/lower.*

student's t [M] A statistical test between the *means* of two distributions to see how alike they are. It is also called the "t test," "t distribution," or referred to as the "t table." It refers to testing the data for a certain level of confidence. William Grosset, a consultant to the Guinness Brewery in Dublin, wrote on this subject under the pseudonym *Student.* See *statistics.*

subcontract [B] A secondary contract, or a firm that receives a contract for work and contracts out some or all the work.

subdirectory [C] A secondary directory for computer files, from the main or root directory.

sublet; sublease [RE] An agreement to allow a tenant to rent the use and occupancy of a property.

subliminal ads [B] Now considered illegal, a practice of split-second images or messages within an ad that tried to reach a consumer just below the threshold of conscious perception.

subordinated security [A] A security issued by a company that is second or third in line to the rights of another security, called the "senior security." Common stock is subordinated to preferred stock, which receives its dividend first. A debenture, a secondary bond, is subordinated to a regular bond, which would receive its interest and principal payments first.

subpoena [L] A formal court order requiring a person to appear in court and give testimony on a certain case.

subscribe/unsubscribe [C] To add, or delete, one's name from an internet list or sign up for a commercial online service.

subscript and superscript [C] In math, or footnoting, smaller numbers or letters placed a little lower or higher than normal:

subscript: $A = p_i + p_j$
superscript: $A = p^i + p^j$.

subsidiary [B] A part of a larger company that is often more autonomous in its operations than the rest of the company. Sometimes refers simply to the various business units of a larger company.

suit [L] Often referred to as a lawsuit, it is the means by which a person or company pursues a remedy in a court of law.

suite [C] A group of software programs packaged together as an integrated unit, such as spreadsheet, word processer, and database all in one.

sum [M] The result of addition. The sum of 4 plus 1 is 5.

sum-of-the-year's-digits depreciation (SYD) [A] A method of accelerated depreciation in which a fraction is written off each year. That fraction is formed with the numerator being the year in question and the denominator being the sum of the asset's years of useful life. For example, the first year's depreciation of an asset with a ten-year useful life would be:

$$\frac{10}{1+2+3+4+5+6+7+8+9+10} = \frac{10}{55}$$

Thus, the first year's depreciation would be the fraction of 10 divided by 55. The second year's depreciation would be the fraction of 9 divided by 55, and so forth. The last year would be the fraction of one divided by 55. See *depreciation*.

summary judgment [L] A legal procedure to have a case resolved before a lengthy trial ensues. The facts are generally stipulated, and the only decision to be made is who is right.

summer rally [F] An often upward trend on stock markets during the summertime. It is thought that during the summer there is a more positive mood on Wall Street because many investors are on vacation enjoying themselves.

summons [L] A legal notice for a person or company to appear in court as a defendant in a case.

sunset provision [L] A provision in the law that ends at a specific time.

> The new law created a temporary excise tax that had a *sunset provision* of December 31, 2002.

Super Bowl predictor [F] A theory about the stock market that says the stock market will rise during the year if a member of the old National Football League, or the current National Football Conference, wins the Super Bowl. The predictor was wrong in 1990 when the San Francisco '49ers won but the market declined, and in 1998 when the Denver Broncos won and the market rose. Also see *January effect*.

superscript [C] See *subscript*.

supervisor [B] A first step of management with responsibility for a small number of employees. In a production facility, a supervisor is often called a "foreman." The next level of management is usually called a "manager."

suppliers [B] Companies that provide parts or subassemblies for other companies.

supply [E] The production of products and services. It is the willingness on the part of businesses and individuals to offer goods and services to consumers. It's one side of "supply and demand." Demand is the desire for specific products and services tempered by the ability to pay for them.

supply and demand [E] The basic economic concept that prices affect what consumers buy. In general, the lower the price, the more a consumer will want to buy, which is the demand. The higher the price, the more the producer will want to sell, which is the supply. The price that is just right balances the supply and demand and is called the "equilibrium price."

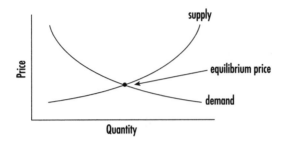

supply chain [S] The entire process of the supplying of products or services to customers for improvement in quality.

supply-side economics [E] The economic philosophy of cutting taxes on individuals and business so there will be a greater stimulus to produce more goods and services. Although taxes are a starting point, the object of cutting taxes is to stimulate the economy by giving individuals more incentive to make money through producing a greater supply of goods and services. See *demand-side economics*.

supply-siders [E] Followers of the supply-side economic philosophy. See *supply-side economics*.

surfing the net [C] The term for browsing through the different web sites on the internet.

surge protector [C] An important device between a computer and the wall socket that protects the computer from unexpected surges of electricity. Yes, surges sometimes happen. The surge protector is usually built into the socket bar where all of the computer and peripheral devices are connected.

surrogate court [L] See *probate court*.

surtax [T] An additional tax.

> The proposed luxury tax was a *surtax*: It would add a 10 percent tax
> to the regular sales tax the buyer already paid on the item.

swap [F] An agreement by two parties to exchange a series of
cash flows, for example fixed-rate payments for floating-rate payments.

swaption [F] An option giving an investor the right to enter into
or cancel a swap at a future date. See *swap*.

sweat equity [S] Term referring to the personal effort one puts
into a start-up business, versus capital investment.

SYD (sum-of-the-year's digits depreciation) [A] See *sum-of-the-
year's-digits depreciation*.

symbols [M] Letter representations for values, mathematical processes, or ideas. Mathematics and statistics are filled with them,
often derived from the Greek alphabet, such as the terms delta
and sigma shown below, or Latin, such as the term integral. One
of the most famous symbols, the peace symbol, was created in
1958 from two semophore (flag) signals, the N (for Nuclear) and
D (for Disarmament):

> delta -   Δ meaning a small increase
> sigma -   Σ meaning a sum
> integral - ∫ used in calculus

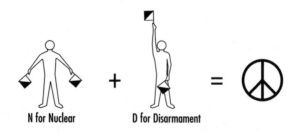

N for Nuclear   D for Disarmament

syndicate [B] A temporary association between two or more
firms, or individuals, in some joint business venture in which the
two members share the gains or losses.

synergy [S] The interaction of two or more entities or ideas that results in something greater than the sum of the parts. When two companies merge, the CEO comments often that the new company will achieve more of a creative synergy than was possible before. Synergy math is often referred to as "two plus two equals five" (that is, greater than the sum of the parts).

sysop [C] An older term for the operator in charge of an internet site or any multiuser system. Sysop is an acronym for SYStem OPerator. The newer term is "webmaster."

System 7 [C] A popular operating system used in Macintosh computers. The latest for the iMac is the MAC OS 8.5 operating system.

T

tab key [C] The key on a computer keyboard that indents text a certain number of spaces at one time.

T account [A] The listing of debits and credits in an accounting ledger that forms the letter T. The debits are on the left and the credits on the right. The T account is used mostly in textbooks, as companies usually keeps three columns, debits, credits, and the balance.

Taft-Hartley Act [B] Legislation enacted in 1947 to amend the National Labor Relations Act to limit some of the more aggressive union labor activities. Among other provisions, it gives authority to the president of the United States to impose cooling off periods in strikes or lockouts that threaten national health or safety.

tailored [S] Term referring to something that has been customized for a particular company or department, as opposed to something off-the-shelf.

take back a mortgage [RE] A situation in which the seller offers to finance part of the purchase through payments such as a mortgage, meaning the seller will take a mortgage rather than cash.

take-charge attitude [S] The disposition of a person who initiates action or leadership and does not have to wait to be told what to do.

takeover [B] A process by which a company changes hands. A takeover may be friendly, if management wants to be sold, or unfriendly, if management fights against the takeover.

tangent (line) [M] The line that touches a circle, or curve, at only one point. A tangent line always forms a right angle to the radius of the circle at that point.

tangible results [S] Specific results that can be measured.

> Cruthers explained that although the marketing campaign produced *tangible results,* no one knew which of the campaign's ads were the most effective.

tangibles [F] An investment that one can actually touch, such as real estate or gold. This is in contrast to intangible investments, such as stocks and bonds, which are only paper representations.

tanken [F] The important Japanese quarterly report on business conditions. Comparable to the Fed's *beige book*.

tape [F] The band of stock quotations that shows each trade on the stock exchanges as it moves along the bottom of a news cable channel or on a computer screen. At one time, the ticker-tape machines clicked away at brokerage offices and provided the fodder for New York's ticker-tape parades. Today, computers have replaced ticker tape so other paper has to be used for these events, though they are still called ticker-tape parades.

tape drive [C] A drive that is used as a backup for computer data.

target [C] The place to which the duplicate of a computer file is sent.

> My *target* for the copy I was making from my hard disk was the "a" drive.

target benefit plan [HR] See *hybrid pension plan*.

target market [B] The group of people who generally buy the type of product being marketed.

> The researchers at Market Corp. told the manufacturers of the new Quik Zip Zipper that their *target market* was women between the ages of thirty-five and fifty and that they should gear their advertisements to that group.

tariff [E] A duty, fee, or tax imposed on the import of goods. Generally, a government tends to make foreign goods more expensive than local ones in order to encourage consumers to buy domestic goods. It often is a way to protect the workforce and business within a country.

task force [B] A temporary team formed with the express purpose of completing a specific task.

> The CEO of Acme Corp. appointed a *task force* to investigate the decline in sales from the last two quarters.

tax abatement [RE] An official reduction or complete suspension of real estate taxes after the initial assessment has been made on a property.

The city *tax abatement* allowed the investors to pay little real estate tax on the property while they renovated it.

taxable income [T] Income subject to tax after all allowable subtractions such as deductions and exemptions, have been made.

Edna was concerned that she would have to pay taxes on all of her $100,000 income but then realized that all her deductions and exemptions reduced her *taxable income* to only $55,000.

tax audit [T] The process through which the Internal Revenue Service determines if an individual paid all of the taxes he owes to the government.

tax brackets [T] The income levels that qualify an individual for different tax rates. Because the United States has a progressive federal income tax, there are different tax brackets individuals might fall into, depending on their income.

Single Tax Rate Schedule for 1999

If taxable income is:	The tax is:
$0 up to $25,750:	15%
$25,750 up to $62,450:	$3,862.50 plus 28% over $25,750
$62,450 up to $130,250:	$14,138.50 plus 31% over $62,450
$130,250 up to $283,150:	$35,156.50 plus 36% over $130,250
$283,150 and over:	$90,200.50 plus 39.6% over $283,150

Married Tax Rate Schedule for 1999

If taxable income is:	The tax is:
$0 up to $43,050:	15%
$43,050 up to $104,050:	$6,457.50 plus 28% over $43,050
$104,050 up to $158,550:	$23,537.50 plus 31% over $104,050
$158,550 up to $283,150:	$40,432.50 plus 36% over $158,550
$283,150 and over:	$85,288.50 plus 39.6% over $283,150

tax break [T] Anything that allows a person to pay less in taxes. Deductions, exemptions, and credits are examples of tax breaks.

Congress enacted a new tax code that gave a *tax break* to families with children.

tax code [T] See *Internal Revenue Code.*

Tax Compliance Measurement Program (TCMP) [T] The dreaded mother of all tax audits. The IRS randomly selects taxpayers who have to verify each and every item on their return. The IRS uses these audits to program its computers to check on all other taxpayers.

The Smiths were chosen for audit through the *TCMP* and had to provide the IRS with complete proof of all their deductions.

tax court [T] See *U. S. Tax Court.*

tax deferral [T] Income that is taxed at a later date. 401(k)s and IRAs (individual retirement accounts) are probably the most common type of tax deferrals. When money is eventually withdrawn, it is taxed with a few exceptions, such as that for the Roth IRA.

tax deferred annuities (TDAs) [HR] Sometimes called 403(b) plans, they are typically a defined-contribution plan available to teachers, hospitals, and nonprofit organizations. However, an organization must sponsor such a plan as contributions are through payroll deductions. Once sponsored, employees generally are able to select from several insurance companies that offer various investment options. The contributions are usually pretax.

tax equalization [T] The process of making the taxes that an expatriate (U.S. citizen working overseas) has to pay equal to what he would pay if he earned his money in the United States. Companies who employee expatriates calculate this equalization for the employee.

taxes [E] Payments to federal, state, and local governments for government expenditures. Taxes come in many forms, such as income, sales, and estate taxes.

tax evasion [T] The act of purposely not paying a tax that is owed.

> The IRS brought Slimy Corp. up on charges of *tax evasion* for purposely not reporting the income it received from Box Co. the year before.

tax exempt; tax-free bonds; tax-free mutual fund [F] An investment in which the interest earned is not taxed. These are generally municipal bonds and are offered by most states, cities, and many counties. If an investor lives in the state in which the bond is offered, then it is usually tax exempt on her federal and state income tax. Out-of-state bonds are only tax exempt on federal tax return. In high-tax states, there are usually a number of mutual funds of tax-exempt bond funds for that state. Treasury issues are tax exempt from state income tax.

tax-free [T] Term describing some income sources, in particular tax-free municipal bond interest, on which one does not have to pay taxes. However, some "tax-free munis," as they are called for short, can incur some AMT taxes, and some tax-free municipals are actually taxable.

tax-free exchange [T] The method allowed in the tax code by which certain assets can be exchanged without taxation. This exchange is usually referred to as a "like-kind" exchange. For example, real estate can be exchanged under Section 1031; this is frequently called "a 1031 exchange." Two investors can exchange real estate under this provision if the two pieces of real estate are considered "like-kind." Also, certain insurance policies or annuities can be exchanged under Section 1035, frequently called "a 1035 exchange." A policy holder can trade in one policy for another, even at another insurance company, if it meets certain conditions.

tax loophole [T] The slang term for "tax break."

taxpayer identification number (TIN) [T] The Internal Revenue Service uses an individual's Social Security number as a reference number for that person. Partnerships, corporations, and trusts have separate taxpayer identification numbers (TINs).

> The tax form asked for the *taxpayer identification number,* so Joey filled in his Social Security number.

tax roll [RE] The list of people or companies who pay property tax in a given municipality.

> After Quick Corp. purchased an office building, its name was entered on the *tax roll* for Smallville.

tax sale [RE] The sale of property to obtain the money to pay property taxes.

> The taxes on the office building downtown were so delinquent that it finally went up for *tax sale*.

tax shelter [T] A legal way to exempt part of one's income from taxation through an investment that generally provides for tax losses. In the 1980s, real estate and oil and gas limited partnerships were popular tax shelters, but as tax laws changed, these partnerships experienced hard times and very dissatisfied investors.

> Because the income Jay put into his IRA was exempt from income tax, it was a great *tax shelter*.

tax software [T] Specialized software that helps individuals and businesses complete their federal and state tax returns; some programs help with tax planning as well. Popular tax software for individuals includes *Tax Cut* and *Turbo Tax*.

tax table [T] The long table in the tax instruction booklet that lists the amount of taxes owed by an individual with a certain income. See *tax brackets*.

Taylor, Frederick [B] See *mass production*.

T-bills; T-notes; T-bonds [F] Treasury securities of different maturities. T-bills are issued for three, six, and twelve months; T-notes are issued from two to ten years; and T-bonds are issued for twenty and thirty years. The thirty-year T-bond is considered the bellwether for long-term interest rates and is usually quoted during daily financial news reports.

TCP/IP (Transfer Control Protocol/Internet Protocol) [C] Two protocol standards by which information is sent over the internet.

t distribution or test [M] See *student's t*.

teams [B] Groups of people working together, usually in small numbers, especially in manufacturing but in other areas of a company as well.

Teamsters [B] The major labor union in the country involved with transportation workers, in particular truck drivers.

techie [C] A computer user with intimate knowledge of the inner working of the computer.

technical analysis [F] One of two approaches to analyzing a particular stock or the stock market as a whole. Technical analysis relies primarily on market volume or price movements to determine the best time to buy or sell stocks. This is in contrast to "fundamental analysis," which analyzes business earnings, balance sheets, and economic factors of a particular company or its business sector to determine if a stock, or group of stocks, should be bought or sold. See *fundamental analysis*.

Technical Analysis: Looking at the Patterns

Market Indicators:	Charting the movements:
market breadth	head and shoulders pattern
market momentum	breakout pattern
insider trading	triple-top pattern
short selling	inverted saucer pattern
moving averages	V-formation

The types of patterns outlined above sometimes emerge in charts that show the graphical plotting of data. For example, if the daily charting of a particular stock began flat, then increased and plateaued, and finally decreased and plateaued again, it is called a "head and shoulders" pattern.

---

technical support [C] The service provided by software or hardware companies to give instruction and help to users.

telecommunications [C] Communication of data, video, text, audio, and other means over long distances.

telecommuting [HR] The act of working at home and contacting the office primarily via telephone, fax machine, and E-mail. See *hoteling*.

teleconferencing [C] A conference among people in different locations all connected by telephone or by both telephone and video.

telemarketing [B] The practice of selling and gathering information about products using the telephone.

> After it did a direct mail solicitation, Zippy Corp. followed up with a *telemarketing* campaign to see if the people who'd received flyers wished to place an order.

telephone tag [S] The situation in which two people keep missing each other, leaving messages at each other's office or on voice mail.

telephonitis [S] A word describing people who are on the phone more than they should be. It is used to describe both the person who constantly interrupts meetings or conversations by taking phone calls and the social person who is always talking to friends on the telephone.

telerate machine [F] The machine that gives the read-out of stock quotations, as the old ticker tape used to.

template [C] A customized, pre-formatted version of a spreadsheet application that is tailored to suit a specific department or organization. Templates streamline the process of creating a spreadsheet by eliminating the need for entering the same formulas over and over.

> The accounting department developed a *template* to be used by all branches for the submission of payroll to the head office.

temporary restraining order [L] An order to preserve the status quo until a hearing is held.

temps; temping; temporary help [HR] Terms related to temporary employment. Temporary employees are hired to complete jobs that companies want to be done for a certain period of time or for a specific project. The workers doing the temporary work are called temps. They refer to their status as temping.

tenancy [RE] A form of ownership of property, usually important in estate matters after one owner dies.

Tenancy Terms—Who Owns It?

joint tenancy with rights of survivorship Two people sharing the ownership of a property, typically spouses. When one dies, the other automatically owns 100 percent of it.

tenancy by the entirety This agreement, specified by certain states to be held only by husband and wife, is essentially the same as joint tenancy with rights of survivorship. A spouse needs permission from the other spouse to dispose of any property.

tenancy in common When two or more people, generally nonspouses, own a specific share of a specific asset, such as a vacation home. When owners die, their wills would specify who gets their share. Also called "joint tenancy."

---

tenancy by the entirety [T] See *tenancy*.

tenancy in common [T] See *tenancy*.

tenant [RE] Someone who occupies property but does not own it.

tender offer [B] An offer by a company to buy another, usually in the form of offering an attractive stock price to the stockholders of the targeted company.

10-K report [A] The financial report that is filed each year by companies traded on any of the stock exchanges. It is filed with the Securities and Exchange Commission (SEC) and is available to the public for all investors to see. It contains complete and audited financial statements.

10-Q report [A] The financial report that is filed each quarter by companies traded on any of the stock exchanges. It is filed with the Securities and Exchange Commission (SEC) and is available to the public for all investors to see. It may or may not contain audited financial information.

terabyte (T, TB) [C] A trillion or so bytes. Actually, it is about 1,099,511,627,776 bytes, or 2^{40}, that is, 2 to the 40th power. See *byte*.

teraflop [C] A term relating to the ability of a computer to complete 1 million calculations per second.

term life insurance [I] See *life insurance.*

testament [T] Technically, a person's testimonial, statement, or wishes expressed at death. Generally, the will is known as the "last will and testament" of a person. Technically, the term "will" deals with the distribution of real property such as real estate, while the term "testament" refers to the distribution of personal property.

testamentary trust [T] A trust usually written into a will that goes into effect when someone dies.

test market [B] A specific geographical area, usually a mid-size city in the Midwest that is considered a representation of the country as a whole. Businesses can market their products and services in those cities to gauge whether the products will be successful in wide release.

test marketing [B] The practice of testing a new product or service. It can generate valuable feedback for predicting the success or failure of a potential product. It can also indicate how a product should be modified to be successful. See *focus group.*

text editor [C] A special program that edits only text files. It doesn't have any of the fancy formatting of many word-processing programs.

text wrap [C] A feature of word-processing and desktop publishing software that automatically positions text around a graphic or picture.

t-group [HR] See *sensitivity training.*

theory [M] A systematic order of knowledge. A theory allows for the analysis and prediction of outcomes. For example, in investments the Modern Portfolio Theory allows for the analysis and prediction of investment results.

theory X, Y, and Z [HR] Three different theories about how to manage people. Theory X promotes the authoritarian approach: People have to be pushed to do their jobs. Theory Y promotes the idea that employees are generally responsible and should be given independence to do their jobs. Theory Z, by William Ouchi in his book of the same name, promotes the Japanese idea of involving workers at all levels in decision making.

thesaurus [C] A tool built into word-processing software or a book that suggests alternate words having the same meaning as a given word.

think outside the box [S] Nonconformist thinking. See *outside-the-box thinking*.

think tank [S] A brainy consulting firm or any group within a company that has really good ideas.

third country nationals (TCN) [HR] Citizens of one country who work in another country and are employed by a company headquartered in still another country (the third). See *expat*.

third world countries [E] See *emerging countries*.

threads [C] In a newsgroup, a series of posts that follow the same topic of conversation. If a user doesn't want to read any more of a certain thread, he or she can give a "kill" or "junk" command and move on to the next topic in the newsgroup.

360-degree feedback [HR] A method of personal evaluation in which executives receive written feedback from superiors and subordinates and then discuss it with a coach to analyze the information and develop a plan of action to remedy any problems that might have been pointed out.

three-six-three [S] An old banker's saying, before the inflation of the 1970s, that referred to the practice of paying bank customers 3 percent interest on savings accounts, charging them 6 percent for mortgage loans, and being on the golf course by 3 P.M. After inflation forced the banks to pay high interest while stuck with long-term mortgage loans, the bankers were up until 3 A.M. trying to figure out a solution.

thrifts [F] See *bank failure*.

tight money [E] The monetary policy of the Federal Reserve (Fed) to make less money available in the economy in hopes of slowing down an overly stimulated economy. It is the opposite of the Fed's "easy" or "loose money" policy.

TIGRs (Treasury Investment Growth Receipts) [F] A trade-marked security of Merrill Lynch providing a stripped Treasury bond.

tilde sign (~) [C] The little wavy line (pronounced TIL-da) that is used in computer spreadsheet macros to represent the Enter key. It comes from the Spanish language, where it is placed over the letter *n* to indicate a nasal sound, or in Portuguese over a vowel to indicate a nasal sound.

time-series analysis [M] The analysis of data over time, such as monthly or yearly.

time to market [S] The length of time it takes to get a product or service to the consumer market from the inception of an idea.

time value of money [M] Financial calculations of present and future value. Time differences influence the value of something, such as an investment. If an investor was promised that his investment would be worth $1,000 in three years but instead wanted the money now, the investment would only be worth $863 if the rate of investment were 5 percent.

timing [F] See *market timing*.

tip [B] Money paid directly to a waiter, taxi driver, bell hop, etc., as compensation for good service. Also called a gratuity. An old story has it that the term *tip* comes from colonial days when tavern keepers would ask for additional donations for the waiters and waitresses in a bowl marked "To Insure Promptness."

TIPS [F] A newer type of U.S. Treasury bond in which the value of the bond increases by the rate of inflation. TIPS is an acronym for Treasury Inflation Protection Securities. They are more frequently referred to as *"I bonds."* See *I bonds*.

title [RE] Proof of ownership. In real estate, the title is exchanged at the closing. It must be clear of all outstanding liens before it is passed on.

title insurance [RE] Insurance that protects a title's validity and the owner's exclusive claim to the property.

titular head [S] Someone who holds a title but doesn't have authority or power.

> Cruthers told the staff in confidence that the new president was only the *titular head* of the division; the real authority was exercised by the head office.

Tobin, James (1918–) [E] See *Nobel Prize for economics.*

today's dollars [M] A measure of how much something in the past or future would be valued in present-day dollars. It is often used with the rate of inflation to illustrate how costs have risen. For example, if a loaf a bread cost $.50 twenty years ago, and inflation rose 3 percent a year, the cost of a loaf of bread in today's dollars would be $.90. However, the actual cost today is about $2. See *present value.*

toggle [C] A switch that turns something on and if pressed again, turns it off. This applies not only to actual keys or switches but also to any program command that turns a function on if used once and then off if used again.

> The Caps Lock key on most keyboards is a *toggle* switch.

token-ring network [C] A local area network developed by IBM in which one person at a time must "grab the token" to transmit. Once finished, another person can grab the token and then transmit to everyone else.

tombstone ad [F] A notice announcing that a security is either being offered for sale or has been sold. Investors check tombstone ads to see what's for sale, the name of the underwriter, the issue, and the date it will be sold.

toner [C] Special black powder used in laser printers that is contained in a cartridge for easy loading.

toolbar [C] A row of icons or items that represent software menu options.

top down [S] A management style in which company objectives are set by upper management as opposed to middle management.

top of mind [S] An item or issue occupying a prime position in the corporate consciousness.

> With the state about to issue a scathing report on its pollution of the nearby river, XYZ Corp. made damage control a *top of mind* concern.

tort [L] A civil wrong outside of a contractual wrong. Libel and slander are examples of torts. They are wrongs causing damages to others that are considered a breach of reasonable conduct in society.

total expense ratio [F] In a mutual fund, the percentage of that fund's assets that are paid as fees.

total quality management (TQM) [B] A fairly new and popular management concept based on the cooperation of both labor and management to improve the quality and productivity of products and service. Simply put, *TQM* is a management approach to long-term success through customer satisfaction. Teams, called quality circles, are usually formed to suggest and implement improvements throughout the manufacturing or service process. Bosses are no longer autocrats, but facilitators assisting in the improvement of quality process.

total return [F] The combination of income plus any gain or loss on an investment. This is in contrast to "current yield," which is just income, and "appreciation," which is the gain or loss. Total return is considered the most meaningful calculation for comparison with other investments. Usually, the total return is given on a yearly basis, January 1 through December 31.

touch pad [C] See *mouse*.

touch screen [C] A technology allowing for selection of choices by pressing options shown on a screen.

touchy-feely [S] A term referring to a nontechnical subject or topic, such as teamwork or human nature. Although such topics are important, they do not lend themselves to technical or mathematical analysis. Because touchy-feely issues are considered the "soft side" of business, the term is sometimes used in a pejorative way.

tower configuration [C] A newer type of computer that sits vertically on the floor, versus the traditional unit that sat under the monitor.

TQM [B] See *total quality management.*

trackball [C] A type of mouse that is built into the keyboard, usually found on a laptop computer.

tract [RE] A piece of land, usually a large parcel, that may be subdivided.

> BPL Construction was looking for an attractive *tract* of land for a new twenty-five-home development.

trade [B] Any business or profession may be called a trade, but the term most often refers to an activity engaged in by a skilled worker.

> The carpenter learned his *trade* from his father and grandfather.

trade, the [B] The segment of the book industry that sells books to the adult public, versus text, professional, or children's books.

trade advertising [B] Advertising directed at retailers and wholesalers, not the final consumer of the goods and services.

trade balance/imbalance; trade surplus [E] An excess of goods sold in one country that are made in another.

trade discount [A] The reduction in price when selling wholesale.

trade magazine or publication [B] Any newspaper or magazine devoted to members of a specific profession. For example, *Advertising Age* is a trade magazine for the advertising industry.

> Whenever he was looking for work, Jones checked the *trade publications* first as they listed jobs in his field.

trademark [L] Legal protection for a specific design, logo, or mark used by a company in the course of business. When approved, a company can use the registered mark ® for ten years, and then it can be renewed if still actively used. Unusual things have been trademarked, such as NBC's three-note sound and MGM's lion roar. See *intellectual property.*

trader [F] A person who executes the buy and sell orders. Traders must be registered, and they charge a fee for making the trade.

trade secret [L] A proprietary idea, process, or formula used in a business. It is usually unique and therefore kept secret. It is given certain legal rights; however, it is not a patent, which is disclosed when applied for. See *intellectual property*.

> The formula for Coca-Cola is a *trade secret* known by only a few people.

trade show [B] A large professional gathering, usually in a hall or convention center, in which different companies within a certain general trade exhibit products and services and make sales to retailers.

trading pit [F] The area on the floor of an exchange, such as a commodity exchange, in which the trading takes place. A pit may be divided into areas for different types of trades.

> The *trading pit* was a sea of activity; to those who didn't work there, it seemed totally out of control.

transfer agent [A] An agent of a company who maintains records of stock ownership for dividend and voting purposes.

transfer payment [E] A payment such as a welfare benefit paid to an individual by the government.

transfer tax [T] Generally considered as estate, inheritance, and gift taxes. It is the tax that may be due upon the transfer of money or property to another person.

transparency [F] The quality of a business or government that allows for easy access to information about the organization's inner workings.

travel and entertainment (T&E) [B] A common term referring to the expenses of business travel.

treasurer [A] The officer of a company responsible for obtaining capital and maintaining cash and investments.

treasury direct [F] An account established to buy and hold Treasury bonds directly through the Federal Reserve Bank. There are no brokers involved in the transactions. The account is usually established through the investor's bank account so everything can be done electronically; interest is automatically deposited into the account.

Treasury issues [F] The variety of U.S. government bills, notes, and bonds issued on a regular basis. Also included are the EE, HH, and the new I bond issues.

treasury stock [A] Stock issued by a company that is owned by the company, usually as a result of repurchasing its shares in the market. The company receives no dividends and has no voting rights because a publicly traded company cannot own itself.

trial balance [A] A listing of all accounts to determine if they balance, that is, whether the debits equal the credits.

triangle [M] A three-sided geometric figure. An isosceles triangle has two sides of equal length; a right triangle has one angle that is 90°; a scalene triangle has no two sides and no angles equal.

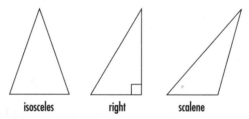

isosceles   right   scalene

trickle-down economics [E] An economic theory and practice that promotes the general economy. If the economy does well, so do most of the people throughout society, including people at lower levels because they are more likely to have jobs. The benefits thus "trickle-down" to all people.

triple A [F] See *AAA rating*.

triple witching hour [F] The hour when options and futures both expire, thus three closings occur together: the regular stock market, options, and futures. This can be a time of considerable volatility in markets as investors scramble to close their positions. The triple witching hours occur four times a year: on the third Friday of March, June, September, and December.

trust [L] A legal entity that holds money or property, such as a charitable trust, a grantor trust, or a pension trust. Parents often set up a trust in their will, for example, in case they both die while their children are still minors. The trust specifies how and when the money is to be distributed to the children.

trustee/trustor [T] In legal talk, a person who holds or manages the money to a trust is the *trustee*, while the person who created and contributed to the trust is the *trustor*.

trustees [A] The group of individuals responsible for specific funds held for the benefit of others, such as the trustees overseeing pension funds.

trust fund [A] Money set aside for special uses. A pension trust fund is one example.

tuition assistance [HR] Reimbursement from a company for some or all of an employee's after-work education.

tulipmania [F] A speculation in tulips in seventeenth century Holland. See *bubble*.

tuple [C] An name for a row in a database.

turnaround [B] A business that has overcome considerable adversity to succeed, often rebounding from a difficult period.

turnkey operation [S] A complete stand-alone operation that can do it all.

turnover [A] The number of times merchandise is sold and then replaced over a specific period of time, often on a monthly, quarterly, and annual basis. It measures the speed of product movement.

[HR] The number of employees who leave a company that need to be replaced. Usually quoted in percentages, as in "Our turnover rate is 15 percent," meaning 15 percent of employees leave each year.

tutorial [C] Immensely valuable for beginners, it is a training program that usually accompanies software. A user can become familiar with the software through the standard examples in the tutorial.

12b-1 fees [F] Technically called a distribution fee, it is a fee for marketing and advertising a mutual fund. This fee is allowed to be charged to investors by the SEC (Securities and Exchange Commission). Some funds specifically indicate that they will not charge such fees. See *mutual fund fees*.

two-bin system [A] An inventory system in which there are physically two bins of parts for manufacturing, one for the regular inventory and one to be used when the first bin is empty. As soon as the first bin is empty, inventory is reordered.

two sets of books [A] The practice of keeping two different accounting ledgers. Sometimes this practice is legitimate, such as when a company has one set of books for regular financial reports and another for credit or tax purposes. Both sets of books are accurate but are kept for different purposes. Sometimes keeping two books is not legitimate, such as when a company tries to deceive vestors, creditors, or the tax authorities by keeping accurate figures for private use but keeping false books for the public.

two-tailed test [M] In statistics, the testing for both ends, or tails, of the bell-shaped distribution curve. This is in contrast to testing only one side for statistical significance.

type-A personality [S] A hard-driving business person. This describes the typical workaholic.

U

UGMA [T] See *Uniform Gifts to Minors Act.*

umbrella policy [I] A policy that provides extra personal liability insurance, usually along with regular property insurance.

> The Smiths had a $2 million *umbrella policy* in case they were sued for any injuries that occurred on their property.

unbundling [B] The separation of complex products or services. For instance, discount stockbrokers have unbundled the trading of stock from the traditional research service.

undercapitalized [A] A company or enterprise that does not have enough capital to either expand as it should or to even carry out its business.

underemployed [HR] The term used to describe someone who is employed at a level or two below his or her education and training.

> After Dr. Bob lost his professorship, he found himself *underemployed* at a burger stand.

underground economy [E] That informal part of the economy that doesn't participate in the official tax system. For instance, art fairs, hobby exhibits, or flea markets are usually operated by weekend entrepreneurs who view that income as covering their expenses.

underlying investment [F] The actual security, such as a stock, that also has options traded on it. The underlying investment is the security itself, not the option.

underwater [HR] The term for a stock option price that is lower than the exercise price. The term could also be used in any financial transaction where the current price of a stock or asset is now lower.

> The executives were grumbling that the stock options they had were worthless because they were all *underwater*.

underwrite; underwriter; underwriting [F] The term *underwriter* refers to brokerage or investment banking firms that assume the financial responsibility for new securities by buying them from the issuer and then selling them to their clients. Thus, the firms guarantee the issuer will receive the desired funds from the new securities.

[I] An *underwriter* is the agent or company who is responsible for determining the insurability of a person for insurance and the rates of insurance if the person is accepted as a policy-holder.

undeveloped country [E] A country whose economy is poorly developed. More commonly referred to as a "less developed country," or LDC for short. See *less developed country*.

undo [C] A computer command that reverses the last action. If a user decides that a change she made was not a good idea, she can undo it with the undo command. It is helpful in word-processing software.

unearned income [T] Income from sources other than salary, wages, or tips. It is generally from investments. Salary and wages are considered earned income.

> John added the income from his investments and rentals and realized that his *unearned income* was much higher than he had originally anticipated.

unemployment [E] The state of having no work for those who are able and willing to work. Those that are unable to work are not included in the figures.

unemployment insurance [HR] Payments an empoyee receives if he loses his job. Employers are required to pay into the system, which is administered by the federal government. There is a limit on the length of time one can collect these benefits.

unfair labor practice [HR] An illegal activity as detailed for unions in the *Taft-Hartley Act* or for employers in the *National Labor Relations Act*.

unfunded liability [HR] Usually refers to a pension plan that does not have enough money in its trust to pay out projected benefits.

unified gift and estate tax [T] The current coordination of federal estate and gift taxes. As of January 1999, each person is allowed to leave $650,000 through an estate or gift while alive without gift or estate taxes. This amount will increase, by schedule, to $1 million in 2006. This is in addition to the annual $10,000 gift exclusion. See *unlimited marital deduction*.

Uniform Gifts to Minors Act (UGMA) [T] A standard set of rules applied in all states that allows parents and family members to give money to minors, generally children under the age of twenty-one. The advantage is its simplicity. The money just goes into a bank account, mutual fund, or brokerage account that bears the child's Social Security number. The adult who manages the money is called a "custodian."

unimproved land [RE] Land that is vacant, with neither buildings nor the necessities required for buildings, such as roads and utilities.

uninsured motorist coverage [I] Auto insurance coverage that pays benefits if the motorist who caused the accident does not have insurance.

union [HR] A recognized organization that represents workers and negotiates working conditions and wages for its members. The percentage of unionized workers has declined over recent years. In 1953 nearly 27 percent of all workers were unionized, whereas in 1999 the figure is now only about 14 percent.

union card [HR] A card identifying a person as an active member of a union.

union shop [HR] A term referring to some companies where all employees are required to be a union member. Often called a "closed shop." In an "open shop," although a union represents all workers, individual workers can decided if they want to be a member of the union.

unisex tables [HR] Certain life expectancy tables that combine male and female life expectancies to get one combined table to be used for everyone. The law stipulates that for pension plan purposes, unisex tables must be used.

unit cost [A] The total cost of one item.

unit investment trusts [F] A static portfolio of municipal bonds that pay out interest and principal in a self-liquidating manner. That is, an initial portfolio of municipal bonds is packaged by a brokerage firm for investors, and then the bonds simply pay out until everything has been liquidated.

unitrust [T] A form of a trust, usually a charitable remainder trust, that pays out a certain percentage of interest each year, such as 7 percent.

universal life [I] A life-insurance policy that earns interest, usually comparable to a money market rate, and also features the ability to increase or decrease the amount of life insurance. Although a money market rate may not seem like a big deal today, it was in 1979 when this type of insurance was first offered. See *life insurance*

universal serial bus (USB) [C] The newest technology in connecting peripherals such as printers, monitors, and the like to a computer. It consists of tiny rectangular ports and software that allows a system to recognize devices after they are plugged in.

UPC [B] See *bar code*.

UNIX [C] An operating system designed by Bell Laboratories in 1969 for a multiuser system. The name came from single user (UN) of an earlier system called MULT "ICS" (IX). Because of federal regulations in the 1970s, Bell could not market UNIX commercially, so it was licensed to many colleges and universities for their multiuser networks. The University of California at Berkeley made considerable improvements to the system. In the early 1980s, AT&T began to consolidate the many versions of UNIX.

unlimited marital deduction [T] A federal estate tax deduction exempting whatever amount of money and property one spouse leaves to the other spouse at death. In the past there was a set amount, but since 1981 the federal estate taxes have an unlimited exemption. Some states, however, have a limited amount that can be passed on without any state estate or inheritance tax. See *unified gift and estate tax*.

upgrade [C] An advancement in a software or computer product. Usually there is a number associated with the upgraded software, which starts out as 1 and then progresses as upgrades are issued. If a decimal is used, then there are usually only small changes. For instance, Windows 3.0 was upgraded to 3.1 and then to 3.11.

uplink [C] In satellite communications, the transmission link between the ground and the satellite.

upload [C] A file or program sent from a computer to a network, or the act of sending the file or program to a network.

> Paul *uploaded* his new file management program to the America Online software area so that other users might be able to take advantage of it.

upstream [B] The movement of ideas or funds from a subsidiary to the parent company. Movement in the other direction is called *downstream*.

uptick rule [F] A 1934 SEC (Securities and Exchange Commission) rule that prohibits the sale of a borrowed stock when the stock is declining. The rule is intended to prevent investors who are short sellers from manipulating a stock downward and making a profit by doing so.

up to speed [S] A term that refers to educating oneself, or someone else, to be prepared to do a job. Frequently used with the verb *get*, as in, "Smith has to *get up to speed* on how to use the web."

URL (uniform resource locator) [C] An address system for the internet. The common http (hypertext transfer protocol) prefix is the URL used for the World Wide Web, as in: http://www.review.com, which is the full address for The Princeton Review. URL is pronounced as U-R-L or Earl.

Some common URLs:

ftp://FTP server
gopher://Gopher server
http://World Wide Web
mail to://E-mail
news://newsgroup
wais://Wide Area Information Server

Uruguay Round [E] The eighth round of international trade negotiations that opened in Punta del Este, Uruguay, in 1986 and concluded in December 1993, generally known as GATT. Previous publicized rounds, or negotiations, were the Kennedy Round (1964 to 1967) and the Tokyo Round (1974 to 1979). It is part of the GATT (General Agreement on Tariffs and Trade) apparatus that began in 1948 to promote good trade relations and practices around the world. See *GATT*.

USB [C] See *universal serial bus.*

useful life [A] The length of time an asset is expected to be used by a company.

Usenet [C] The "user's network" is a collection of discussion groups called "newsgroups." Usenet is not the same as the internet but can be accessed from the internet. Many internet sites carry Usenet, one of the most popular features of the internet. It was born in 1979 as a result of a joint project between the Defense Department's Advanced Research Projects Agency, the National Science Foundation, and universities.

user [C] Anyone who uses a computer.

user-friendly [C] An adjective for a program or computer system that is relatively easy to use, especially for a beginner.

> The Macintosh icon-based software is said to be very *user-friendly*: A user needs only to click on an icon to bring up a program, rather than remembering many commands.

user ID [C] The name by which a user and his account are known online. Most people use some variation on their name or a nickname. Pronounced user eye-dee.

use tax [T] A commonly ignored state tax that is a sales tax paid to one's own state when he or she buys something in another state.

U.S. Savings bonds [F] See *EE, HH,* and *I bonds.*

U.S. Tax Court [T] The court where IRS tax claims are contested.

usufruct [T] The right in some states, often community property states, of a surviving spouse to live in the marital residence (also called a "homestead right") for as long as he or she is alive, even if the house is left to the children or someone else. Pronounced YOO-za-fruct.

utilities [RE] Public services, such as water, gas, electricity, and telephone.

> The cost of *utilities* in our county is much more than in neighboring counties.

utility [C] A program in an operating system that does file management—sorting, deleting, and copying files; formatting disks and diskettes; and renaming stored files.

> The human resources department used a sort *utility* program to sort the company's database files by employee number.

[E] A basic and useful concept widely used by economists to describe why consumers buy products and services: people find *utility* in them. In noneconomic terms, people want, desire, or receive gratification from things they buy. The demand for a product or service is usually satisfied after some level of use. Thus, the economist will say that the demand decreases on the margin, or after each use. The term "marginal utility" refers to this diminished satisfaction by consumers after use. However, some products or services tend to have an increasing demand at the margin, such as potato chips or cigarettes.

> Jane could only stand to see three movies a month; she would be said by economists to have a decreasing *utility* at the margin until three, at which point there would be no *utility* at all for her.

V

vacancy rate [RE] Ratio of vacant space in a building to total space. May also refer to the ratio of total rents for the vacant space to the total rents for the building.

> Alice Corp. has had a terrible time renting out office space in its new downtown building—it has a *vacancy rate* of almost 100 percent.

vacation home [T] A recreational home to which certain tax rules apply depending on if and how long it is rented out during the year.

vacation pay [HR] Compensation sometimes given if all of one's vacation days are not taken. Some companies follow the use-it-or-lose-it approach. Others allow retirees and other employees leaving the company to be paid for their unused vacation.

valuation [RE] The estimating of value. A real estate appraisal report may also be called a "valuation report."

> Bradley and Co. did a *valuation* of the insurable assets of the company for its insurance forms.

value added [B] A term used in a variety of ways but generally meaning the adding of features, characteristics, or worth to make something more attractive—and usually more expensive—to a consumer. Frequent flyer credits is a *value-added* service to basic business travel. Packaging jam in ornate jars for reuse is a "value-added" practice. Consultants who provide useful insights or creative ideas provide *value-added* service.

value added tax (VAT) [T] A form of tax, especially popular in Europe, where governments tax each step of the production process at which value is added. The tax is calculated on the amount of value added.

> Marie couldn't believe how much higher the prices were in Britain than in the United States until she remembered that Britain included a *VAT*, which she could have refunded later.

value chain [S] The linking of various business resources within a company to create value. This could include a new business department that comes up with new products, a design department that gives it a desirable form, an engineering department that is able to fit the internal workings into the design, a production department that can produce it under tight deadlines and quality standards, and marketing and advertising departments that can help introduce and sustain the product successfully. It is the linking of all of these resources of a company that produce value. The concept was introduced by Michael Porter in his 1985 book *Competitive Advantage.*

value stocks [F] See *growth versus value.*

vaporware [C] Software that has not yet been produced but is being touted and even advertised. Thus, some software is just hot air, or vapor.

> Microhard's new office-management software looked great on television, but when eager consumers tried to purchase it they found out that it was *vaporware*, and thus not available for sale.

variable [M] A changing value. Or, as a mathematician would say, the replacement set containing more than one element. In an algebraic formula, a variable is often represented with letters like x or y. See *constant* and *dependent and independent variables.*

variable annuity [I] An annuity that offers the policy holder a choice of investments, such as a growth stock fund, a balance fund, a bond fund, or a money market fund. Depending on which investments the policy holder chooses, the amount of annuity increases.

variable costs [A] Expenses, or costs, that vary directly with the amount of goods manufactured. These costs are often the raw materials for the goods and the costs of labor. This is in contrast to "fixed costs," which are those that generally do not vary but remain fixed, such as the basic cost of keeping the factory running.

variable life [I] A whole life insurance policy that offers holders several funds to choose from for their cash value investments, such as a growth stock fund, a balanced fund, a bond fund, or a money market fund. See *life insurance.*

variable rate mortgage [RE] See *adjustable rate mortgage (ARM).*

variance [A] The difference between expected cost and actual cost in a standard cost.

variance account [A] In cost accounting, an account used to record the difference, or variance, between the actual manufacturing cost and the standard cost.

variance analysis [A] In cost accounting, the investigation of the difference between the actual and standard costs.

variety store [B] A retail store selling a wide range of low-cost merchandise.

vector [M] In science and engineering a quantity that has magnitude (size) as well as direction. An example of a vector is wind velocity, which can blow at, say, 15 m.p.h. toward the Northeast. This is in contrast to a "scalar," which has magnitude only, such as in the temperature.

velocity of money [E] The speed at which money circulates in an economy.

vendor [B] A business or individual that supplies products or services to companies at any step of production or distribution.

Venn diagram [M] A diagram representing two or more sets of numbers, and how and if they are combined. It is usually shown as circles inside a rectangle. Each circle represents a set of numbers. If the circles have some overlap, then those parts are common to both. Named after John Venn (1824–1923).

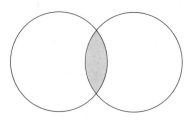

venture capital [F] Money from investors who seek out and offer capital to new and speculative enterprises. These investors are often referred to as "venture capitalists." They seek to make money available to companies who have difficulty obtaining regular loans because of the speculative nature of their companies. Venture capitalists usually seek significant stakes in these new companies and hope for significant returns on their investments.

venture capitalist [F] See *venture capital*.

verdict [L] A final decision by a court, often after a jury has made its decision.

vertical analysis [B] Analysis of an industry's products and companies from raw goods to customers. In the service industry, this could be an analysis of the movie studios and then the distribution channels such as television and cable. This is in contrast to "horizontal analysis," which is the analysis of companies in the same business. See *horizontal analysis* and *integration*.

vesting [HR] The point at which one has been at a company long enough to be entitled to a benefit. For instance, one may have to be at a company for five years in order to be entitled to a pension plan. This is not to be confused with the normal one-year rule before one can start to contribute to a 401(k) plan. Although one is always entitled to his contribution, frequently the company also contributes to the 401(k), and the employee is not entitled to these contributions for a few years. When one is entitled to the company contributions, it usually takes one of two general forms of vesting.

Vesting in Company Contributions in Your 401(k) Plan:

cliff vesting After a specific number of years, often three years and usually not more than five, one is entitled to all past company contributions and thereafter to all future company contributions. This is sometimes referred to as "full vesting." The purpose of this vesting is to recognize that an employee has been with a company for a certain number of years, and so he may have the money immediately, making the employee feel at home.

graduated vesting Sometimes called "step-vesting." After a certain number of years, say three years, one is entitled to 20 percent of all company contributions made up until that point. The next year, one would be entitled to another 20 percent, and so forth until one would be entitled to 100 percent of contributions, in this case, eight years.

V-formation [F] See *technical analysis.*

VGA [C] See *monitor.*

viatical settlement [I] The sale of a life insurance policy by a person who is terminally ill to a third party in return for an immediate payment of a percentage of the policy amount. The viatical company would collect the full policy amount upon the death of the person. Thus, this is a way of providing needed funds for pressing medical costs. Some viatical companies are now even buying policies from older people who are in good health. Viatical is pronounced vi-AT-a-cul.

virtual [B] A word that has crept into business jargon that generally means a traditional outward appearance, but inside it's very nontraditional. Virtual corporation, virtual leadership, and virtual office are such examples. The term comes from the virtual reality concept of games. See *virtual reality.*

virtual memory [C] A method of organizing the computer memory so that it appears to have more memory than in actuality, allowing larger programs than normal to run.

virtual office [HR] The array of technology and equipment, such as a cellular phone, pager, fax, and access to the internet that allows some employees, especially salespeople, to operate as if they had an office, even when they don't.

virtual reality [C] An interactive computer system with devices such as helmets and gloves that allow the user to artificially interact with a simulated 3-D reality.

virus [C] A computer program which, like a real-life virus, spreads by duplicating itself into other software and causing damage. Viruses are malicious—in recent years, virus checks and vaccines have been developed to locate and remove viruses before they do any real damage. A virus can be set to attack at a specified time, as is the case with the Michelangelo virus, which is set to go off each year on March 6, the artist's birthday. This mysterious virus, which some experts doubt actually exists, is designed to erase a hard drive's data.

vision [B] The perception of the overall mission and strategy for a company. It allows for a common understanding of company goals and standards to which employees can aspire and by which they can be judged. It can also be part of morale building within an organization.

Visual Basic software [C] A popular BASIC software specialized for Windows applications.

voice mail [C] An automatic computer answering system that allows callers to leave a verbal message that can be digitized and stored on disk for later replay. Callers to the system can also be transformed to other extensions.

voice recognition [C] Software technique allowing speech commands to operate programs, versus the keyboard or mouse commands. Although currently limited, it is expected that in the future this type of software will be able to use a large vocabulary to operate the computer. The user first needs to "train" the software to the user's voice by giving it samples. The title of Microsoft's department developing this type of software is aptly named "The Wreck a Nice Beach Group," a term that has the same wave patterns as "The Recognized Speech Group." This points out the difficulty in getting computers to recognize words because the same wave pattern can represent different words.

voir dire [L] The formal questioning of prospective jurors for a case. In French it means *to speak the truth*, which is what is expected of each person who is a prospective juror.

volatility [F] The amount of variation or fluctuation of something. An example is the volatility of the stock market. The more volatility, the greater the risk or uncertainty. The opposite is a "stable," or "boring" market. Active investors and speculators like volatile markets for the potential price swings and potential profits to be made.

volume discount [B] Per-unit reduction in price because of the large amount of products purchased.

voodoo economics [E] A general term applied to economic theories or practices that are considered odd or unworkable from the speaker's point of view. First used by George Bush in the 1980 presidential race to describe the supply-side economic plans of his then-opponent, Ronald Reagan.

voucher [A] A form that gives authorization to pay specific expenditures.

Brown sent his signed expense *voucher* to accounting so he would be reimbursed for his recent travel.

vulture fund [F] A fund that specializes in buying depressed real estate, investment limited partnerships, or stocks in the hopes that these investments can be turned around for a handsome profit.

W

wage [HR] Pay for work performed, especially in manufacturing employment. Often quoted as an hourly rate. See *minimum wage*.

The workers negotiated a *wage* increase up to $10 per hour.

wage and price controls [E] Governmental action to control wages and prices. Sometimes called "wage stabilization" or "wage freeze." The last time this occurred was in the 1970s when inflation was unusually high.

Wagner Act [HR] See *National Labor Relations Act*.

WAIS (wide area information server) [C] A system used to search and retrieve information from different databases and libraries on the internet. The user specifies which databases she wants to search and gives a list of keywords to search for; the WAIS (pronounced as WACE) server will give the user a list of articles that she may be interested in. WAIS will display the chosen article after it conducts the search.

waiting line theory [M] See *queuing theory*.

waiting period [I] The period of time before an insurance policy goes into effect.

waiver [L] A declaration that one has knowingly given up a right, such as when a person admits his guilt and *waives* his right to a trial.

waiver of premium [I] A provision of many life insurance policies that the insurance company will forego, or *waive*, the premium if the policy-holder becomes disabled or seriously ill.

wake up and smell the coffee [S] An expression used to instruct a person to snap back to reality and realize what's really going on in a certain situation.

walkout [HR] Another word for a worker strike. See *strike*.

Wall Street [B] Usually denotes the main financial markets in the United States but can specifically refer to the main street in New York where the New York Stock Exchange resides. Also called the Street. In the early history of New York, there was an actual wall that protected the small city. The street now stands where that wall once stood.

***Wall Street Journal* [B]** The popular daily newspaper of business and investments. It is the primary newspaper of the U.S. financial markets and company activities. It is published Monday through Friday.

warehouse [B] A building that stores goods temporarily until such goods are shipped to retail stores for final sale.

warm boot [C] See *boot*.

warrant [L] A court order directing a police officer to arrest a person.

warrants [F] A security that gives an investor the right to buy the company's common stock at a predetermined price by a certain date. For instance, a company may offer a warrant that gives the investor the right to purchase shares of stock at $25 up until December 31, 2003.

> We purchased 100 *warrants* at $1 each to buy Spamo Corp. stock for $20 a share. When the stock price soared to $26, we exercised the warrant, bought the stock for the $20, and made a $5 profit on each share, for a total profit of $500.

warranty [B] A written guarantee by a manufacturer that its products are of the highest quality and free of defects. A manufacturer may promise to replace or fix the product if defective.

wash sale [F] The rule that prohibits the buying and selling of the same security within thirty days in order to take a tax loss. The IRS disallows the loss.

wasting asset [A] A natural resource asset that gets used up. As examples, gas, timber, and minerals are depleted as they are consumed.

water rights [RE] The rights of owners who have water flowing through, bordering on, or underneath property they own. See *riparian rights*.

waybill [B] A record or statement used in shipping that states the name of the shipper, the route the cargo will take, the weight of the cargo, and the shipping costs.

The shipper checked the *waybill* on the packages before he loaded his truck.

weak dollar [E] See *dollar is higher/lower*

web, the [C] See *World Wide Web*.

web browser [C] Browsers for the World Wide Web that allow one to link to other sites with only a few clicks of the mouse. The most popular web browsers are Netscape Navigator, Microsoft Explorer, and Mosaic.

webmaster [C] A person responsible for managing a web site. The older term was "sysop" (SYStem OPerator).

web sites [C] Addresses on the World Wide Web that have homepage information.

weighted average [M] An average where each item is multiplied by a *weight* or factor relative to the whole.

welfare plan [HR] A general term used in employee benefits to mean any nonwage benefits such as medical and disability insurance, as well as benefits such as vacation and educational assistance.

welfare state [E] A term used to indicate widespread use of government programs for the poor in a society.

wellness programs [HR] Any one of a variety of company programs to maintain good health, such as a physical exercise program or yoga classes to learn how to deal more effectively with stress.

what ifs [S] Scenarios used to figure out the results given different assumptions. In more technical terms, this is called "sensitivity analysis." See *model*.

white-collar worker [B] Officers and managers in a business, as opposed to factory workers. Traditionally, white-collar workers wore white shirts or blouses.

white elephant [S] An asset, often real estate, that is too expensive to maintain.

white goods [B] Large household appliances such as refrigerators, stoves, and dish washers. The name comes from their original color; they were all white.

white knight [B] A friendly company that comes to the rescue of another company that is the target of a takeover.

white noise [B] The artificial noise that is sometimes generated by a machine to create a more normal environment, versus a too silent and uncomfortable space.

Whitney, Eli [B] See *mass production*.

whole life insurance [I] A form of life insurance in which cash values are accrued. Thus, a whole life policy is a vehicle for both investment and insurance. Sometimes whole life is called "permanent life insurance;" however, a policyholder can stop the policy anytime by stoping premium payments. See *life insurance*.

whole numbers [M] The set of counting numbers, such as 1, 2, and so forth, including 0.

wholesale; wholesale prices [B] The step before retail. Generally referred to as buying in bulk.

> The appeal of those large food stores is that they are able to offer *wholesale prices* on bulk purchases.

wholesaler [B] A person who buys in large quantities from a manufacturer and in turn sells to a retailer.

widget [S] A make-believe object produced by hypothetical businesses in case studies and other examples.

widows and orphans [C] See *orphans and widows*.

wiggle room [S] Flexibility that allows one to modify his or her position if necessary.

wildcat strike [HR] An unauthorized worker strike or an isolated strike at one of a company's plants.

will [L] A written document specifying who is to get what at a person's death. Generally, it is known as the "last will and testament." Technically the term "will" means the giving of real property, like real estate, and the term "testament" refers to personal property.

will substitutes [T] Methods of passing money and property at death without a will. Most commonly refers to naming a beneficiary to such assets as IRAs (individual retirement accounts) and titling real estate or brokerage accounts as "joint tenancy with rights of survivorship." See *joint tenancy with rights of survivorship*.

Wilshire 4500/5000 [F] Two useful indexes of all U.S. stocks. The Wilshire 5000 consists of all domestic stocks of the United States, while the Wilshire 4500 consists of all stocks except the largest 500, which comprise the S&P 500. The Wilshire 4500 represents about 30 percent of the entire stock market whereas the S&P 500 represents about 70 percent. (There are about 6,000 actual individual stocks at any one time combined in all of the markets.) See *Russell 2000*.

window [C] A generally rectangular portion of a computer screen that contains some sort of information, often used with a graphical user interface (GUI).

window dressing [S] An attractive outward appearance that covers up what may not look so good under further scrutiny. This is sometimes used in accounting by presenting a more favorable financial picture of a company than the facts warrant.

window of opportunity [S] A narrow time frame in which an opportunity exists for an individual or company to take advantage of a situation.

Windows 3.1; Windows 95; Windows 98; Windows NT [C] Various versions of Microsoft's advanced operating system, which replaced the old DOS operating system. The evolution began with Windows 1.0 in 1985 and continues now through Windows 98 and Windows NT (New Technology).

win-lose [S] See *win-win*.

Wintel [C] A term combining Windows and Intel, referring to the giants of the personal computer industry. The popularity of Windows and the Intel chips have made computers popular and relatively inexpensive.

win-win [S] A strategy where everyone wins. It comes from game theory, where usually one person is pitted against another, or one company against another. However, business is not really a game, and it's not always a win-win outcome. In fact, there are a number of possibilities:

Let's Play the Game:

no-win An outcome where no one wins. For instance, a negotiation where the boss didn't want to give a large raise but does, because the employee used hard-ball tactics; the employee doesn't really win either because the boss now harbors ill feelings.

no-lose An outcome where no side loses. For instance, a negotiation where a company accepts the average bid, with the company not having to pay top dollar, nor the winning firm working for low pay. Neither side lost.

win-win An outcome where both sides win. For instance, a negotiation where a company picks the best supplier, and the supplier gets the best deal. Both win because they both got what they wanted.

win-lose An outcome where one side wins, and the other side loses. When two companies bid for the same business, one usually wins and the other loses.

lose-lose An outcome where both sides lose. For instance, a negotiation where the bidding is so low the bidder loses (because it won the bid but cannot afford it) and the company loses because the winning bidder cannot afford good service.

zero-sum game A premise that one person's gain must be matched with another person's loss. Someone wins and someone loses.

---

wire house [F] A traditional name for a large brokerage firm. The name comes from the past when the firms received confirmation of stock market trades by wire from the floor.

wireless [C] Various technologies to communicate without wires, namely via radio transmissions. Cellular, infrared, microwave, and satellite are all wireless.

wire transfer [F] The movement of funds from one account to another by electronic means, namely telephone or computer.

withholding [T] A portion of money taken out of one's paycheck for various taxes, employee benefits, and money for credit unions. Specifically the taxes are federal, state, and Social Security (FICA) taxes. Two forms provide witholding information: W-4, in which an employee estimates her withholding; and the W-2, in which is a statement of what was withheld. See *FICA*.

> When Marty filled out a new W-4, he added the extra exemption for his dependent children to reduce the amount of *withholding* and increase his weekly take-home pay.

witness [L] A person under oath or affirmation who gives testimony in a court of law. A "character witness" is a person who testifies as to the good character of another person. A "material witness" gives testimony that is central to a case.

Word [C] The popular Microsoft word-processing software.

word of mouth [S] The method of finding out about something through others, from one mouth to another.

> April couldn't find the web site on granola, but she knew by *word of mouth* that it did exist.

word of mouth advertising [B] Informal communications between people about products and services that they like or dislike. Considered the best kind of advertising, if positive, of course.

WordPerfect [C] A popular word-processing software program.

word processing; word-processing software [C] Software designed for producing text documents. Microsoft Word and WordPerfect are popular examples.

workaholic [S] See *type-A personality*.

workers' compensation [HR] A state system of medical and disability coverage for on-the-job accidents and illness. Each state has differing coverage, different rules, and different rates. Companies pay the premiums.

work force [HR] The total employment of a company or country.

working capital [A] The excess of current assets over current liabilities. Also called *net working capital*.

work-in-progress inventory [A] Goods being manufactured but not yet finished. Sometimes called "goods-in-progress."

workout [A] The process of renegotiating a company loan.

World Bank [E] Created by the Bretton Woods agreement in 1944, it lends money to countries who have difficulty getting loans from private sources. The more developed countries contribute funds to the bank. The bank is more formally called the International Bank for Reconstruction and Development. See *Bretton Woods* and *International Monetary Fund.*

world class [S] The best, or among the best, in the world. Countries compete now in the global business community and thus measure themselves in that sphere, not just in one country.

World Wide Web (Web) [C] One of the most popular services on the internet, it includes multimedia, graphical, and hyperlinks to other sites. In fact, to most people, the internet and the web are one and the same. The web is noted as part of the beginning of most popular internet addresses (www.). The total number of users in this country has risen dramatically. In September 1997 there were an estimated 58 million users, and by June 1998 that had increased 36 percent to an estimated 78 million.

worst-case scenario [S] The absolute worst outcome that could arise.

wrap-around account [F] A brokerage account where the firm offers a named professional investor that will provide the investment advice for the individual's account.

wraparound mortgage [RE] A mortgage that is added to and includes an old mortgage. In a wraparound mortgage, the new lender will assume the obligation to pay off the old mortgage.

> When the Barklees' sold their home, they issued a *wraparound mortgage* to the Joneses—that would encompass their old loan plus the additional amount the Joneses needed.

writ [L] A legal order that is issued by a court to compel a person to do something, such as leash a dog.

write protect [C] Refers to the ability to set a floppy disk so it cannot be erased or changed. A little plastic switch on the upper right of the disk can be positioned open to write-protect it.

writing an option [F] The process of starting a stock option in motion by offering stock for the action required in a call or put option. By "writing an option," the investor offers stock as a payment, called a "premium," and then waits until the option either expires or is acted upon by the option buyer (or seller). If the option expires and no action is taken, then the investor is free and clear, having received additional money for the stock put up. Investors will offer their stock when they think the price will be stable. The investor then earns extra money on the stock. If the stock rises (or decreases with a put option), and the option is exercised, then the investor losses his stock and is not able to earn the profit from the increased stock price.

writing down; writing off [A] The reduction in value of assets, either by circumstances or because the initial value was determined to be too high.

writing up [A] The increasing of asset values in an attempt to keep the value of the asset current.

wrongful death [L] Basis for a law suit in which survivors sue for monetary awards from a person or company that caused the death of another person.

wrongful termination [L] The basis for a law suit in which a person seeks monetary damages from a company she claims terminated her in violation of the law, such as termination because of age or sex.

www (World Wide Web) [C] See *World Wide Web*.

WYSIWYG [C] Pronounced WIZ-ee-wig, it stands for What You See Is What You Get. In word-processing or desktop software, it means the printout will look like what is on the screen.

X

x-axis [M] In graphing, the horizontal axis. See *y-axis* and *z-axis*.

Xerography [C] The copyrighted process of producing a copy of a document by depositing ink on paper. Invented in Astoria, Queens, in 1938, it is the technology that has changed the way offices operate. It is so pervasive that the Xerox company has to caution the business community that a "Xerox" copy is a registered trademark, and in fact the phrase should be copy or photocopy this."

Xerox Palo Alto Research Center [C] The center of much of the personal computer research in California beginning in the 1970s.

Xmodem [C] The initial protocol, or standard, for transferring files through modems. It operates by transmitting blocks of 128 bytes. Ymodem is faster. See *Ymodem* and *Zmodem*.

XO chart [F] A method to track movements of the stock market by putting an X if the market is up and an O if it is down. Also called a "point-and-figure chart." See *technical analysis*.

Y

Yahoo! [C] A popular World Wide Web site that, while often referred to as a search engine, is actually a large directory of web sites. It maintains an extensive dictionary of web sites through human compilation.

Yankee bond [F] Bonds sold by foreign bond issuers to American investors that are denominated in dollars rather than their own foreign currency. This eliminates the uncertainty of currency fluctuations for the American investor.

y-axis [M] In graphing, the vertical axis. See *x-axis* and *z-axis*.

yellow-dog contract [HR] An illegal business practice of getting a worker's promise not to join a union if hired. It was outlawed in the 1935, National Labor Relations Act. See *National Labor Relations Act*.

yellow page advertising [B] Business advertising appearing in the nonresidence section of phone books, printed on yellow paper.

yield [F] The income earned on an investment, either interest as in a bond or dividend as in a stock.

yield curve [F] A chart showing the current Treasury interest rates for different maturities. It is a curved line starting with short-term interest rates on the three-month Treasury bill continuing all the way out to the thirty-year Treasury bond. It represents to investors the current risk-free investment yields at any maturity.

yield to call [F] The total return on a bond to the potential call date on the bonds, usually selling at a premium. Bonds normally can be called five or ten years after they are issued. If interest rates decline, meaning that the bonds have increased over par— par being the majority value of the bonds—then the issuer can call the bonds before maturity, pay only par to the bondholders, reissue them at a lower interest rate, and save considerable money. See *callable bond*.

yield to maturity [F] The total return on a bond to its maturity date. If an investor bought a bond either at a premium (bond was higher than par) or at a discount (bond was lower than par), that decrease or increase to par—which is the maturity value—is calculated along with the interest earned to maturity to give a true total return of the bond.

Ymodem [C] An enhanced protocol for transferring files through modems. It operates by transmitting blocks of 128 to 1,024 bytes. It is faster than Xmodem but not as sophisticated as Zmodem. See *Xmodem* and *Zmodem*.

Y2K [C] A dogged computer problem related to the COBOL language. *Y* stands for year, *2K* stands for 2000. To save on valuable memory space in the early days of computers, programmers used only the last two digits to represent the year, with the first two digits assumed to be 19. Thus, when the computer gets to the year 2000, it interprets it as 1900. This has the potential to cause a host of problems throughout the business and government sectors. For example, in the Social Security system, it would mean that everyone would be deemed over 100 years old and entitled to a benefit. Fortunately these systems have been corrected and tested so that won't happen. However, there are people who will not schedule a flight while the clock will be turning from 1999 to 2000 because they fear the air traffic system will stop working at that point.

yuppie [S] This is the original Young Urban Professional. A number of demographic groups have recently been identified and given their own acronyms like DINK, for Dual Income with No Kids, and one of the latest, SOD, for Start-Over Dads who remarry and start another family.

Z

z-axis [M] In graphing three dimensions, the additional third dimension from the *x*- and *y*-axis. See *x-axis* and *y-axis*.

zero [M] Neither positive nor negative; nothing. As a mathematician would say, it is an element that when added to a number results in the number itself.

zero-based budgeting [A] A budgetary system in which all expenditures are reassessed anew each year from the bottom up. This is in contrast to the practice of adding an incremental increase to budgets. It allows a fresh look at ongoing business activities and their expenses.

zero-coupon bonds [F] A bond that pays no current interest but instead pays it all when it matures. Thus, an investor buys the bond at a discount, and it increases in value until it matures. That discount is the present value of $1,000, the traditional bond par value.

zero defects [B] The ideal manufacturing situation: No product is manufactured with any defects. It is either a goal, or more likely, a target that a company works toward. See *six sigma* and *total quality management*.

zero-sum game [S] See *win-win*.

zip code [B] The U.S. Postal Service's system, inaugurated in 1963, that designates geographic areas for mail sort and delivery. The common codes are five digits, but the Postal Service is promoting its nine-digit code, called "zip plus 4." Zip stands for Zone Improvement Plan.

Zip drive; Zip disk [C] The copyrighted disk storage technology by Iomega Corp. The Zip disks typically handle 100 megabytes of data, versus the standard 3.5-inch disk, which handles 1.4 megabytes. The Zip disk is just a bit larger than the standard disk and requires a special Zip drive.

Zmodem [C] Currently the most popular protocol for transferring files through modems because it can handle noisy and changing line conditions. The earlier protocols were Xmodem and Ymodem.

zoning; zoning board; zoning ordinances; zoning variance [RE] *Zoning ordinances* are laws communities pass to designate how land will be used, such as for residential, commercial, and industrial uses. A *zoning board* is available to hear individuals or companies who wish to alter existing zoning, and if given that right after a hearing, they receive a *zoning variance*.

zoom [C] The ability to make a computer software window larger or smaller.

z score or measure [M] In statistics, the measurement of the number of standard deviations. A z score of 2 means it is 2 standard deviations from the mean, or average.

Appendix I

Acronyms and Abbreviations

AAAA American Association of Advertising Agencies

AAA American Accounting Association

ABA American Bankers Association

ACA American Compensation Association

ADA Americans with Disabilities Act

AD&D accidental death and dismemberment

ADEA Age Discrimination in Employment Act

ADP automated data processing

ADV investment advisor form (SEC)

AFDC Aid to Family with Dependent Children

AFL-CIO American Federation of Labor—Congress of Industrial Organizations

AFR applicable federal rate

AGI adjusted gross income

AI artificial intelligence

AICPA American Institute of Certified Public Accountants

AIREA American Institute of Real Estate Appraisers

AMA American Management Association

AMEX American Stock Exchange

AMI alternative mortgage instrument

AML adjustable mortgage loan

AMT alternative minimum tax

AOL America Online

APB Accounting Principles Board

APR annual percentage rate

ARM adjustable rate mortgage

ASAP as soon as possible

ASCII American Standard Code for Information Interchange

ASREC American Society of Real Estate Counselors

ASTD American Society for Training and Development

ATM automated teller machine

BBB Better Business Bureau

BBS bulletin board system

BD broker dealer

BIOS basic input/output system

BLS Bureau of Labor Statistics

bps bits per second

BOL bill of lading

CAD/CAM computer-aided design and computer-aided manufacturing

CAI computer-aided instruction

CAPM capital asset pricing model

CATV cable television

CBO Congressional Budget Office

CBT Chicago Board of Trade

cc carbon copy

CD Compact disc or certificate of deposit

CD-ROM compact disk, read-only memory

CEBS certified employee benefits specialist

CEO chief executive officer

CERN Conseil Européen pour la Recherche Nucleaire

CFC chartered financial consultant

CFO chief financial officer

CFP certified financial planner

CFTC Commodities Futures Trading Commission

CGA color graphics adapter

CGI common gateway interface

CIF cost, insurance, freight

CISC complex instruction set computer

CLU Chartered Life Underwriter

CME Chicago Mercantile Exchange

CMO collateralized mortgage obligation

c/o care of

CO certificate of occupancy

COB coordination of benefits

COBE Chicago Board Options Exchange

COBOL Common Business Oriented Language

COBRA (health insurance) Consolidated Omnibus Budget Reconciliation Act of 1985

COD cash on delivery or collect on delivery

COLA cost of living adjustment

COLI corporate-owned life insurance

comps comparable properties

COO chief operating officer

CPA certified public accountant

CPCU chartered property and casualty underwriter

CPI Consumer Price Index

cpi characters per inch

CPM cost per thousand

cps characters per second

CPU central processing unit

CRE counselor of real estate

CRT cathode ray tube

CUSIP Committee on Uniform Securities Identification Procedures

CYA cover your ass

D&B Dun & Bradstreet report (credit report on a company)

DBA doing business as

DCR debt coverage ratio

DDB double-declining-balance depreciation

DIF discriminate function system

DJIA Dow Jones Industrial Average

DNS domain name system

DOL Department of Labor

DOOM deep out of the money

DOS disk operating system

DOT Department of Transportation or designated order turnaround

Dow the Dow Jones Industrial Average

DP data processing

DTP desktop publishing

EA enrolled agent or enrolled actuary

EAFE Europe, Australia, Far East

EAP employee assistance program

EC European Community

EEC European Economic Community

EEOC Equal Employment Opportunity Commission

EER energy efficiency ratio

EFT electronic funds transfer

EGA enhanced graphic adaptor

EIB Export-Import Bank

EMU [European] Economic and monetary union

EOQ economic order quantity

EPA Environmental Protection Agency

ERISA Employee Retirement Income Security Act

ESOP employee stock ownership plan

FAA Federal Aviation Administration

FAQ frequently asked questions

FAS free alongside ship

FASB Financial Accounting Standards Board

fax facsimile transmission

FBI Federal Bureau of Investigation

FCC Federal Communication Commission

FDA Food and Drug Administration

FDIC Federal Deposit Insurance Corporation

Fed Federal Reserve System

Fedex Federal Express

FHA Federal Housing Administration

FHLMC (Freddie Mac) Federal Home Loan Mortgage Corporation

FICA Federal Insurance Contributions Act

FIFO first in, first out

FMLA Family and Medical Leave Act

FMV fair market value

FNMA (Fannie Mae) Federal National Mortgage Association

FOB free on board

FOMC Federal Open Market Committee

FORTRAN Formula Translation

FTC Federal Trade Commission

FTP file transfer protocol

FV future value

FYI for your information

G or GB gigabyte

G-7 Group of Seven Nations

G-10 Group of Ten Nations

GAAP generally accepted accounting principles

GAO General Accounting Office

GATT General Agreement on Tariffs and Trade

GenX Generation X

GC general contractor

GDP gross domestic product

GIC guaranteed investment contract

GIF graphic interchange format

GIGO garbage in, garbage out

GIM gross income multiplier

GNMA (Ginnie Mae) Government National Mortgage Association

GNP gross national product

GO general obligation bond

GPM graduated payment mortgage

GPO Government Printing Office

GRM gross rent multiplier

GTC good till canceled

GUI graphical user interface

HBR Harvard Business Review

HDTV high density television

HHS Health and Human Services Department

HMO health maintenance organization

HP Hewlett Packard

HR human resources

HTML hypertext markup language

HTTP hypertext Transport Protocol

HUD Housing and Urban Development

Hz hertz

IBM International Business Machines

ICC Interstate Commerce Commission

IMF International Monetary Fund

Inc. Incorporated

I/O input-output

IP internet protocol

IPO initial public offering

IRA individual retirement account

IRC internet relay chat

IRR internal rate of return

IRS internal revenue service

ISBN International Standard Book Number

ISDN Integrated Services Digital Network

ISO incentive stock option

ISSN International Standard Serial Number

ITC investment tax credit or International Trade Commission

ITO International Trade Organization

JIT just-in-time inventory or just-in-time manufacturing

K or KB kilobyte

KISS keep it simple stupid

LAN local area network

LAWN local area wireless network

LBO leveraged buyout

LCD liquid crystal display

LDC less developed country

LED light-emitting diode

LIBOR London Interbank Offer Rate

LIFO last in, first out

LTC less than carload

LTV loan to value ratio

M1, M2, and M3 money supply

MAI member, Appraisal Institute

MB or Megs megabyte

MBA master of business administration

MBO management by objectives

MFN most-favored nation

MGIC Mortgage Guarantee Insurance Company

MHz megahertz

MICR magnetic ink character recognition

MIPS million instructions per second

MIS management information systems

MLM multi-level marketing

MLS multiple listing service

MPT modern portfolio theory

MS-DOS Microsoft disk operating system

MSA medical savings accounts

MUD multi-user dimension

munis municipal bonds

NAFTA North American Free-Trade Agreement

NAHB National Association of Homebuilders

NAM National Association of Manufacturers

NAR National Association of Realtors

NASA National Aeronautics and Space Administration

NASD National Association of Securities Dealers

NASDAQ National Association of Securities Dealers Automated Quotation

NAV net asset value

NFA National Futures Association

NIMBY not in my back yard

NLQ near letter quality

NLRB National Labor Relations Board

NOI net operating income

NOL net operating loss

NOW negotiable order of withdrawal

NPV net present value

NQSO non-qualified stock option

NR not rated

ns nanosecond

NTIS National Technical Information Service

NTSB National Transportation Safety Board

NYSE New York Stock Exchange

OASDHI Old Age, Survivors, Disability, and Hospital (Social Security)

OBL ocean bill of lading

OCR optical character recognition

OECD Organization for Economic Cooperation and Development

OEM original equipment manufacturer

OJT on-the-job training

OMB Office of Management and Budget

OPEC Organization of Petroleum Exporting Countries

OPM other people's money

OSHA Occupational Safety and Health Act

OTC over-the-counter

P&L profit and loss statement

PAC Political Action Committee

PBGC Pension Benefit Guarantee Corportion

PBX private branch exchange

PC personal computer

PC-DOS personal computer disk operating system

PCS personal communications services

PDA personal digital assistant

P/E price/earnings ratio

PERT Program Evaluation Review Technique

PGIM potential gross income multiplier

PIC personal identification code

PIN personal identification number

PMS Pantone matching system

POP point-of-purchase display

PPI producer price index

PPO preferred provider organization

PPP point-to-point protocol or purchasing power parity

prefab
prefabricated house

PSA public service announcement

PUD planned unit development

PV present value

Q-TIP qualified terminable interest property

QDRO qualified domestic relations orders

R&D research and development

RAM random access memory or reverse annuity mortgage

REIT real estate investment trust

RFP request for proposal

RGB red, green, and blue

RIF reduction in force

ROI return on investment

ROM read-only memory

RTC Resolution Trust Company

S&L Savings and Loan Association

SBA Small Business Administration

SBDC Small Business Development Centers

SBIR Small Business Innovation Research Program

SDR special drawing rights

SEC Securities and Exchange Commission

SEP simplified employee pension

SERP supplementary executive retirement plan

SIG special interest group

SIPC Securities Investor Protection Corporation

SKU stock-keeping unit

SLIP serial line Internet protocol

SLMA Student Loan Marketing Association

SMSA standard metropolitan statistical area

SOB son of a bitch

SOP standard operating procedure

spec on speculation

SPD summary plan description

SSA Social Security Administration

SSI supplemental security income

STRIPS
Separate Trading Registered Interest and Principal of Securities

SVGA super video graphics array

SYDsum-of-the-year's-digits depreciation

T or TB terabyte

T-bills, T-notes, and T-bonds Treasury securities

T&E travel and entertainment expense

TCMP Tax Compliance Measurement Program

TCP/IP transfer control protocol/ internet protocol

TDA tax deferred annuities

TIN taxpayer identification number

TQM total quality management

UGMA uniform gifts to minors act

UPC universal product code

UPS United Parcel Service

URL uniform resource locator

user ID user identification

VA Veteran's Administration

VAT value added tax

VGA video graphic array

VP vice president

VRM variable rate mortgage

WAIS wide area information server

WPI wholesale price index

WWW World Wide Web

WYSIWYG
  what you see is what you get

YTD year-to-date

ZBB zero-based budgeting

APPENDIX II

Government Contacts

Truly the world's center for acronyms. It has been estimated that more acronyms per square foot have been created inside the Beltway than anywhere in the world.

The Key Players

The White House
1600 Pennsylvania Avenue, NW
Washington, DC 20500
202/456-111
www.whitehouse.gov

U.S. Senate
The Capitol
Washington, DC 20510
202/224-3121
www.senate.gov

U.S. House of Representatives
The Capitol
Washington, DC 20510
202/224-3121
www.house.gov

The Supreme Court of the United States
United States Supreme Court
Building
One First Street, NE
Washington, DC 20543
202/479-3000

The Alphabet Soup

Useful web sites:
www.fedworld.gov (central gateway to governmental agencies)
www.law.vill.edu (Villanova Law Center—Federal Web Locator)

Bureau of Economic Analysis
1441 L Street, NW
Washington, DC 20230
202/606-9600

Bureau of Labor Statistics (BLS)
2 Massachusetts Avenue, NE
Washington, DC 20212
202/606-7800
stats.bls.gov

Census Bureau
Department of Commerce
Washington, DC 20233
301/457-2794
www.census.gov

Commodity Futures Trading
Commission (CFTC)
  2033 K Street, NW
  Washington, DC 20581
  202/254-6387

Congressional Budget Office
(CBO)
  Second and D Streets, SW
  Washington, DC 20515
  202/226-2700

Consumer Product Safety
Commission
  East West Towers
  4330 East West Highway
  Bethesda, MD 20814
  301/504-0580
  www.cpsc.gov

Council of Economic Advisers
  Old Executive Office Building
  Washington, DC 20500
  202/395-5062

Department of Commerce
  14th and Constitution Avenue, NW
  Washington, DC 20230
  202/482-2000
  www.doc.gov

Department of Health and
Human Services (HHS)
  200 Independence Avenue, NW
  Washington, DC 20201
  202/619-0257
  www.os.dhhs.gov

Department of Housing and
Urban Development (HUD)
  451 7th Avenue, SW
  Washington, DC 20410
  202/708-1422
  www.hud.gov

Department of Labor (DOL)
  200 Constitution Avenue, NW
  Washington, DC 20210
  202/219-5000
  www.dol.gov

Department of Transportation
(DOT)
  400 7th Street, SW
  Washington, DC 20590
  202/366-4000
  www.dot.gov

Department of the Treasury
  1500 Pennsylvania Avenue, NW
  Washington, DC 20220
  202/622-2000
  www.ustreas.gov

Environmental Protection Agency
(EPA)
  401 M Street, SW
  Washington, DC 20460
  202/260-2090
  www.epa.gov

Equal Employment Opportunity
Commission (EEOC)
  1801 L Street, NW
  Washington, DC 20507
  202/663-4900

Export-Import Bank (EIB)
  811 Vermont Avenue, NW
  Washington, DC 20571
  800/565-EXIM
  www.exim.gov

Federal Aviation Administration
(FAA)
  800 Independence Avenue, SW
  Washington, DC 20591
  202/267-3111
  www.faa.gov

Federal Bureau of Investigation
(FBI)
  935 Pennsylvania Avenue, NW
  Washington, DC 20535
  202/324-3000
  www.fbi.gov

Federal Communications Commission (FCC)
1919 M Street, NW
Washington, DC 20554
202/418-0200
www.fcc.gov

Federal Deposit Insurance Corporation (FDIC)
550 17th Street, NW
Washington, DC 20429
202/393-8400

Food and Drug Administration (FDA)
5600 Fishers Lane
Rockville, MD 20857
301/443-1130
www.fda.gov

Federal Maritime Commission
800 North Capitol Street, NW
Washington, DC 20573
202/523-5707

Federal Mediation and Conciliation Service
2100 K Street, NW
Washington, DC 20427
202/606-8100

Federal Reserve System (Fed)
20th and C Streets, NW
Washington, DC 20551
202/452-3000
www.frbchi.org

Federal Trade Commission (FTC)
Pennsylvania Avenue and 6th Street, NW
Washington, DC 20580
202/326-2222
www.ftc.gov

General Accounting Office (GAO)
441 G Street, NW
Washington, DC 20548
202/512-3000

Government Printing Office (GPO)
North Capital and H Streets, NW
Washington, DC 20401
202/512-0000
www.access.gpo.gov

Internal Revenue Service (IRS)
500 N. Capitol Street, NW
Washington, DC 20013
202/874-0700
www.irs.ustreas.gov

International Monetary Fund (IMF)
700 19th Street, NW
Washington, DC 20431
202/623-6180

International Trade Administration
Main Commerce Building
Washington, DC 20230
202/482-5145

Library of Congress
101 Independence Avenue, SE
Washington, DC 20540
202/707-5000
www.thomas.loc.gov

National Aeronautics and Space Administration (NASA)
300 E Street, SW
Washington, DC 20546
202/358-1000
www.nasa.gov

National Labor Relations Board (NLRB)
1099 14th Street, NW
Washington, DC 20570
202/273-1000

National Technical Information Service (NTIS)
703/487-4223
www.fedworld.gov

National Transportation Safety
Board (NTSB)
490 L'Enfant Plaza, SW
Washington, DC 20594
202/382-6600

Occupational Safety and Health
Administration (OSHA)
1120 20th Street, NW
Washington, DC 20036
202/606-5100
www.osha.gov

Office of Management and
Budget (OMB)
Executive Office Building
Washington, DC 20503
202/395-3080

Organization for Economic
Cooperation and Development
(OECD)
2001 L Street, NW
Washington, DC 20036
202/785-6323

Patent and Trademark Office
2121 Crystal Drive
Arlington, VA 22202
703/305-8341
www.uspto.gov

Pension Benefit Guarantee
Corporation (PBGC)
1200 K Street, NW
Washington, DC 20005
202/326-4000
Railroad Retirement Board

844 North Rush Street
Chicago, IL 60611
312/751-4776

Securities and Exchange
Commission (SEC)
450 5th Street, NW
Washington, DC 20549
202/942-4150
www.sec.gov

Small Business Administration
(SBA)
409 3rd Street, SW
Washington, DC 20416
202/205-6605
800/8-ASK-SBA
www.sbaonline.sba.gov

Social Security Administration
(SSA)
6401 Security Boulevard
Baltimore, MD 21235
410/965-1234
800/SSA-1213 or 800/772-
1314
www.ssa.gov

United Nations Information
Center
1775 K. Street, NW
Washington, DC 20006
202/331-8670
www.un.org

U.S. Chamber of Commerce
1615 H Street, NW
Washington, DC 20062
202/659-6000
800/638-6582
www.uschamber.org

U.S. Postal Service
475 L'Enfant Plaza, SW
Washington, DC 20260-0010
202/268-2000
www.usps.gov

Veterans Administration (VA)
810 Vermont Avenue, NW
Washington, DC 20420
202/273-4900
www.va.gov

About the Author

Paul Westbrook is a noted financial and retirement planning expert who is tapped frequently by major publications for his views. He also gives seminars and speeches on a variety of financial and retirement related topics. Mr. Westbrook began his career as a human resources professional at several major corporations, later moving on to consulting. He instituted and headed a national practice in financial and retirement planning at a major international benefits consulting firm. For the past several of years, Mr. Westbrook has run his own financial and retirement planning firm based in Ridgewood, New Jersey. His mix of corporate, consulting, and entrepreneurial experience has provided him with an ideal background for the writing of this book.

NOTES